ELIZABETH GURLEY FLYNN

Ceres: Rutgers Studies in History

Lucia McMahon and Christopher T. Fisher, Series Editors

New Jersey holds a unique place in the American story. One of the thirteen colonies in British North America and the original states of the United States, New Jersey plays a central, yet underappreciated, place in America's economic, political, and social development. New Jersey's axial position as the nation's financial, intellectual, and political corridor has become something of a signature, evident in quips about the Turnpike and punchlines that end with its many exits. Yet New Jersey is more than a crossroad or an interstitial "elsewhere." Far from being ancillary to the nation, New Jersey is an axis around which America's story has turned, and within its borders gather a rich collection of ideas, innovations, people, and politics. The region's historical development makes it a microcosm of the challenges and possibilities of the nation, and it also reflects the complexities of the modern, cosmopolitan world. Yet far too little of the literature recognizes New Jersey's significance to the national story, and despite promising scholarship done at the local level, New Jersey history often remains hidden in plain sight.

Ceres books represent new, rigorously peer-reviewed scholarship on New Jersey and the surrounding region. Named for the Roman goddess of prosperity portrayed on the New Jersey State Seal, Ceres provides a platform for cultivating and disseminating the next generation of scholarship. It features the work of both established historians and a new generation of scholars across disciplines. Ceres aims to be field-shaping, providing a home for the newest and best empirical, archival, and theoretical work on the region's past. We are also dedicated to fostering diverse and inclusive scholarship and hope to feature works addressing issues of social justice and activism.

For a complete list of titles in the series, please see the last page of the book.

ELIZABETH GURLEY FLYNN

THE REBEL GIRL, DEMOCRACY, AND REVOLUTION

MARY ANNE TRASCIATTI

RUTGERS UNIVERSITY PRESS
New Brunswick, Camden, and Newark, New Jersey
London and Oxford

Rutgers University Press is a department of Rutgers, The State University of New Jersey, one of the leading public research universities in the nation. By publishing worldwide, it furthers the University's mission of dedication to excellence in teaching, scholarship, research, and clinical care.

Library of Congress Cataloging-in-Publication Data

Names: Trasciatti, Mary Anne, author.
Title: Elizabeth Gurley Flynn : The rebel girl, democracy, and revolution / Mary Anne Trasciatti.
Description: New Brunswick, New Jersey : Rutgers University Press, [2025] | Includes bibliographical references and index.
Identifiers: LCCN 2024047471 | ISBN 9781978817562 (paperback) | ISBN 9781978817579 (hardcover) | ISBN 9781978817586 (epub) | ISBN 9781978817609 (pdf)
Subjects: LCSH: Flynn, Elizabeth Gurley. | Communists—United States—Biography. | Women labor leaders—United States—Biography. | Women civil rights workers—United States—Biography.
Classification: LCC HX84.F5 T73 2025 | DDC 335.0092 [B]—dc23/eng/20250213
LC record available at https://lccn.loc.gov/2024047471

A British Cataloging-in-Publication record for this book is available from the British Library.

Copyright © 2025 by Mary Anne Trasciatti
All rights reserved
No part of this book may be reproduced or utilized in any form or by any means, electronic or mechanical, or by any information storage and retrieval system, without written permission from the publisher. Please contact Rutgers University Press, 106 Somerset Street, New Brunswick, N.J. 08901. The only exception to this prohibition is "fair use" as defined by U.S. copyright law.

References to internet websites (URLs) were accurate at the time of writing. Neither the author nor Rutgers University Press is responsible for URLs that may have expired or changed since the manuscript was prepared.

∞ The paper used in this publication meets the requirements of the American National Standard for Information Sciences—Permanence of Paper for Printed Library Materials, ANSI Z39.48-1992.

rutgersuniversitypress.org

In memory of my parents,
Dominick Trasciatti and Ruth Gilboy Trasciatti

CONTENTS

INTRODUCTION 1

1 **STRATEGIZING FROM THE SOAPBOX**
   Free Speech Fights in Missoula and Spokane 7

2 **THE FIGHT FOR FREE SPEECH IN PATERSON, NEW JERSEY** 41

3 **WAR AND CIVIL LIBERTIES**
   An Oxymoron? 73

4 **FROM CIVIL LIBERTIES ICON TO COMMUNIST MENACE** 119

5 **FROM THE LITTLE RED SCARE TO THE BIG RED SCARE** 163

6 **THE SMITH ACT TRIALS OF COMMUNISTS IN NEW YORK** 199

7 **THE STRUGGLE CONTINUES**
   Flynn's Final Years 245

EPILOGUE 291

ACKNOWLEDGMENTS 295

NOTES 299

INDEX 357

ELIZABETH GURLEY FLYNN

Introduction

ELIZABETH GURLEY FLYNN is one of the most important figures in the history of the U.S. Left. Her participation in "the working-class movement," as she called it, spanned nearly six decades, from 1906 to 1964. As a Socialist, then a Wobbly syndicalist, then a Communist, she organized workers into unions, led strikes in a variety of industries, supported anti-imperialist movements around the globe, galvanized resistance to fascism, protested deportation of immigrants, advocated for prison reform, championed labor and political rights for women, fought for civil rights for Black Americans, and defended civil liberties for labor activists of all ideological stripes. It is no exaggeration to claim that Flynn was involved in just about every major campaign of the Left in the first two-thirds of the twentieth century.

The long arc of Flynn's activist career, the many issues to which she devoted her prodigious energy, and the combination of characteristics that earned her admirers as well as enemies—fierce wit, sharp intellect, fearlessness, personal warmth, a way with words, determined optimism, and absolute devotion to workers and their struggles—make it possible to tell her story in different ways. This is not the first biography of Flynn, but my approach to telling her story differs from earlier books in that I foreground Flynn's commitment to civil liberties as a characteristic and enduring element of her activism and a force that shaped her life.[1] My assumption throughout the book is that civil liberties work is a through line that connects the various phases of Flynn's political career and the different campaigns in which she was involved. From her Wobbly years to her leadership of the Communist Party of the United States (CPUSA), Flynn was a trailblazer in the American civil liberties movement, an ardent and active defender of the right to hold and express one's own political views and to associate with like-minded people in peaceful pursuit of economic, social, and political change. Rather than surrender responsibility for civil liberties to the courts, she advocated and practiced what legal scholar Larry Kramer has called "popular constitutionalism," the idea that ordinary people are capable of defining and protecting their rights through vigorous debate of the Constitution and active supervision of the judiciary.[2]

Had I written this book earlier, the previous statements would have been met with skepticism or, quite possibly, scorn. Until fairly recently, the Cold War paradigm that prevailed in just about every facet of U.S. society left no room for complex thinking about Communists. The idea that one could be a Communist and a sincere champion of the Bill of Rights would have strained the boundaries of believability among many liberals and conservatives alike. As demonstrated by the American Civil Liberties Union (ACLU) expelling Flynn from its executive board in 1940 solely because of her membership in the Communist Party, this way of thinking about her originated well before the start of the Cold War. Yet a clear-eyed examination of the historical record shows that Flynn's commitment to civil liberties matched or even exceeded that of others in the movement, including and especially those among the ACLU board who judged her and found her wanting. It was her politics, not her commitment to the Constitution, that bothered her critics and relegated her to the margins of civil liberties history. It is certainly possible and even worthwhile to question some of the political choices that Flynn made as a Communist. Her alignment with William Z. Foster against efforts to realign the CPUSA away from the international Communist movement toward a more United States–centered approach to economics and politics after World War II and again after Khrushchev's revelations of Stalin's crimes are examples of choices about which we might speculate and disagree. Yet if Flynn's commitment to internationalism sometimes blinded her to realities within the United States and the Soviet Union, it never entailed a rejection of the Constitution. The end of the Cold War has made it possible finally to write her into the center of civil liberties history where she belongs.

Flynn's understanding of civil liberties was inseparable from her socialist politics. She believed that freedom of speech, press, assembly, and the right to a fair trial by jury are necessary for democracy. However, she did not advocate civil liberties as a matter of individual rights. On the contrary, she recognized that in a capitalist state such as the United States, where material resources are unevenly distributed, some individuals (typically members of the capitalist class) wield greater power than others (typically members of the working class). The only way to remedy the imbalance of power between these "haves" and "have nots" is collective action by the latter. Collective action is impossible without civil liberties. In other words, without guarantees of free speech, press, assembly, and a fair trial, workers could not possibly hold union drives, conduct strikes, organize against exploitation, resist oppression, advocate for worker-friendly policies, or do any of the things required to secure basic needs and a share of the good life, what labor activists poetically refer to as "bread and roses."

As most biographies do, this one takes a chronological approach. I consistently weave elements of Flynn's personal life into the story of her political career. Her early exposure to stories about the Irish freedom struggle from her parents, her friendships with Irish revolutionaries like James Connolly and Jim Larkin, and the way in which she understood and expressed her Irish identity, for example, are very important, but the focus is always on Flynn as a public figure. This choice reflects the way she lived her life. Flynn enjoyed a close relationship with her family, especially her mother and her sisters; loved her son dearly, if often in absentia (his death from cancer at the age of twenty-nine was a devastating blow); and had warm friendships, a short-lived marriage, and numerous love affairs, most notably with Italian anarchist Carlo Tresca, but the working-class movement was her lifeblood. For this reason, I am far more interested in exploring her journey from Wobbly free speech fighter and strike leader, to Workers' Defense Union and ACLU founder, and to Communist Party head challenging laws that criminalize certain forms of political thought than in pondering the breadth and depth of, say, her romantic attachments.

I also steer away from evaluating Flynn's feminism. Although she advocated for women's social and economic equality, encouraged women's active participation in organizing drives and strikes, had numerous female friends in a variety of political movements—including, when she joined the CPUSA, women like Claudia Jones who helped her appreciate the particular forms of exploitation and oppression perpetrated against Black women—and was a leading figure in the global antifascist women's network that emerged after World War II, Flynn did not call herself a feminist. As a young woman, she did not campaign for suffrage because she believed it was a distraction from the immediate concerns of working women. In this, she was a typical Wobbly, espousing direct action in the workplace as the only path to liberating workers from wage slavery. Flynn did not even vote until she cast a ballot for New York City mayoral candidate Fiorello LaGuardia on November 2, 1937. She considered that act to be the moment she ceased being a Wobbly.[3]

Flynn supported her friend Margaret Sanger's campaign for women's access to information about sex and reproduction and to birth control, but the issue of reproductive rights was never as important to her as were issues like the right to picket during a strike. Like many women in the CPUSA, she did not endorse the Equal Rights Amendment because she believed it would undermine labor laws that protected women in the workplace. Her first commitment was to the class struggle—all other issues mattered to the extent that they advanced that struggle to the benefit of the working class. Therefore, I take my cue from Flynn and evaluate her on the things that she found important.

In her younger days, Flynn toyed with the idea of becoming a constitutional lawyer. It is hard to imagine her poring over legal tomes, preparing memoranda, filing briefs, and the like. Such tasks were not where her talent lay nor where her heart led her. She was an orator, and what an orator she was! After she joined the Industrial Workers of the World (IWW), she quickly became one of the union's most popular figures, drawing crowds on street corners and in meeting halls and making headlines in the press nearly everywhere she went. Flynn's youth and beauty undoubtedly contributed to her appeal, but it was her capacity to connect with an audience; her ability to communicate empathy and compassion along with compelling arguments, witty observations, and forceful emotional appeals; and her obvious and unshakable faith in the dignity and goodness of the working class that made her truly remarkable. Numerous individuals recalled being profoundly moved by the experience of hearing young Elizabeth Gurley Flynn speak, sometimes decades after the occasion.

Unlike youth and beauty, Flynn's affability and talent for connecting with audiences did not desert her with age, although in her later years with the CPUSA her audiences were more likely to be readers of a pamphlet, magazine article, or column for the *Daily Worker* than listeners of a speech.[4] However, even as the bulk of her work shifted from the medium of speech to that of writing, Flynn retained the audience-centered perspective of an orator. Her language was simple and straightforward but never patronizing. She never trafficked in abstract theoretical concepts at the expense of concrete, experiential realities. She appreciated her audience's intelligence, whatever their level of formal education, but also understood their need to *feel* as well as think. In short, she liked and respected her working-class audiences, and they, in turn, liked and respected her.

That Flynn was a talented orator is of central importance to my telling of her story. It helps explain her popularity; her success as an organizer, strike leader, and fundraiser for numerous labor defense campaigns; and her overall approach to civil liberties. For Flynn, speech was not an abstraction; it was a type of action without which organizing, striking, labor defense campaigns, and all other forms of collective political action were impossible. Like many socialists of her generation, she saw freedom of speech and all First Amendment rights as part of the revolutionary legacy of the United States. She consistently used the language and symbolism of Americanism to claim that revolutionary legacy for working-class movements. Flynn's talent for oratory also helps explain her status within the Communist movement. Her male comrades among the party leadership did not take Flynn seriously. Their attitude derived partly from sexism and partly from elitism. Flynn's ability to talk to working-class audiences and the obvious delight she took in doing so were taken as evidence that she was an intellectual and political lightweight. Ponder the irony.

As befits an activist for whom civil liberties were inextricably tied to the class war, the chapters that follow are organized around the various "battles" that Flynn fought in defense of First Amendment rights. Chapters 1 and 2 explore Flynn's early career in the IWW, particularly her leadership of free speech fights in Missoula, Montana; Spokane, Washington; and Paterson, New Jersey, from 1909 to 1915. Although she fought against local efforts to silence speech with a labor-themed message, Flynn's popularity and her moxie garnered widespread attention for the free speech fights and sparked a conversation about civil liberties that reverberated around the United States and the globe. Chapter 3 considers how World War I and Flynn's break with the IWW expanded the scope of her civil liberties activism beyond the local to the national and even the international. Increasingly, she and her allies in the burgeoning civil liberties movement—which was inspired by the brutal repression visited upon working-class labor activists who refused to support the war or to tamp down their organizing activities or strikes and upon middle-class conscientious objectors in the United States—saw their work as part of a global effort on behalf of political prisoners connected to labor and anticolonial movements throughout the United States and Europe, as well as in India and Mexico, and integral to the success of the young Bolshevik government in Russia.

Chapter 4 continues to explore the national and international implications of Flynn's civil liberties activism in the 1920s and 1930s. She was among the founding members of the ACLU and made important contributions to the work of the fledgling organization and to antifascist movements in the United States and Italy. Her 1937 decision to join the CPUSA caused many liberals in the ACLU to turn on her and led to her controversial expulsion from that organization three years later, an act that fed the juggernaut of the Cold War by granting the seal of liberal approval to anti-Communism. Chapter 5 discusses Flynn's opposition to repression of the CPUSA at the federal level in the years before World War II and her work to generate support for the fight against fascism after the United States entered the war. The chapter also covers Flynn's increasing involvement in the struggle for Black liberation—specifically her opposition to practices such as police brutality, housing discrimination, lynching, and the poll tax—and considers how anti-Communism encouraged divergent trajectories for the civil rights and civil liberties movements. The chapter concludes with a discussion of Flynn's role in the conflict that arose over Browder's decision to transform the CPUSA into a political association, which resulted in his expulsion from the party in 1945.

Chapter 6 covers Flynn's leadership of defense campaigns during the Smith Act trials of Communist Party leaders—including herself—in New York. I consider how pervasive anti-Communism and her own misreading of the political situation in the United States constrained Flynn's efforts to generate popular support for Communists whose civil liberties were being violated. Chapter 7 follows the final decades of Flynn's career from her release from federal prison, where she was sent following her Smith Act conviction, to her death in the Soviet Union in 1964. I discuss Flynn's growing feelings of isolation in the United States, which she attempted to mitigate by traveling to Communist countries and other places where communist parties enjoyed significant influence; her commitment to "party discipline," which kept her at the forefront of the fight against political repression even when she would have preferred to retire; and her final civil liberties fight: a defense of the right to travel, which she undertook when the State Department revoked her passport. The epilogue considers how historical memory of Flynn has been and continues to be shaped more by anti-Communism than by appreciation for her significant contributions to civil liberties and working-class movements in the United States and around the globe.

If readers of this book come away with an appreciation of the extraordinary work that Elizabeth Gurley Flynn did to defend the rights of speech, press, assembly, and a fair trial for labor activists of all kinds and with a clear sense of why a robust defense of the First Amendment is necessary for the functioning of democracy, especially in a capitalist state, then I have achieved the goal I set for myself in writing this book. If, in addition, Flynn's story inspires future generations of activists for civil liberties or any number of the other causes for which she fought doggedly over a period of almost sixty years, all the better.

CHAPTER 1

Strategizing from the Soapbox
Free Speech Fights in Missoula and Spokane

> The Working Class and the Employing Class Have
> Nothing in Common—Not Even the Streets.
> —*Industrial Worker*, August 12, 1909

IN THE SUMMER of 1906, at the tender age of fifteen, Elizabeth Gurley Flynn, a member of the Socialist Labor Party (SLP), launched her career as a street corner speaker in New York City. "I took to it like a duck to water," she recalled in her autobiography.[1] No surprise there. Flynn's parents had joined the Socialist movement when their firstborn daughter was young. Her American-born father worked in the quarries before studying engineering at Dartmouth and dropped out to become an itinerant mapmaker when his family could no longer afford tuition. Galway-born Annie Gurley worked as a seamstress until the second of the couple's four children was born. The Flynn family moved around several times before settling in New York. Poverty dogged them wherever they went. Flynn spent many hours at home—and at countless meetings to which her father "dragged" her—listening to conversations and debates about such topics as the exploitation of workers in various industries, union organizing drives, and the evils of imperialism (British and otherwise). These experiences and her encounter with books like Edward Bellamy's *Looking Backward*, combined with her family's poverty and the suffering she witnessed among the working-class families around her, steeled Flynn's hatred for capitalism and formed her into a militant socialist with an internationalist outlook.

Flynn's charisma and talent for debate—she won a silver medal in school—provided her the tools she needed to transform her political

7

commitments into action. In no time, the supremely gifted teenage orator was drawing crowds wherever she spoke. It was not long before Flynn's speeches drew the attention of law enforcement as well. In August 1906, she mounted a soapbox to deliver a speech on women and socialism in New York's Theater District. Before she finished the speech, police ordered her down from the makeshift platform and arrested her for speaking without a permit and blocking traffic in Times Square. The incident earned her the first of several nicknames, "Daughter of the Reds," bestowed on her by fellow socialists. She did not object to the moniker. "The red flag does not mean riot, bloodshed and anarchy," she explained to a reporter with all the confidence of a precocious rising star in the movement. "It means the red, healthy blood of the people. I am in that sense a daughter of the reds and I love in that understanding the red flag."[2]

Flynn's youthful ardor notwithstanding, the incident was not unusual. Soapbox speaking was a well-established feature of urban life in the early twentieth century.[3] The practice took its name from the crate on which outdoor speakers stood to elevate themselves above their audience—literally, a wooden box in which manufacturers delivered soap to stores for retail sale. Soapbox speaking was popular because it allowed communicators to bring their message directly to people in the places where they lived and worked, giving public presence to issues, ideas, individuals, and groups that might otherwise never be seen or heard. Orators held forth on a variety of topics, providing education and entertainment to audiences to save souls for the afterlife or to recruit bodies in the here-and-now for labor, suffrage, civil rights, and other social movements. In the 1870s, city governments began requiring permits for outdoor speaking to exercise control over the use of public space. Orators who were considered too radical or disruptive were simply denied a permit. Knowing they would be denied, many radical speakers never bothered to request a permit and instead played a kind of cat-and-mouse game with police, speaking surreptitiously until caught, at which time they abandoned the soapbox (or took it with them) and ran away or, in Flynn's case, surrendered to the forces of law and order.

Flynn Joins the Wobblies

The same year that Flynn was arrested for soapbox speaking, she became an organizer for the Industrial Workers of the World, also known as the IWW or the Wobblies, joining New York's "mixed local" Number 179. It was a natural match. Flynn was young, whip-smart, possessed of a flair for the dramatic, and fiercely anticapitalist. The IWW was an audacious organization of rebels dedicated to the abolition of capitalism and the emancipation of working people. Founded in 1905 in Chicago, the IWW's mission was to organize all workers in all industries into "one big union." The industrial unionism of the IWW appealed to segments of the working classes that the conservative and exclusive American Federation of Labor (AFL), which organized only skilled tradesmen along craft lines, chose to ignore: migratory and unskilled workers, immigrants, Blacks, and women.[4] As its name suggests, the IWW was part of a global upsurge of early twentieth-century working-class radicalism.[5] Its impact on the U.S. labor movement was greater than the size of its membership, which during the time of Flynn's active involvement may have been as many as 60,000 and as few as 2,500.[6] As Flynn observed, a fierce fighting spirit animated the IWW and solidified its role as the nemesis of corporate interests: "The IWW was a militant, fighting, working-class union. The employing class soon recognized this and gave battle from its birth. The IWW identified itself with all the pressing immediate needs of the poorest, the most exploited, the most oppressed workers. It 'fanned the flames' of their discontent."[7]

Flynn's first foray into civil liberties work began a year after her arrest for soapboxing, when she spoke in defense of William "Big Bill" Haywood, Charles Moyer, and George Pettibone, officers of the Western Federation of Miners (a union that was at the time affiliated with the IWW) who were wrongfully accused of planting a bomb that killed former Idaho Governor Frank Steunenberg.[8] During the defense campaign, she met James Connolly, member of the IWW, founder of the Irish Socialist Federation of New York, and revolutionary leader of the movement for Irish independence from England. Connolly admired the young champion of the working class, and the two became firm friends. When another friend, Scottish socialist John Carstairs Matheson, asked Connolly what to make of "La Belle Flynn," whom Matheson called an "infant prodigy," Connolly assured him that Flynn was all right. "Like you," he explained, "I have a distrust of prodigies. But Lizzie is entirely free from the stereotyping characteristic. In fact, the really wonderful thing about her is the readiness [with] which she evinces a desire to learn, and to abandon her former opinions when they are proven untenable. She started out as a pure Utopian, but now she laughs at her former theories."[9] Connolly befriended Flynn's parents as well, and he and his family were frequent guests at the Flynn family residence. Flynn's relationship with the Irish Republican nationalist, internationalist, and anti-imperialist Connolly was another formative influence on her politics.

Flynn, Connolly, Patrick Quinlan, and other Irish and Irish Americans established the Irish Socialist Federation in 1907. As described by Connolly, the federation's aims were "to assist the revolutionary working-class movement in Ireland by a dissemination of its literature, to educate the working-class Irish of this country into a knowledge of Socialist principles and to prepare them to co-operate with the workers of all other races, colours and nationalities in the emancipation of labour."[10] Active involvement in defense campaigns was an essential component of the federation's plan for labor's emancipation. Leaders of the organization believed their history of oppression had bestowed upon the Irish a responsibility to stand up for fellow workers whom the law targeted because of their participation in the class struggle. In response to criticism of a demonstration in support of Haywood, Moyer, and Pettibone, members of the federation's governing committee wrote "An Irish Manifesto" in which they observed, "In that onward march of the working class, the sons and daughters of the Emerald Isle are taking and will take the part worthy of the traditions of a race that never faltered in the face of danger, that for over 700 years has never surrendered in its struggle against injustice. Fellow countrymen: In our own land we have long seen the packed juries give our best and bravest to the hangman's rope, shall we stand idly by while the same atrocious crimes of power are consummated here?"[11] Flynn's name topped the list of signatories.

At its 1908 annual convention in Chicago, the IWW declared itself a syndicalist union, which meant that it focused its energies on achieving socialism through direct action in the workplace and the general strike rather than the political process. It trumpeted its take-no-prisoners militant syndicalism in the revised preamble to its constitution, which declared "The working class and the employing class have nothing in common" and pledged unrelenting struggle "until the workers of the world organize as a class, take possession of the earth and the machinery of production, and abolish the wage system."[12] True to its word, in the first five years of its existence alone, the IWW led or supported strikes in numerous industries and locations, including tinners and slaters in Youngstown, Ohio; miners in Goldfield, Nevada; cooks and waiters in Reno, Nevada; electrical workers in Schenectady, New York; lumber workers in Portland, Oregon; silk workers in Paterson, New Jersey; metal workers in Bridgeport, Connecticut; quarry workers in Marble, Colorado; loggers in Seattle, Washington; and railroad workers in Prince Rupert, British Columbia, to list just a few.[13]

Flynn was a delegate to the 1908 IWW convention, and she heartily endorsed the union's embrace of syndicalism. Her presence caught the attention of the press. Articles praised her for having stamina enough to journey from New York by freight train. Her appearance also garnered attention. One account described her as attired "in jaunty felt hat and a long, romantic cape such as Rosalind [the heroine of Shakespeare's *As You Like It*] might have worn in the forest of Arden." Flynn's husband, John Archibald "Jack" Jones, an ore miner whom she had met on the Mesabi Iron Range in Minnesota, accompanied her. The two had married in January, and almost immediately after the marriage, he had been arrested and charged with attempting to dynamite a mine captain's home in Aurora, Minnesota. She had returned to New York at the insistence of her worried family, but Jones was released after eight days for lack of evidence. He joined her in New York some time afterward and traveled with her to Chicago.[14] After the Chicago IWW convention, Flynn left the SLP and concentrated her efforts on organizing with the Wobblies.

Flynn would eventually become a recognized expert at organizing defense campaigns for labor activists who were targeted for repression by local, state, or federal authorities, but she made her reputation as a civil liberties advocate on the street corner soapbox as a free speech fighter. Street speaking was an essential component of the IWW's organizing strategy.[15] Between April and September of 1908, a handful of speakers from the New York City propaganda league conducted "a systematic agitation throughout Manhattan," consisting of four indoor meetings, one large mass meeting in Union Square, and fifty-six street meetings around the borough. Altogether they reached an estimated twenty thousand wage workers with the message of industrial unionism.[16] The best Wobbly orators were audacious and fearless. One famous trick street speakers used to draw an audience was to shout "Help! I've been robbed!" When a sufficient number of passersby had gathered around, the speaker would add "by the capitalist system" and launch into an attack on various and sundry forms of exploitation perpetrated on wage workers by the employing class.[17] Called "jawsmiths" in IWW parlance, Wobbly soapboxers acted as if they owned the streets, and for those moments when they held a crowd spellbound, they *did* own the streets.

It was not long before Wobbly street speakers met with resistance. Beginning in 1908, several city governments, primarily in the West, attempted to thwart IWW organizing efforts by passing laws against outdoor speaking or stepping up enforcement of existing laws. The Wobblies fought back by calling free speech fights, essentially coordinated and sustained campaigns of nonviolent resistance to the law. The IWW free speech fights have come to be regarded as significant moments in the history of civil liberties in the United States.[18] As legal historian David Rabban has noted, Wobblies were the first to claim a First Amendment right to use public places.[19] Veteran soapboxer Flynn devised many of the tactics that Wobblies used to claim their First Amendment rights.[20] The story of how she did so begins in Missoula, Montana.

The Missoula Free Speech Fight

Founded in 1860 as the Hellgate Trading Post, the settlement that would be Missoula moved five miles upstream by 1866, where it was rechristened Missoula Mills before taking the shortened form of its name. Missoula was incorporated as a town in 1883, the same year that saw the arrival of the Northern Pacific Railway. An 1885 history referred to Missoula as "the very garden of all Montana," most probably referring to the extensive vegetable and flower gardens surrounding a log cabin on Front Street, a downtown thoroughfare. The name stuck, and Missoula began to promote itself as "The Garden City."[21] Missoula was also an industrial city of some importance, but the coming of the railroad and founding of the U.S. Forest Service headquarters in 1908 made the lumber industry a major engine of the local economy.

Workers in Montana's lumber camps toiled in unsafe and unsanitary conditions that rivaled those of workers in urban factories. Shoddy housing, poor sanitation, rancid food, inadequate bathing facilities, and a generally unclean and unhealthy atmosphere were the norm.[22] Lumber workers started organizing in the IWW in 1907. The need for improved sanitary conditions in the logging camps was a main argument of Wobbly organizers who blamed capitalism for the filth and disease that lumber workers faced.[23] Organizing drives were conducted on the trains that carried loggers from one camp to another and in the pages of IWW newspapers.[24]

Migratory workers regularly flowed in and out of Missoula on their way to lumber camps in the region and mining towns in places like Anaconda and Butte. The city billed itself as a labor-friendly place, mostly around Labor Day, when elected officials and business leaders extolled the virtues of AFL-style craft unionism and cooperation between capital and labor for the production of wealth.[25] Their vision of the virtuous, intelligent, reasonable working man, controlled by his superiors for his own and the greater good, suited the interest of boosters who promoted Missoula as a "City Beautiful."

The City Beautiful Movement emerged in the fields of architecture and urban planning after the Chicago World's Columbian Exposition in 1893. It was based on the perception that rapid urbanization was turning cities into ugly places, physically and morally. City Beautiful advocates saw a connection between beauty—defined in terms of classical monumental forms (think of an ancient Greek temple)—order, and morality. They sought to make the urban landscape more physically attractive, and hence more orderly, so that residents would respond with a surge of civic pride, which would in turn regenerate morality.[26] City Beautiful committees sprung up in municipalities around the nation. The Missoula City Beautiful committee endeavored to promote their metropolis as a better looking, more orderly, and more peaceful alternative to the crowded, boisterous cities back East. To make the case, they ignored those things that Missoula had in common with its older, industrial counterparts: wealthy residents living in beautiful houses and working in pleasant surroundings, while the resident working classes lived far less comfortably; factory smokestacks filling the air with black residue.[27] Missoula's saloons and brothels catered to migratory workers. Unkempt, unwashed, and undisciplined, these workers subverted the idealized vision of labor trotted out annually and tarnished the image that city boosters strove to present to would-be developers, investors, and "respectable" residents.

The IWW did its best to explode idealized images of the West as a land of freedom and promise. "There is no East and there is no West," opined an article in the Wobbly newspaper the *Industrial Worker*. "The homeless worker—the tramp—from New York meets at the campfire with the man who has just escaped from the chain gang of Seattle."[28] Wobblies saw the real promise of the West in its potential as a site of class struggle. When she joined the IWW, Flynn, who had been born in New Hampshire and lived most of her young life in the Bronx, organized primarily in the industrialized cities of the Northeast, especially New York. Her perspective broadened when she made her first trip west with the IWW in the summer of 1909. In her own words, she realized that "New York is a very small part of the revolutionary movement, at least."[29]

Flynn's tour began in Chicago, where she set out "in a spirit of high adventure . . . to see [her] country and to meet its people." Her recollection exudes appreciation for the natural landscape of the West, which she called the "spacious bosom" of the nation. "The western country still had traces of the frontier. It was sparsely settled and had a natural wild beauty," she wrote. "I fell in love with my country—its rivers, prairies, forests, mountains, cities, and people."³⁰ Flynn's travels took her from Chicago to Minneapolis, Butte, Great Falls, Seattle, Spokane, British Columbia, and finally Missoula. She arrived there in August 1909 to join Jack Jones, who had been organizing workers in the city since his arrival in fall 1908.

Flynn was struck by Missoula's natural beauty.³¹ "The surrounding hills are very picturesque," she observed in the *Industrial Worker*, "and the town is verdant with a splendid variety of trees and flowers, which is responsible for its title, 'The Garden City.'"³² She was less positive about the built environment, noting, "The houses are old-fashioned, the streets are the natural dust and mud of Montana, and the sidewalks, treacherous wood."³³ City officials earned even lower marks for their proposal to recruit migratory workers for a low-wage public works project to build cement sidewalks.³⁴

Upon her arrival in Missoula, Flynn set about finding affordable space in which to set up headquarters for the local—or, as she called it, a "home" for the lumberjacks and other workers—which would include a reading room filled with Socialist and labor newspapers, pamphlets, and books.³⁵ She and Jones finally found space in the basement of the Harnois Theater, next to the Missoula Chamber of Commerce. Joined by fellow IWW organizer Frank Little, they began holding outdoor meetings on the nearby corner of Higgins and Front Streets. Their choice of location was strategic: the commercial center of Missoula radiated from this intersection, as did the saloons and brothels of the red-light district that tempted men with money in their pockets.³⁶

The trio held five street meetings in a week, drawing crowds of migratory workers and curious onlookers with a banner emblazoned with the letters "IWW" and classic IWW sayings and fiery speeches in which they championed the cause of industrial unionism and excoriated local employment agencies for selling fraudulent jobs.³⁷ Missoula was home to a number of agencies that charged migratory workers a fee to find them work in the lumber camps. The practice of selling jobs was common throughout the region, and the system was corrupt, so much so that employment agents were called "sharks." Often a worker would pay for a "job ticket" in the city and head out at his own expense to a far-flung lumber camp only to find that the job he had purchased did not exist. Other times, the selling of job tickets was little more than a scheme to recruit replacement workers, or scabs, for the lumber companies.

Flynn and other Wobblies referred to that part of the city where jobs were bought and sold as the "slave market" and those who worked for wages as "wage slaves."³⁸ They used the vocabulary of slavery to convey the lack of freedom and autonomy entailed by the wage system. In a world in which working for wages is completely normal, it may be hard to imagine the profound impact that the institutionalization of the wage system had on people who had been accustomed for millennia to working for themselves as farmers or purveyors of a craft or trade. The transition to capitalism that began in medieval Europe transformed labor from a self-sustaining activity into a commodity. Silvia Federici explains, "By transforming labor into a commodity, capitalism causes workers to submit their activity to an external order over which they have no control and with which they cannot identify."[39] In sixteenth- and seventeenth-century Europe, the wage system was so feared and despised that many peasants and artisans became vagrants, vagabonds, or criminals to avoid selling their labor to the highest bidder.[40] Wage work became institutionalized in the United States with the emergence of the factory system in antebellum New England. Here, as in Europe, white working people feared and resented the dependence and loss of autonomy that resulted from having to sell one's labor to an employer. They understood the distance between their own situation and that of chattel slaves in the South as a matter of degree rather than kind.[41] A vocabulary of slavery permeated antebellum labor rhetoric on both sides of the Mason-Dixon Line. In the North, wagons driven by recruiters for the storied Lowell textile mills were known as "slavers." In the South, proslavery advocates used the term *Lowellization* to mean the radicalization of Black and/or white workers.[42]

The specter of slavery continued to haunt U.S. labor into the twentieth century. The AFL made its peace with the wage system (so much so that AFL president Samuel Gompers defined free labor as wage labor) and sought job security and good pay for its members, hence its motto of "a fair day's wage for a fair day's work."[43] In contrast, the IWW's revolutionary program aimed to abolish the wage system altogether. Western employment agencies were singled out as one of the system's most nefarious elements, on par with slave markets in the antebellum South. This 1908 polemic against the "sharks," published in the *Industrial Worker*, is illustrative.

> Today, in the industrial centers, North and South alike, we have also the wholesale and retail dealers in slaves—white, black, and yellow. Especially is this the case in the towns of the Pacific Northwest. Transient laborers form the working class in the majority of this part of the country. The jobs are mostly on railroad or construction work or in the many

logging camps and lumber mills, where the demand for men and the jobs for them are alike temporary and uncertain.

To supply the men and to distribute them to the various battlefields in the industrial war with speed and keen competition among the workers, the modern slave trade—called the employment agent—grows fat and rich from the misery of his victims. Like Haley, in "Uncle Tom's Cabin," he is secure in the protection of the law and in the well-paid blindness of its hirelings.[44]

Calling the area of the employment agencies a slave market identified that space as the hub of a perverse job system in which workers were expected to pay for their own bondage, as buying a job essentially amounted to paying one's way into wage slavery.

Public speaking in front of the "slave market" was not limited exclusively to radical labor organizations. The corner also played host to the Salvation Army, a charitable, evangelical Christian organization founded in England in the 1860s. In 1880 the organization made its way to the United States to convert the most destitute members of society.[45] Diane Winston describes the Salvation Army in its early years as "a living metaphor bent on territorial conquest."[46] Despite municipal laws that discouraged outdoor preaching, Salvationists dove into late nineteenth-century urban street culture. They competed with the IWW for control of space and appealed to the same constituency. Calling the city their "open-air Cathedral," they attracted audiences for a message of meek submission to the Christian gospel with lively tactics that included parading, vocal and instrumental music, and minstrel shows and other types of dramatic performance.

Flynn mocked the organization for ignoring workers' basic bodily needs in pursuit of saving souls. "The Salvation Army marches forth to exhort the lumberjacks on the condition of their souls," she wrote in the *Industrial Worker*. "'Are you living in sin?' they ask. 'I don't know if that's what you call it,' I heard one worker say, 'but it's a lousy bunk-house out in the woods!'"[47] In truth, the Salvation Army provided an extensive array of social services to complement its spiritual work.[48] A main source of its rivalry with the IWW was the evangelicals' pretense to exclusive ownership of the streets.[49]

The IWW and Salvation Army shared the streets grudgingly until Flynn's quick wit provoked disciplinary action against the IWW from Missoula law enforcement. Missoula had its own public order law, a city ordinance passed in 1899 that decreed any person who makes "any improper or unusual noise, riot, or disturbance, or who shall commit any breach of the peace . . . use profane, obscene or offensive language, or in any way disturb the peace or quiet of any street . . . shall be guilty of a misdemeanor."[50] For the first couple of weeks that Flynn was in town, no effort was made to enforce the law. Then on September 27, soldiers from Fort Missoula complained that she was harassing them and threatened to sweep the IWW off Missoula's streets. Police intervened to protect Flynn and her comrades. The Wobblies would not relinquish their soapbox, however, which caused business owners to lodge complaints. The next day, two speakers were arrested. Speaking continued the following day, and two more arrests were made. All the speakers arrested were men. At their trial on September 30, the men were found guilty of disturbing the peace and sentenced to fifteen days in the county jail. As reported in the *Butte Miner*, "It is alleged that the men, assisted by one woman, occupied prominent positions on platforms constructed of boxes and barrels from which they addressed the general public and they are said to have hurled uncomplimentary remarks at passersby who failed to respond to their entreaties to stop and listen to their pleas for public recognition."[51]

Essentially, Flynn and fellow Wobblies got in trouble with the law for heckling soldiers and other passersby. Heckling was a standard element of street speaking, part of the back-and-forth between speaker, audience, and bystanders that made soapbox oratory spontaneous, lively, and entertaining.[52] In other words, it was part of the show. When police intervened to stop Flynn from doing what all good soapbox orators do, they steeled Wobbly determination to remain on the streets in violation of the public order. In court the IWW defendants contended that the Salvation Army made more noise than they did, with their singing, performing, and parading in the streets. However, Judge Small ruled that claim irrelevant. In pronouncing sentence, he gave the option of a suspension, provided the men promised to refrain from making further speeches on the streets; they refused the offer and were remanded to jail.[53] Their commitment to keeping the fight for free speech in the streets was perfectly consistent with the union's philosophy of direct action, which held that the place for workers to fight capitalism was not at the ballot box or the negotiating table but on the job, at the point of production. In this case, Wobblies adapted the philosophy of direct action to the ban on street speaking by challenging the law in the streets.

Flynn did not return to the soapbox after the incident with the soldiers (she was pregnant at the time, although it is unclear whether her IWW comrades knew of her condition), but she remained active in the free speech fight. After the trial concluded, she sent a telegram to IWW headquarters in Spokane and to the Western Federation of Miners in Butte, explaining the situation in Missoula and asking for assistance. Her telegram prompted a notice on the front page of the September 30, 1909, issue of the *Industrial Worker* titled "FREE SPEECH BATTLE; FIGHT OR BE CHOKED." With this notice, local Missoula chronicler George Venn observes, "what appeared to be a small town struggle against a few outspoken transients and a girl began to enlarge."[54]

The notice in the *Industrial Worker* merits a look for what it reveals about Flynn's importance to the free speech fight and the persuasive tactics that the IWW used to recruit participants:

> Elizabeth Gurley Flynn is a 19 year old girl. She has been speaking in Missoula, Mont., as an organizer for the Industrial Workers of the World. Industrial union number 40, IWW, of Missoula has been telling the lumber workers that they must unite in one union to fight the bosses. Her husband and fellow worker Little are now in jail for speaking on the street. It may be necessary to fill the Missoula jail and it is up to you, IWW men, to go to Missoula and, if necessary, be arrested for the crime of speaking on the street. The unions of the IWW invite every free born "American" and every man who hates the tyrannical oppression of the police to go to Missoula and help the workers there to win out.[55]

Two things are noteworthy about the notice. First, and hardly surprising, the message was targeted to appeal to male Wobblies. "IWW men" were specifically called upon to go to Missoula and help their fellow workers win a union. If the appeal to working-class solidarity proved an insufficient motivator, Flynn's young age and the fact that she was a girl— and a girl whose husband had been thrown in jail, no less—provided the added incentive of coming to the aid of a female in distress. The notice also illustrates how a radical labor organization used the language of Americanism to appeal to its constituency and frame its position on public expression.

Americanism emerged as a political language, according to Gary Gerstle, in the second and third decades of the twentieth century as the result of a "medley of factors," most of which involved efforts to impose from the outside a set of material conditions and ideological structures on working people.[56] However, the origins of this political language are much earlier, dating back to the IWW free speech fights. As James Barrett has observed, working people had their own definitions of what it meant to be

American, which they refined and transmitted in working-class organizations.[57] Since the union's founding in 1905, radicals in the IWW had crafted their own phrases, symbols, and historical lineages to separate capitalism from democracy and express their program of revolutionary unionism as a quintessentially American endeavor. In the call for recruits to the Missoula free speech fight, quotation marks around the word *American* in the phrase "free born 'American,'" suggested an inclusive vision of American identity that was open to anyone who embraced freedom, regardless of race, ethnicity, or place of birth. In this vision immigrants, whether they had naturalized, were Americans too. By implication, tyrannical, oppressive police, who had made a crime of speaking in the street, were foreign and un-American. This rhetorical tactic would become increasingly important in radical campaigns for free speech.

The call for volunteers continued with pointed rhetorical questions about bravery and loyalty:

> Are you game?
> Are you afraid?
> Do you love the police?
> Have you been robbed, skinned, and grafted on?
> If so, then go to Missoula and defy the Police, the courts, and the people who live off the wages of prostitution.[58]

And it ended with a warning for Missoula authorities:

> NOTICE—WE WOULD SUGGEST TO THE MISSOULA POLICE, THAT NO I.W.W. MEN BE SHOT nor CLUBBED. THAT NO I.W.W. WOMEN BE RAPED nor INSULTED.[59]

Clearly, the notice appealed to a sense of camaraderie forged among migratory workers by the shared experience of life on the streets.[60] It also implied an audience of gallant and courageous men who willingly face difficulties and dangers in order to shield women from harm.[61] This chivalry is the kinder and gentler side of "virile syndicalism," Francis Shor's term for the courageous, physical, unfettered working-class masculinity celebrated and performed by the IWW in its protest activities.[62] C. L. Filigno, secretary of the Spokane IWW, with whom Flynn would be tried in that city's free speech fight weeks later, confirmed the chivalrous motive for IWW sojourners in Missoula. As quoted in the *Daily Missoulian*, he promised, "There are 100 men now in route from Seattle and about as many from Portland headed for Missoula to help Girley [sic] Flynn in her fight for free speech."[63]

In calling for soapbox reinforcements, Flynn exploited the subversive potential of migratory workers' mobility. Ordinarily, the mobility required of migratory workers defined them as criminals under vagrancy or tramp laws that made the state of being poor and without ties to a particular place illegal. Employers and the police used random arrests for vagrancy to undermine migrant worker organization and enforce social control.[64] The same lack of status and disconnection from a particular place that made them vulnerable to arrest, however, also allowed radicalized workers to slip away unnoticed and "act quickly, moving from scene of confrontation to scene of confrontation with relative rapidity."[65] In other words, the ability to circulate freely is what enabled a vulnerable migrant workforce to fashion itself into what Matthew May calls a hobo orator union, "a body that, in order to follow the seasonal patterns of migrant labor power, primarily constitutes itself in the sphere of social reproduction through the embodied practice of soap-box oratory."[66]

Flynn's importance to the free speech fight is evident in press coverage of the struggle. "Woman Would Fill City's Prisons," reported the *Daily Missoulian* after word of Flynn's telegram was made public. Quoting from the *Spokane Chronicle*, the article continued, "The old order has changed. The men are now chasing the police."[67] Incensed at the "serious charges" leveled against them, Missoula police tried to suppress the notice, to no avail.[68] IWW members flocked to the city via freight cars and formed a kind of oratorical assembly line. As soon as one speaker was arrested, another took his, or her, place. The use of railroad freight cars held a special kind of irony. Typically, these freight cars transported resources and products of industrial capitalism; now they transported workers for a human assembly line to challenge the brutalizing effects of that same system upon those workers. Here was an early twentieth-century example of capitalist logic being folded against itself.

As the audience for IWW soapboxers increased, city officials became more aggressive in their efforts to suppress street meetings. Police beat Wobbly speakers, sometimes brutally. Jack Jones was clubbed and arrested, then beaten unconscious in prison for singing "The Red Flag" against the sheriff's orders.[69] Audiences were punished too. Firemen turned their hoses on street crowds, ostensibly to keep traffic moving. An October 2, 1909, article in the *Butte Miner* reported, "When the IWW began their outdoor séance tonight a crowd of 1,000 men and women congregated at Higgins Avenue and West Front Streets, effectively blocking the streets, and it became necessary to make a demonstration with the fire hose in order to disperse the multitude."[70] Given that the population of the entire county at the time was just under thirteen thousand people, the size of the crowd must have unnerved police and local business interests.[71] Not every instance of street corner speaking drew an enormous crowd or ended with a soaking from the fire house, but any time large numbers of bodies spilled into the streets to engage with Wobbly orators, they temporarily halted the flow of pedestrian and vehicular traffic and transformed the space into a site of public protest. Speaking in front of the employment agencies, Wobblies not only argued the case against dishonest labor brokers; they confronted the power of the "sharks" directly and disrupted their operations.[72]

Typically, an IWW speaker went into a district and stayed there for an extended period, "until the speaker was worn out or the local audiences got tired."[73] The wealth of available speakers in response to her notice inspired Flynn to try a new tactic: Instead of speaking only at the intersection of Higgins and Front, Wobbly orators were to "select leaders of small squads and distribute them about town, thus giving each a chance to gather a crowd before the police became cognizant of the movements of the IWW."[74] When Flynn recruited volunteers from outside Missoula to hold forth on a soapbox in the Garden City and deployed them in this fashion, speaking simultaneously from different street corners, she frustrated efforts to silence orators and created the impression that the IWW was pervasive in the city and throughout the region.[75]

Missoula law enforcement, politicians, business leaders, and residents recognized Flynn as the unquestioned leader of the free speech movement. The *Butte Miner*, for example, characterized her as an "arch disturber, organizer and leader of the Industrial Workers of the World, a woman of considerable power as a speaker and of unquestioned courage."[76] On October 4, 1909, when city and county jails were filled to capacity, police arrested Flynn, hoping that her removal would signal the end of the soapboxing.[77] They understood the symbolic and practical value of female leadership for the free speech fight, and so, it seems, did the Wobblies.[78] Upon Flynn's imprisonment, the *Butte Miner* reported, another woman, "lieutenant of Mrs. Flynn," Mrs. Edith Frenette, a socialist newly arrived from Spokane, stood ready "to take up the burden where the recognized leader was compelled to lay it down."[79]

While she was in jail, Flynn continued to rally support for the cause, sending a letter to comrades in Spokane in which she vividly described the conditions of her imprisonment and lauded a member of the Forestry

Department for mounting the soapbox and getting arrested on behalf of free speech.[80] Flynn's case was dismissed without a trial, and she was released the next day. The following evening, October 6, violence erupted. Edith Frenette had just been arrested and was being escorted to the county jail when someone in the crowd allegedly threw a rock and hit a policeman. "There were more than 100 men in the bunch, which followed the officers to the very jail door, demanding the release of the woman," reported the *Anaconda Standard*, "and in the darkness the person who threw the missile could not be seen and no one was arrested."[81] Coverage in the *Billings Daily Gazette* was more sensational. Frenette's arrest, it was reported, "almost precipitated a riot." She was "hurried to the county jail, followed by a howling and jeering mob, some of whom stood on the jail steps and defied the officers to arrest them."[82] The *Great Falls Daily Tribune* similarly observed, "A large and angry mob surrounded the police and made a threatening demonstration and during the melee a number of rocks were hurled at the police escorting the woman."[83]

Arguably, the call to protect IWW women from sexual assault encouraged the angry response to Frenette's arrest, as did Flynn's own imprisonment. (The arrest of the two women also drew professors from the University of Montana into the free speech fight on the side of the IWW.) However, Flynn reported that she and Frenette, both of whom were placed in the witness department of the county jail because there were no separate cells for women, "were treated with kid gloves by the sheriff and his wife, although [Flynn's] husband had been badly beaten up in the jail by this same Sheriff Graham."[84] Like Flynn, Frenette was released without charge.

Despite, or perhaps because of, the arrest of Flynn and Frenette, IWW speakers continued to claim the streets as their own. They stubbornly insisted on what French philosopher Henri LeFebvre called "the right to the city." According to LeFebvre, the right to the city entails "the right of users to make known their ideas on the space and time of their activities in the urban area" and "the right to the use of the center, a privileged place, instead of being dispersed and stuck into ghettos."[85] Thus, a night that saw thirty-five speakers arrested for soapboxing also had hundreds of Wobblies and supporters marching and singing along Higgins Street.[86] This impromptu parade showed the union's moxie.[87] It forced people who had so far managed to avoid the crowded intersections where soapboxers were holding forth into direct contact with workers and their issues. Normal power dynamics were turned upside down as bosses and other high-status individuals who usually determine the course of social interaction had no choice but to yield and allow workers to pass. In an effort to placate IWW organizers and reinstitute their own sense of ownership of the streets, city officials offered a place to speak without interference away from the corner at Front and Higgins—and beyond the side streets one block east and west. The Wobblies refused.[88] Consent to this kind of free speech zone away from the employment agencies, the Salvation Army, and commercial foot traffic would have blunted the force of their message, limited its reach, and allowed the exploitation of workers in the slave market to go uncontested.

Flynn's tactics ensured a Wobbly victory for free speech in Missoula. In the glare of the spotlight, its jails filled to capacity, with the Wobblies threatening to recruit an additional five hundred volunteer orators, the city surrendered.[89] Garden City officials agreed to treat the IWW and the Salvation Army equally under the law, allowing both organizations to orate on the streets. Having acquiesced to these demands, authorities now focused on the task of rebuilding Missoula's image as a City Beautiful and turned their attention to preparations for the upcoming Western Montana Apple Show. As Flynn later explained, residents eventually "tired of the unfavorable publicity and excitement. The taxpayers were complaining of the cost to the little city, demanding it be reduced." In the end, she wrote, "The authorities gave up. All cases were dropped, and we were allowed to resume our meetings. We returned to our peaceful pursuit of agitating and organizing the IWW."[90] Peaceful, indeed. Flynn left Missoula soon after the free speech fight ended and returned to Spokane. The city was stepping up its campaign against street speaking and her presence was needed to lead another resistance.

The Spokane Free Speech Fight

Settled in 1871, Spokane (originally named Spokan Falls for its location near the falls of the river named after the Spokan, or Spokane, Indian tribe) was incorporated as a city in 1881, the same year that saw the arrival of the Northern Pacific Railway, just like Missoula two years earlier. Discovery of gold, silver, and lead in the nearby Coeur d'Alene region of Idaho in 1883 brought a flood of prospectors to the area. With its transportation infrastructure and proximity to the mines, Spokane emerged as an important regional trading center, and its population grew rapidly. Although the Great Fire of 1893 destroyed much of the city's downtown area, this event did not halt Spokane's growth. An initiative to rebuild downtown combined with the arrival of the Great Northern Railway made Spokane into a transportation hub for the Inland Northwest, known also as the Inland Empire. By 1910 Spokane's population of 104,000 had surpassed that of Walla Walla, its rival for commercial dominance in the region, and there was hope among residents that their city, now the largest of the Inland Empire, would surpass Seattle to become the largest city in all of Washington.

Spokane and Missoula were similar in other ways: both cities played host to migratory workers, who came there to look for seasonal employment in the mines and lumber camps and hold over for the winter season, and to a number of local establishments that sought their patronage, among them dishonest labor brokers selling fraudulent jobs (the infamous "sharks") as well as saloons, brothels, and gambling halls. Spokane also had its share of boosters who worked actively to sell the city as a desirable place to live and do business. They were businessmen and politicians as well as charitable clubwomen and female social reformers. Economic stability and respectability were twin pillars of their promotional rhetoric.[91] Their challenge was to promote economic opportunities afforded by the region's mineral wealth while simultaneously minimizing the visible social and environmental impact of the mining and logging industries.[92]

Spokane also had its own City Beautiful committee. Founded in 1906, the committee aimed to make Spokane "more cleanly, healthful, and attractive" so that the city "shall be a source of justifiable pride to her citizens of the present and of the future."[93] The committee exhorted residents to pick up trash, keep their houses and yards neat, and support efficient government. They also called for large-scale beautification projects. Fearful that Spokane's existing park system, comprising less than two hundred acres, was insufficient to accommodate its ever-rising population and that too much of the remaining natural landscape was being surrendered to developers for unsightly and unhealthy industrial use, the City Beautiful committee and the 150,000 Club—an organization dedicated to increasing Spokane's population to 150,000 within ten years (an ultimately unrealized goal)—endorsed an amendment to the city charter that called for establishment of a new Park Commission. Voters in the 1907 election approved the amendment, and almost immediately after the committee's formation, members moved to hire the nationally prominent Olmsted Brothers landscaping firm to develop a comprehensive plan for the development of city parks, parkways, and streets.[94] Providing street space for migratory workers was not part of the plan.

In 1907, city boosters helped elect Herbert Moore as mayor on a platform of moral reform that included controlling prostitution, gambling, and drinking—vices associated with the slave market. In December 1908, as part of the plan for moral reform, Billy Sunday was invited to Spokane for a six-week revival. Sunday's mission, so to speak, was to lead the working classes away from sins of the flesh toward a life of temperance, self-discipline, and respect for authority, civil as well as religious. "An ex-baseball player turned evangelist, thundering his gospel of the sawdust trail," Sunday "burst upon Spokane with telling effect," observes local author Lucile F. Fargo.[95] His tent sermons were lively affairs during which he pounded the lectern, contorted his body, and broke furniture.[96] As many as ten thousand people crammed into "the tabernacle," a temporary wooden structure that served as his place of worship, while thousands more crowded outside.[97] Although his Christian gospel appealed primarily to middle-class women, his Christian charity was popular among men in dire economic circumstances.[98] A 1907 economic depression left scores of men unable to find work, and the effects of that depression lingered into the winter of 1908–1909. Sunday offered the unemployed a place to sleep on benches in the tabernacle, followed by free breakfast in the morning. Hundreds took advantage of the offer.[99] Despite complaints from residents about the spread of lice and disquiet about increasing numbers of hoboes in Spokane, Sunday refused to rescind the hospitality, and the jobless men kept coming. More than a thousand unemployed workers migrated to the city that winter for sustenance.[100]

Sunday competed with the IWW for the loyalty of Spokane's working classes. Wobblies considered him a hypocrite who fed the poor a meager meal while he made himself rich with his sermons.[101] They countered his message and the appeals of the Salvation Army, which had established a beachhead in the city nearly twenty years earlier, with the gospel of industrial unionism. Their organizing campaign began in earnest when James H. Walsh arrived in the city in November 1908. Walsh was leader of the "Overalls Brigade," a group of workers clad in denim overalls and red bandannas that trekked from Portland, Oregon, to Chicago for the IWW convention, recruiting members at various hobo camps along the way. Upon his arrival in Spokane, he and fellow "missionaries in the class war," as he called them, immediately began recruiting for the local.[102] Walsh was a talented organizer, and membership in the union quickly surged. Buoyed by the increase in members—over a thousand new recruits—the local rented space for a union hall on Front Street, launched the *Industrial Worker*, and stepped up its local campaign against fraud among Spokane's labor brokers. The "Don't Buy Jobs" campaign had IWW orators on soapboxes in front of employment agencies in the central business district on Stevens Street—the heart of Spokane's own "slave market"—where they excoriated brokers as predators, urged a boycott of the agencies, and exhorted workers to seek jobs through the union. Even the Spokane Central Labor Council, local arm of the normally antagonistic AFL, unofficially supported the Wobbly campaign against the "sharks."[103]

Members of the Spokane city government knew about the fraudulent practices of the employment brokers and the city council debated measures to regulate the agencies. Wobbly soapboxers pushed that debate beyond the confines of government chambers and into the street, where people most affected by the "sharks" could make their respective views known to residents and politicians. Owners of the hiring firms responded to the IWW campaign with a demonstration of their own class consciousness and formed the Associated Agencies of Spokane. The organization pressed the city council to pass an ordinance banning outdoor meetings.[104]

Although city boosters supported efforts to regulate hiring practices, they also feared Spokane's reputation as a place to invest and relocate would be marred if the city became known as a refuge for migratory workers and a stronghold for the IWW. In the end their affinity for order and desire for respectability proved stronger than their commitment to regulating the "sharks," and they threw their support behind the drive to ban street meetings. On December 22, 1908, the city council passed a law that decreed, "It shall be unlawful for any person or persons to hold any public meeting or make any speech, give any show, performance, or exhibition, or do any other such act which shall tend to draw or collect a crowd upon any street, alley, or sidewalk within the fire limits"—that is, within the thirty-two-block range touched by the Great Fire of 1893—essentially, throughout the downtown area.[105] The law took effect January 1, 1909, and subjected violators to a maximum penalty of one hundred dollars, thirty days in city jail, or both. Supporters claimed the measure was designed to keep meetings from blocking traffic, a justification that had been used to pass a similar law in 1891.[106] In an article titled "Streets Are for All the People," the *Spokesman-Review*, mouthpiece for city boosters, explained why the new law was needed: "The streets are for traffic, and street meetings block traffic and are therefore in conflict with the essential purpose of public highways."[107] The article also allowed that the ordinance would help restore Spokane's good name by sweeping undesirables off the street: "Street gatherings had become a nuisance and a disgrace in Spokane. They drew together idle and vicious characters, interfered with the orderly course of business and gave the city a disreputable appearance which had long been criticized by visitors from other towns."[108]

This claim hinted at an insidious double standard regarding who belonged in the city and who did not. Most of the so-called upstanding citizens of Spokane were originally from somewhere else. Boosters worked hard to entice more residents from outside the region, particularly those from the eastern United States who had already made the decision to migrate westward. They were especially committed to selling the Pacific Northwest to settlers who might otherwise have gone to California.[109] Somehow these new arrivals were perfectly welcome, as were those Irish immigrants who constituted the city's police force, but migratory workers and IWW organizers, whether they hailed from other countries or other parts of the United States, were vilified as "foreigners," "aliens," and "outsiders."[110]

When the IWW pointed out that Spokane had muzzled free speech, supporters of the law pointed out that outdoor meetings in public parks and vacant lots were allowed. As was the case in Missoula, however, the free speech zone kept orators and their audiences out of public view and away from the very people and activities with which they had issue. No surprise, Wobblies wanted no part of it, but they did agree to cancel a planned protest of the law after police assured them that IWW speakers would not be arrested if streets and sidewalks were not blocked.[111]

Police left the IWW alone until a group of men who had been fleeced by the sharks held a demonstration at which someone threw rocks through the windows of several employment agencies on Stevens Street on February 16, 1909.[112] The February 16 unrest was the second time that disgruntled workers had vented their anger at the "sharks" in the course of a month. Walsh arrived on the scene and kept demonstrators from doing further damage, and the union disavowed any role in the incident. Nonetheless, the police chief warned that the ordinance against street speaking would be enforced from that point forward—only for Wobbly orators. Religious speakers were free to hold forth on the streets without fear of reprisal providing they did not disturb the peace.

Wobblies reacted with a plan to generate a test case for challenging the constitutionality of the law by holding a street meeting and having Walsh speak.[113] It failed. Walsh was arrested and found guilty. Fred H. Moore, a relatively unknown socialist attorney at the time who would later gain international recognition as chief counsel for Italian anarchists Nicola Sacco and Bartolomeo Vanzetti, prepared an appeal to challenge the law in court. The appeal was eventually dropped because Walsh left the state, but the IWW rank and file continued to speak in the street until the onset of spring, when workers left the city in search of jobs in the mines and lumber camps.

On August 10, 1909, the city council codified the preference for religious speakers by amending the original ordinance to include a clause permitting the mayor to "grant a permit to any regular religious organization to hold religious meetings" in the downtown area, thus granting the Salvation Army leave to renew its street corner soul-saving work. The masthead of the *Industrial Worker* heralded this blatant double standard with a turn of phrase adapted from the preamble to the Wobbly constitution: "The Working Class and the Employing Class Have Nothing in Common—Not Even the Streets."[114] The *Spokesman-Review* remained steadfast in its position that banning IWW street corner oratory contributed to Spokane's beautification.[115] In turn, Wobblies mocked the City Beautiful philosophy for being fixated on urban aesthetics and having no regard for the material conditions of ordinary people's lives.[116]

Wobblies again used Flynn's tactic of recruiting orators to violate the city ordinance when President William Howard Taft stopped in Spokane a month later and addressed an outdoor audience of approximately twenty-five thousand people, blocking streets "so tight that workmen could not get home to their dinner." Now IWW organizers had the evidence they needed to argue that claims about traffic and congestion were merely pretext for getting the union out of the city.[117] They refused to relinquish the streets. On October 25, police arrested IWW organizer James Thompson for street speaking. His trial date was set for November 2. Word went out via a headline in the *Industrial Worker*, "Wanted: Men to Fill the Jails of Spokane," and a follow-up letter to all IWW locals declared, "November 2nd. Free Speech Day. All lovers of free speech are asked to be in readiness to be in Spokane on that date."[118]

The Spokane free speech fight officially began on November 2, 1909. Judge Mann dismissed the case against Thompson and declared the new law giving preferential treatment to religious speakers unconstitutional but ruled the old ordinance, which forbade street speaking of any kind, still in effect.[119] As in Missoula, Wobblies planned to raise the cost of enforcing the ban on outdoor speech beyond what the city was willing to bear, in terms of money and lost prestige, by filling prisons and clogging the court system, all while generating constant propaganda. Police Chief John Sullivan, undoubtedly aware of what had happened in Missoula, beefed up his on-duty force by calling all members to work on November 2.[120] Police made 103 arrests that day. Within a few weeks, five hundred people had been rounded up. IWW members were charged with disorderly conduct and sentenced to thirty days and one hundred dollars.

Organizers were charged with criminal conspiracy, a felony publishable by a prison term. This two-tier system was intended to end the campaign quickly by decapitating the union. Police also pressured owners of meeting halls in the city not to rent to the IWW.

Flynn arrived soon after the campaign began. She framed the struggle to speak on the streets as a battle to reclaim public space unjustly seized by public authorities to serve private economic interests, and she cast the IWW in the role of a heroic volunteer army struggling against paid professional forces with far greater armaments but far less heart. In the November 10, 1909, issue of the *Industrial Worker*, she wrote, "This fight is serious. It must be won.... These men are brave, loyal supporters of a great cause. They are heroes in the battle of labor."[121] Others used the martial frame as well. The *Tacoma Times* reported on the "bitter industrial war" being waged in Spokane for the right to stand on a soapbox and talk.[122] In New York, anarchists and socialists in the Free Speech League, an organization committed to defending free speech for all viewpoints, pledged to raise a "free speech army" of unemployed men from around the country to send to Spokane "to become martyrs to the free speech campaign being inaugurated in that city."[123]

As recruits poured into Spokane, Flynn's tactic of circulating speakers throughout different streets to confuse and frustrate police became a key element of the battle plan. Richard Brazier describes this tactic in some detail in his recollection of the free speech fight.

> The cops were massed in full force all through the Slave Market section and, evidently were expecting us to gang up in front of the Employment Offices and do our spieling there. But we had many Wobblies infiltrating the crowds and sizing up the position the cops had taken. Their layout was reported back to the Wobbly Hall and then, instead of sending our speakers out to where the cops were waiting, we sent them two or three blocks away. Soon the cops were running helter-skelter in all directions. The Wobblies in the crowds knowing exactly where the speakers were, headed and herded the crowds in the right direction.[124]

A battle frame permeates Brazier's writing. He likens Wobbly free speech fighters to guerrilla combatants on spatial reconnaissance, reporting the maneuvers of a better armed but less wily and flexible enemy force. "There were times," he observes, "when these hit and run tactics were varied by small mass forays that generally caught the cops off base." Police would then scurry "to round up the many small bunches of Free Speech fighters who brashly invaded their territory and were speaking on their sacred streets."¹²⁵

In addition to the "hit and run" tactic Wobblies used sound in important ways. Vocal and instrumental music worked to draw crowds, drown out rival speakers, and once an outdoor meeting was finished, lead the audience into the union hall. While they paraded, Wobblies sang "The Red Flag" and "The Marseillaise." They even adopted the latter as their official song.¹²⁶ The "Little Red Songbook," a now-legendary compilation of working-class anthems, many of which married pious melodies with irreverent verses, was born in Spokane the year of the free speech fight.¹²⁷

In an era before public address systems were widely available, resonant speaking voices also worked to draw attention where it was needed. Brazier recalls how one speaker, a man possessed of a "stentorian voice" that could raise the dead "and make quite a good talk," moved stealthily through the slave market calling audiences for soapboxers on various corners: "Once the crowd had assembled he introduced the other speaker, then moved on to another spot where another speaker was to do his stuff, and there repeat his stentorian call to arms until another crowd had assembled."¹²⁸ The deep-voiced man, Jim Patten by name, was a Londoner who reported learning how to orate in Hyde Park, "where you had to shout long and hard to be heard."¹²⁹ By making the union and the migratory workers it represented audible as well as visible, the free speech fights made it even harder for the good citizens of Spokane to ignore them.

As was the case in Missoula, eloquence was not a requirement to participate in the Spokane free speech fight. Most orators were pulled from the soapbox almost immediately after they said just a few words. Men and women who feared or were just plain bad at public speaking read from the Declaration of Independence or some other appropriate document. Some who took to the soapbox simply shouted "Fellow workers and friends!" and then waited to be arrested.

Women played a visible role in the Spokane free speech fight. On the second day of the campaign, police arrested three women: Edith Frenette, who had returned to the city after the Missoula free speech fight and was picked up for street speaking, and Ann Arquett and Isabella Huxtable, who were arrested when police raided the IWW hall.¹³⁰ Arquett was one of four female members of the IWW band in Spokane.¹³¹ At least two more women joined them, so that five Wobbly women awaited trial by November 10.¹³² On December 28, six more women—Mrs. Emile Hermann, Mrs. Floyd Hyde, and four other members of the newly organized United Wage Workers—left Seattle to "offer themselves as martyrs" for the right to speak on the street in Spokane.¹³³ They were hardly the footloose hoboes of Wobbly lore, free to follow their desires and revel in the camaraderie of being "on the bum."¹³⁴ According to the *Industrial Worker*, one of the women had a child under two years old at home and the other was pregnant. It is likely that one of the four unnamed women who set out with them was Bessy Fiset, assistant editor of the *Seattle Socialist*, a weekly Pacific Northwest newspaper. Bisset sold copies of the *Industrial Worker* on the corner of Main Street in Spokane.¹³⁵

Once again, locals recognized Flynn as the leader of the free speech fight. Her femininity, youthful good looks, intelligence, and eloquence caught people's attention and, in some cases, earned her grudging admiration.¹³⁶ An increasingly obvious pregnancy only intensified locals' curiosity.¹³⁷ It has been claimed that she chained herself to a lamppost so as to frustrate any effort to arrest her and cart her off, but alas, the story is an urban legend.¹³⁸ Flynn's mobility through Spokane's outdoor spaces was limited not by chains but by pregnancy and the cultural conventions around it. "When I came to Spokane," she wrote, "the all-male committee was somewhat disconcerted to be told that I was pregnant." Jack Jones had chosen to remain in Missoula, and consequently, Flynn's male Wobbly comrades took it upon themselves to define the bounds of her public activity. The IWW was at war in Spokane, and the front lines of the battlefield were no place for a pregnant woman: "They decided I was not to speak on the forbidden streets but confine myself to speaking in the IWW hall, to clubs and organizations willing to give us a hearing, and in nearby places to raise defense funds."¹³⁹

Concern for Flynn's safety was reasonable considering the methods used to control Wobbly orators and their audiences. As in Missoula, water hoses were used to disperse a crowd, and police wielded clubs freely. Those who were arrested and imprisoned were fed a diet of bread and water when they refused to work on the rock pile, packed into a small room known as the "sweatbox" for hours, and then moved to a freezing cold cell without blankets or cots, blasted with icy, cold water if they complained too vigorously.¹⁴⁰ When Spokane's jails filled up, the unused and unheated Franklin Elementary School building on Stevens Street was put to use as a makeshift prison. Once a week, despite the cold weather and regardless of whether they had appropriate clothing, Franklin School inmates were forcefully marched to the city jails for a bath.¹⁴¹

City officials and the press waited for Flynn to appear somewhere on a soapbox, but she never did.¹⁴² Instead, she created and used other spaces for resisting the ordinance. She was principal speaker at a city council hearing on the law, and she addressed crowds in the IWW hall, where she challenged the constitutionality of a ban on public speaking, ridiculed police and local officials, and urged comrades to take their place in the outdoor assembly line of orators. When city authorities closed down the hall and prohibited the IWW from renting private auditoriums, Flynn addressed a public meeting in a city courtroom and dubbed the site a "temple of injustice," a scornful reference to the judicial proceedings normally conducted there. In a speech to the Butte Miners Union, she said Spokane police looked and acted like "gorillas." In the *Industrial Worker* she depicted the Spokane jail as "a black hole or torture chamber"; called Judge Mann "a lackey of the parasites" and "almost illiterate"; described Chief of Police Sullivan as a "long, lank, gila-like monster"; and berated police officers as "hired thugs," "Cossacks," "a herd of gorillas," and "fat-jowled Hibernians." She was especially harsh on the Irish among Spokane's police force. "Some of the big, fat Irishmen who arrested our brothers," she wrote, "had such thick brogues that the stenographers were unable to take down their testimony." Spokane officials were not the only ones to suffer the lash of Flynn's sharp words. She also lambasted the AFL, which did not support the free speech fight, for being "craven," "contemptible," and "yellow."[143]

The audacity of women Wobblies challenged the authority of Chief of Police Sullivan, and he reportedly asserted, "Any woman who attempts to speak on the streets will be treated the same as a man."[144] That assertion turned out to be false. Female free speech fighters who were arrested and imprisoned were not subjected to the same kind of physical violence as their male counterparts, but several of them faced allegations about their sexual conduct or endured sexual assault. The sexualized nature of punishment meted out to female Wobblies supports claims by feminist scholars that penal discipline in mixed-sex environments where men are in charge works not only to enforce institutional order but also to reinforce men's dominance over women.[145]

Edith Frenette, veteran of the Missoula free speech fight, was arrested and charged with disorderly conduct for standing on a private porch near the Franklin School and singing "The Red Flag" to encourage prisoners. Sullivan and six other police officers testified against her. According to Flynn, "They swore that she acted as if she were drunk, that she had carried on in a disorderly manner on the streets since this trouble started, and one said she acted like a 'lewd woman.'"[146] Police were not the only ones to question the morals of women associated with the IWW. When presiding over a case involving eight newsboys arrested in the raid on the union hall, Judge Hinkle said of the mother of one of the boys, herself a Wobbly sympathizer, "The IWW hall is no fit place for a woman. And no good woman frequents it."[147] He offered an awkward apology a few days later when men and "women who [visited] the hall regularly" packed his courtroom in protest.[148]

Whereas Frenette's accusers leveled their attack on her sexual morals in the recognized public forum of the courtroom, Flynn and another female Wobbly, Agnes Thecla Fair, reported being sexually assaulted while in prison. Flynn described Fair, a poet whose livelihood derived almost exclusively from sales of a collection of her poems titled "Songs of the Sourdoughs," as "a slight, delicate woman, very intense ... the first woman hobo [she] met."[149] Histories of the IWW contain stories of how Wobblies imprisoned during the free speech fights displayed solidarity in the face of physical and mental torture, but these prisoners were all men. The relatively few women Wobblies who were arrested and thrown in prison did not enjoy the company of comrades, and their isolation and gender left them vulnerable in a way the men were not.

Fair was arrested in early November for addressing a crowd at the intersection of Howard and Riverside Streets. Her description of how the Spokane police treated her reveals an acute awareness of the gender dynamics of police power. "My offense was mixing in free speech fight and behaving so different from other women arrested," she recalled in a letter published in the November 20, 1909, issue of *The Workingman's Paper*. Fair declined to walk to the station and asked for a ride in the "hurry-up wagon." The crowd continued to grow while she waited for transportation. The car finally arrived, Fair waved a red handkerchief as she entered, and "cheers went up for Free Speech."[150] She was put into a prison cell with a female prostitute who was immediately asked to leave the cell, after which Fair was threatened with rape. She reported the incident in some detail: "They put me in a dark cell, and about ten, big burley bruises came in and began to question me about our union. I was so scared I could not talk. One said 'We'll make her talk.' Another said, 'She'll talk before we get through with her.' Another said, 'F--k her and she'll talk.' Just then one started to unbutton my waist [blouse], and I went into spasms which I never recovered from until evening."[151]

This ordeal had hardly finished when Fair was sexually assaulted by a male prison guard disguised as a woman. She recalled, "I thought it was a drunken woman until the officers went out. Then I felt a large hand creeping over me. It's too horrible to put on paper." The experience left her severely agitated, a not uncommon reaction among female victims of sexual assault: "I jumped out into an enclosure, screaming frantically and frothing at the mouth. Had not two of our girls been arrested and brought in just then I do not think I would ever come to."[152] Fair was released on the recommendation of a doctor three days later, and fellow Wobblies carried her back to her room on a stretcher. Her account was disputed by prison officials and a female representative of the Salvation Army who claimed that Edith Frenette did not believe Fair. The IWW, however, was steadfast in its support.[153] The edition of the paper in which her account was published was confiscated as "indecent literature."[154]

Flynn was arrested while walking down the street and charged with conspiracy on November 30. In an account obviously designed to arouse indignation, the *Industrial Worker* reported, "[She] is in a delicate maternal condition [and] much concern for her health was in evidence last night on learning that she was undergoing a hard sweating conducted by the Gila monster, the Pug and the gang of gumshoe snakes always in attendance."[155] In her own account of her prison experience, Flynn expressed awareness of women inmates' vulnerability at the hands of male prison guards and—no doubt influenced by Agnes Thecla Fair's ordeal—described a feeling of relief at not being alone in a cell.

> I was placed in a cell with two other women, poor miserable specimens of the victims of society. One woman is being held on a charge that her husband put her in a disorderly house. The other is serving 90 days for robbing a man in a disorderly resort in Spokane. Never before had I come in contact with women of that type, and they were interesting. Also, I was glad to be with them, for in jail one is always safer with others than alone. One of the worst features of being locked up is a terrible feeling of insecurity, of being at the mercy of men you do not trust a moment, day or night.[156]

Her cellmates treated her kindly, but Flynn discovered during the night that they were part of a prison prostitution ring orchestrated by the guards. "Taking a woman prisoner out of her cell at the dead hours of the night several times to visit sweethearts," she exclaimed, "looked to me as if she were practicing her profession inside of jail as well as out!" The greater offense occurred when she herself was mistaken for a prostitute by one of the guards: "Early in the morning a man by the name of Bigelow, jailer, I presume, came into the cell with breakfast. Instead of leaving it in the ante-room of the cell and going about his business, he marched straight into the room where we were all still in bed. He laid his cold hand on my cheek and I awoke with a start. My anger blazed up and said, 'Take your hand off me, I didn't come here to be insulted.' He murmured some inarticulate excuse, 'Of course not,' or words to that effect, and got out."[157]

Flynn used the idea of feminine modesty to argue that the guard, whom she called "a brute of a man," had violated her right to privacy. Her story boomeranged beyond the Spokane city limits and back. That the virtue of a young, beautiful, married, pregnant woman—one of their own, no less—was compromised in so gross a manner spoke directly to the Wobbly ideal of chivalrous masculinity and was incorporated into appeals for more volunteers. Flyers announced, "Elizabeth Gurley Flynn, a girl organizer only 19 years old, soon to become a mother, was arrested, charged with criminal conspiracy, confined in jail with prostitutes and insulted by an officer of the law."

Leonard Abbott, prominent New York Socialist and associate editor of *Current Literature*, published a letter in that periodical asking Spokane Mayor Nelson Pratt to answer the allegations. The mayor responded in a public missive defending Officer Bigelow's "good name" and calling Flynn's charges "wild and hysterical," thus dismissing her by questioning her sanity on account of her gender, a timeworn strategy for silencing women. Not to be outdone, Flynn answered the mayor with a letter, which she mailed to the press. In her letter, Flynn requested the mayor either "make an amended statement in the public press of this city ... apologizing" for his "inadvertent suggestion" regarding the condition of her mind or that someone connected with an official body of Spokane file a complaint against her for criminal libel.[158] When the mayor refused to either apologize or press charges of libel against Flynn, she responded by filing her own suit. Members of the Spokane Women's Club, some of whom had put up money for Flynn's $5,000 bail, were appalled at "the specter of prostitution thriving in Spokane's jails" and "horrified that someone with the nationwide audience that Flynn enjoyed could be criticizing the morals of Spokane's officials."[159] Her charges reignited a moribund campaign for a female prison matron. The *Industrial Worker* reported, "That she endured and lived is due only to the strength of her mind and courage of her soul. For Mrs. Flynn has within her a new life that is to come into the world."[160]

Male Wobblies supported one another through the prison experience by singing songs, telling jokes, haranguing prison guards, staging performances, giving speeches, devising tactics for the fight, and recruiting for the local. Wobbly prisoners even staged what is believed to be the first hunger strike of the labor movement.[161] Through these actions they transformed the site of their incarceration into the functional equivalent of a union hall and turned their shared suffering into an expression and experience of solidarity.[162] In contrast, neither Flynn nor Fair enjoyed the company of other female Wobblies upon their initial imprisonment. Lacking enough female free speech fighters to make a sizable prison cohort, female Wobblies could not use their numbers to subvert prison norms. Left on their own, Flynn and Fair were subject to the conventional logic of the prison regime, including sexual assault by male prison employees. Upon their release from prison, both women brought public attention to bear on their experiences by publishing first-person accounts in the press. Their respective accounts left them open to questions about their sexual morality, though Flynn's high profile and status as a married, pregnant woman shielded her against accusations of immorality. Her story served as a powerful tool for recruiting volunteers and exposed city officials to allegations of hypocrisy for crusading publicly against vice while presiding over a secret prison-based prostitution operation.

At her first conspiracy trial, Flynn was convicted, sentenced to ninety days in prison, and released on bail. She was then tried on appeal. She was originally to face trial alone, but she asked to be tried with IWW Secretary C. L. Filigno, who was facing the same charges. Flynn wanted to secure a victory for free speech, and she believed that if she were tried alone and acquitted, people would think the sympathy of the jurors had been aroused because she was a woman.[163] During the trial, which ran from February 9 to February 25, anonymous sources from around the United States inundated Spokane with postcards bearing messages designed to shame the jurors, such as "Aren't you ashamed?" and "What do you think of the Constitution?"[164] The tactic was partially successful. The jury found Filigno guilty and acquitted Flynn, much to her dismay and the dismay of the judge who held her responsible for the civil unrest that had engulfed the city.[165] Her pregnancy undoubtedly played a role. Accounting for the verdict years later, she observed, "By this time I was obviously pregnant and even the fast-fading Western chivalry undoubtedly came into play."[166]

Male jurors were not the only ones to react to Flynn's obvious maternity. When her condition became unmistakable, her Wobbly comrades no longer considered it appropriate for her to speak in any public spaces. Early twentieth-century women orators, perhaps most obviously the celebrated organizer of coal miners Mary Harris "Mother" Jones, deployed motherhood successfully as a rhetorical and organizing tactic, but pregnancy was another matter.[167] Although more women were going out during daylight hours in maternity clothes in the early twentieth century, the idea that pregnancy was a private concern, that pregnant bodies signified matters inappropriate for public display and consideration like sexual reproduction and the birthing process, lingered. A large-bellied pregnant organizer addressing predominantly male working-class audiences was a disturbing prospect. Flynn recalled how one Wobbly, a "fussy old guy," protested about her public appearances: "It don't look nice. Besides, Gurley'll have that baby right up on the platform if she's not careful."[168] It seems labor was to remain invisible in the male-dominated labor movement.

Despite the best efforts of Spokane officials, the free speech fight continued through the winter unabated. When police raided the local IWW office, Wobblies moved their headquarters to Coeur d'Alene, Idaho. When they arrested eight editors of the *Industrial Worker*, the paper moved to Seattle. When police pulled Wobbly orators off the soapbox and hauled them off to jail, more Wobblies took their place.

The situation in Spokane spawned conversations about free speech around the United States and internationally. The conversation involved immigrant as well as U.S.-born workers. Comparisons were made between Spokane city government and repressive regimes in tsarist Russia; Mexico, then ruled by the military dictator Porfirio Diaz; and Spain, where government forces were cracking down on demonstrations in Barcelona protesting the execution of anarchist educator Francisco Ferrer.[169] Radicals also made connections with the situation in Spokane and efforts to enact so-called gag laws in other U.S. and Canadian cities.[170] The Irish Socialist Federation of New York, Scandinavian Socialist Local of Minneapolis, and Finnish Socialists of Astoria, Oregon, passed resolutions supporting the IWW, as did the city of Minot, North Dakota, led by a socialist mayor, and workers in other cities across the United States, including Butte, Seattle, Oakland, Denver, Reading, and Rochester.[171] English, German, and Swedish Wobblies protested the brutal treatment accorded them by Spokane law enforcement to their respective governments.[172] Solidarity with the free speech fighters was conveyed from socialists in France and as far away as Australia.[173] And radicals were not the only ones to support the Wobblies' right to speak in the streets.[174] Mainstream commentators claimed Spokane's ordinance was unconstitutional.[175] Others denounced the methods used against Wobbly soapboxers. One Missouri paper vilified Spokane police for committing the "horrors and outrages of the Spanish Inquisition."[176]

Not all reactions were positive. Some critics opposed the very idea of free speech as license to violate decorum and disrupt social order.[177] Others saw the free speech fight as a diversion from the more important work of organizing. One editor in Wenatchee Washington claimed the Wobblies were "suffering martyrdom" for a "silly ordinance" designed to keep streets and sidewalks clear when they should have been putting their energies toward righting a "deepseated social wrong."[178] Not surprisingly, Spokane police and the local press were unmoved by the free speech claims made by Wobbly orators. When Detective Alexander McDonald spied a man preparing to put a box in the street for use as a platform, he promptly made an arrest. When the would-be orator protested "I'm an American citizen and I want my rights," McDonald replied "That's what they all say" and, according to the *Spokesman-Review*, smashed the box "so it might not serve for any more unkempt Ciceros."[179]

Eventually, both sides grew weary of the struggle. Just a few days after Flynn's acquittal, an IWW committee held a conference with Mayor Pratt regarding the ban on street speaking. Flynn described the union's rationale for the overture: "The hall had been closed down, the defense office had been moved to Coeur d'Alene, Idaho, in charge of Fred Heslewood. Over 600 men had been arrested. Our forces were seriously depleted, although we were boldly and publicly announcing a spring renewal of the free speech fight. The committee resorted to a tactical move at the suggestion of [William Z.] Foster. They approached the mayor offering to negotiate an end of hostilities. The city was full of floaters and the authorities feared they were all IWWs."[180]

A conference with Police Chief Sullivan followed. Subsequent negotiations between representatives of various parties in the free speech fight led to restoration of the union's right to hold meetings in indoor places and to hold peaceful outdoor meetings. Prisoners were released as well, and measures were taken to rescind the licenses of the worst "sharks." The ordinance against outdoor speaking, however, remained on the books. Both sides declared victory. But Flynn and the Wobblies had clearly succeeded in popularizing the idea that ordinary people had a right to use the streets. To illustrate, an article published in the *Republic* out of Rockford, Illinois, praised Spokane for having reinstated the Constitution and restored the right of free speech to its citizens with the observation "The city again became American."[181]

Flynn left Spokane not long after the conclusion of the free speech fight and returned to New York where her son Fred was born May 19, 1910. She later joked, "He had the strange record of being twice in jail for free speech before birth."[182] It was quite a thing for a Wobbly agitator to leave the soapbox for the maternity ward, and Fred's birth was considered a newsworthy item. One Spokane paper reported the blessed event with a headline that read, "Gurley Flynn Is Mother. IWW's Leader Ends Warfare to Care for Infant Son."[183]

Soon after the birth of her son, Flynn's marriage to Jack Jones ended. Her contributions to the IWW free speech fights, on the other hand, were more enduring. The format and tactics that Flynn devised in Missoula and brought to Spokane became the model for the campaigns that followed in Fresno, San Diego, Seattle, and elsewhere in the West. Moreover, she helped launch a conversation about working people's First Amendment right to use public places for purposes of organizing and demonstrating, which reverberates to this day. This conversation was not, as critics of the IWW free speech fights have claimed, about abstract rights divorced from the material realities of working-class life and the imperatives of organizing campaigns.[184] On the contrary, for immigrant workers it was a way of coming to understand the United States for themselves, part of the process Barrett called "Americanization from the bottom up."[185]

By its own admission, the IWW was on the front lines of a class war. The terrain of that struggle comprised streets, squares, public parks, meeting halls, factory floors, and the courts. With the possible exception of privately owned meeting halls, working people could not assume unfettered access to any of these places. Every effort by municipal authorities to limit speech somewhere was, in effect, a campaign to capture terrain from labor and hold it for capital. Continued unabated, this process would eventually eradicate labor from existence. This reality was not lost on Flynn. During the Spokane free speech fight, she made it clear that the criminal conspiracy charge brought against Filigno for recruiting soapboxers to Spokane was not merely a way to halt the IWW's organizing drive but an effort to destroy the union: "If it is criminal conspiracy to write for men, it is criminal conspiracy for those appealed to to come to Spokane. If it is criminal conspiracy to come yourself, it is criminal conspiracy to send money to help out. If it is criminal conspiracy to help your organization with money donated, it is criminal conspiracy to pay your dues to help out."[186]

Free speech, then, is not an abstract consideration separate from the everyday struggles that make up an organizing drive. On the contrary, in a capitalist state where moneyed interests conspire to silence workers, the defense of free speech is a necessary tool for organizing to seize control of the means of production.[187] For Flynn, the best way to defend free speech was to occupy a terrain, claim your right to do so—with justification from the Declaration of Independence or the Constitution articulated with the language of Americanism—and speak. She led this defense from the soapbox in the streets of Missoula and Spokane, transforming an ordinary, disposable artifact of the industrial city into a symbol of resistance. She continued to lead it on the streets and in meeting halls back East, most notably in Paterson, New Jersey, where business interests and local law enforcement tried to break a strike of primarily immigrant silk workers by driving the Wobblies out of the city altogether.

CHAPTER 2

The Fight for Free Speech in Paterson, New Jersey

> You may have the right, but we have the power.
> —John Bimson, Paterson chief of police

FLYNN'S WESTERN SOJOURN, particularly her leadership of the Missoula and Spokane free speech fights, demonstrated her immense value to the IWW. She began organizing workers in the cities of the industrial East while her son Fred, known affectionately by family and friends as Buster, was still an infant in the winter of 1910–1911.[1] Her decision was motivated by economic necessity as well as a desire to be back in the throes of the struggle. She was estranged from her husband and living with her parents and siblings, her father was often unemployed, and the $21 weekly salary she earned from the IWW helped pay the bills.[2]

A National Reputation

The next few years were eventful for Flynn and the IWW. In 1911, she met socialist legends William "Big Bill" Haywood and Eugene Debs for the first time.[3] That same year she spoke to striking shoe workers in Brooklyn and female garment workers in Minersville, Pennsylvania.[4] While speaking at street meetings to organize employees laid off from the Baldwin Locomotive Works in Philadelphia, she was arrested twice for blocking traffic—both times the judge threw out her case. She later noted that the police officer who initially arrested her was the first to call her "'an outside agitator,' a name [she] heard often in the next few years."[5] Such was Flynn's growing reputation for eloquence, audacity, and commitment to the struggles of working people that a newspaper in Bridgeport, Connecticut, where she had participated in her first strike nearly five years earlier and was to speak again by invitation of a recently organized local of the Brotherhood of Machinists, labeled her "perhaps the most interesting personality in the labor movement both East and West of the Mississippi" and noted, "Her zeal, her earnestness, the convincing manner of her speech, attracts audiences of thousands to listen to her wherever she goes." The paper also praised Flynn's leadership during the free speech fights claiming that she "delivered some of the most remarkable speeches throughout the northwest, that ever came from a champion of labor."[6]

Part of Flynn's reputation came from her tendency to speak her mind freely.[7] Bosses who exploited workers, police officers who broke up labor meetings, corrupt politicians, and other servants of capitalism were not her only targets. In a 1911 speech to metalworkers and machinists in Harrison, New Jersey, for example, she offered sharp criticism of union leaders who worked for their own benefit rather than that of the members: "We have too many leaders travelling around smoking good cigars and living in a state of luxury beyond the dreams of avarice. We keep these men in official positions, paying them good salaries, and the first thing we know they lose sight of our welfare and only seek to accomplish that which will be of greatest benefit to themselves." Her comments surprised some of her listeners, especially the union leaders among them, and endeared her to many more who appreciated having such a staunch and fearless ally.[8]

In 1912, Flynn went to Lawrence, Massachusetts, along with Haywood to help lead a strike of textile workers who had walked off the job in protest against a pay cut implemented without their consent in response to a state law that shortened the workday. The original strike leaders, Joseph Ettor and Arturo Giovannitti, were behind bars on trumped up charges of killing a striker named Anna LoPizzo. Although Flynn was a well-known figure in the labor movement with a growing national reputation, when the Lawrence strike began, the Wobblies were still relatively unknown outside the West. It was not long before their determined opposition to capitalism and audacious tactics struck fear in the hearts of purveyors of the status quo on the eastern side of the country as well. One *New York Times* reporter called the IWW "the most serious menace the present system of society has ever been called upon to face."[9]

In part, the IWW was so fearsome because it was so American. While the union was part of an early twentieth-century "global upsurge of anarchism and syndicalism," its roots were firmly planted in the United States.[10] The IWW had been founded in Chicago, and as the Spokane and Missoula free speech fights illustrated, Wobblies spoke the language of working-class

Americanism in their U.S.-based campaigns. Although the union organized among immigrant workers, many of its most militant members were born in the United States.[11] These factors gave lie to the claim that anticapitalist ideas and movements were brought to the country by dangerous "foreigners." Flynn's mother, Annie Gurley, emphasized the American nature of the IWW in an interview she gave about her daughter and the union during the Spokane free speech fight. She noted that Elizabeth was a "New York girl," and nearly all the other free speech fighters were "American born and many of them had a long American lineage."[12]

In Lawrence, the "New York girl" Flynn demonstrated her ability to connect with immigrant workers. Immigrant women were the driving force behind the strike, and Flynn held special meetings where they could address issues that were relevant to them. On weekends, she traveled to cities as far away as Pittsburgh, Pennsylvania, and Wheeling, West Virginia, where she spoke to workers of various nationalities at meetings to raise money for the Lawrence strike fund.[13] At the suggestion of Italians in the IWW and the Italian Socialist Federation, she also organized a campaign to place the young children of striking workers in the homes of sympathizers in places like New York City and Barre, Vermont.[14] This tactic, which had been used successfully in strikes in Italy, removed children from a tense and sometimes violent strike situation and conveyed a poignant message about hunger and material deprivation among the families of the strikers. That message was amplified when police efforts to prevent children from leaving turned violent. The children's exodus and other innovative tactics garnered extensive press coverage, aroused public sympathy, and secured a victory for the twenty-three thousand strikers as well as a pay increase for textile workers around the state. The union was further vindicated when a jury acquitted Ettor and Giovannitti.

It was during the Lawrence strike that Flynn met Carlo Tresca, an anarchist from Sulmona, Italy, who would become the love of her life. When she returned to New York after the strike, Tresca left his wife, Helga, and daughter, Beatrice, to move in with Flynn and her family. Together the pair led a strike of hotel and restaurant workers in New York in early 1913. Flynn made news during that strike for her bold ideas, including doing away with the practice of tipping waiters and instead instituting what she called a "living wage" and urging striking restaurant workers to make signed affidavits that unfit food was being served even in "swell" restaurants along Broadway. When asked about the affidavits, she replied, "We want the capitalist to know when he sits down to his dainty dinner that his daintiness rose out of a vile pot like a lily out of a mud pool."[15] Another item that made news during the strike was the revelation of Flynn's affair with Tresca. Newspapers around the country reported that a volume of Elizabeth Barrett Browning's poems, *Love Sonnets*, had fallen out of Tresca's pocket during a scuffle between strikers and the police. Inscribed in the volume was "I love you, Carlo. Elizabeth, December 11, 1912."[16]

Flynn's prominent role in the free speech fights, the stunning success of the Lawrence strike, and her daring leadership of the hotel workers strike solidified her national reputation as a formidable champion of the working class.[17] Her fame, or infamy, depending on one's perspective, followed her to Paterson, New Jersey, where she went to lead a strike among silk workers, which erupted on January 27, 1913. The Paterson strike illustrates the lengths to which local law enforcement, municipal government, and business interests collaborated to criminalize speech and assembly to squash a strike and, in the process, eviscerate a union. It also showed the resilience and flexibility required of Flynn and other organizers and striking workers to hold their ground, literally.

The Paterson Strike

Unlike the newer cities in the West and Pacific Northwest, Paterson had more than a century of history behind it when the IWW arrived. Established in 1791 about fifteen miles west of Manhattan and centered around the Great Falls of the Passaic River, Paterson was the first planned industrial city in the United States. Alexander Hamilton, with backing from the Society for Establishing Useful Manufactures (SUM), which held seven hundred acres above and below the falls, envisioned it as a way to harness the power of the falls for manufacturing domestic goods and reduce the fledgling nation's reliance on imported products.

Paterson grew steadily in the first decades of the nineteenth century. Its citizens were primarily workers in the local factories. Firearms and railroad locomotives were manufactured there, but textiles were a mainstay of local industry. By 1825 Paterson was known as "the cotton town of the United States." The first factory strike and the first sympathy strike took place in 1828 when cotton workers walked out to protest against a change in the lunch hour and demand a shortening of the workday from thirteen and a half hours to twelve hours; the strike was crushed by militia after a week. In 1835, nearly two thousand textile workers, almost all of them children between ten and eighteen years old, most of them female, struck for a shorter workday. They succeeded in getting a sixty-nine-hour workweek (twelve-hour days during the week and nine hours on Saturday).

Silk manufacturing began in 1840, after cotton production moved to New England. By 1870, two-thirds of raw silk imported to the United States was processed in Paterson. The city was attracting a sizable population of immigrants from Ireland, Germany, Russia, and Italy to work in the industry. In 1913, Flynn recalled, Paterson "hummed with silk factories." She did not remember it as an especially attractive place: "The city was a typical textile town with the same poor shabby firetrap wooden houses for the workers, dreary old mills built along the canal. The people were poorly dressed, pale and undernourished."[18] Despite their beleaguered appearance, Paterson's working-class residents engaged in continuous, active struggle against harsh labor conditions. Local historian Marcia Dente observes that "between 1880 and 1910, the city recorded at least 140 strikes and work stoppages."[19]

The 1913 strike began with a walkout by eight hundred employees of the Doherty Mill after four of their co-workers were fired for trying to get the company's management to eliminate the four-loom system. This system, known as the speedup, required operators who previously had run two looms to run three or four looms, which increased the physical exertion and output of each weaver and decreased the number of workers in the mills, without increasing wages. Workers who walked out of Doherty and other mills rejected the four-loom system and called for an eight-hour day, a minimum wage of twelve dollars per day for dyers' helpers, and a 25 percent increase for other silk workers. Histories of the strike have typically characterized the Doherty walkout as a spontaneous action, but groundwork for this action was laid over several years by Italian immigrant anarchists in the city.[20]

Paterson's polyglot silk workforce included English speakers as well as Germans, Eastern European Jews, and Italians. By 1913, Italians were the largest ethnic group in the silk mills. Many among them embraced syndicalism, anarchism, and socialism that dated back more than a generation. The anarchist community was especially vibrant and active. Paterson anarchists published one of the most widely circulated and influential Italian-language anarchist newspapers in the United States, *La Questione Sociale* (The social question), and several of the movement's outstanding figures were associated with the city. Errico Malatesta, the charismatic organizer and writer who was exiled from Italy after the repression of worker uprisings in the 1890s, assumed editorship of *La Questione Sociale* during his 1899 Paterson sojourn. In 1893, Maria Roda, famous for her defiant attitude toward an Italian judge who had her imprisoned at age fifteen for carrying on and singing seditious songs at a rally, migrated to Paterson from Italy and formed a women's "Emancipation Group" that inspired similar groups in a number of other cities with Italian immigrant neighborhoods.[21] In 1900, Italian-born silk worker Gaetano Bresci traveled from Paterson back to Italy and assassinated King Umberto I to avenge the killing of dozens workers in Milan for demonstrating against rising food prices during protests that swept through Italy in May of 1898.[22] Bresci's act earned Paterson the label "world capital of anarchism."[23] Luigi Galleani, who had escaped from an Italian prison where he was being held on charges of conspiracy, came to Paterson in 1901. In 1902, a strike erupted in the silk mills, and Galleani played a leading role; he was wounded in the face when shots rang out during a clash between striking workers and police. In 1913, when another strike broke out, Italians generally and Italian anarchists in particular comprised the militant core.[24]

After their rebellion against the speedup, strikers decided to organize under a union umbrella. As in Lawrence, their radicalism did not incline them to the American Federation of Labor, and the conservative, anti-immigrant craft union did little to attract them. On the contrary, the AFL United Textile Workers of America (UTW) had signed an agreement with the Doherty Mill to accept the four-loom system in 1909. A more immigrant friendly alternative was the IWW Silk Workers' Union Local 152, established by Paterson anarchists in 1906.[25] After the 1913 walkout, Local 152 offered leadership, and the striking workers accepted. "Leadership," however, is a misleading term. Throughout the strike, the relationship of the IWW to the strike was advisory.[26]

An alliance between silk workers and the militant union meant IWW organizers would be coming to Paterson. The local press and silk manufacturers looked upon this prospect with a combination of disdain and dismissiveness. On February 21, an editorial in the *Paterson Evening News* lamented, "the untold injury" visited on Paterson by the "pernicious activities" of "professional organizers who [came] from other cities and in a professional way [endeavored] to stir up strife in the mills and among the workers [there]."[27] Silk manufacturers expressed with confidence, "Our thousands of respectable workers will pay no attention to the howl of the IWW for a general walkout."[28] According to manufacturers, "respectable workers" accepted conditions in the mills uncomplainingly.

It soon became clear that the Paterson strike was as much a conflict over the right to plan, access, occupy, and use urban public space—the right to the city—as it was a struggle over the four-loom system, wages, and the length of the workday.[29] Silk interests claimed an exclusive right to the city. That they felt a kind of ownership of Paterson was not surprising, given that it had been planned as an industrial city, with buildings and thoroughfares designed to facilitate production and distribution of goods. The economic, social, and recreational interests of working-class residents were secondary (at best) concerns in a space created solely to generate profit. The challenge for striking workers was to claim their own right to Paterson by stifling the productive capacity of factories and transforming streets and sidewalks from conduits for distribution into forums for collective resistance and, at times, direct confrontation between capital and labor. Flynn and other IWW organizers joined the strike to facilitate this process.

Flynn and Tresca arrived in Paterson about a month after the strike began. It was not Flynn's first time in the city. In the summer of 1907 she spent a week there and spoke at the IWW hall every night.[30] She returned just a few weeks before the 1913 strike began and spoke to a group of shirt makers, after which, she recalled, "300 girls joined the I.W.W."[31] Upon her return the morning of February 25, she and Tresca addressed an audience of nearly five thousand mostly Italian and Jewish broad silk weavers at Turn Hall, urging them to join the Doherty workers in a general strike. Police Chief John Bimson, "who looked like a stupid moustached walrus," according to Flynn, could not understand why she was so concerned about "foreigners." He wasted no time in showing where he stood on the issue of free speech in Paterson.[32] Bimson branded the speakers "outside agitators" and arrested Flynn and Tresca along with fellow Wobbly Patrick Quinlan. Quinlan, who had arrived late to the meeting, was accosted as he walked down the aisle to the speaker's platform before he said a word to the audience. Flynn's arrest did not sit well with strikers—1,500 of them protested loudly outside the hall and accompanied her to the police station, jostling with police all the while.[33] She and the other "outside agitators" were released on bail and ordered to stay away from the city. The trio returned to Paterson two days later in defiance of the order. They were rearrested as they stepped off the train at the Erie Depot and charged with conspiracy to cause an unlawful assemblage of persons and inciting to riot. All three continued to speak in Paterson while they awaited trial.

On March 7, Big Bill Haywood joined the trio of Flynn, Tresca, and Quinlan. Police immediately arrested Haywood upon his arrival at the depot. Bimson denied the arrests were intended to suppress workers' right to strike, but he claimed control over who could speak about labor issues in Paterson. "We have no objection to our own people conducting a strike," he explained, "but the day of the out-of-town agitator carrying on his profession is past."[34] However, neither the silk manufacturers' bravado nor

Bimson's arrests succeeded in containing the strike. Instead, outrage at the abrogation of their right to decide who could speak to them and in what spaces fueled the decision of ribbon weavers to join.[35] The ranks continued to swell until twenty-five thousand workers—nearly all the silk workers in Paterson—were on strike. Close to three hundred mills were shut down.[36]

One tactic that mill owners used to tamp down militancy during the strike was to threaten workers with a "blacklist." Any worker whose name appeared on that list would be denied employment in the city's mills when the strike was over. This threat was meaningless to Flynn and other IWW leaders, so authorities instead had them arrested and "deported" from Paterson. Against criticism that he was violating the right of free assembly and free speech by having IWW organizers arrested, Paterson Mayor Andrew McBride claimed "an ancient right of cities" to prevent "undesirable strangers from invading."[37] McBride drew a distinction between the rights of workers who belonged in Paterson and IWW organizers, who had no real interest in the city except to tarnish its reputation as a hospitable place for industry. When strikers asked McBride to restore civil liberties in Paterson, the mayor declared that workers had the right to free speech and assembly, but outside agitators did not: "'I am a workingman,' the Mayor said, 'I worked to obtain my education as a doctor, and I am daily among the people, but I cannot stand for seeing Paterson flooded with persons who have no interest in Paterson, who can only give us a bad name.'"[38] By "bad name," McBride meant a reputation for being inhospitable to the new industries that Paterson was seeking to attract. He had been openly criticized by silk manufacturers for risking industrial development in the city by not taking a hard enough stance against radicals and was evidently looking to redress the matter.

McBride and other city officials attempted to drive a wedge between IWW organizers and the rank and file by claiming the union came to Paterson only to stir up trouble and would abandon them before the strike was over. Flynn refuted this claim in a speech to an assembly of strikers: "They say that out of town agitators have been brought here and now that they have stirred up all the trouble they are going to leave. How can we? Most of us are under bonds to remain within the State; so how can we possibly leave."[39] But her real reason for remaining in Paterson was not legal restriction: Flynn was committed to the strike and would remain in Paterson until it was finished.[40] Moreover, because she was invulnerable to the threat of blacklisting, she could take risks and say things about the silk manufacturers that workers could not. Wobbly organizers, she told workers, "are simply your phonograph and you make the record."[41]

Silk manufacturers also tried to use patriotism as a weapon against the Wobblies. They declared March 17 Flag Day, festooned the mills with American flags, and offered strikers a choice between the red flag of revolutionary and foreign socialism or the stars and stripes.[42] Of course, Flynn and fellow Wobblies were no strangers to using the vocabulary and symbolism of Americanism to legitimate their cause. After all, they had defended their right to free speech in Spokane, Missoula, and numerous other localities by standing on a soapbox and reading the Declaration of Independence. On March 17, strikers marched through Paterson wearing American flag pins supplied by local socialists and carrying a banner that read, "We wove the flag; we dyed the flag. We live under the flag; but we won't scab under the flag."[43]

Flynn's commitment to the strike went beyond talk. On April 25, a grand jury indicted her for incitement to riot and advocating destruction of property. She was in New York at the time, but together with Tresca, who had also been indicted, Flynn returned to Paterson the next day to be placed under arrest. A crowd of five hundred strikers gathered at the train station to watch as Paterson police hustled her into a waiting car. As the car pulled away, the crowd gave her a rousing cheer of encouragement: "We'll stick it out even if you are in jail, Miss Flynn!" After a short stay in jail, Flynn was released on $3,000 bail. She expressed no worry about the charges against her, confident as she was that they would be dropped as soon as they were heard by the jury. Her first act upon leaving the sheriff's office was to send a telegram to her mother in New York. "Mother worries a great deal about me," she explained, and being a dutiful daughter, Flynn wanted to set her mother's mind at ease.[44]

Silk manufacturers refused to acknowledge that workers had risen in revolt on their own. Instead, they insisted the IWW was directing the strike and vying to wrest control of the city and its workforce away from them. As part of their effort to drive the union out of Paterson, manufacturers banded together and formed a press committee, which paid for a series of articles in the *Paterson Evening News* to present the current situation from their perspective. In their opening salvo, manufacturers claimed the general strike that grew from "an incipient beginning" involving one mill was caused by "the sinister influence of the organization known as the Industrial Workers of the World." As evidence of the union's "sinister influence" they cited the free speech fights in Los Angeles and San Diego, during which Wobbly organizers were indicted by grand juries "for inciting riots," and the Lawrence strike, during which the Wobblies "were charged with having incited riots that resulted in murder." Manufacturers insisted that order, progress, and prosperity could be restored in Paterson only by themselves: "men who have had a hand in the upbuilding of the city; men who are engaged in educational, charitable and uplifting endeavors; men who can look their fellows and their employees in the face with the consciousness of fair dealings always."[45] Local newspapers amplified this sentiment and called for the formation of vigilance committees to force the Wobblies out of town.[46]

Flynn issued a rejoinder to these claims in a speech to a sympathetic audience of small business owners, which was later elaborated and published in *Solidarity* under the heading "Figures and Facts." In the speech, she contested manufacturers' claims about good wages, noting that an examination of pay envelopes proved workers were paid far less than their bosses had claimed. She also posed a series of questions to challenge the presumption that silk manufacturers' interests were coequal with the city's interests.

> Does the Silk Association have its banquets here? No, they dine in the Waldorf-Astoria in New York City. Have they their spacious offices here? No, their address is 354 Fourth Avenue, New York City. Do their wives and daughters buy their gowns (silk or otherwise), their furs, jewels or automobiles in Paterson? Do they attend the opera in Paterson? . . . Do the employers build their homes, attend church or send their children to school here? How many grocery, clothing, shoe, drygoods or drug stores, meat markets, coal dealers or doctors and dentists could exist if they depended on the mill owners for patronage? We address these plain words to the businessmen of Paterson. The manufacturers and stockholders are not your customers. The workers are![47]

In Flynn's alternative vision of the city, silk manufacturers were the real "outsiders" because profits they earned in Paterson filled the coffers of businesses in New York City and the economic well-being of silk workers was what ensured stability and prosperity for the city. She made the same case while she was under interrogation by Police Chief Bimson: "You look at Paterson different than I do, chief. You see Paterson when you look at the manufacturers and the businessmen of the city, but I look at Paterson as 25,000 silk workers who are struggling hard to make a living under poor conditions."[48]

The State of New Jersey also refused to believe that Paterson's silk workers had sufficient reason or rebelliousness to wage an industry-wide general strike on their own. In its annual report, the New Jersey Bureau of Industrial Statistics, precursor to the Department of Labor, faulted the Wobblies for stirring up discontent among workers and unnecessarily enlarging the strike beyond shops that were directly impacted by the speedup. The report insisted that Paterson's resident silk workers would not have engaged in an industry-wide strike had they not been aroused by outsiders "masquerading as representatives of an organization working for the welfare of labor" who seized control of the strike and made intemperate appeals to further their revolutionary agenda.[49]

The claim that IWW organizers manipulated silk workers for their own ends obscured the strikers' very real grievances. This fact was not lost on at least one contemporary observer. John Fitch, an author of the landmark 1909 Pittsburgh Survey, the first major U.S. sociological study of an industrial community, wrote after he visited Paterson, "It cannot be without cause that working people numbering tens of thousands continue on strike, their incomes absolutely cut off, for a period of three months," and yet he reported hearing very little talk, outside the ranks of the strikers, about the grievances, real or imagined, of the silk workers.[50] Instead, he noted, "In the offices, stores and cafes, in the meetings of the ministerial association, in the Charity Organization Society, in most of the papers and at the firesides of the more comfortable citizens, there is but one topic of conversation—the I. W. W."[51]

Clearly, for all their insistence on the docility of their workforce, silk manufacturers and their allies worried that the IWW's success in Lawrence would be repeated in Paterson. Their fears were not without grounds. Paterson's history of radicalism meant that the core of the strike consisted of workers who were more experienced and skilled in struggle than were their Lawrence counterparts. And they could benefit from lessons learned in Lawrence. To that end, Wobblies brought to New Jersey some of the tactics that had been used successfully during the Lawrence strike. They organized a general strike committee that had complete authority over all decisions to ensure that the strike belonged to the workers. Most of the committee's members were non-IWW, and all proposals formulated by the committee were sent to the rank and file for approval.[52]

Another tactic brought from Lawrence was the mobile picket line, which marched up and down the sidewalks in front of each of the mills every day. The continually moving chain of pickets supplanted the tactic of small, static groups that had been used in previous strikes, including the famed shirtwaist makers strike in New York in 1909. Essentially a type of parade, the moving picket line was a performance of solidarity, a form of communication, and a mode of resistance. When strikers walked back and forth on streets and sidewalks in front of the mills singing, carrying signs, and chanting slogans, they took up physical and acoustic space and made themselves seen, heard, and impossible to ignore.[53] The act of picketing this way engaged and unified otherwise idle and disparate workers physically and mentally; provided visible proof of the power of collective action for strikers, employers, and other members of the community; and kept the strike a public issue. Arguably, the most important function of the picket was to grind production to a halt by physically blocking the factory entrance and psychologically intimidating men or women who approached with ideas of going back to work.[54]

The primary importance of picketing to stop production was not lost on Flynn, or on the Paterson police. In 1913 picketing was not a legally protected category of political speech, and police routinely arrested picketers, often for alleged acts—or planned acts—of violence. To thwart such accusations, Flynn cautioned workers on the picket line to keep their hands in their pockets so that police could not plant rocks or other objects in them and claim that picketers were planning to use the planted objects to break windows or commit other violent acts.[55] When arrested strikers were brought to trial in the Passaic County Courthouse and crowds of fellow strikers demonstrated in protest outside, she insisted that the demonstrators return to the picket line to keep strikebreakers from entering the mills: "I cannot make it too strong. Get up in the morning and see to it that no one returns to work. Don't devote your interest to the Court House because it will be foolish to concentrate your attention there. You don't have to picket the Court House, because the scabs will not go there."[56]

Flynn also excoriated jurors who found picketers guilty. Although any informal congregation on streets or sidewalks could be construed as an unlawful assemblage, she observed that only striking workers were arrested and charged.

> Walking on the streets is not a crime in the United States of America, if it is, they will have to put us all off the earth. Then we will have to suspend ourselves in the air and the clouds. The capitalistic courts admit that you have the right. Picketing is not yet a crime. If a dog is killed or hurt on the street, in an instant a crowd will congregate. Is that unlawful assemblage? If it is unlawful to picket the mills then it is unlawful to watch the baseball score on the boards of the newspaper office. If it is unlawful to picket, then it is unlawful to look at street store windows.[57]

It was not up to the police to decide which kinds of activities constituted appropriate gathering and where such gatherings might take place. Flynn insisted that silk workers had as much lawful right to access, occupy, and use Paterson's streets and sidewalks as did anyone else. She also insisted that strikers continue picketing despite arrests. To relinquish the picket line was to relinquish the right to be in Paterson's streets, to cede the city to Paterson's business interests and thereby surrender the strike. On this point, she was unequivocal: "For you to relax on the picket line will make you a traitor to your fellow workers."[58]

Paterson police showed little concern for the constitutional rights of silk workers. Their loyalty was to the silk manufacturers. They patrolled city streets in a car furnished by the National Silk Dyeing Company, subjecting IWW organizers, strikers, and anyone suspected of being a striker to verbal harassment, physical violence, and arrest for any number of legal acts, such as walking, gathering and talking in groups, carrying a Socialist newspaper, or whistling.[59] Approximately 1,850 strikers, most of them Italians or Jews, were arrested on charges of unlawful assemblage and inciting to riot. In most cases penalties ranged from ten days to six months in the county jails with fines from $10 to $500. Not all punishments were meted out in court. Police and "special detectives" from the O'Brien Detective Agency of Newark employed by one of the manufacturers beat, kicked, and clubbed strikers. Two men were murdered: Modestino Valentino, an innocent bystander to a scuffle between picketers and strikebreakers, was shot and killed by company detectives on April 19; Vincenzo Madonna, a striker, was shot and killed by a strikebreaker on July 13.[60] In defiance of efforts to keep them from gathering in the streets, Wobblies held mass funerals for both men that filled the city's thoroughfares with mourners. Valentino's funeral cortege stretched for ten blocks; thousands of workers marched in the procession to the cemetery, where they heard fiery eulogies by Tresca and Haywood that honored Valentino and vilified silk manufacturers, police, and detectives. A seemingly endless parade of mourners then filed by and dropped red carnations on the casket.[61] Madonna's funeral was smaller but still noteworthy for its size. Fifteen hundred men and 350 women marched in the funeral procession, which passed from 120 Belmont Avenue, where he lived, through the center of the city.[62] Both murders went unpunished.

Women were an important part of the workforce in Paterson, and they played a vital role in the strike. They led or marched on picket lines and strike parades, got up on soapboxes to exhort fellow workers on streets and sidewalks, and spoke from the stage in meeting halls. A group of teenage Italian girls who walked out of the Bamford Mill addressed a meeting in Madison Square Garden in New York City about working conditions in the mill.[63] Silk worker Hannah Silverman marched with a contingent of fifteen other strikers from Paterson approximately thirty miles to Coney Island, Brooklyn.[64] A few of the women were seasoned radicals, but many others found their voice during the strike. Flynn reached out to them at women-only meetings and helped many to

FIGURE 1. Elizabeth Gurley Flynn (seated, right) with Eva Botto (standing) and an unidentified Paterson striker, 1913.
Credit: American Labor Museum / Botto House National Landmark

overcome their fear of public speaking. She also insisted upon absolute loyalty to the union. Just before the policemen's ball, she warned that "any girl who attended or danced with a policeman would be thrown out of the union."[65] She was twenty-two years old at the time, and her youth, vitality, dedication to the union, and apparent fearlessness made her enormously popular among the young women workers, who saw her as a model for activism and leadership. But Flynn's popularity extended beyond the young women of Paterson's silk mills. Beloved by male and female workers of all ages, immigrant and U.S.-born alike, she was the main link between the IWW and the strikers.[66] In his history of the strike, Steve Golin notes, "This woman, more than anyone, was the leader of the Paterson strike."[67]

Femininity afforded little in the way of protection or status for striking silk workers. A quarter of the strikers arrested were women.[68] Some of the more outspoken and militant strikers, such as Hannah Silverman and Mary Gasperano, were arrested multiple times for a variety of "offenses," including speaking to picketers and intimidating strike breakers. Women strikers were targets of physical violence too. Ninfa Baronio was clubbed on the picket line in front of her young son for the "offense" of trying to help a striker bloodied and knocked unconscious by a blow to the head and defending a ten-year-old boy who was being kicked by a policeman.[69] Alexander Scott, editor of the Socialist *Passaic Weekly Issue*, testified to seeing a woman, eight months pregnant, "pushed in the abdomen very roughly by a policeman, and knocked down" for pleading with police not to arrest her husband.[70] Scott himself had been arrested and charged with "advocating hostility to the government of Paterson" for criticizing Bimson in his paper.[71]

Squeezing the IWW out of the City

A strike of such magnitude and with such determined opposition required extensive coordination. Strikers met regularly to discuss and devise tactics, socialize, forge alliances, exchange information, and reenergize. The typical lineup was mass meetings in the morning, shop meetings in the afternoon. Meetings for women and for members of Local 152 and other groups were held on various evenings.[72] Like many associations of immigrant and working-class people, the IWW did not have resources to construct or purchase a building in which to hold meetings and had to use borrowed or rented spaces. Fortunately, early twentieth-century Paterson was dotted with meeting halls. The largest and most important of them were Turn Hall and Helvetia Hall. Owned by Italians Thomas

Cappa and James Cangianelli, Turn Hall was the principal meeting place of the strikers; Helvetia Hall served as IWW headquarters. Smaller venues like Probst's Hall, Degelman's Hall, the Union Athletic Club, and the Workingmen's Institute held the shop meetings, more sober gatherings where decisions about strategy typically were made. Not every hall proprietor was willing to rent to the strikers; the union called a boycott of the Germania Assembly Rooms after the proprietor refused to rent space for meetings of the hard silk weavers.[73]

Flynn was far and away the most popular speaker. The mere mention of her name drew cheers of "hurrah!" and sent crowds of workers to the stage to find the best vantage point.[74] Besides Flynn, Tresca, Quinlan, and Haywood, other prominent radicals who spoke at mass meetings included labor poet and Lawrence strike leader Arturo Giovannitti; Harlem soapboxer Hubert Harrison, also known as the "Black Socrates"; and Socialist Frederic Sumner Boyd, editor of the *New York Call*. Meetings were not closed: police attended and had stenographers on hand to record what transpired. It was not unusual to begin with an instrumental musical performance to enliven the crowd and for evening meetings to morph into a dance or some other festive social event.

Paterson's blue laws, which banned all secular business on the Christian Sabbath, meant that strikers could not hold meetings on Sundays.[75] To

FIGURE 2. Elizabeth Gurley Flynn in Paterson with Hubert Harrison (seated, left), William "Big Bill" Haywood (seated, right), Patrick Quinlan (standing, second from left), and other IWW members, 1913.
Credit: American Labor Museum / Botto House National Landmark

keep momentum going at the beginning of the strike, socialists suggested nearby Haledon as an alternative location for Sunday meetings. Mayor William Brueckmann, elected on the Socialist ticket, welcomed strikers to town. The first meetings were held outside in a spot called Barbour's Grove. An estimated twelve to fifteen thousand men, women, and children braved wind, rain, and mud for the strike meeting on March 2. The site lacked a good speaker's platform, and some in the audience climbed trees for improved visibility, but they had to return to earth because of high winds. Flynn, who was one of the speakers at the meeting, caught a cold from being outdoors in wet weather for so long and went back to New York City to recuperate.[76]

Things took a turn for the better in April, when Italian silk workers Pietro and Maria Botto granted IWW organizers and strikers access to their Haledon property at 93 Norwood Street. Built in 1908, the Botto house functioned as both a home and a source of income; the family always kept the first floor for their own use and typically rented rooms on the second and third floors. During the strike, especially on Sundays, the house was transformed into a vibrant political space. The design lent itself to this kind of transformation. Building and grounds made a perfect outdoor amphitheater. The three-story concrete-block and clapboard house sat on a hill overlooking a large green that was almost entirely enclosed by trees; a second-floor balcony functioned as an elevated speaker's platform. Whereas the smaller Paterson halls required workers to meet separately within their distinct occupational groups, the grounds of the Botto house were spacious enough to accommodate all the strikers. Upwards of thirty thousand people representing nine ethnic groups gathered on the lawn, where they picnicked, sang songs, enjoyed band performances, and applauded speeches by Flynn, Tresca, Haywood, Quinlan, local Wobbly Adolph Lessig, Upton Sinclair, Hubert Harrison, and others.

Those who attended the "monster meetings," as they were called, experienced solidarity directly and powerfully as they looked out on the large crowd and heard and felt themselves eating, singing, laughing, booing, and cheering in concert with so many fellow workers. After the strike was over, Flynn explained the importance of the Haledon meetings for militating against feelings of social isolation and material deprivation and encouraging solidarity among workers. The original reason for going to Haledon, she recalled, went deep into the psychology of a strike.

> Because Sunday is the day before Monday! Monday is the day that a break comes in every strike, if it is to come at all during the week. If

FIGURE 3. Elizabeth Gurley Flynn in front of the Botto House, 1913.
Credit: American Labor Museum / Botto House National Landmark

you can bring the people safely over Monday they usually go along for the rest of the week. If on Sunday, however, you let those people stay at home, sit around the stove without any fire in it, sit down at the table where there isn't very much food, see the feet of the children with shoes getting thin, and the bodies of the children where the clothes are getting ragged, they begin to think in terms of "myself" and lose that spirit of the mass and the realization that all are suffering as they are suffering. You have got to keep them busy every day in the week, and especially on Sunday, in order to keep that spirit from going down to zero.[77]

Photos of the meetings published in the press conveyed the size of the crowd and suggested the magnitude of the Haledon experience.[78] IWW leaders, strikers, and the women of the Botto family, whose hard work maintaining the house and tending to the needs of the speakers made the events possible, recalled the meetings as tremendously exhilarating occasions.[79]

As the strike continued, police punished the owners of Turn and Helvetia halls by threatening to revoke their liquor licenses and fining them for running a "disorderly house" after strikers held a dance without first seeking a dance hall permit. These financial disincentives proved ineffective at keeping the hall owners from renting to strikers. On May 19, a month after Valentino's murder, a meeting at Turn Hall threatened to erupt into violence when a policeman brandished his gun after strikers heckled detectives in the audience and tried to eject the official stenographer, Sydney Turner. The next day, Mayor McBride ordered Turn Hall and Helvetia Hall closed. Police also ordered streets around the mills closed and prevented strikers from using three thoroughfares: Beech Street, Summer Street, and Railroad Avenue.

Reports of police brutality, street closings, hall closings, and the conviction and sentencing of Patrick Quinlan to two to seven years' imprisonment sparked a debate in Paterson and around the country about civil liberties.[80] Strikers and their supporters actively participated in the debate and took action to protect their constitutional rights. A committee of strikers voiced complaints about street closings. As happened during the free speech fights, comparisons between the United States and tsarist Russia were made.[81] The owners of Turn and Helvetia halls brought suit against Mayor McBride, Chief Bimson, and the police commissioner and sought an injunction against closing the halls until the case was heard.[82] Unfortunately, the struggle between city officials and the union continued to get more attention in the press than did the conditions in the mills that gave rise to the strike. Disagreement centered on who were the primary lawbreakers: police and Mayor McBride, for transgressing state and federal constitutional provisions by limiting free speech and assembly, or the IWW, for supposedly encouraging riotous behavior and threatening property with calls for sabotage.[83]

The closing of Turn, Helvetia, and other halls around the city forced Wobblies to find creative solutions to the lack of meeting space. Flynn petitioned local churches for permission to hold women's meetings on their premises to ensure that women could meet in a warm and safe place off the street.[84] Although she was unsuccessful, it is a testament to her talent for improvisation that a radical socialist would seek space in houses of worship. Churches were important community organizations, and to secure their support for the strike would have been a significant achievement. The IWW also tried to borrow or lease privately owned residential spaces, perhaps in hopes of repeating the success of the Haledon meetings at the Botto House. A man who owned real estate at 51 and 53 Ellison Street permitted strikers to hold meetings outside in the backyards, which abutted one another. An audience of two thousand, including men, women, and children, jammed into the space, and hundreds were turned away. Local organizer Ewald Koettgen told the assembled crowd, "They can close halls and do other things against you but they can't stop us from meeting in the open air when the owner of the land decides that they will give you the privilege of assembling on their property."[85]

Koettgen's remarks reveal that the IWW tethered its free speech claim to a private property claim, another notable tactic, given the union's strong anarchist influence. The tactic succeeded. By granting his consent to strike meetings, the owner of the Ellison Street lots transferred the rights that inhered to him as a property owner to the union and the strikers. The problem of state intervention thus solved, at least for the moment, Koettgen announced that meetings would be held in the lots every morning until the halls reopened. That plan soon proved unworkable. So many workers crowded onto the porches there was fear they would collapse under the weight and cause injury.[86]

A few days later, IWW organizer Adolph Lessig signed a lease for the Doremus Estate on Water Street. The oldest homestead in the city, reported to have been the headquarters of President George Washington when he was in the area, it was a pleasant, comfortable colonial residence, "built of big brown stone blocks, with low white eaves, spacious rooms, a hall running through the centre, and plenty of light and air."[87] The spacious grounds could hold as many as twenty thousand people for open-air meetings. In what was by now characteristic fashion, the Wobblies used the language of Americanism to describe the significance of using the historic estate for their own brand of revolutionary activism. *Solidarity*, the IWW paper based in Cleveland, Ohio, heralded the acquisition of "Historic Headquarters for IWW Strikers." The paper offered a historical narrative of the building that linked the kind of work performed there by the eighteenth-century president with activities of twentieth-century striking silk workers, noting, "Rooms once occupied by the greatest American protagonist of political freedom are now the meeting place of the strike committee, the forerunners of industrial freedom."[88]

Although weather would still be an issue, there could be no question about strikers' right to assemble: because the estate was leased to Lessig, it was effectively property of the union. Even the local press recognized the IWW's property claim: the May 28, 1913, headline of the *Paterson Evening News* read "Strikers Meet in Pouring Rain on Their Own Property." The union used its property rights to make the Doremus Estate into a quasi-public meeting space; Wobblies communicated the inclusiveness of the space by labeling building and grounds "The Workers' City Hall."[89] Having once again settled the matter of meeting space, Lessig told the two-thousand-plus strikers who assembled on the lawn for the first Water Street meeting, there was no longer a need to worry about police closing up their halls. Strikers could get back to the picket line and see that no one returned to work.[90]

Despite Lessig's assurances, conflict over strike meetings in Paterson did not end with the leasing of the Doremus Estate. About a week later, members of the congregation of the Grace Methodist Episcopal Church composed a petition to the Board of Public Works against open-air meetings there. That strikers were meeting in the same space where President Washington once held counsel no doubt offended the sensibilities of men like Samuel McCollum, a prominent church leader and representative of the silk manufacturers as well as the husband of Margaret M. Doremus, whose family name graced the estate. Strikers responded with their own petition, endorsed by five hundred signatories who supported the meetings.[91] Conflict between strikers and Grace Methodist Episcopal turned audible the next day, when a drum corps held rehearsal on church grounds during an open-air strike meeting across the street. The sound of the drums drowned out Lessig as he was addressing fifteen thousand strikers assembled at the Doremus Estate. A group of about three hundred strikers went to the church and asked the corps to stop playing, but the drumming continued unabated, and the strike meeting was halted for several minutes. Fearing retaliation, members of the church called police to the scene. After the drumming finally stopped, a large automobile with a sign advertising a church picnic drove down the street, with young men blowing horns and ringing cowbells. Flynn, who was speaking at the time, fell silent. After the car passed and the cacophony was over, she told strikers that if they had done anything like that in the city, they would have been arrested for inciting to riot.[92]

Starving Workers into Submission

Squeezing the IWW out of Paterson was only one tactic used to break the strike. Starving the workers into submission was another. Silk manufacturers had developed industries in Pennsylvania to counter the militancy of Paterson's workers with the desperation of coal mining families. The labor force in these Pennsylvania communities was primarily women and children, who worked more hours per week for less pay than their counterparts in Paterson. As the strike ground on through the spring, Wobbly organizers tried to shut down the Pennsylvania operations. Flynn spoke to girls in a Pennsylvania silk mill, who were doing Paterson work, to no avail.[93]

Flynn, Tresca, and other IWW organizers also traveled around New Jersey to raise awareness of the strike and money for the strike fund. In Hackensack, New Jersey, the halls were closed to them, and they had to address workers on the outskirts of the city on the lawn of a sympathizer. Efforts to overcome hostilities did not always meet with success. In Bayonne, four unidentified IWW speakers were refused permission to speak and escorted out of town on order of Mayor Matthew T. Cronin.[94] Another IWW veteran of the Lawrence strike, Joseph Ettor, was denied a permit for hall space in New Haven, Connecticut, when he attempted to speak on behalf of Paterson strikers.[95]

To alleviate hunger and deprivation among strikers, Flynn oversaw another exodus of the children, like the one she had organized to such great success in Lawrence. It began on May Day when one thousand strikers and a busload of eighty-five strikers' children swelled the ranks of the New York City parade. Crowds "constantly cheered" as the bus wended its way through Manhattan, and they gave the children an ovation when they reached Union Square.[96] After the parade, the children were distributed among New York families who were to care for them for the duration of the strike. In all, seven hundred Paterson children were placed with sympathetic families in New York and New Jersey. However, unlike in Lawrence where violence erupted when police intervened to prevent the children from leaving, the tactic did not attract widespread attention or generate significant financial support, probably because Paterson police let the children leave without interference.[97]

The Paterson Pageant

With hunger continually nipping at the heels of the strikers, some Wobbly organizers turned to the bohemian set in Greenwich Village for help. These cultural radicals had provided crucial support in terms of publicity and money, but it was not enough to fill the bellies of twenty-five thousand workers and the families that depended on them for sustenance. Haywood and a few other organizers met with a group of artists and writers to brainstorm ways to bring the story of the strike to other potentially sympathetic New Yorkers who would donate needed funds. They came up with a plan to reenact the strike on stage in the form of a pageant. On June 7, a group of one thousand strikers performed before an audience of fifteen thousand, including three thousand strikers, in a theatrical production at Madison Square Garden created by journalist and poet John Reed and financed by Mabel Dodge. Hannah Silverman led the pageant parade of strikers-turned-performers singing the *Marseillaise* and the *Internationale* up Fifth Avenue to the Garden.

Flynn—who believed strikes were fought at the workplace, not in the theater—opposed the pageant from the start because it distracted workers from the picket line. She did not raise her objections publicly at the time, but in her postmortem of Paterson, she derided the pageant as the event that "started the decline" of the strike. Instead of holding the line at the mills, she argued, the most energetic and strongest workers were "playing pickets on the stage." While they were absent from the picket line, the first scabs entered the mills. Adding insult to injury, the pageant did not deliver on its promise to fill the coffers of the strike fund.[98]

In the end, it is hard to imagine how the pageant—or any artistic collaboration—could have succeeded in turning the tide of the strike. Silk interests proved less attached to the city of Paterson than the strikers and more able to capitalize on geographic mobility than the IWW. While strikers suffered hunger and other forms of material deprivation, manufacturers continued production by sending orders to factories in Pennsylvania, where, despite Flynn's best efforts, the wives, daughters, and sisters of poorly paid miners were willing to work for low wages. Outlasted by the manufacturers, one by one, dyers, then broad silk weavers, then ribbon weavers, then dye workers returned to work.

Conspiracy Trial

Flynn was tried twice for the charge of conspiracy to cause an unlawful assemblage of persons and inciting to riot. Her first trial opened on June 30, 1913. In response to a petition from defense attorney Henry Marelli, State Supreme Court Justice James Minturn ordered "foreign" juries for her trial and that of the other IWW organizers to be drawn from Hoboken, Jersey City, and other locales outside the county.[99] Fellow Wobblies predicted that the trial would draw the attention of the press because, as one writer for *Solidarity* put it, Flynn, with her youth and ability, "makes good copy."[100] They were right. On the day she was called to testify on her behalf, Flynn brought her mother, Annie, and toddler son, Buster, to court with her, a not-unprecedented act, as both had accompanied her to the courthouse in Lawrence for the murder trial of Joseph Ettor and Arturo Giovannitti.

It is impossible to discern whether Flynn intended their presence at her Paterson trial to provide a tactical advantage, but having mother and especially son present suggested to jurors that in addition to being a radical revolutionary, she was a beloved daughter and mother. Buster endeared himself to the press and, almost certainly, the jury as well. The *Paterson Evening News* reported that the child possessed "long flaxen curls" and a "beautiful little head." His appearance and "scampering" around the courtroom made him the center of attention.[101] Most affecting was the "little tot's" behavior when lunch was brought to the jury.

> A little picture that touched the hearts of many, occurred shortly after 3 o'clock yesterday afternoon, when a caterer arrived with the dinners of the jurymen. As the door of the jury room swung open and the men entered carrying the large baskets filled with good things the little tot was seen to run in the open door and stand peeping in open eyed wonderment at the faces of the twelve stern men seated around the table discussing the fate of his mother. He stood there for nearly a moment before he was noticed, and then he was tenderly picked up by one of the court attaches, who carried him away out of the sight of the men within.[102]

This performance of family ties and maternal obligation brought Flynn's private life into the formal, public space of the courthouse. The domestication of public space must be considered at least partially responsible for the jury's inability to render a verdict after twenty-five hours of deliberation.[103]

The strike effectively ended not long after the end of Flynn's trial, on July 28, 1913. On August 3, workers held their last Sunday meeting in Haledon, but at Cedar Cliff Woods instead of the Botto House. Pietro Botto, fearful of reprisals from manufacturers against his family for the prominent role they had played during the strike, had refused to allow further use of his house and yard. His concern was not unwarranted: about two thousand men and women who had participated in the strike were blacklisted and struggled to find work.[104] Yet the strike was not a complete failure. Although workers did not win an eight-hour day, twenty-one factories agreed to reduce the workday from ten to nine hours. Two-loom assignments, rather than the three- or four-loom systems that pervaded elsewhere, remained the industry standard in Paterson. Their solidarity fragmented after 1913, but Paterson silk workers continued to strike, albeit on a much smaller scale, in the months, years, and decades that followed.[105]

Although Flynn struggled with chronic bronchitis after months of shuttling between New York City and Paterson and speaking outdoors in inclement weather, she returned to address workers several times after the strike ended. She was less successful when attempting to speak in other New Jersey cities and towns—including Trenton, Bayonne, and Jersey City—to raise money for the defense of Quinlan and also Boyd, who had been arrested and convicted of sedition during the waning days of the strike for advocating sabotage.[106] Quinlan's conviction was particularly egregious because, according to his own testimony and that of thirty witnesses, he had not even spoken at the meeting where he was arrested. However, nine policemen testified to the contrary, and the jury found their testimony more credible.[107] Efforts to shut out Quinlan's advocates were not limited to the Garden State. In New York City, the Paterson Defense Conference was denied use of the storied Great Hall at Cooper Union. The ban elicited protest from the well-heeled Edith Cram, a supporter of Flynn's and a granddaughter of Peter Cooper, to no avail.[108]

The winter of 1914 was cold and bleak. A recession left scores of people unemployed around the United States. As Flynn noted, "There were growing breadlines, homeless men were sleeping in doorways and cellars, families were in dire distress."[109] After several unemployed men were arrested for taking shelter in a New York City church, Flynn helped organize the IWW Unemployed Union of New York to coordinate demands for food, clothing, and jobs. She spent much of the remainder of the year recuperating from bronchitis, relaxing with Tresca, and tending to her son, who had also taken ill.[110]

The Paterson Free Speech Fight

Flynn was back on the circuit in the spring of 1915. After a months-long speaking tour that took her to forty-seven cities and nineteen states, she returned to New York in the fall.[111] In early September of 1915, amid talk of another strike, silk manufacturers and the chamber of commerce pressured Mayor McBride's successor, Robert Fordyce, to keep the Wobblies from returning to Paterson by issuing a written order prohibiting IWW meetings.[112] Fordyce complied, citing as precedent similar actions by officials in other cities around the United States.[113] The Paterson ban was officially implemented when Flynn and Tresca came to address a meeting of silk workers on September 3, 1915. Chief Bimson ordered the hall closed and the meeting dispersed. Tresca, who had been arrested more times than any other IWW leader during the strike, slipped away.[114] Police took Flynn to the station, where she was interrogated by Bimson. After the interrogation, Bimson ordered Flynn to be escorted to the Erie Depot and put on a train to New York. In an uncharacteristically candid assessment of the situation with regard to free speech in Paterson, he quipped, "You may have the right, but we have the power."[115] Undaunted, Flynn refused to ride in the police car and insisted on walking the route from the police station to the train station. Of course, she was recognized almost immediately (surely that was her intent) and before long a crowd of about five hundred people joined her, making a kind of spontaneous parade and demonstration. Supporters at the depot cheered her as she boarded the train.[116]

Fordyce's order sparked renewed debate about free speech in Paterson. "We understand that Paterson, N.J., has seceded from the United States," announced the *New Republic*. "The chamber of commerce, the mayor and the chief of police among them have abrogated the constitution and have decided that they will use force to prevent Miss Elizabeth Gurley Flynn from addressing the mill workers. The rulers of Paterson are about the most dangerous citizens this country harbors."[117] Not all reactions were critical. Praise for the ban on IWW speakers came from various quarters. A *New York Times* editorial, titled "Good for Paterson," is illustrative: "Free speech is a noble and an indispensable right," declared the paper. "The New Jersey city of Paterson has suffered long and been excessively magnanimous to public enemies on account of its praiseworthy devotion to free speech. It has been too hospitable to perilous guests. Friday night it drew the line at last."[118] The editorial continued, "In view of the $15,000,000 or so at which Paterson estimates its loss by the mischief making of the IWW two years ago, it may well feel that its generosity to rattlesnakes has gone on long enough."[119] The *Times*'s urban vision matched that of the manufacturers: business interests constituted the city of Paterson; consequently, anything that threatened the profits of business interests was harmful to the city.

IWW organizers had grown used to having the content of their speech monitored and (often falsely) reported during a strike, and as the Paterson example illustrates, they were remarkably resourceful at creating and using space where speech and other forms of active participation could happen, but Fordyce's preemptive measure was a different matter. "This," recalled Flynn, "culminated in a free speech fight."[120] Haywood fired off telegrams to President Wilson and Mayor Fordyce protesting that Flynn had been "deported from Paterson" in violation of New Jersey's own constitutional protections and threatening a call to the general membership "to fight this issue and re-establish the right to free speech and free assembly."[121] Both Flynn and Haywood knew that the stakes in an established East Coast city with a history of labor conflict were different than they were in a place that was banking on its reputation as a pleasant alternative to older industrial centers. Moreover, the existence of a resident workforce vulnerable to blacklisting required different tactics from free speech campaigns among migrant workers in western and midwestern locales. The Wobbly newspaper *Solidarity* amplified this message: "Paterson is not Spokane. It is a city of 'home guards,' not migratory workers. A free speech fight, in the Spokane way, is not possible; not at least until passive resistance has been tried and a favorable atmosphere has been created." But passive resistance was not to be confused with acceptance of the status quo: "The fight is by no means ended yet."[122]

Flynn and the Wobblies could not count on an army of hoboes to make their way to Paterson and mount the soapbox in assembly line fashion as they did in Missoula and Spokane, but support did come from other allies, among them the libertarian radicals in the Free Speech League.[123] The league had had its own conflict with Paterson police just after the end of the strike. In December of 1913, anarchist Emma Goldman was prohibited from delivering a lecture on "The Spirit of Anarchism in the Labor Struggle." A month later, the league held a protest meeting at which journalist Lincoln Steffens, anarchists Goldman and Alexander Berkman, and other free speech advocates spoke, unmolested.[124] After the 1915 ban on IWW meetings was enacted, the Free Speech League scheduled another protest meeting. That meeting was suppressed by police on the grounds that the hall owner had no permit. "This was merely a subterfuge," league president Leonard Abbott later reported. "The actual cause of the suppression of the meeting seems to have been the fear that Elizabeth Gurley Flynn or Carlo Tresca would attempt to speak."[125] Abbott was right. As Flynn explained in a letter urging socialist and friend Rose Pastor Stokes to attend the meeting, organizers had signed a contract specifying "no IWW speakers permitted," but the plan was to have Flynn and Tresca address the audience anyway and then "put it up the authorities either to discriminate against [them] or drop the matter."[126]

Ultimately, the Paterson free speech fight boiled down to a contest between Paterson authorities and Elizabeth Gurley Flynn. One reporter who witnessed a failed attempt by Flynn to address a meeting in Paterson recounted it as "the burly [police captain] and the little labor leader ... confronting each other on the steps of the hall."[127] Another called the struggle "Elizabeth Flynn's contest with Paterson."[128] As justification for her presence in the silk city and part of an effort to create a more formal, centralized organizational structure, the IWW announced that Flynn had been appointed organizer for Paterson and vicinity. Adolph Lessig's statement regarding Flynn's appointment asserted for U.S. citizens a fundamental right to mobility—especially for the purpose of employment—within and between states: "Miss Flynn is a citizen of the United States and we claim the right to move freely from one section of the country to another and accept whatever positions might be tendered us, whether in the interests of labor or otherwise."[129] Lessig's claim that U.S. citizens had complete freedom of movement between and within states was a challenge to Paterson authorities who barred Flynn from the city on grounds that she was a dangerous outsider attempting to stir up unrest among locals.

Flynn's own effort to thwart suppression of her right to speak in Paterson involved sartorial subterfuge. On November 12, she disguised herself with glasses, a coat, hat, furs, and a large muff in which she hid her face, which she had borrowed from wealthy suffragists. Her plan was to slip past police unnoticed, enter the hall where a protest meeting had been scheduled, ascend the platform, reveal herself, and speak. The tactic was devised at a conference of women held at the Hotel Brevoort in New York City and possibly inspired by a similar effort by Irish labor activist James Larkin, who disguised himself with a beard to subvert a legal order that banned him from speaking to striking workers during the 1913 Dublin Lockout. Whereas Larkin made his way through the crowd unnoticed, ascended to a balcony, and then ripped off the beard to address a cheering crowd of workers, Flynn was immediately recognized as she ran up the stairs of the meeting hall and "held on the hall steps while the meeting went on inside."[130]

The demonstration for Flynn's right to free speech was led by Henrietta Rodman, a high school teacher. Flynn described Rodman as "a truly remarkable woman" who "fought the school system on a dozen fronts—for the right of married teachers to have children and continue to teach, and many other issues more or less accepted today." In contrast to the "respectable" women of Spokane, who would not make common cause with a rowdy radical IWW, Flynn praised Rodman and her other suffragist allies in the Paterson free speech fight for not being "scared off by the red baiting of the time."[131]

Flynn and Rodman were both members of the Heterodoxy Club, a Greenwich Village–based feminist salon for "unorthodox women" founded by suffragist Marie Jennie Howe.[132] It was through Heterodoxy that she likely met many of the distinguished, well-dressed ladies who escorted and/or supported her in her struggle against the muzzle imposed on her by Paterson authorities. In addition to Howe and Rodman were Inez Milholland, an attorney and suffragist who helped organize the 1913 suffrage parade in Washington, D.C., and who led the parade wearing a crown and a long white cape while riding atop a large white horse named "Gray Dawn"; Jessie Ashley, a New York City attorney and member of the Socialist Party of America (SPA) who helped with the production of the Paterson Pageant and offered legal counsel to unemployed demonstrators in 1914; and Fola La Follette, daughter of Wisconsin Senator Robert M. "Fighting Bob" La Follette and in her own right a suffragist, actor, and labor activist who walked the picket line with female garment workers on strike in New York City in 1913. A day after her failed attempt to disguise her way into the protest meeting, the Passaic County prosecutor revived Flynn's 1913 indictment for inciting to riot. Her female supporters and a few noteworthy men, including Reverend John Haynes Holmes and Walter Lippmann, formed the Elizabeth Gurley Flynn Defense Committee, chaired by another Heterodoxy member, Marion Cothren.[133] Flynn's defense committee raised over a thousand dollars to pay legal fees and other expenses associated with the trial.[134]

While she battled Paterson authorities, Flynn also fought for the life of Joe Hill, a Swedish immigrant and Wobbly organizer and songwriter who had been arrested for the murder of a Salt Lake City grocery store owner in 1914. Despite the circumstantial nature of the evidence against him, a jury found Hill guilty.[135] While Hill languished in prison, he struck up a correspondence with Flynn, and the two became friends. In May 1915, while she was on a cross-country speaking tour for the IWW, Flynn met with Hill in prison. She was the first person to see him after he had been sentenced to death. The experience moved her deeply, and she committed herself to working for his exoneration. She gave numerous speeches to call attention to the injustice of his trial and death sentence and once again enlisted the help of her well-connected ally Edith Cram, this time to help her persuade Woodrow Wilson to intervene on Hill's behalf. Flynn and Cram met first with Wilson's private secretary Joseph Tumulty, who offered to forward an appeal to Wilson. Soon after, the president granted Flynn, Cram, Cram's husband John (president of the New York Public Service Commission), and Cram's brother-in-law Gifford Pinchot (former chief of the U.S. Forest Service) an audience at the Oval Office. Wilson agreed to appeal to Utah Governor William Spry, but his overture had no effect. Hill was executed by firing squad on November 19, 1915. While he was in prison, Hill was inspired by Flynn to compose (or complete) a song, "The Rebel Girl," thus bestowing that label upon her for posterity.[136]

Conspiracy Trial Redux

If Flynn began her December 1915 trial with a heavy heart, she did not let it show. She was accompanied by Rose Pastor Stokes and physician, anarchist, and birth control advocate Dr. Marie Equi.[137] That she had the support of prominent women, observed her father, Thomas Flynn, in an article he wrote for *Solidarity*, likely contributed to the equitable treatment accorded her by presiding Judge Abram Klenert. Even the judge's wife was positively disposed. "A sweet faced, kindly looking little woman," he observed, she "continued to talk in earnest subdued whispers despite the judge's repeated rapping" and "openly wept with evident sympathy for Miss Flynn when lawyer Marelli was delivering his plea at the end of the trial."[138] This time, the "foreign" jury deliberated for only a few minutes before acquitting Flynn on the same charges that had Quinlan serving a prison sentence. "Freedom of speech has triumphed over loranorder [law and order]," she quipped in her characteristic wry fashion.[139] Joseph Ettor sent a telegram to *Solidarity*: "Fight for free speech, triumph."[140] After her acquittal, Flynn continued to work for Quinlan's release.[141] She also vowed to continue speaking in Paterson and announced that she was thinking of getting a restraining order against Police Chief Bimson to keep him from interfering with meetings.[142] For his part, Bimson retorted that he would continue to prohibit Flynn from speaking until the order against the IWW was rescinded.[143] Fordyce did not relent, but newly elected Mayor Amos Radcliffe rescinded the order in January 1916.[144]

FIGURE 4. "The Ladies Tilt Their Lances at Free Speech Dragon," *New York Tribune*, November 21, 1914.
Credit: Library of Congress Chronicling America online collection

Throughout the four-month-long Paterson free speech fight, the press made light of women's civil liberties advocacy with comments about Flynn's size, references to her supporters' "shrill" comments, and headlines like "The Ladies Tilt Their Lances at Free Speech Dragon."[145] Nonetheless, the ideological diversity of Flynn's female supporters and their joint determination to defend the First Amendment did not go unnoticed. One article published just before her December trial, titled "Women Trying to Save Paterson Orator," identified Mrs. Rose Pastor Stokes and Mrs. O. H. P. Belmont as among Flynn's chief defenders and noted the diverse political views of the group and their commitment to the cause of free speech: "Miss Flynn is pretty near an anarchist, while Mrs. Belmont is an ardent suffragist and Mrs. Stokes is a socialist. These women, along with many others, believe the Paterson police are tramping on the right of Free Speech in trying Miss Flynn, and they propose to make her case of national moment and carry it to the highest courts."[146]

Pressed to identify a reason why suffragists might make common cause with a class warrior like Flynn, commentators highlighted the bonds of female friendship: "Their [suffragists'] support could be explained only by their belief in the sincerity of the labor leader whom they called friend," opined a writer for the *Outlook*.[147] Whatever their political differences, women like socialist Stokes and suffragist Belmont had reason beyond friendship to support Flynn's cause: socialists were increasingly under surveillance and silenced by police and government authorities; suffragists had recently adopted soapboxing and street meetings as a method of informing and recruiting for their cause—in fact, suffragists had been inspired to these tactics by observing labor organizers in England and the United States—and they were sensitive to what they considered extralegal efforts to curtail the rights of women speakers.

Not long after Paterson, the IWW ceased its free speech fights. There was disagreement among Wobblies about whether fighting for free speech was too great a diversion from the more necessary and important task of organizing workers on the job.[148] But Flynn could never separate free speech work from organizing work. She was not concerned with an abstract conception of rights—what fellow Wobbly Fred Thompson called "free speech on its own account." On the contrary, she believed without the right to occupy and use public space to represent the interests of working people, unions were impotent, and without unions, the most vulnerable members of society would be helpless against rapacious capitalism. Therefore, a vibrant labor movement required constant struggle against "force and violence" used by the ruling class to deny workers the right to organize, to strike, and to picket.[149] Events in Paterson both during the strike and afterward demonstrated the extent to which labor rights are inseparable from constitutional rights. Silk manufacturers waged a two-pronged assault against striking workers that attempted to squeeze the union out of the city by denying the right to picket or to meet without interference while simultaneously outlasting strikers by sending work to impoverished, unorganized regions of Pennsylvania. The link between labor rights and constitutional rights would become even more evident and crucial when the United States plunged into the war against the Austro-Hungarian Empire in Europe accompanied by a war against all forms of political dissent at home. Once again, Flynn would play a leading role in the struggle against repression.

CHAPTER 3

War and Civil Liberties

An Oxymoron?

> Master enough independence of thought to look at the havoc created by the Iron Heel of Capital with your own eyes.
> —Workers' Defense Union flyer, 1919

TWO DEVELOPMENTS COMBINED to shift the focus and tactics of Elizabeth Gurley Flynn's activism after the Paterson free speech fight. One was war in Europe and the subsequent entry of the United States into the conflict. The other was Flynn's break with Haywood and resignation from her position as an organizer and strike leader for the IWW.

The War to End All Wars

While Flynn was fighting for free speech in Paterson, the "war to end all wars" raged in Europe and elsewhere around the world. The rapid onset of the conflict and expectations that it would be brief and relatively painless made it possible for belligerent nations to secure popular support and amass resources when war was declared in the summer of 1914.[1] In theory the European Left was antiwar, although there were divisions between revisionists who maintained that socialism could only occur within the framework of the nation and anti-imperialist Left radicals who argued that competition among capitalist nations for control of the noncapitalist world would inevitably result in global catastrophe and herald the end of the nation state as a vehicle for human progress.[2] The Second International unanimously passed antiwar resolutions at several of its congresses in the name of working-class solidarity in the first decade of the twentieth century, but in the end, the various socialist parties that comprised it found the lure of nationalism too hard to resist.³ Although a number of Left radicals declared their opposition to the conflict, socialist parties in Germany, France, Britain, Belgium, Austria, and Hungary supported the war policies of their governments. The only large socialist party that remained opposed to the war was the Italian, and Italy was neutral at the time.⁴

In general, working-class activists in the United States viewed the war with a critical eye. Throughout the period of official U.S. neutrality, a lively debate about the war and preparedness ensued within the labor movement and among working-class radicals. This debate played out differently in different organizational contexts. In the American Federation of Labor, there was significant support for neutrality and against preparedness, and the antiwar culture remained vibrant even after AFL president Samuel Gompers announced his support for President Woodrow Wilson's campaign for a military buildup in late 1915 and 1916. The majority wing of the American Socialist Party broke from precedent set by their European counterparts and opposed the war abroad as well as the preparedness movement at home, although there was some disagreement over which nation bore most of the responsibility for the conflict. The IWW, which espoused international solidarity and opposed all wars as products of a capitalist system and class conflict, taunted Gompers for jumping on the preparedness bandwagon in its newspaper *Solidarity* but did not issue an official position against the war. Instead, the decision of whether to oppose the fighting was left to the conscience of individual members.⁵

Flynn was antiwar during the period of official neutrality and had scathing words for the preparedness movement. Her criticism was influenced as much by her Irish American identity as her socialist politics: "The glory of war! Hah! Money and religion have caused all the wars. While England defends little Belgium, she puts her heel on Ireland's face," she told an audience at an antiwar demonstration in St. Louis. "Defend your country! What ground do you own? Not even enough to stand on, perhaps, much less enough to bury yourself in."⁶

Like many Wobblies, however, Flynn focused most of her activist energy at this time on organizing for the class struggle. In 1914, the United States was in a deep economic recession. Increasing numbers of orders from the Allies for military and nonmilitary goods turned the economy around. During the period of neutrality, U.S. industrial production rose 32 percent and the GNP increased by almost 20 percent. The private sector workforce added 2.5 million workers, mostly in manufacturing.⁷ At the same time, prices of food skyrocketed. The high employment rate coupled with the increased cost of living emboldened workers to militant action. The year 1915 saw a record 1,593 strikes. In 1916, that number was surpassed with 3,789 strikes.[8] "While war raged abroad and President Wilson campaigned in 1916 on the slogan 'He Kept Us Out of War,'" Flynn later explained, "we in the IWW doggedly stuck to our knitting. Our self-appointed task was to organize the unorganized workers and lead them in struggles for better wages, shorter hours, and decent working conditions. Our concentration was bound to be in basic industries, where the war profits were soaring."[9]

Labor Defense in Minnesota and Washington

One of those 1916 strikes ended Flynn's career as a Wobbly organizer. It occurred among the multiethnic mix of immigrant ore miners on the Mesabi Iron Range in Minnesota, where she had met her now ex-husband almost a decade earlier.[10] Iron from the Mesabi Range fed the mills of U.S. Steel, which produced ships, guns, and other war-related items from the durable metal. With more orders from the Allies than it could handle, the steel industry was turning record profits.[11] In 1916, U.S. Steel posted $1.2 billion in sales (up from $727 million the previous year) and $313 million in profits (up from $110 million in 1915).[12] Meanwhile, the iron ore miners lived in wretched conditions and earned wages insufficient for maintaining an adequate standard of living for a family. Miners were paid on the "contract system" for how much ore they mined rather than how many hours they worked. Contract rates for 1915–1916 averaged between $2.80 and $3.25 per day.[13]

The strike started on June 2, 1916, with a spontaneous walkout at the St. James mine, near Aurora, Minnesota. The walkout was led by an Italian immigrant miner, Joe Greeni, after he opened his pay envelope and found that his wages had been cut. Before long, the strike spread throughout the entire region. When striking miners asked the IWW for assistance, the union obliged in spades. Nunzio Pernicone notes that "by the third week of June, the IWW had sent 34 organizers—a record number—to direct 10,000 miners."[14] The large number of organizers was indicative of the union's commitment to mirror the nationalities it sought to bring together.[15] Among the organizers sent to the Mesabi Range were Irishman James Gilday, half–Native American and half-white veteran of the Missoula free speech fight Frank Little, and Flynn's political ally and romantic partner, also a crackerjack organizer of Italian workers, Carlo Tresca.

When strikers issued their demands—which included an eight-hour day, pay raises, and greater control over the conditions of work—owners responded by recruiting armed guards to harass and beat them.[16] After a clash between strikers and guards resulted in the death of a miner, police began arresting IWW organizers.[17]

One evening, police raided the home of one of the strikers, Philip Masonovich, ostensibly looking for an illegal still, and assaulted him and his wife. The Masonoviches and their boarders fought back, a scuffle ensued, and a deputy was shot and killed. Police then arrested the Masonoviches and a boarder along with Little, Gilday, and Tresca, who was not present when the shooting occurred. On orders from Haywood, Flynn and Joseph Ettor traveled from New York to Minnesota to replace the imprisoned organizers. Flynn was joined by Mary Heaton Vorse and Marion Cothren.[18] The three women were friends as well as political allies with a history of collaboration. In 1912, Vorse's reporting brought much-needed attention to conditions in Lawrence before and during the strike; Cothren chaired the defense committee when Flynn was arrested during the Paterson strike in 1913.

Flynn, Vorse, and Cothren toured throughout the Mesabi Range to encourage sympathy and raise funds for the defense of the strikers and the IWW organizers.[19] However, their valiant efforts along with those of the strikers themselves, their families, and other IWW organizers and supporters were no match for the brutality of the guards and dwindling funds. The strike was called off on September 17, 1916.[20]

After the strike ended, the task of getting Tresca out of jail remained. Flynn and Ettor led the defense campaign. In December 1916, the trio of Flynn, Ettor, and Tresca brokered an out-of-court settlement in which three strikers, including Masonovich, pled guilty to first-degree manslaughter in exchange for the release of Tresca and the other prisoners. The settlement, which Flynn later regretted, infuriated Haywood, who saw it as a violation of the IWW's general rule against striking deals in court and claimed that it sold out the strikers. He officially reprimanded Flynn (the two were already at odds over how strike relief and donations to the defense fund were to be handled, a skirmish in the larger battle over centralization of the union—in short, Flynn opposed centralization).[21] In response, she severed formal ties with Haywood and never organized another IWW strike. Although she parted ways with IWW leadership, Flynn's commitment to the principle of direct action and to the workers who were the IWW's core constituency did not diminish. For the next several years, she continued to urge workers to join the One Big Union and defended the rights of Wobblies whenever they were targeted for repression.

Flynn's next labor defense campaign on behalf of the IWW was in early 1917. After a brief sojourn in New York to spend the Christmas holiday with her son, she left for Seattle, where a group of Wobblies had been arrested and jailed on murder charges. The charge stemmed from a bloody confrontation that had taken place in Everett a few weeks earlier. On November 6, 1916, members of the IWW had traveled from Seattle to Everett, aboard the steamships *Verona* and *Calista*, to mount the soapbox and speak in support of a strike by shingle weavers, whose free speech rights were being violated in typical brutal fashion by local law enforcement. A band of citizen deputies were waiting for the ships and refused to let them land. Shots were fired, and at least five Wobblies and two deputies were killed. The ships turned around and returned to Seattle, where 38 IWWs from the *Calista* and 236 from the *Verona* were arrested as they disembarked. Nine days after the arrests, all but seventy-four men were released. Those who were detained faced a charge of "constructive murder"—that is, murder resulting from the commission of a so-called dangerous act, in this case, participating in a demonstration against the exploitation of workers.

Flynn spent several months speaking on behalf of the prisoners in Montana and throughout Washington State.[22] She was not the only woman involved in the defense campaign—veteran free speech fighter Edith Frenette, socialist lawyer Caroline Lowe, and Portland doctor Marie Equi also played active roles—but Flynn, described as a "human storm signal" by one reporter, garnered the lion's share of attention. Students in the school of journalism at the University of Montana were even required to attend and report on her speech in Missoula.[23] She used the attention showered on her to highlight the serious nature of the charge leveled against the imprisoned Wobblies. Constructive murder, she explained, was a more serious charge than simply a charge of murder: "If a man can be charged with murder because he was speaking to or was a member of a crowd to which murder occurs, then anybody—the police or the sheriffs, or anybody who wishes—can start a riot in any crowd and thereby cause the speaker to be charged with murder."[24] The campaign yielded positive results: charges against the imprisoned Wobblies were dropped, and only one, Tom Tracy, was tried for murder. He was acquitted.

The Everett Massacre was a swan song for the Wobbly soapbox orator. Under Haywood's direction, the wild and woolly organization was changing from an itinerant association into a structured and centralized entity that eschewed impassioned oratory and daring street performance to focus on the nuts and bolts of organizing for the long term. This revised organizational form did not entail a shift in political orientation—the IWW was to remain a syndicalist union.[25] The turn to long-term organizing was intended to make the union a permanent presence in the workplace that could deliver higher wages, shorter hours, and more control over the job to the marginalized workers who remained its core constituency.[26]

U.S. Labor and the War

The IWW was not the only labor organization that was positioning itself to take advantage of the opportunities presented by World War I. For years, conservative AFL leaders portrayed their brand of unionism as a respectable alternative to the "thuggishness" of socialists and the IWW. Julie Greene has documented how AFL president Samuel Gompers traded on the union's respectability to lobby for prolabor policies. She has also detailed the active role that Gompers and the AFL played in getting trade unionists on the ballot and supporting prolabor candidates, mostly on the Democratic ticket, in the elections of 1906, 1908, and 1910.[27] When the United States entered the war, Gompers was a familiar political actor in Washington and well positioned to capitalize on opportunities for labor created by a wartime economy.

Gompers pressed the advantage for the AFL by putting himself in a position to help direct the war effort and frame government policies toward labor. A key element of this strategy was to crush the rival IWW. Relations between the AFL and the Wobblies had been antagonistic since the IWW's founding in 1905. Gompers was not above collaborating with employers, and he hired detectives and state and local law enforcement to squash IWW organizing drives in industries where the AFL wished to establish or retain dominance. Now he collaborated with federal law enforcement as well. Along with Ralph Easley of the National Civic Federation, he hired a detective to monitor Wobblies and anarchists. Obsessed with the issue of loyalty and subversion, Gompers fed surveillance reports of supposed IWW collaboration with German agents to the Bureau of Information (BI).[28]

In October 1916, Gompers's willingness to be a stool pigeon for federal agents along with his support for Wilson's military preparedness initiatives garnered him an appointment as a civilian advisor on the Council for National Defense (CND), a federal agency created to coordinate preparedness efforts. In March 1917, at a meeting of the AFL's Executive Council, he rammed through a statement that committed the AFL to war if Congress declared it. Once war was declared, Gompers, as part of the CND's commission on labor, penned what appeared to be a no-strike pledge, although the CND later denied that it was such and maintained that labor had not ceded the right to strike as a last resort.[29] Whatever Gompers intended, the strike wave that began in 1915 did not recede when the United States went to war. On the contrary, there were 6,205 recorded strikes between April 6, 1917, and November 11, 1918.[30] As David Montgomery has noted, it was "the abundance of employment" that "gave millions of workers the confidence to quit jobs and search for better ones and to go on strike on a scale that dwarfed all previously recorded turnover and strike activity."[31]

How the rivalry between the AFL and a hierarchically structured IWW would have played out is anybody's guess. The U.S. declaration of war provided justification for the federal government, with a wink from Gompers and the AFL, to crush the IWW and repress all expressions of political dissent and anticapitalist agitation. But seeds of the federal and state repression that characterized the home front were sowed well before the United States entered the war.[32]

Political Repression

The first laws against the radical Left had targeted anarchists. New York State led the way with the Criminal Anarchy Law, passed one year after the assassination of President William McKinley. McKinley's assassin, Leon Czolgosz, was a second-generation Polish American who claimed to be an anarchist. Whether Czolgosz actually was an anarchist is debatable—he did not belong to any anarchist group—but authorities wasted no time in adding his crime to a growing list of recent anarchist assassinations that included various European heads of state: French President Sadi Carnot (1894), Spanish Prime Minister Antonio Canovas (1897), and Austrian Empress Elizabeth (1898).[33] The 1902 law made being an anarchist or associating with anarchists criminal acts. As defined by the law, criminal anarchy was the doctrine advocating the overthrow of organized government by force, violence, assassination, or any unlawful means. To advocate this doctrine by speech or writing, or to join a society or attend a meeting for teaching or advocating anarchy, was a felony.[34] Not to be outdone by New York State, the federal government passed its own antianarchist law at the urging of McKinley's successor, Theodore Roosevelt. The 1903 "Anarchist

Exclusion Act" prohibited anarchists—as well as epileptics, beggars, and importers of prostitutes—from entering the United States and allowed for the deportation (within three years of arrival) of anarchist aliens already in the country. It marked the first time in U.S. history that immigrants could be excluded because of their political beliefs.

These state and federal statutes laid the groundwork for more stringent antiradical laws that would be passed in the restive atmosphere of strikes, support for revolutionary movements abroad, and social divisions over preparedness in the years that preceded U.S. entry into the war. In February 1917, Congress passed an immigration law that mandated a literacy test for immigrants, barred most Asian immigration, doubled the head tax on immigrants from $4.00 to $8.00, and expanded the list of excluded persons to include not only anarchists and "idiots, imbeciles, epileptics, alcoholics, poor, criminals, beggars, any person suffering attacks of insanity, and ... polygamists" but also "those who were against the organized government or those who advocated the unlawful destruction of property and those who advocated the unlawful assault of killing of any officer." It also stipulated that "any alien who at *any time after entry* [emphasis mine] shall be found advocating or teaching the unlawful destruction of property, or advocating or teaching anarchy, or the overthrow by force or violence of the government of the United States" be deported.[35] President Wilson vetoed the bill primarily because of the literacy test, which he described as a "penalty for lack of opportunity," but Congress overrode his veto, and the law went into effect on May 1, 1917.[36]

The law's provision against property destruction specifically targeted the IWW. Beginning in 1912, editorials encouraging sabotage had begun to appear regularly in the Wobbly press along with an image of a black cat with bared teeth (the "sab cat"). The tactic, theorized as a means of struggle by French syndicalists in the mid-1890s and reinterpreted by the IWW, became the subject of much debate after the arrest and conviction of Frederic Sumner Boyd for advocating sabotage during the Paterson strike.[37] Boyd's was the first sabotage case to come before the U.S. court system.[38] In 1914, the IWW officially endorsed sabotage as a tactic at its annual convention.

During the Paterson strike, Flynn endorsed sabotage in a speech she gave after Boyd's arrest, which the Cleveland Publishing Bureau made into a pamphlet titled *Sabotage: The Conscious Withdrawal of the Workers' Industrial Efficiency*. In her speech, Flynn defined sabotage as "the guerrilla warfare" of the class struggle and a counterpart of the "open battle" of the strike.[39] "Sabotage," she explained, "is a means of striking at the employer's profit for the purpose of forcing him into granting certain conditions, even as workingmen strike for the same purpose of coercing him. It is simply another form of coercion."[40] She outlined several forms of sabotage, including interference with the quality of goods; interference with the quality of service by revelation of unsavory information about a product, so-called open mouth sabotage (the tactic she had encouraged during the hotel workers strike); strict compliance with workplace rules; and removal of vital pieces of machinery, or "putting the machine on strike."[41] Flynn's goal, as Rosemary Feurer points out, was to reclaim the word sabotage and render it nonviolent, and her analysis of the tactic as a mode of direct action by workers was brilliant and insightful.[42] Nevertheless, it was a tactical error to say such things in a public forum, and the mistake was made worse when the speech appeared in pamphlet form because Flynn could not claim her words were being deliberately misunderstood or taken out of context. The misstep would dog her for the rest of her activist career.

As the pamphlet was going to press, Boyd signed a petition for pardon in which he renounced sabotage and "all other subversive ideas." A coda by the publishers noted Boyd's "apparent cowardice" in the face of his conviction. Not long after it was printed, the pamphlet was pulled from circulation by the IWW General Executive Board, which apparently never approved the original printing. In 1917, the pamphlet was reprinted over Flynn's objection. By then, the notion that she endorsed the ruin of businesses and wanton destruction of property was firmly fixed in the popular imagination.[43]

Criminal Syndicalism

Just two weeks after passage of the federal immigration act, the first of many state laws against the IWW was introduced into the Idaho legislature. The law and an antisabotage law passed at the same time were sought by lumber and mining interests to halt Wobbly organizing efforts underway in those industries. State Senator W. G. Walker, chief sponsor of the criminal syndicalism law, gave a speech against the IWW when he introduced the legislation. Copies of IWW literature were left with each senator when the bill came under consideration. The bill passed the Senate by a vote of 32–3. Similar tactics were used in the House, where the bill passed by a unanimous 60–0 vote.[44]

The Idaho statute defined criminal syndicalism as the "doctrine which advocates crime, sabotage, violence, or unlawful methods of terrorism as a means of accomplishing industrial or political reform" and made the advocacy of such doctrine a felony. The law also made it illegal to publicize criminal syndicalism; justify by word of mouth or in writing "the commission of or the attempt to commit crime, sabotage, or violent methods of terrorism"; establish or hold membership in a criminal syndicalist organization; and teach or provide physical space for the teaching or advocacy of criminal syndicalism. Essentially, the law criminalized any sort of challenge to industrial capitalism.[45] Although there was no appeal to patriotism or the war when the bill was enacted, the tone shifted when the United States joined the fight. As Robert C. Sims observed, "It was easy to mobilize home guards for military purposes, and finding no 'huns' around, vent that patriotic fervor against the Wobblies."[46] By framing IWW-led strike activity as disloyalty, Idaho businessmen could use the law to arrest Wobbly organizers and strikers and thus cripple the union. And use it they did. Within five years of the law's passage, hundreds of Wobblies were arrested and prosecuted.

Idaho's criminal syndicalism law became a prototype for anti-Wobbly legislation passed in other states. Within a month of the Idaho law's passage, Minnesota enacted a similar statute. Between 1917 and 1920, twenty-one states and two territories passed their own criminal syndicalism laws, several of which were copies of the Idaho legislation. Whatever their wording, all the laws used the concept of criminal syndicalism to outlaw membership in the IWW, halt the union's organizing drives and strike actions, and strengthen the position of business interests. Ahmed A. White proposes that this legislation was "perhaps the most explicit, straightforward, and altogether remarkable effort in modern America to use the power of the state, backed by law, to stamp out a radical organization."[47]

Wilsonian Rhetoric

A climate of acceptance for consolidating state power to repress dissent was fostered by President Wilson, a former collegiate debater with a keen awareness of how presidential rhetoric could be used to crystallize public opinion and motivate congressional action on policy proposals (he was the first president since John Adams to deliver a State of the Union address). During his first term of office, he made his disdain for working-class militancy clear. For example, in his 1914 Fourth of July speech at Independence Hall, the president reproached labor organizers who criticized the status quo, and he expressed preference for top-down efforts to improve working peoples' lives. Although the United States was in a deep recession with widespread unemployment, Wilson declared, "I know from a wide observation of the general circumstances of the country taken as a whole that things are going extremely well."[48] He then scolded those who disagreed with his rosy assessment of the nation's economic situation: "I wonder what those who are crying out that things are wrong are trying to do. Are they trying to serve the country, or are they trying to serve something smaller than the country? Are they trying to put hope into the hearts of the men who work and toil every day, or are they trying to plant discouragement and despair in those hearts? And why do they cry that everything is wrong and yet do nothing to set it right?"[49] Even assuming there was an economic problem, the solution, according to Wilson, was not for workers to organize themselves but for them to cooperate with their betters in finding a solution: "If they love America and anything is wrong amongst us, it is their business to put their hand with ours to the task of setting it right."[50]

As he embraced preparedness, Wilson stepped up his rhetorical assault on those who did not endorse an idealized image of what he called "the full freedom and opportunity of America."[51] In December 1915, his third State of the Union address warned of the grave internal threat posed by those within the nation's borders who, he said, "have poured the poison of disloyalty into the very arteries of our national life." He urged passage of federal laws to crush out "such creatures of passion, disloyalty, and anarchy."[52]

Wilson returned to the poison metaphor as he fostered a mentality of national defense that fed fears about unpatriotic labor organizations, disloyal immigrants, and foreign radicals. In 1916 remarks delivered upon his acceptance of the Democratic nomination for a second term of office, he observed, "The seas were not broad enough to keep the infection of the conflict out of our own politics."[53] As a result, he continued, "the passions and intrigues of certain active groups and combinations of men amongst us who were born under foreign flags injected the poison of disloyalty into our own most critical affairs, laid violent hands upon many of our industries, and subjected us to the shame of divisions of sentiment and purpose in which America was condemned and forgotten."[54] Wilson then committed himself to "act with unmistakable purpose in rebuke of these things, in order that they may be forever hereafter impossible."[55]

But Wilson's rhetoric was a double-edged sword. Along with thinly veiled threats about the consequences of dissent, he used language that seemed to endorse popular uprisings against imperial powers. In a 1916 address to the League to Enforce Peace, Wilson articulated the foundational elements of what would become his geopolitical vision for the postwar order: popular sovereignty, which he would later rephrase as "national self-determination," and the equality of all nations. Thus he declared, "We believe that every people has a right to choose the sovereignty under which they shall live" and "the small states of the world shall enjoy the same respect for their sovereignty and for their territorial integrity."[56] In January 1917, just months before the United States declared war on Germany, Wilson delivered his "Peace without Victory" speech in which he offered a critique of European imperialism and reaffirmed his commitment to popular sovereignty as the basis for lasting peace: "No peace can last, or ought to last, which does not recognize and accept the principle that governments derive all their just powers from the consent of the governed, and that no right anywhere exists to hand peoples about from sovereignty to sovereignty as if they were property."[57]

Wilson's rhetoric of national self-determination gave hope to activists in anti-imperialist liberation struggles in India, China, Egypt, Korea, Indochina, and Ireland, hope that would be dashed at the Versailles Peace Conference.[58] Anti-imperialist activists in the United States did not have to wait until Versailles to be disappointed. In the case of Ireland, Wilson supported the moderate Home Rule movement that sought self-government within the United Kingdom but regarded more militant Irish nationalists and their supporters in the United States as pro-German and a threat to neutrality.[59] On March 5, 1917, he issued an explicit condemnation of offering aid to anti-imperialist struggles abroad in his second inaugural address, delivered a month before the United States declared war on Germany and just ten days before Czar Nicholas II was forced to abdicate the throne in Russia. "The community of interest and of power upon which peace must henceforth depend," he intoned, "imposes upon each nation the duty of seeing to it that all influences proceeding from its own citizens meant to encourage or assist revolution in other states should be sternly and effectually suppressed and prevented."[60] Although he welcomed what he saw as the overthrow of Russian autocracy by democratic forces (that view would change when the Bolsheviks overthrew the provisional government established after Nicholas's abdication), Wilson opposed efforts by outsiders to provide material aid or otherwise attempt to influence the course of events.[61]

The Espionage Act

While the United States was officially neutral, Wilson made it clear that political dissent was a threat to the national interest and, consequently, that criminalizing dissent was a reasonable option. The U.S. declaration of war on Germany made dissenting opinion an apparently greater threat because it undermined the unity of purpose necessary for a successful war effort. Concerned that open disagreement would make it hard to muster the resources—especially manpower—needed for a successful American military campaign to "make the world safe for democracy," Wilson pressed for a law to protect the nation from "the insidious methods of internal hostile activities." In June, Congress obliged by passing the Espionage Act, which authorized up to twenty years of imprisonment and up to $10,000 in fines for anyone who interfered with military recruitment or encouraged "disloyalty." The terms of the Espionage Act were strengthened by the enactment of amending legislation, the Sedition Act of 1918. This law authorized penalties for speaking against the U.S. government, Constitution, flag, or uniform; interfering with wartime production; promoting the cause of America's enemies; inciting refusal of military duty; obstructing military recruitment, and more. It also criminalized advocating or suggesting any of these activities.[62]

Not a single person was convicted of spying under the Espionage Act during the war, but the law was far from ineffective. Together, the Espionage and Sedition Acts provided legitimacy for the federal government to silence critics of the war and capitalism. More than two thousand people were prosecuted under the wartime laws for written or oral expressive activities, and more than half of the cases resulted in convictions.[63] Press and speech were key battlefronts in this war on dissent.[64]

The Espionage Act empowered postal officials to censor the press by making it illegal to mail any written, printed, or visual matter advocating or urging "treason, insurrection, or forcible resistance" to the law. Penalties for attempting to use the mail for such ends were a fine of not more than $5,000, a prison term of not more than five years, or both. Although the Fourth Amendment protected first-class mail from being opened or inspected without a warrant, newspapers were typically mailed at the less expensive second-class rate, which left them vulnerable to search and seizure. Under the terms of the Espionage Act, Postmaster General Albert Burleson could declare nonmailable any publication with offending content; more important, he could revoke second-class mailing privileges for any paper that published nonmailable content frequently enough to justify the presumption that it would continue to do so. In October of 1917, Congress passed the Trading with the Enemy Act, which further empowered Burleson by mandating prepublication review of all articles and editorials about the war or the belligerent parties in the foreign-language press. Under the terms of the Sedition Act, moreover, Burleson could refuse to deliver mail to individuals or organizations who, in his estimate, used the mail in violation of the law.[65]

Burleson was not shy about exercising the authority vested in him by the law. By the end of the war, he had barred more than one hundred publications from the mail.[66] Whereas prewar efforts to shut down troublesome newspapers like the *Industrial Worker* during the Spokane free speech fight had been thwarted by simply moving the press to another location, wartime federal censorship was a different matter. Denial of second-class privileges forced many papers to shut down because they could not afford the higher first-class postal rate. Foreign-language papers ceased publication because they could not sustain the cost and delays incurred in translating articles for government approval. Loss of their papers dealt a serious blow to organizations for whom the press was an essential medium for sharing news and information and disseminating propaganda.

Repression of speech played out in meeting halls, on street corners, in parks, and other public spaces. Before the start of the war, radicals in the United States had enjoyed a rich and vibrant oratorical culture. The institutional elements of this culture were largely created by the Socialist Party. In 1911, for example, the party organized a Socialist Lyceum Bureau, which offered a course of five lectures to be given by a speaker designated by the bureau. Three hundred locals availed themselves of the program in its first year.[67] Another Socialist institution, the Rand School of Social Science, regularly hosted spirited debates on current issues by notable public figures.[68] The Rand School also offered public speaking classes as a standard part of its curriculum. The program was integrated: A. Philip Randolph and Chandler Owen lectured on "The Economics and Sociology of the Negro Problem," and classes were open to Black students as well as white.[69] Alongside these institutional forms was a lively vernacular culture of street speaking. Soapbox oratory was a staple of socialist and Wobbly organizing, but street speakers of all political stripes held forth in cities and towns on history, economics, politics, literature, and the necessity of the class struggle.[70] The most talented orators attained celebrity status and regularly attracted crowds at street corner meetings and organized assemblies. As we have seen, access to these spaces, particularly for socialists, syndicalists, and anarchists, was not always guaranteed. Local governments and law enforcement collaborated with business interests to deny a platform to speakers with a prolabor message through legal and extralegal means, sometimes involving physical violence, and labor activists often had to fight for their right to public spaces. Before the war, these struggles were primarily local and sporadic. After the United States declared war, these loosely coordinated state and local efforts to disrupt public meetings and criminalize certain kinds of speech gave way to a coordinated federal apparatus to squash dissent that pervaded every level of society.

Federal laws against dissent made it nearly impossible for radicals to claim and use space to gather, offer an alternative vision of the war, and issue a challenge to the political and economic status quo. In this environment, there would be no more friendly towns with socialist mayors. No more meeting halls rented from fellow immigrants. No more houses rented and/or repurposed for use as meeting halls. No more local prisons transformed into protest spaces.

How one measures the effect of the war and repression on the U.S. labor movement depends on what part of the labor movement one chooses to focus on. Gompers had a cozy relationship with the Wilson administration and was a presence in wartime federal agencies, such as the Council for National Defense and the National War Labor Board (NWLB), a voluntary agency created by presidential proclamation after the United States declared war to settle labor disputes that might interrupt war production. Former president William Howard Taft and labor lawyer Frank Walsh co-chaired the NWLB. Walsh had also chaired the Commission on Industrial Relations (CIR), which had been established by Congress six years earlier in response to increasing conflict and violence between capital and labor to investigate and report on labor conditions in the principal industries of the United States.[71] Walsh was a known friend of labor, and the NWLB was seen as legitimating workers' demands for the right to organize, good wages, and workplace democracy.[72]

Filtered through the ideological prism of Wilson's rhetoric of democracy and self-determination, these wartime agencies fostered the impression among workers that the federal government would protect them from the predations of greedy employers. For the duration of the war, at least, this impression proved largely accurate. Wartime labor militancy secured an eight-hour day, higher wages, and better working conditions for large segments of the labor force. The AFL enjoyed a surge in membership between 1917 and 1919.[73] But these gains were not shared evenly by all workers, and they came at a cost: total acquiescence in the war effort. As we shall see, they would also prove ephemeral. Labor activists and organizations beyond the pale of this symbiotic arrangement were subjected to governmental and extragovernmental repression on an unprecedented scale.

Local federal attorneys and judges enjoyed considerable autonomy when prosecuting and sentencing alleged Espionage Act offenders. Enforcement of the law was particularly aggressive in districts where the IWW was active or where the Socialist Party had done well in the November 1917 elections.[74] In an atmosphere in which patriotism was synonymous with acquiescence, it was not necessary to prove that a speaker had directly incited to illegal activity to secure a guilty verdict. Prosecutions in the lower federal courts typically relied on the bad tendency test, which determined the illegality of speech on the basis of its tendency to bring about any violation of the law, no matter how small.[75] Among those convicted for seditious speech were leading lights of various radical movements, including socialist Eugene Debs, arrested for giving an antiwar speech in Canton, Ohio; socialist Kate Richards O'Hare, arrested in Fargo, North Dakota, and sentenced to five years in prison for discouraging enlistment in the armed forces; economist Scott Nearing, indicted for his authorship of an antiwar pamphlet, *The Great Madness: A Victory for the American Plutocracy*; and anarchists Emma Goldman and Alexander Berkman, arrested and imprisoned for two years for interfering with military recruitment and then deported upon their release from prison.

It is important to recognize that the impulse toward repression of antiwar opinions and actions was not simply a response to top-down propaganda efforts. On the contrary, there was considerable "horizontal" pressure to embrace the war.[76] A volunteer army of citizen soldiers, aglow with the fire of patriotism and eager to combat enemies of the state wherever they found them, lent their efforts to the federal government's campaign against dissent. Such popular surveillance and disciplinary actions were not unprecedented. Americans had been claiming the authority and obligation of citizens to police one another as an inherent aspect of self-government since the founding of the republic, and legal and extralegal methods had always coexisted.[77] The 1850s saw a transformation of vigilantism from "frontier vigilantism," a periodic and temporary form of civil justice rooted in the ostensibly natural and democratic right to violence, to "bourgeois vigilantism," a method of enforcing class and racial privilege.[78]

With its fierce anticapitalist agenda and commitment to solidarity across boundaries of race, sex, and nation, the IWW was a favored target of bourgeois vigilantes, especially during the free speech campaigns. Michael Cohen has argued that attacks on the union during World War I and the postwar era inaugurated a new phase in the history of American vigilantism, "one in which the distinctiveness of extralegal, community-based violence transcended local imperatives and became part of the nationalist and state building project of the Progressive Era."[79] Some Americans acted on their own or as part of informal vigilante groups, like the one that tortured and then murdered Frank Little in Butte, Montana, on August 1, 1917.[80] Others enlisted in "legitimate" patriotic societies that sprung up at the beginning of the war, such as the National Security League and the American Defense Society, where efforts to suppress radical movements for the sake of "100 per cent Americanism" were bankrolled by powerful business interests.[81]

The most active and widespread of these vigilante groups was the American Protective League (APL). Founded by Chicago entrepreneur Albert M. Briggs to ferret out pro-German spy operations, the APL worked closely with police and federal agents in surveillance units approved by high-level government officials, including Attorney General Thomas Gregory and the chief of the Bureau of Investigation, A. Bruce Bielaski.[82] Members were savvy businessmen who seized upon the war as an opportunity to link pacifism, anti-imperialism, and any critique of the capitalist state with treason, and the organization provided forward momentum for the federal government's antiradical campaign. APL members were instrumental in Eugene Debs's arrest, conviction, and imprisonment. When he arrived in Canton to speak, local operatives, along with reinforcements from Cleveland, filtered through the audience and transcribed the speech. After he finished speaking, Debs was arrested for violating the Espionage Act. APL operatives turned over several transcripts of the speech to the Department of Justice (DOJ) to be used as evidence. During the trial, members of the APL searched people admitted into the courtroom and stood guard throughout the proceedings. When Debs was convicted and imprisoned, they proudly boasted of their role in the affair.[83]

Assault on the IWW

On September 5, 1917, APL members and local police officers helped DOJ agents raid Wobbly headquarters and the homes of IWW officials in Chicago, Fresno, Seattle, Spokane, and every other city in the United States in which the IWW had an office. Raiders confiscated several tons of materials, including membership records, minutes of meetings, newspapers, pamphlets, correspondence, office supplies, personal possessions—from mailing lists and love letters to rubber bands and empty beer bottles—and even pictures of Frank Little, who had been lynched only a few weeks earlier.[84] DOJ and APL lawyers sifted through the mass of confiscated papers and used what they found to charge the union with five counts of violating the Espionage Act by conspiring against the government, conspiring to injure citizens in their civil rights by means of sabotage and similar acts, conspiring to cause insubordination and discourage enlistments in the army, and conspiring against postal laws by using the mails to achieve the aforementioned goals. In addition to Chicago and Fresno, federal grand juries handed down indictments in Sacramento, Wichita, and Omaha.

As White explains, the doctrine of conspiracy makes it a crime for defendants to agree to pursue a criminal purpose. Prosecutors in a conspiracy trial need only to demonstrate such agreement; they are not required to prove that the defendants actually did anything illegal. Moreover, although conviction requires proof of "an overt act" committed to further the conspiracy's purpose, the act need not have been criminal in nature, and only one defendant need have committed it. The conspiracy charges against the IWW derived from opinions expressed in IWW literature (prosecutors introduced fifteen thousand documents in evidence) rather than expressly illegal acts committed by individuals, an approach that essentially put the IWW itself on trial. As members of the union, each of the nearly two hundred indictees was accused of every crime. The counts totaled ten thousand.[85]

Flynn was among 166 suspected IWW members—and the only woman—indicted by the Chicago federal grand jury. Given her reputation as a firebrand speaker, organizer, and strike leader, her arrest was probably inevitable. She had not uttered or authored anything in direct opposition to the war once the United States entered; charges against her were based on her authorship of the *Sabotage* pamphlet. Arrested along with her were Carlo Tresca, Joseph Ettor, and Arturo Giovannitti. Almost immediately, friends and supporters sprang into action and organized a defense committee to raise money and agitate for Flynn's release. After she was released on bail, Flynn set about devising a legal strategy for herself, Tresca, Ettor, and Giovannitti. Noting the frequency with which she was called upon to save male comrades from trouble with the law, she quipped to Giovannitti, "All my life men have demanded I get them out of jail!"[86] That she should take the lead in this endeavor made sense for several reasons, none of which was directly connected to her sex: She was the most well connected of the group, the most experienced in matters of labor defense, and unlike Tresca and Giovannitti, both of whom were

Italian-born, she was an American citizen and thus invulnerable to the threat of deportation.

As Flynn set about organizing the defense campaign, it was clear that the higher stakes entailed by war and greater resources of the federal government necessitated a change in tactics. This time there would be no running an end game around the law and no embarrassing elected officials into capitulating to IWW demands, as she and fellow Wobblies had done in Missoula, Spokane, Paterson, and elsewhere. Audacity may have secured victory in the prewar free speech fights, but it was not going to work against wartime federal indictments. A month after the initial raids, Wobblies formed the General Defense Committee to consolidate resources and coordinate a national publicity and fundraising effort for the trials. Under the leadership of William Haywood, who was named in the Chicago indictment, the General Defense Committee raised over $1 million in contributions.[87] Haywood urged the Wobblies to surrender themselves and stand trial together. Flynn disagreed, believing that a series of separate trials would clog the federal judicial system and buy time until the war hysteria had worn off. When her idea did not prevail, she along with Tresca, Ettor, and Giovannitti moved to have their cases severed from the Chicago case.[88]

During the IWW free speech fights, Flynn goaded, harangued, and heckled mayors and police chiefs. With the stakes too high to risk a flippant response, she turned instead to conciliation and moral suasion. In January 1918, she made a plea for clemency in a letter of petition to President Wilson that she wrote on the advice of Joseph Tumulty, Wilson's private secretary and political advisor, whom she had met when she traveled to Washington to ask for a stay of execution for Joe Hill in 1915.[89] In the letter, she challenged the reputation she had acquired as a labor agitator by claiming that her activism was necessitated by maternal obligation. Nationalist rhetoric of the era linked motherhood to patriotism and support for the war, and Flynn exploited this connection to argue that she could not possibly be an antiwar radical because she was devoted to her child and siblings.[90] She wrote, "For seven years I have supported my child, and helped to educate two sisters (one of whom is now a teacher) and a brother, who is now eligible for the draft. This is, of course, only what other women are doing and has been a labor of love, but it is rather incompatible with the popular conception of a 'labor agitator.'"[91] Clearly, she was dissembling, and motherhood gave her more than adequate cover.

In addition to rejecting the moniker of labor agitator, Flynn disavowed membership in the IWW "due to violent disagreements that arose in the organization last December." Here she alluded to the conflict with Haywood during the Mesabi Range strike. She then closed the letter with a supplicating tone. After claiming that Wilson's war aims were consistent with her own aspirations for labor (another dubious assertion, to say the least) she begged for the chance "to prove at least that such ideals are free from sordid motives, that they are forward-looking, social and liberal in character and that it is inconceivable and loathsome to one whose darkest moments are lit by dreams of freedom, to ally oneself with German militarism and its fiendish autocracy ... as one idealist to another."[92] Strategic bending of the truth was not new for Flynn—recall her threat to city officials in Missoula that five hundred more hoboes were wending their way to the Garden City to continue the fight for free speech. What was different here was her tone. Militancy and audacity had given way to humility and obsequiousness.

However problematic they might seem in retrospect, lying, humility, and obsequiousness proved successful tactics. Flynn's severance motion succeeded, and her lawyers were able to drag out the proceedings until after the armistice, when the government dropped the charges. She also helped Tresca, Ettor, and Giovannitti obtain severance and avoid trial. Having thus begged her way out of a difficult situation, she returned to activism—although, as part of her clemency agreement, she did not speak out against the war—and became a dedicated advocate for anyone imprisoned on account of their political beliefs or involvement with the labor movement. In contrast, Haywood proved himself a much less shrewd tactician. He was convicted, sentenced to twenty years in prison, and fined $10,000. He subsequently jumped bail and fled to Moscow, where he died in 1928. So much for standing on principle.

Women, War, and Civil Liberties

When Flynn commented to Giovannitti after the Chicago indictment was handed down that men in her life have always demanded she get them out of jail, she hinted at a larger truth about women and civil liberties work. The wartime civil liberties movement burgeoning around her was rooted in the peace culture that emerged in New York City in the early days of the conflict, a culture that was largely the province of women. Feminists marched down Fifth Avenue as early as the fall of 1914 to protest against war and the militarization of U.S. society.[93] The peace movement grew larger even as the drumbeat for war grew louder, involving socialists and liberals, men as well as women; women remained a strong presence through their leadership of various organizations like the Women's Peace Party (founded in 1915 by a group of over three thousand women), the Emergency Peace Federation, and the American Union Against Militarism. After the U.S. declaration of war—when the federal government intensified its campaign against radicals, pacifists, and conscientious objectors—liberals took action against legally sanctioned press censorship, denial of space for public discussions, infiltration of meetings, prosecution of speakers on the flimsiest of evidence, rounding up of "slackers," and office raids. Many of the newly minted civil libertarians were members of the privileged class, well educated, and well connected. Before the war, they had shown little sympathy for constitutionally protected individual rights, believing that excessive individualism prevented the realization of much-needed social reform policies. They saw the value of free speech for democracy and tolerated disagreement in the public sphere insofar as it aimed for positive social transformation, but they had no truck with arguments about the inevitability of class conflict and the need for a radical restructuring of society. The zealous persecution of dissent unleashed by the Espionage Act, however, challenged their faith in a benevolent government and awakened them to the importance of constitutional rights. Even some who supported the war, like John Dewey, grew concerned about the antidemocratic policies inspired by the conflict on the domestic front.[94]

During the war, women took the lead in organizing to defend civil liberties for dissenters. In May 1917, a group of feminist-pacifists founded the New York Bureau of Legal First Aid, later renamed the Bureau of Legal Advice (NYBLA), to provide free legal advice and counsel for conscientious objectors, draft resisters, and others whose opposition to the war put them at odds with the wartime statutes. Start-up funds came from the Women's Peace Party and the Emergency Peace Federation. Officers included lawyer and journalist Marion Cothren (chair), lawyer and birth control advocate Jessie Ashley (treasurer), and pacifist Fannie May Witherspoon (secretary), all of whom were friends and allies of Flynn.[95]

Flynn and the women of the NYBLA enjoyed a mutually supportive and cooperative relationship.[96] As was the case during the Paterson free speech fight, a shared commitment to civil liberties provided an opportunity to unite the often-divergent priorities of the women's movement and the labor movement. Ashley, who had volunteered legal services when Flynn was called to trial for unlawful assembly and disturbing the peace during the Paterson strike, once again worked on Flynn's defense committee when she was arrested for violating the Espionage Act. Cothren chaired that committee. When the bureau expanded the scope of its activities to assist radicals and labor activists after the armistice, Flynn provided Witherspoon, whom she knew from the IWW-led unemployment demonstrations of 1914, with valuable information about how the labor movement worked and advice on how to contact unions whose members might wish to avail themselves of the bureau's services.[97]

Soon after the Bureau of Legal Advice was created, Roger Baldwin and Crystal Eastman of the pacifist American Union Against Militarism (AUAM) formed a national organization to advocate for the rights of conscientious objectors and antiwar activists. Originally called the Bureau of Conscientious Objectors, then the Civil Liberties Bureau of the American Union Against Militarism, it eventually became the National Civil Liberties Bureau (NCLB). The bureau obtained legal counsel for the cases it endorsed, generated publicity on behalf of the defendants, and raised funds. Whereas labor defense groups were staffed primarily by radicals who lacked connections to influential persons in the government, bureau members included preeminent citizens like Baldwin, Unitarian minister John Haynes Holmes, and John Lovejoy Elliott, head of the New York Society for Ethical Culture. Their social status and personal contacts made it possible to lobby government officials directly on behalf of bureau clients, which expanded to include IWW members under federal indictment.[98] Women like Eastman and Helen Phelps Stokes, daughter of a wealthy philanthropic family and central figure of the Intercollegiate Socialist Society, made significant contributions to the bureau, but most women involved in conscientious objector and civil liberties work gravitated toward the NYBLA and other organizations where there was a stronger female presence.

The Workers' Defense Union

The alphabet soup of organizations was just one part of the hotbed of civil liberties activism that was New York in 1918. Harlem socialists A. Philip Randolph and Chandler Owen defended free speech as necessary for the overthrow of tyranny in all its forms in their newly launched monthly magazine, *The Messenger*.[99] Elsewhere in Manhattan, socialists and trade unionists met and pledged to work together on behalf of imprisoned IWW comrades and to enlist the support of conservative American Federation of Labor unions in the "struggle between the employer and the employee." Radicals in the Borough of Kings organized the Brooklyn

Labor Defense Council to help "the many Socialist, I.W.W. members and other political prisoners in the United States."[100]

The expansion of civil liberties activism beyond defense of conscientious objectors required new organizational forms and tactics. In March 1918, a coalition of socialists and liberals including Flynn, Baldwin, Holmes, Norman Thomas, and Fannie Witherspoon founded the Liberty Defense Union (LDU) "to organize popular support on behalf of persons prosecuted for the exercise of their constitutional rights of free speech and free press."[101] Within a month of its founding, the LDU launched a nationwide campaign to provide funds and lawyers for any persons arrested for exercising the right to free speech or press, regardless of political beliefs or affiliation. Although it had the support of prominent liberals and radicals around the country, ringing endorsements from the radical press, and a bevy of popular speakers on the circuit, the fledgling organization lacked the staff and structure to meet the needs of its many constituents.[102] There was a particular need for an organization that focused exclusively on labor-related cases. To meet this need, a conference of radical and trade union delegates was called in July to form the Workers' Liberty Defense Union.[103] That organization lasted until the end of the war. After the armistice was signed, the need for an organization dedicated to labor-related civil liberties work was greater than ever. Flynn estimated that as many as 1,500 men and women were either in prison or under indictment, the majority for holding, expressing, or acting in accord with antiwar, anti-imperialist, or anticapitalist ideas.[104]

In November 1918, Flynn organized the Workers' Defense Union (WDU) under the auspices of the National Civil Liberties Bureau to advocate specifically for the hundreds of labor activists who had been prosecuted under wartime laws for activities that were deemed as interfering with the war effort. The two organizations enjoyed a close and cordial relationship, and the NCLB provided crucial financial assistance as the WDU was taking shape, including paying Flynn's salary for nine weeks. As she later recalled, "We were like a godchild to the Civil Liberties Bureau."[105]

In January 1919, Flynn convened a meeting of delegates to the WDU. They elected Fred Biedenkapp of the Brotherhood of Metal Workers as treasurer and Simon Schachter of the Furriers Joint Board as secretary. Flynn retained the title of organizer. Ella Reeve Bloor later joined the group as field officer. The WDU combined traditional labor defense tactics with new forms of civil liberties activism. Its stated goals were as follows:

1. To secure amnesty for all prisoners jailed before and during the war for labor-related activities;
2. To provide legal counsel and material assistance to defendants in labor cases under indictment or appeal;
3. To protest the government's policy of deportation of foreign workers on account of their political opinions;
4. To advocate for the establishment of a recognized status for political prisoners (such as existed in Europe);
5. To champion the rights of free speech, press, and assemblage guaranteed by the United States Constitution.[106]

Operations were set up in space made available by the Brotherhood of Metal Workers from its own offices at the People's House, a six-story building at 7 East Fifteenth Street that was owned by the Rand School of Social Science. These were not luxurious digs. Flynn described the space as small, dark, and gloomy, with polluted air and bars on the windows.[107] The modest space soon became an important site for working-class struggles around the globe.

Flynn steered the WDU into an activist program that included mass meetings and demonstrations, visits to unions, and leafletting as well as fundraising for legal defense and bail.[108] The WDU's activist agenda also included organizing letter writers to correspond with jailed labor and antiwar activists; sending inmates money, books, games, musical instruments, clothing, and other items; obtaining special diets; and protesting solitary confinement and unsuitable work assignments.[109]

The winter of 1918–1919 must have appeared to Flynn and her allies a propitious time to launch an organization dedicated to defending the rights of radicals in the United States. The surprising success of the 1917 Russian Revolution and the Bolsheviks' tenacious hold on power during the ensuing civil war, despite Allied support for the counterrevolutionary White forces, raised the prospect of a global anticapitalist insurrection for many on the Left. After Lenin led the Bolsheviks to power with only eleven thousand party members, anything seemed possible. Lenin himself insisted that the Russian Revolution was merely a prelude to a European revolution that would eventually spread around the world.[110] The establishment of (short-lived) Soviet Republics in Hungary and Bavaria in the spring of 1919 demonstrated the reach of communism. That a Bolshevik-led revolution might erupt in the United States was not a hard sell in an atmosphere of social and economic unrest nurtured by high unemployment, inflation, and ethnic and racial discrimination.

Postwar Political Unrest

While the scent of revolution in the air may have excited radicals like Flynn, it evoked a fierce reactionary impulse from political conservatives and business interests as well as Gompers, who denounced the regime as a tool of Germany and insisted the United States should not recognize the Bolshevik government.[111] The elections that took place just days before the armistice were "devastating" for the Democrats and, consequently, for unions, as Republicans and employers who opposed wartime labor policies established common ground with Southern antilabor conservatives who resented efforts to organize among Black workers.[112] No sooner was the armistice signed than the uneasy working relationship between capital and labor facilitated by the National War Labor Board began to collapse. Thousands of workers lost their jobs as factories quickly reconverted to peacetime production levels. The newly unemployed were forced to compete with over four million returning soldiers for the limited jobs that were available. Things grew worse as President Wilson's curtailment of price and profit controls resulted in a spike in the cost of living so that many who found jobs had a hard time making ends meet, despite working as many as twelve hours a day, seven days a week. Workers responded with a wave of strikes that rippled throughout 1919. Over four million workers participated in labor stoppages that year. The postwar epidemic of strike fever began with a general strike in Seattle. It spread to encompass a police strike in Boston, a textile strike in Lawrence, a strike of 425,000 miners in the coal fields, and the "Great Strike" of 350,000 workers against U.S. Steel. Whereas prewar labor unrest was blamed on "outside agitators," in the postwar shadow of the Bolshevik Revolution, business leaders and those who sympathized with them claimed the strikes were fomented and led by "alien radicals."

Immigrant labor radicals made a convenient scapegoat for the nation's bleak postwar economic situation. The steel strike illustrates how business interests used antiradicalism and xenophobia to crush working-class militancy. In its report on the strike, the Interchurch World Movement found that "despite the fact that the demands were for better working conditions, a six-day week, eight instead of ten, twelve or fourteen hours a day, and for recognition of labor's right to organize, etc., the newspapers before and during the strike asserted and reasserted in various direct forms and in various ways of implication that the objects of the strike were 'revolutionary' and 'Bolshevik' and that the strikers were 'disloyal' and 'un-American.'"[113]

Mainstream newspapers were not the only entities to cooperate in vilifying strikers as foreign subversives. In the towns of western Pennsylvania, where state and local authorities were subservient to the interests of the steel industry, strikers were met with brutal suppression of civil liberties.[114] The sheriff of Allegheny County forbade outdoor meetings anywhere in the county and deputized five thousand strikebreaking employees of U.S. Steel to enforce the order. Indoor meetings were forbidden throughout the region as well. In Monessen, many Russian strikers were rounded up and jailed on charges of "radicalism." State police clubbed strikers of other nationalities off the streets and into their homes. Strikers in Braddock were beaten, jailed, and fined from ten to sixty dollars. In New Castle, police beat and arrested strikers and held them in prison until the strike was over. Police in other Pennsylvania towns adopted these methods.[115]

The steel strike marked the beginning of the end of the coalition between labor Democrats, unionists, and Progressive activists that characterized the war years. Workers discovered that the rhetoric of democracy and the principle of self-determination did not apply to them in the postwar period. Now that the war was over, the federal government, extricated from the role of mediator between capital and labor, showed where its real loyalty lay by using the strike as an opportunity to quell a growing labor insurgency. The DOJ conducted "red raids" against workers, locking up and deporting immigrant radicals. In Gary, Indiana, the National Guard occupied the city and banned parades. Strikers, among them uniformed ex-soldiers, who defied the order and held an "outlaw parade" were arrested. Guardsmen broke up picket lines and rounded up union officers in other trades. The guard remained in Gary until the strike was broken.[116]

The postwar wave of militancy involved Black workers as well as white. Before and during the war, thousands of Black workers left rural communities in the South for jobs in Northern industrial cities, a mass movement that has come to be known as the Great Migration. In addition to economic opportunity, World War I represented to some Black Americans a chance to challenge false assumptions of their inferiority and demonstrate their patriotism and One Hundred Percent Americanism.

It has been estimated that half of the Black population of the United States supported the war to one degree or another.[117] W. E. B. Du Bois's argument that "if this is our country, then this is our war" exemplified the commitment of Black Americans to serve.[118] More than 350,000 Black soldiers did serve in the military, mostly as support troops. Their hopes for social acceptance were largely unrealized, as they served in segregated units in which the commanding officers, with few exceptions, were white. Although many Black soldiers served proudly and with distinction, implicit and overt racism undermined morale, and the desertion rate for Blacks was more than three times that of whites.[119] The other half of Black America was apathetic or openly antiwar. Local draft boards deferred proportionally fewer Blacks than whites, and thousands of draft-age men deliberately evaded conscription. Some did so to take advantage of new employment opportunities in a booming wartime economy; others were simply unmoved by appeals to fight for democracy for Europeans when it had yet to be won at home for Black Americans.[120] Among the latter group were A. Philip Randolph and Chandler Owen, who regularly defied the law and exhorted readers to resist military service in the pages of *The Messenger*.

The war and the migration of hundreds of thousands of Black Americans from the South to the North inspired a level of activism unequaled until the modern civil rights period.[121] Blacks fought back against violence and other forms of mistreatment by whites, sparking race riots in several cities. The deadliest of these riots occurred during the war in East St. Louis, when anywhere from forty to two hundred Blacks were killed after owners of the Aluminum Ore Company hired Black workers to replace white strikers. After the war, racial violence peaked again during what James Weldon Johnson of the National Association for the Advancement of Colored People (NAACP) called the "Red Summer" of 1919. The longest and bloodiest of the riots was in Chicago, which lasted for thirteen days and left almost forty people dead (over half of the casualties were Black), over five hundred injured, and hundreds of Black homes and businesses destroyed. This type of violence was largely, but not exclusively, an urban phenomenon. Violence was likely to erupt whenever and wherever Blacks asserted their humanity. A report commissioned by the U.S. Senate in fall 1919 found that white violence against Blacks had caused twenty-six different riots over the course of the year. Retribution was brutal when Black workers engaged in explicitly classconscious activities. In the rural community of Elaine, Arkansas, somewhere between one hundred and two hundred Blacks and five whites were killed during a conflict that erupted when Black sharecroppers tried to organize a union. As they did with white workers in the steel strike, law enforcement blamed Black Communists for stirring up discontent. Only this time it was not local police but the nascent Bureau of Investigation that sounded the alarm.[122]

Antiradical Hysteria

In this atmosphere of economic uncertainty and political unrest, the loyalty of returning war veterans was an important consideration. Men like newspaper editor Arthur Guy Empey worked hard to stoke antiradical sentiments among veterans who struggled financially upon their return from combat. Empey was an American who served in the British army until he was wounded at the Battle of the Somme. He published an account of his experiences in a bestselling novel, *Over the Top*, which was used to recruit soldiers after the United States entered the war. In 1918 he produced, directed, and starred in a film based on the book.[123] In the spring of 1919, Empey became managing publisher of *Treat 'Em Rough*, the magazine of the army tank corps. The phrase was originally the corps motto, devised for this branch of the military by its members.

Empey's chief goal was to discourage out-of-work soldiers from faulting the U.S. government and business interests for their woes. To that end he created a scapegoat enemy in the Bolsheviks: "Do not forget that while you were fighting 'over there' or training 'over there' at thirty dollars per month, these Bolsheviks were fighting you and were trying to undermine your Government in order to impede the prosecution of the war."[124] Soldiers who were frustrated by a lengthy job search were encouraged to let off steam through the "sport" of beating up radicals: "Millions of men cannot suddenly find employment. It takes time. Some will have to wait longer than others for that job. If you are one of the unlucky ones, show the stuff in you and grin and bear it. It won't be for long. Do not become a Bolshevik. If you feel like fighting go out and smash a Red—it is a great sport knocking them off soap boxes."[125]

Empey made no distinction between anarchism, socialism, communism, and syndicalism: all were forms of Bolshevism, a pestilence that had to be destroyed before it overran the nation. "It is the duty of every red-blooded American, whether in uniform or not," he wrote, "to destroy these vermin. A good, right-handed swing on the jaw will do more in 2 minutes to convince the soap-box orator that he is wrong than all the coddling and misdirected attempts at education that can be instituted. If the Bolsheviks in this country want war, *we will give them war*. If they talk of revolution, *we will put them in a place where revolution will do some good, and that is hell*."[126] Empey's magazine advertised itself and its politics in eye-catching fashion. Every night for a month, a rented electric billboard on the north side of Times Square flashed "Treat 'Em Rough Declares

War on the IWW" and "Treat 'Em Rough Declares War on Bolshevism" alternately for several minutes.[127]

Radicals and their allies pushed back against Empey's vitriol. The Socialist *New York Call* deplored his inflammatory rhetoric, raised questions about his military background, and published criticism of him by army officers. National Civil Liberties Bureau Director Albert DeSilver wrote a letter to Secretary of War Newton D. Baker asking him to repudiate Empey.[128] Despite these efforts, some quarters were fertile ground for Empey's words. The rallying cry for the May Day rioters who violently broke up meetings and attacked parade marchers was "Treat 'Em Rough."[129]

Superpatriots like Empey and employers looking to crush strikes were not the only entities wanting to continue the campaign against radicals at home even after the war overseas had ended. Congress debated extending wartime federal antisedition laws into peacetime. The effort failed, but state legislatures succeeded in passing a variety of antiradical measures. Thirty-four states enacted criminal anarchy, criminal syndicalism, and sabotage statutes. In some cases, wartime laws were automatically extended into peacetime or adapted with slight changes. The criminal anarchy and sedition laws, patterned after the New York Anarchy Act of 1902, defined "criminal anarchy" and "sedition" as "the doctrine that organized government should be overthrown by force or violence or by assassination . . . or by any unlawful means."[130] Criminal syndicalism laws modeled after the Idaho legislation defined "criminal syndicalism" as "any doctrine . . . advocating the commission of crime, sabotage . . . or unlawful acts of force and violence . . . as a means of accomplishing any change in industrial ownership or control, or effecting any political change." "Sabotage" was defined as "willful and malicious physical damage or injury to physical property."[131] All the laws made it a felony to advocate any of the doctrines described in speech or writing or to join an organization advocating them.[132]

State-level efforts to criminalize radical politics also targeted visual rhetoric. Between 1917 and 1925, twenty-eight states adopted "red flag laws." Some of the laws forbade the display of the red flag in parades or public meetings; others made possession of an emblem "distinctive of Bolshevism, anarchism, or radical socialism" a misdemeanor. As might be expected, civil liberties advocates were critical of the Red Flag Laws, but opposition also came from unexpected places. Although the Massachusetts Supreme Court found the state's Red Flag Law constitutional, the law was repealed when state legislators realized that it criminalized the crimson flag of Harvard. Red flag laws in other states remained viable until 1931, when the U.S. Supreme Court decided by a seven-to-two vote in *Stromberg v. California* that laws banning red flags violated the first and fourteenth amendments.[133]

New York contracted its own strain of the postwar antiradical fever that affected the nation. Fearful that New York City was the national center point of a Bolshevik agitation (Chicagoans might have disputed that notion: both communist parties were born in the Windy City in September 1919), members of the State Assembly passed a resolution to create a committee to investigate Bolshevist or revolutionary activities. Thus was born in March of 1919 the Joint Legislative Committee to Investigate Radical Activities in New York State, otherwise known as the Lusk Committee after its chair, Senator Clayton R. Lusk.[134] The Lusk Committee carried out highly publicized raids on the Soviet Bureau (an unofficial embassy set up by the Bolshevik government to secure diplomatic recognition by the United States and encourage trade with American businesses) and the Rand School as well as the IWW and various branches of the Communist Party, and they investigated publishing houses and meeting halls.[135]

Miraculously, the Workers' Defense Union was spared. Although it was in the same building as the Rand School, Flynn's name appeared on the committee's list of dangerous radicals, and agents infiltrated meetings at which she spoke and transcribed her speeches, the offices of the WDU were not raided. Most likely due to poor organization, the WDU was absent from the committee's list of organizations in the People's House, nor was its office included in the layout of the building drawn up for the raid.[136]

A "United Front" of Radicals

Unity was essential in the face of such intense hostility toward labor, generally, and radicalism, particularly. Fortunately, Flynn was extremely talented at building coalitions. She recruited delegates from over 170 organizations of various ideological bents into the WDU, making it arguably the one truly "united front" created by radicals in the United States.[137] Groups as diverse as the International Association of Machinists, United Hebrew Trades, Teachers' Union, Consumers League of the Bronx, Socialist Party, New York Vegetarian Society, and Italian Bakers Federation counted among its affiliates.[138]

The WDU succeeded in uniting diverse constituencies because it did not concern itself with propagating one set of ideas. Instead, Flynn focused the organization on the one goal shared by all labor organizations across the ideological spectrum: "freedom of its spokesmen and the establishment of civil rights for workers."[139] As Flynn explained, the decision to exclude deliberation or action on "extraneous subjects" not directly connected to this goal went a long way to cementing the ranks "because everybody—from extreme anarchists on the left to conservative trade unionists on the right—felt strongly about the injustice of wartime prosecutions of fellow Americans and was willing to fight for their release. The imprisoned comrades, of whatever persuasions, were a bond of unity."[140]

The solidarity of the capitalist class was another inspiration for unity among workers and their allies. WDU literature exhorted workers to see how the "Iron Heel of Capital" was using postwar legislation to intensify its campaign against labor by persecuting the movement's most active and outspoken members, whatever their ideological commitments: "Workers are thrown into dungeons for the crime of thinking, whether they be affiliated with the IWW or the A.F. of L., the Communist groups or the Socialist Party."[141] While capital's henchmen rounded up labor's most active champions as one undifferentiated mass of "Reds," they used vagrancy, criminal anarchy, and criminal syndicalism laws as well as deportations to breed fear and foster distrust and dissension among the rank and file: "They define a dissatisfied migratory worker as a 'vagrant'; they brand a reader of a labor paper as a 'criminal syndicalist'; they dub every idealist 'seditionist, spy, traitor, anarchist'; they pillory as an 'undesirable' the alien who joins his American fellow workers in the fight for a better world. Categories of capital's making these are! Will labor succumb to such superficial strategy? Will it stone and crucify its spokespersons?"[142]

In addition to worming away at working-class solidarity, these laws threatened to debase the material conditions of workers' lives. A Kansas law against vagrancy, for example, that criminalized the refusal to work "when work at fair wages is to be procured in the community" empowered the courts to decide what constituted a fair wage and left any worker on strike for higher pay subject to being jailed as a "vagrant." The criminal syndicalism law of California left every worker in a union subject to a fourteen-year prison term if an act of violence were committed during a strike conducted by that union.[143] Threat of deportation made immigrant workers everywhere in the United States fearful of organizing into unions and demanding better wages and working conditions.[144]

The issue of deportation was extremely important to Flynn and the WDU. In October 1918, Congress passed "An Act to exclude and expel from the Unites States aliens who are members of the anarchistic and similar classes." This law, known as the Deportation Act, built on earlier immigration laws to authorize deportation of any immigrant who opposed organized government, belonged to an organization that advocated overthrow of the government by violent means, or belonged to any organization that taught these views. The provisions of the law were applicable to any immigrant irrespective of time of entry. Although anarchists were the explicit target of the law, immigrants who belonged to any organization that was found to support violent revolution, such as the communist parties, were subject to deportation. Looking back on the law a quarter century later, Flynn called it "the granddaddy of all repressive legislation."[145]

The Bureau of Immigration, at that time under the Department of Labor, typically decided who would be deported under the law. They were ably assisted by the DOJ under the direction of Attorney General A. Mitchell Palmer. Flynn thought Palmer was obsessed: "He saw 'reds' in schools, at dances, in plays, in unions, under the bed—just everywhere."[146] The fire of Palmer's obsession with radicals was stoked when a bomb planted by anarchist Carlo Valdinoci, part of a coordinated attack against government officials, exploded at Palmer's Washington, D.C., home on the evening of June 2, 1919. No one in Palmer's family was hurt, but Valdinoci was blown to bits when he tripped on the steps while trying to place the bomb. Palmer's response to the attack was swift and fierce. He authorized his assistant, J. Edgar Hoover—described by Flynn as "a roundfaced, bullnecked, eager beaver"—to arrest foreign radicals.[147]

Acting without warning or warrants, federal agents forced their way into union offices and the meeting places of Communists, anarchists, and Socialists. In December 1919, Palmer's agents seized 249 resident aliens, including Emma Goldman and Alexander Berkman, and put them on a ship (the *Buford*) bound for Russia. In January 1920, they raided homes and headquarters in over seventy cities and arrested as many as ten thousand people, including seven hundred in New York. Immigrants picked up by the Palmer Raids, as they have come to be called, were held on Ellis Island in New York, Deer Island in Boston, Fort Wayne in Michigan, and elsewhere, where they languished in miserable conditions. In many cases their loved ones had no idea where they were. Held without charge and denied rights of due process, they were subject to deportation if they admitted to holding radical ideas or belonging to a radical organization. Before public pressure put an end to the raids, over five hundred immigrant workers were deported, "some to certain death in their homelands."[148]

Flynn understood deportation as an instrument of repression designed to divide American-born and immigrant workers and keep the latter fearful, docile, and submissive. From May to December 1919, the WDU raised over $23,000 bail, much of it posted for deportees.[149] The money was dispersed through the Deportees Defense and Relief Committee, which Flynn and Baldwin had organized at the request of the fledgling Communist Party after the first Palmer Raids.[150] When the Communist Party pulled out, the committee was absorbed by the WDU. Between January 5 and February 12, 1920, the committee raised over $4,000 to address what it called "the greatest menace that the American labor movement has ever faced."[151] The money funded legal work on behalf of individuals facing deportation, publicity about various cases, bail for imprisoned workers, and material aid to families.[152] The WDU rallied its delegates to support the committee's work with appeals to working-class solidarity and descriptions of the awful conditions faced by prisoners awaiting deportation: "Workers! Stand by your persecuted alien brothers. Deportation is the last resort of a panic-stricken system. Its application by the Department of Justice and Labor has no humanity in it. Families are destroyed. The victims are herded into crowded quarters, where disease spreads among them. Several have died on Ellis Island. There are some among the detained aliens who are not connected with any organization. They happened to be in the raided halls or houses, and they happen to be working men and women."[153]

The Deportees Defense and Relief Committee disbanded in March 1920. Its work was carried on by a committee organized by the deportees themselves. Flynn's commitment to supporting workers who faced deportation—and their families—did not end when the committee disbanded or when the workers left the United States. She would continue to oppose deportation as a tool of political repression for the rest of her political career.

By the early 1920s, the WDU was a recognized leader in labor-related civil liberties work.[154] The go-to labor defense organization for the Civil Liberties Bureau and the nascent ACLU, it served as a model for similar organizations in Baltimore, Albany, Denver, and Kansas City.[155] Although the organization's activities centered on cases in New York, it functioned as a clearinghouse for labor-related cases at the state and federal level throughout the United States, especially those involving workers with no national reputation or strong labor group to support them. Flynn insisted that lesser-known prisoners not fall through the cracks of labor defense. In a speech she delivered at a civil liberties conference in New York, Flynn informed fellow activists, "For every one of the cases you know about, there are 100 hundred about which you know nothing at all."[156] Left on their own, these workers—"obscure and almost forgotten"—would have difficulty navigating an unfamiliar legal system; an endorsement from the WDU enabled them to benefit from the organization's knowledge of the legal process and gave them access to competent and committed lawyers, not to mention fundraising and publicity channels.[157] Attorneys who represented WDU clients included Charles Recht, general counsel for the Bureau of Legal Advice; Harry Weinberger, attorney for Emma Goldman and Alexander Berkman; and Walter Nelles, pacifist, counsel for the National Civil Liberties Bureau, and founding member of the ACLU.

Among the well-known "political offenders" who received some sort of assistance from the WDU were Eugene Debs, Kate Richards O'Hare, Emma Goldman, and Alexander Berkman as well as Rose Pastor Stokes, a prominent New York socialist sentenced to ten years in prison for allegedly attacking war profiteering "in a daily newspaper of large circulation," and Victor Berger, a member of the Socialist Party Executive Committee and Congressman-elect from Wisconsin who was tried in Chicago under the Espionage Act for conspiracy to hamper the government in the conduct of war, convicted, sentenced to twenty years in prison, and denied his seat in Congress. In addition, the WDU publicized and donated to the defense campaigns for IWW members indicted in Chicago, Wichita, and Omaha. Despite having severed formal ties with the union over her disagreement with Haywood, Flynn's name was still linked with the IWW, and she remained personally involved in the defense effort, using her fame and public speaking ability to champion the union and raise money for Wobbly comrades imprisoned at Leavenworth and elsewhere.

The WDU also endorsed a great many cases of lesser-known (at the time) individuals arrested during and after the war, including the following:

> *Rocco De Blassis*, Italian immigrant, charged with rioting in Rome, New York, for taking a gun away from an assailant who was firing into a crowd of pickets during a strike of the Sparco electrical works, deported to Italy along with his wife and children in July 1920.
> *William Krispenz*, Communist labor organizer from Detroit, arrested in Chicago and ordered deported to Hungary, held on Ellis Island despite cancellation of his deportation order.
> *Morris Zucker*, Socialist and dentist from Brooklyn, New York, convicted under the Espionage Act and sentenced to fifteen years' imprisonment for giving a speech in which he predicted the triumph of socialism in the United States.

Dr. Marie Equi, anarchist living in Portland, Oregon, convicted under the Espionage Act and sentenced to three years in prison and fined $500 for making statements derogatory to the army and navy in a speech at which two officers from the Army Intelligence Bureau were present.

Dr. Elizabeth Baer and Charles Schenck, Philadelphia Socialists sentenced to ninety days and six months, respectively, for their complicity in the distribution of an anticonscription leaflet; the latter's case made its way to the Supreme Court as *Schenck v. the United States*, and in a unanimous opinion written by Justice Oliver Wendell Holmes Jr., the court upheld Shenck's conviction as constitutional and thus laid the foundation for the "clear and present danger" standard for free speech.

Mollie Steimer, nineteen-year-old anarchist, arrested and sentenced, along with three other young men, to twenty years' imprisonment for passing out a leaflet opposing military intervention in Russia and encouraging a general strike among munitions workers.

John Summerfield Randolph, IWW member from Auburn, New York, and descendant of a signer of the Declaration of Independence, charged under the Espionage Act and sentenced to ten years in the Atlanta Federal Penitentiary for expressing sympathy with Debs and opposition to the war.

Albert Brooks, IWW member, convicted in Dillon, Montana, and sentenced to prison for distributing an IWW leaflet written before the war entitled "War and the Worker."

Joseph M. Coldwell, Socialist Party organizer in Rhode Island, sentenced to three years in the Atlanta Federal Penitentiary for expressing sympathy for three conscientious objectors who were sentenced to twenty years each.

Flora Foreman, Socialist schoolteacher, arrested in Amarillo, Texas, charged under the Espionage Act for expressing nonsupport for the Red Cross, convicted, and sentenced to five years in prison, despite chronic respiratory problems.[158]

Lovett Fort-Whiteman, Black Communist, arrested in St. Louis, where he gave a speech to members of the Communist Labor Party of America in 1919, and charged under the Espionage Act for allegedly advocating "resistance to America."[159]

Joseph J. Jones, IWW member, arrested in Boston for allegedly advocating criminal anarchy propaganda among Black workers.[160]

Defense of Black Workers

As the Fort-Whiteman and Jones endorsements reveal, the WDU's commitment to unity included defense of Black workers' rights. Flynn drew upon her experience as an organizer for the IWW to campaign for class solidarity in the face of white supremacy. In July 1919 she spoke at a "Red-Hot Mass Meeting" at the Palace Casino in Harlem to raise money for *The Messenger*, which had been denied second-class mailing privileges after editors A. Philip Randolph and Chandler Owen criticized the hypocrisy of a nation that fought to "make the world safe for democracy" while allowing its own Black citizens to be terrorized by white racists.[161] Their piece, titled "The Hun in America," mimicked sensationalist reporting of German wartime atrocities against Allied civilians to offer a scathing and graphic critique of complacency in the face of lynching and other violent crimes committed by whites against Blacks in the United States during so-called peacetime.

> In CIVILIZED AMERICA (?) a boy just blossoming into manhood in the shadow of the Court-house in Waco Texas was burned up to the amusement and delight of fifteen thousand white American citizens. Children were permitted to sell the bones as souvenirs. It was a HOLIDAY. In Georgia, the abdomen of a woman, upon the eve of bearing a child, was ripped open, the form emptied upon the ground, while American HUNS buried their heels in its brains. THINK OF IT! The Huns of Germany pale into utter insignificance beside the nameless and indescribable fiendishness of the American HUNS.[162]

At the Harlem meeting Flynn, who was billed as a "most gripping and scholarly Irish woman orator," shared the stage with Randolph and Owen as well as Norman Thomas; Jamaican-born W. A. Domingo, a leader of the Harlem Socialist Party; and Second Lieutenant William N. Colson, a contributing editor of *The Messenger*.[163] In her speech, she warned her audience against manipulation into interracial conflict by the capitalist class. Although she was no longer an official member of the IWW, she spoke from an insider's perspective when she exhorted Black workers to join the union: "In the IWW we do not preach class distinction, or creed or color. We are all bound together for the betterment of the workingman." The response to Flynn was quite enthusiastic, and the meeting raised almost $500 in bonds for *The Messenger*.[164]

In November 1919, Flynn spoke again in Harlem, this time at a meeting called by the Committee of Justice to the Negro to protest the killing of

RED-HOT
Mass Meeting

10,000 Harlem Citizens will protest against unjust interference with Negro Publications in Mails by

BURLESON OF TEXAS

COME and HEAR why the NEGRO PROBLEM is growing more acute every minute.

LISTEN to the cool, dispassionate Logic and Eloquence of the following Brilliant Orators:

ELIZABETH GURLEY FLYNN
Most Gripping and Scholarly Irish Woman Orator

GEORGE FRAZIER MILLER

A. PHILIP RANDOLPH and CHANDLER OWEN
Instructors, Rand School of Social Science

W. A. DOMINGO, Editor Negro World will Preside.

PALACE CASINO
135th Street and Madison Avenue

Sunday Afternoon, July 13th, at 3 Sharp

ADMISSION FREE

FIGURE 5. Flyer advertising "Red-Hot Mass Meeting" in Harlem, 1919. Credit: Image courtesy of the New York State Archives NYSA_L0038-78_B1_F19

more than one hundred Blacks during the Elaine Massacre and demand justice for the twelve African Americans sentenced to death for crimes related to the violence (no whites were charged). Other speakers that day included James Weldon Johnson of the NAACP and Norman Thomas. Flynn was the last to take the podium. She spoke against the "legalized lynching of Arkansas farmers," exhorted Black workers to organize, and urged white workers to welcome Black fellow workers into their unions.[165]

Authorities feared the consequences of cross-racial working-class solidarity, and agents of the Lusk Committee—or "Luskers," as they were called—closely monitored meetings that promoted unity between Black and white workers. One of those agents attended the Harlem meeting and transcribed the proceedings, including Flynn's speech. The Lusker's transcription gives a sense of her skill in building rapport and the enthusiasm with which she was received by the audience. Flynn drew upon her Irish ancestry and offered the experiences of migration and the struggle for freedom from oppression as a common bond between herself and the Black workers in the audience and, by extension, all Black and white workers.

> We are gathered here together, liberty-loving, justice-loving men and women. It does not matter what the color of our skin may be. It does not matter from which corner of the earth we may have come. My ancestors came here willingly. Your ancestors came here unwillingly. (Applause). My ancestors came here because they were seeking from America—which they could not find in Ireland at that time—your ancestors came here in slavery and oppression; and we are standing here together today, the descendants of those pilgrims of days gone by, demanding the liberty that this country has promised the entire world.[166]

In addition to her gift for oratory, Flynn had an extraordinary talent for fundraising. After her speech, she presided over the ritual passing of the hat with witty and relentless running commentary: "If you want liberty for those men, justice for those men, liberty for yourselves, you have got to be willing to invest your money, as well as your enthusiasm in that effort."[167] As the collection box circulated the room, she cajoled people into depositing bills, rather than silver, and commented approvingly when white workers practiced class solidarity by donating to the cause, "I am glad it is going to be one of our white workers over here who is going to give the first bill, and here is another and another."[168] She gently chided those who tried to leave the assembly without making a contribution:

"Now, do not anybody go, because I know most of you, and I would like to state who you are, and that would be very embarrassing." Even law enforcement agents assigned to observe the meeting, presumably most of them Irish American, were expected to donate: "Do not forget the Bomb Squad, if there are any of them in the hall. I am sure they would be willing to give a small contribution for justice, in the name of Irish freedom, if not in any other kinds of freedom. (Applause and laughter.)"[169]

At the conclusion of the event Flynn issued a final call for solidarity and commitment to action that resonated with her audience: "Let us pledge ourselves. Hand in hand, shoulder to shoulder, heart to heart, to go forward until justice, liberty, and civilization are enthroned from one end of this great country to another. (Applause.)"[170] Her language—specifically, the invocation of political ideals, such as "justice" and "liberty," and assertions of national greatness—suggests a second noteworthy characteristic of the WDU: its framing of labor-related civil liberties work as an endeavor deeply rooted in American political traditions.

The WDU: An American Organization with an International Perspective

WDU literature framed civil liberties work as an epic struggle on behalf of "an idealistic vanguard known as the radicals" against self-serving moneyed interests that had seized on the war as an opportunity to extend their control of U.S. political institutions and reverse the democratic revolution set in motion by the founders of the nation.[171] Flynn and her WDU allies criticized the Espionage Act as a regressive law that reestablished constructive offenses against the government—that is, crimes based not on evidence of any overt act but built up by the court through inference and implication (recall the charges against Wobblies after the Everett Massacre). In language that called to mind eighteenth-century Republicanism, they asserted, "Tyrants have always punished their rebellious subjects for 'constructive' activities."[172] They drew moral authority from the Declaration of Independence, "a very clear statement upon the right of agitation," and legal authority from the Constitution: "The wording is clear and hardly to be misinterpreted. Congress should make no law abridging the freedom of speech or of the press. Nevertheless in direct violation of this amendment and of the spirit of the Declaration of Independence, Congress has passed a series of laws the effect of which was to suppress freedom of discussion, to curtail free speech, free press and free assemblage all over the United States."[173]

Nineteenth-century abolitionists such as Wendell Phillips of Massachusetts, who defended the right to free speech even when it violated the so-called property rights of slaveholders, were held up as exemplary Americans.[174] The deportation law was criticized as a departure from American ideals, "a flagrant contradiction of the past history of America as an asylum for political refugees—to whose idealism this nation owes much of its vigor and social progress."[175] Repeal of the law was deemed necessary to "re-establish this country as a haven of refuge for the persecuted in all lands."[176] More recent history was also tapped for strategic ends. The drive to raise bail for imprisoned comrades co-opted the language of the campaign to raise funds for the war effort, imploring union members and allies of the labor movement to make a "Liberty Loan" to "open the jails for one of your fellow workers, suffering indescribable tortures, eaten alive by the white plague."[177] These historical allusions helped the WDU position itself as the inheritor of a U.S. tradition of struggle against political repression. As the founders of the nation threw off the yoke of British tyranny in the eighteenth century and abolitionists challenged Southern cotton interests in the nineteenth, so the WDU fought to prevent capital's henchmen from reducing workers to servile status in the twentieth.

Although the WDU was rooted in American political culture, its outlook extended beyond national borders. The campaign to secure political prisoner status for the men and women who had been arrested for antimilitarism or involvement in the labor movement and to obtain a general amnesty for these political prisoners is illustrative. The case for amnesty hinged on the argument that European countries had long since recognized a difference between common crimes and political crimes, and the United States lagged behind. As one WDU pamphlet expressed it, "While every other country of any degree of enlightenment is repealing its war measures and releasing political prisoners, in the United States political offenders are still receiving savage sentences."[178] The analogy, of course, entailed a critique: the United States heralded itself as a haven for political prisoners from other lands even as it repressed political dissent within its own borders.

Flynn considered everyone held under the Espionage Act or targeted by the Palmer Raids a political prisoner, and she spoke frequently about the issue.[179] Representatives of the WDU put forth resolutions at meetings of various labor and radical organizations.[180] Along with a variety of labor unions, the Socialist Party, the Civil Liberties Bureau / ACLU, and newly established general amnesty organizations such as the Political Prisoner

Defense and Relief Committee and the League for Amnesty of Political Prisoners (Flynn was a member of the league), they rallied around the cause of political prisoners to address concerns about the impact of the war and the Bolshevik Revolution on civil liberties and secure greater tolerance for dissent in the future.[181] At a time when the forces of reaction were running roughshod over civil liberties with the ostensive aim of preventing the "Reds" from launching another successful revolution, the general amnesty campaign must be credited with inspiring public deliberation about the nature of political dissent and the question of whether the United States should recognize political prisoners.[182] But while the campaign provided a counterweight to hyperpatriotic mobs and overzealous prosecutors, it could not effect a change in the legal status quo.[183] The last of the Espionage Act prisoners would not be pardoned until President Franklin Roosevelt's Christmas Amnesty Proclamation of 1933.

Authorities intended incarceration as a means of disrupting political activities, but like the male soapbox orators jailed during the free speech fights, many of the prisoners for whom Flynn and the WDU advocated continued their political activities behind bars. The use of prison as an instrument of political activity was a relatively new phenomenon in the early twentieth century, according to Padraic Kenney. It was brought into being in part by the emergence of collective social movements in Europe, chief among them the socialist movement in its various forms. Suppression of these movements required incarceration of numbers of like-minded people, which, in turn, allowed for the creation of community inside prison.[184] Arguably, the best-known U.S. prisoner to use a jail cell as a site for politics was Eugene Debs. Already a towering figure among mainstream and radical labor activists when he was arrested under the Espionage Act, Debs used his prisoner status to continue the struggle against rapacious capitalism alongside his comrades outside of prison. In 1920, he ran for president on the Socialist Party ticket for the fifth time, winning nearly a million votes from his jail cell.

Prison was also a space for practicing politics beyond national boundaries. In 1918, Mexican revolutionary anarchist Ricardo Flores Magón, who was being closely watched on both sides of the border, was apprehended in Los Angeles, California, and charged under the Espionage Act for publishing an antiwar pamphlet. He was sentenced to Leavenworth Prison. At Leavenworth, Magón interacted with radicals of different races, ethnicities, nationalities, and political ideologies. Together, explains Christina Heatherton, they transformed the prison into "a convergence space of radical internationalist traditions," creating affinities, generating new political understandings, and devising tactics for international, revolutionary, anticapitalist struggle.[185]

The WDU endorsed Magón's case. Leavenworth was not the first time he had been imprisoned in the United States for his revolutionary activities. In 1907 and 1912, as part of a cross-border counterinsurgency campaign, he was arrested and imprisoned for publishing the anarchist newspaper *Regeneración* allegedly in violation of neutrality laws between the United States and Mexico. But repression was not the only thing to traverse the United States–Mexico border. Cross-border solidarity helped drive the organizing campaigns of IWW locals in Los Angeles and around the Southwest, where Mexicans played an important role.[186] Socialists fighting against the open shop in Los Angeles found common cause with the Magonista movement while Magón was imprisoned there.[187] By the time of his Espionage Act arrest, Magón was known and admired among many U.S. radicals, including Flynn. She called him a "heroic fighter" and noted how the struggle that he and other Mexican comrades waged against a repressive political regime and exploitative U.S. corporations resonated deeply on this side of the border—so much so that "many American IWWs and Socialists, in the tradition of Lafayette and Kosciusko, crossed the border to join the Mexican revolution."[188]

The WDU's working-class, revolutionary internationalism extended well beyond the North American continent. The organization endorsed the international "Hands Off Russia!" campaign, which opposed giving aid or sending troops to bolster anti-Soviet forces during the civil war that engulfed Russia from the end of the October Revolution until the Bolsheviks defeated the White armies in 1921. Space was made at the offices at 7 East Fifteenth Street for the Society for Technical Aid to Soviet Russia, founded to expedite and coordinate emigration to Soviet Russia by skilled workers.

Another group that made its temporary home with the WDU was the Friends of Freedom for India (FFI), founded by members of the IWW, the Socialist Party, and liberal Americans (with a Hindustani advisory board) to defend members of the multiethnic, anti-imperialist, revolutionary Ghadar Party who had been arrested in the United States under the Espionage Act and threatened with deportation for their anti-British activities.[189] At least nineteen of these Indian activists were convicted for having violated neutrality laws before the United States even entered the war, in 1915. The aims of the FFI, which counted W. E. B. Du Bois, Margaret Sanger, Franz Boas, Upton Sinclair, and Roger Baldwin among its members, were to maintain the right of asylum for political prisoners from India and to agitate for Indian independence. In the WDU space at Fifteenth Street, the FFI printed a weekly news bulletin, *India News Service*, which reported on the activities of Indian revolutionaries around the world, as well as a variety of pamphlets and books.[190] At least one of these publications, Basanta Koomar Roy's *The Labor Revolt in India*, which compared the situation of Indian Labor and of India generally with that of other countries, was banned by British authorities in India.[191]

In addition to providing office space for the FFI, the WDU endorsed the cause of the Indian deportees and raised money to help defray their legal expenses. Flynn represented the WDU at the first convention of the FFI, held at the Hotel McAlpin in New York City on December 5, 1920. She was one of the over four hundred delegates representing one hundred organizations in attendance. The program included a symposium on "Conditions and Problems of India," led by the Indian delegates. As part of the symposium, Flynn took part in a discussion on "America's Duty towards India's Independence Movement" along with Baldwin, Du Bois, Mary White Ovington, and Rose Schneiderman.[192] The focus of the convention was expansive. Among the many resolutions passed were a call for a fair trial by jury for all aliens threatened with deportation and condemnation of the British opium monopoly. Attendees also sent greetings to Mahatma Gandhi and greetings to the leaders of movements for independence in Ireland, Egypt, Mesopotamia, and South Africa.[193] The final resolution laid out a series of indictments against British colonial rule in India and called for the creation of the India Investigation Commission, "whose duty it [would] be to proceed at once to India to make a thorough and impartial investigation of these charges" and report back to the FFI and the American people.[194]

Indian revolutionaries made common cause with Irish freedom fighters in the struggle against British imperialism. In the early twentieth century, the two groups forged a local alliance in New York that was nurtured by a strong and dynamic U.S.-based Irish Republican movement and liberal press laws that allowed both groups to publish nationalist propaganda and distribute it domestically and around the globe.[195] The alliance remained intact during and after World War I. It was likely strengthened by the shared experience of surveillance and repression meted out against radical critics of empire.[196] In fact, the Friends of Freedom for India was named after the Friends of Irish Freedom, which had been founded in New York to counter pro-British sentiment in the United States and advocate for Irish independence a month prior to the Easter Rising of 1916.

Flynn's support for the cause of a free Ireland had been instilled in her from birth by her parents and was nurtured by her friendship with republicans like James Connolly and Jim Larkin. The two led the Irish Transport and General Workers Union during the Dublin Lockout of 1913, a dispute that politicized the working classes of the city and led to the formation of the Irish Citizen Army, which played a major role in the Rising. In 1914, when Larkin came to the United States, he went on Connolly's advice to the Flynn family's apartment in the Bronx. A "magnificent orator and an agitator without equal," according to Flynn, Larkin "thundered against British imperialism" at antiwar and strike meetings, often under the green banner of the Irish Socialist Federation given to him by Flynn's mother, Annie Gurley.[197] Connolly, one of the leaders of the Rising, was executed by firing squad while sitting down (having been injured during the fighting, he was unable to stand) on May 12, 1916. After the Rising, Flynn and her family assisted Irish Republicans who sought them out while in the United States on fundraising tours, including Connolly's daughter Nora and Hannah Sheehy Skeffington, in a variety of ways from providing a quiet place to grieve to babysitting.[198] Larkin lambasted moderate, "respectable" Irish Republicans, whose support for Irish independence stopped short of armed rebellion. In 1919, he was elected a delegate to the founding meeting of the Communist Party in Chicago. The same year he was arrested in New York and charged under the state's Criminal Anarchy Law. Flynn helped organize a delegation to lobby Irish Republican leader Eamon de Valera for funds for Larkin's defense, and the WDU supported Larkin's case and offered him a platform to speak at meetings.[199] He was sentenced to five to ten years in Sing Sing Prison but was pardoned by Governor Al Smith and then deported by J. Edgar Hoover in 1923.

Flynn's commitment to helping build a workers' republic in Ireland and the penalties she saw exacted on friends who were directly involved in the struggle made her naturally supportive of others who were working to free themselves from British rule. In her autobiography, she recalled facilitating a meeting of Indian and Irish revolutionaries that resulted in a contingent of Indians marching in the Saint Patrick's Day Parade down Fifth Avenue. That non-Irish would participate in this "sacred event" was evidence, according to Flynn, that "feeling ran high against England."[200] As her 1919 speech in Harlem demonstrated, Flynn also saw parallels between working-class Irish immigrants and Blacks in the United States. She drew upon the shared experience of migration and discrimination at the hands of Anglo-American elites to build alliances with Black radicals for union organizing drives and campaigns against the Ku Klux Klan. The solidarity that Flynn felt with the struggles of Black workers was reciprocated by

A. Philip Randolph. In 1921, Randolph, Flynn, and Joseph Cannon of the United Mine Workers shared the stage at a meeting of the National Association for the Promotion of Labor Unionism among Negroes. The meeting had been called to unite Black and white workers in a fight to keep the Klan from gaining a foothold in the North. In an obvious show of support for the Irish freedom struggle, Randolph, secretary of the association, called the Klan the "black and tans of America," a reference to the band of former British soldiers recruited to assist the Royal Irish Constabulary in maintaining control over the Irish Republican Army during the War of Independence, which they did with a degree of violence and brutality that earned them the deep and abiding hatred of the Irish.[201]

In 1923, President Calvin Coolidge commuted the sentences of the last remaining IWW prisoners detained at Leavenworth. The WDU closed shop after release of the IWW prisoners. Throughout the organization's five-year existence, Flynn showed that it was possible to work across ideological, racial, and national divides to coordinate publicity, legal strategies, financial resources, and political connections in defense of anyone targeted for their activities on behalf of working-class movements. Her efforts provided a model for how to build a radical civil liberties organization in an intolerant political climate and within a hostile legal system. This model would inspire the International Labor Defense, one of the most important civil liberties / civil rights organizations in U.S. history, which was founded under the auspices of the Communist Party in 1925.

Looking back on her work with the WDU, Flynn regarded it as a formative experience that broadened her horizons considerably. Prior to the war, she had been "a devoted IWW," but the WDU brought her into contact "with Socialists, anarchists, trade unionists, Communists, suffragists, pacifists, liberals, Indian and Irish nationalists, and official representatives of both the Soviet and Irish republics."[202] Although she continued to frame her work as defending constitutionally guaranteed rights to free speech, press, association, and due process, her activism had expanded considerably beyond street corners and meeting halls in the small towns and cities of the United States. By the early 1920s, she and her free speech allies in the WDU saw their work as part of a global effort on behalf of political prisoners connected to labor and anticolonial movements throughout the United States and Europe as well as in India and Mexico, and they were deeply committed to the success of the young Bolshevik government in Russia. Flynn's internationalist perspective would continue to inform her activism and influence the civil liberties movement in the 1920s and '30s.

CHAPTER 4

From Civil Liberties Icon to Communist Menace

> I don't relish the prospect of her going forth as a martyr on this forthcoming lecture trip of hers, but I can swallow it a darned sight better than the prospect of her going forth as a victor in the fight, a reborn Joan of Arc.
> —John Haynes Holmes

ON JANUARY 12, 1920, a group of nearly two dozen activists met at the Civic Club on West Twelfth Street in New York City with the goal of reorganizing the wartime National Civil Liberties Bureau into a permanent organization for the defense of civil liberties. At the meeting, Roger Baldwin read aloud the names of those who had accepted the invitation to join in the work of reorganization. Among them were Jeanette Rankin, U.S. Congresswoman from Montana, one of only fifty House members who voted against the declaration of war on Germany; James Weldon Johnson, field secretary (soon to be appointed executive secretary) for the NAACP; Rose Schneiderman, labor organizer and president of the New York Women's Trade Union League; Jane Addams, social worker and president of the Women's International League for Peace and Freedom; Morris Hillquit, labor defense lawyer and founder of the Socialist Party of America; Helen Keller, revolutionary socialist and disability rights advocate; and Elizabeth Gurley Flynn.[1]

Baldwin had been director of the National Civil Liberties Bureau from its founding in October 1917 until his resignation prior to refusing to register for the draft, which had been extended to men up to the age of forty, in September 1918. His refusal to serve in the military constituted a violation of the Espionage Act, and he was sentenced to a year in prison.

At the 1920 meeting, Baldwin questioned the expediency of listing his or Flynn's name among the members of the national committee of the reorganized association, which the group voted to name the American Civil Liberties Union (ACLU). He reasoned that their respective prosecutions under the Espionage Act would expose the nascent organization to attack. He was outvoted by the other members of the group on the principle that their commitment to civil liberties had earned the two a place on the new organization's masthead.[2] Two decades later, the question of whether Flynn was an asset or a liability to the ACLU would be revisited because of her decision to join the Communist Party, and the governing body of the organization would reach a different conclusion. For now, however, Flynn's name recognition, organizing ability, extensive network, and dedication to the intertwined causes of labor and civil liberties made her a highly valued member, worth facing whatever criticism of the ACLU her presence might invite.

The East Side Joan of Arc

Although it would be a stretch to say that Flynn was a household name in the 1920s, she was arguably the most well-known woman radical in the United States at the time. Readers of this book are likely familiar with the moniker "Rebel Girl," which Joe Hill bestowed on her before he was executed by a firing squad in 1915. In the early twentieth century, Flynn was more often referred to in the press with some form of the name that novelist Theodore Dreiser gave her at the start of her career, the East Side Joan of Arc. Although she disliked the name because she was not religious, it is not hard to understand why it stuck. Like the iconic Joan of Arc, Flynn was an attractive young woman—one newspaper described her as "petite, well formed, with almost faultless features, dusky hair, and great starlight eyes"; another simply as "a pretty little Socialist from New York's East Side"—whose courage, conviction, and absolute dedication to a cause had elevated her to a position of leadership.[3] Whereas Joan had dedicated herself to doing God's will by leading an army to battle for the cause of France, Flynn's dedication was to the cause of labor. It rested not on religious principles but on the conviction that class conflict was inevitable in a capitalist state and that the struggles of working people in the United States were inseparable from movements against capitalism, racism, and imperialism around the globe. Moreover, like Joan and countless other women activists before or since, Flynn refused to let traditional gender roles define her or limit her sphere of activity. Her unapologetic anticapitalist, antiracist, and anti-imperialist politics combined with her refusal to tamp down her activism and submit to the normal constraints of marriage and motherhood made Flynn an aberration to some and a hero to others.

Since she first became a public figure, Flynn's personal life had been garnering media attention. She did not fit neatly into any of the available frames for women activists. Her politics were not borne of rebellion against her family, and she did not refuse to marry, like anarchists Emma Goldman and Voltairine de Cleyre. She was not a widow who transformed grief into activism, like Mother Jones. Although she married, she did not perform traditional domesticity, and despite having a child, she refused to be defined by motherhood. The mainstream press did not quite know what to make of this beautiful young woman with a fierce intellect, fiery eloquence, and revolutionary agenda from a tight-knit, Irish American, socialist family in the Bronx. After the *New York Sunday World* published a piece on her marriage to Jack Jones, Thomas Flynn spoofed that paper's traditional gender framing of his daughter's relationship in a letter to a New York socialist newspaper, the *Daily People*: "Elizabeth is supposed to speak:—'but comrade Jones knows more than I do,' etc. That Elizabeth Flynn should admit that anyone knows more than she does, is startling information to me, who have carried on many strenuous arguments with her on nearly every possible subject since she was merely four years of age and even younger."[4]

The elder Flynn's comments gave a sense not only of the *World*'s attempt to cast his daughter in a traditional role she had no interest in playing but also of the relationship between father and daughter. Rising to her father's challenge, the younger Flynn had the last word in a postscript appended to his letter: "Recalling the proverb about a woman's postscript being the most important part of the letter, let me just add, in connection with the sentiment just expressed above that Elizabeth would admit of anyone knowing more than she, is startling and wonderful—Elizabeth is usually called 'the daughter of her father.'"[5]

Flynn's pregnancy was another newsworthy item, and here again, although she was anything but traditional, an effort was made to frame her within a narrative of traditional domesticity. At a loss to explain why such a "sweet-faced girl" in a "delicate condition" would subject herself to the horrors of prison during the Spokane free speech fight—and all while using her maiden name despite clearly being happily married—the *Tacoma Times* surmised that "ten miserable years of childhood spent in squalid, poverty-ridden tenement districts of New York" had filled her with "a spirit of revolt against existing industrial systems."[6]

The marriage between Flynn and Jones ended shortly after the birth of their son, but Jones did not file for separation until July 1920. That information also made it into the press.[7] Jones, alas, was unlucky in love. His next wife, Anna Mitchell, drowned in a boating accident while the two were on their honeymoon after having eloped in August 1920. Although Jones had been an organizer for the IWW and founded the Dill Pickle Club, a well-known Chicago hub for radical politics and art, every article about the tragedy identified him as the former husband of Flynn, and more than one identified the second Mrs. Jones as the "wife of Elizabeth Gurley Flynn's divorced husband."[8]

Flynn's gift for public speaking, particularly her ability to engage and move an audience, brought her the greatest attention. Her eloquence and tactical acumen had caused locals to see her as the unquestioned leader of the free speech fights in Missoula, Spokane, and Paterson. In 1917, the *Industrial Worker* called her "the best woman labor speaker in America."[9] In the 1920s, her ability as a compelling speaker was a source of both fear and awe. A reporter for the *St. Louis Post-Dispatch* remarked that Flynn was "without doubt the most brilliant female labor agitator in the United States" and noted, "She holds her audience under a magnetic spell from beginning to end of her vituperative denunciations of the capitalist system."[10] Given her supposed ability to mesmerize an audience with anticapitalist invective, Flynn's mere presence at an event was often enough to evoke negative sanctions. In 1921, when Philadelphia police learned that she was one of the speakers at a meeting for Sacco and Vanzetti, they immediately rushed to the hall, shut down the meeting, and lugged off the "Bolshevist Princess," as she was called by the *Public Ledger*.[11] A year later, the City of Brotherly Love again showed itself to be anything but when it came to Flynn. As part of its campaign to crack down on "red propaganda," the superintendent of police assigned two hundred police officers to arrest any speaker associated with the "notorious radical."[12] In contrast, organizers of the Ford Hall Forum in Boston, a public lecture series intended to foster freedom of speech and open debate on a variety of issues, invited Flynn to speak precisely because she possessed a "reputation for unrestrained radicalism" couched in a "calm, logical, and orderly" manner of speaking.[13]

The Early ACLU: Serving the Cause of Labor

Even without Flynn to attract attention, the nascent ACLU was bound to be the target of criticism. The organization had dedicated itself to a radical project: aiding the class struggle by protecting workers' rights of free expression and assembly.[14] It had been conceived with this project in mind. "The cause we now serve is Labor," declared an undated, unsigned memo, "Suggestions for Reorganization of the National Civil Liberties Bureau," almost certainly written by Roger Baldwin in 1919.[15] A 1920 statement issued to announce the ACLU's founding made clear the organization's mission: "The industrial struggle is clearly the essential challenge to the cause of civil liberty today. The whole gamut of activities aimed at 'reds, radicals, Bolshevists, and I.W.W.' is in substance only the one purpose of suppressing the revolt against intolerable industrial autocracy." The announcement also made clear that suppression of civil liberties was not confined to radicals; it extended to all labor. To meet this threat required a kind of all-purpose labor defense organization: "No association is organized to deal broadly and generally with these issues in the struggle of labor. Each labor group makes its unaided fight, without relation to the common problems they face together."[16] The ACLU positioned itself as just such an organization.

In its early years, the ACLU modeled its civil liberties work on the direct-action approach of the IWW. One of the organization's initial campaigns involved free speech fights to challenge local ordinances against labor-themed outdoor meetings reminiscent of those waged by the Wobblies a decade earlier, except the ACLU soapboxers were socially prominent individuals rather than an army of hoboes. On October 12, 1920, ACLU members John Haynes Holmes, Rose Schneiderman, and Norman Thomas held an outdoor meeting during which they read from the Constitution atop a soapbox before being arrested by police in Mount Vernon, New York. That same evening in Norwich, Connecticut, Boston Brahmin Elizabeth Glendower Evans and socialist Albert Boardman spoke from a soapbox before being arrested. Reverend William Fincke, Presbyterian clergyman and head of the Brookwood School in Katonah, New York, did the same in Duquesne, Pennsylvania.[17] These efforts suggest the extent to which the fledgling civil liberties organization looked to the storied labor union for inspiration.

In terms of substance and style, Flynn was a natural fit for the early ACLU. She and Baldwin collaborated on several initiatives in the early 1920s. For Labor Day 1920, the WDU and ACLU joined with the IWW Defense Committee to test labor's right to hold open-air meetings in Union Square. These Labor Day meetings, the first since 1917, were intended as fundraisers to secure bail money for the IWW prisoners in Chicago, Wichita, and Sacramento. The Socialist *New York Call* billed them as a "non-partisan effort to secure the release of men suffering in prison for their efforts or their views in political and economic matters."[18] When the organizers of the Union Square rally were denied a permit, they moved the meeting to a variety of indoor locations around the city.[19] Interestingly, while radicals saw Labor Day as a chance to redress wrongs committed against labor activists during the war, the conservative AFL reaffirmed its embrace of U.S. militarism by passing a resolution to observe labor's national holiday as Lafayette-Marne Day, in honor of the birth of General Lafayette and the First Battle of the Marne, the first significant Allied victory in World War I.[20]

In the spring of 1921, Flynn embarked on a speaking tour with Baldwin that had the pair traveling to Rochester, New York, and various Midwestern cities including Cleveland, Toledo, Detroit, Chicago, Milwaukee, St. Louis, Indianapolis, Cincinnati, and Pittsburgh. Flynn addressed amnesty for the IWW, and Baldwin spoke on the general issue of civil liberty and industrial conflict. Another joint endeavor was the Amnesty Alliance for New York State Political Prisoners, founded to advocate for the release of Communists who had been rounded up at the behest of the Lusk Committee in November 1919 and prosecuted under New York's Criminal Anarchy Law. James Larkin, Benjamin Gitlow, Charles Ruthenberg, and Harry Winitsky were among those arrested and imprisoned. Flynn served as secretary-treasurer for the group. As was typically the case with Flynn's civil liberties work, the Amnesty Alliance was nondenominational, declaring, "We serve ALL labor groups, without regard to their views or doctrines."[21] Other affiliates included the Italian Chamber of Labor, Socialist Party of the Bronx, and the Workers' (Communist) Party. Flynn and Baldwin also served together on the National Executive Committee of the Labor Defense Council, which was formed to advocate for Communists who were arrested in a raid on a meeting by local and federal law enforcement (acting on a tip from a Bureau of Investigation informant) and indicted under the Michigan criminal syndicalist law in 1922. Among those arrested were William Z. Foster, Earl Browder, and Charles Ruthenberg. Like the Workers' Defense Union, the Labor Defense Council spawned several local chapters.[22]

The Sacco and Vanzetti Case

Arguably, the most high-profile collaboration between Flynn and the ACLU was the campaign to save Italian immigrant anarchists Nicola Sacco and Bartolomeo Vanzetti from the electric chair. The case began on May 9, 1920, when the two men were arrested while riding a streetcar in Brockton, Massachusetts. They had unwittingly fallen into a trap that police set for another Italian anarchist: Mario Buda, suspected driver of a getaway car used in a robbery and double murder at a shoe factory in nearby Braintree, Massachusetts, a month earlier. All three Italians were members of a circle of anarchists devoted to the teachings of Luigi Galleani, who preached a militant form of anarchism that advocated the overthrow of government by any means necessary, including violence.

Given the nature of their politics and their immigrant status, Sacco and Vanzetti initially believed they were being rounded up for deportation as part of the Palmer Raids. Understandably reluctant to admit their anarchist politics or their acquaintance with Buda for fear of being deported, the men lied to police about both. Police construed these lies as a cover-up for their involvement in the Braintree crimes, and both men were charged with robbery and murder. The prosecution's case against Vanzetti was weak, so he was tried and convicted of another crime (a bungled robbery in the nearby town of Bridgewater, Massachusetts, the previous New Year's Eve) to establish a criminal record for him before the trial for the Braintree crimes. That second trial opened in Dedham, Massachusetts, on May 21, 1921. After six weeks, despite flawed evidence and dubious testimony, the jury decided unanimously that the two were guilty. Immediately, their lawyer, Fred Moore, filed a series of supplementary motions for a new trial, all of which failed. Moore's successor, William Thompson, was also unable to get the men a new trial or a stay of execution.

When their trial began, Sacco and Vanzetti were, in Flynn's words, "very humble and obscure foreign-born workers," largely unknown outside the Italian anarchist circle in which they traveled.[23] Announcement of the verdict was regarded as local news. The front page of the *Boston Herald* reported that two Italian immigrants had been found guilty of first-degree murder. Outside of Boston, the case was largely irrelevant. The *New York Times* reported the verdict several pages into the paper in a short piece next to an advertisement for golf supplies. The next day, another New York–based daily newspaper called *Il Progresso Italo-Americano* (Italian American progress), the most prominent Italian-language newspaper in the United States, published a similarly brief piece on the outcome of the trial.[24] By the time the case reached its ultimate conclusion, however, the two men were internationally recognized symbols of the barbarity of American "justice" and no part of the world was untouched by protests demanding their release. Almost a century later, scholars, artists, writers, and activists are still inspired by their story, and the men's guilt or innocence is still debated.

What happened to transform the plight of two unknown immigrant anarchists into a global cause célèbre with lasting historical resonance? The transnational anarchist network to which they belonged deserves part of the credit for spreading the word, mobilizing resistance, and providing funds for their legal defense throughout the lengthy appeals process.[25] But although this network reached around the world, it was invisible to potential allies in the United States with the power to intervene in the case. A liaison between the transnational radical network and potentially sympathetic elements of American society with the capacity to sustain a legal battle on the men's behalf had to be found. That liaison was Elizabeth Gurley Flynn.

As a syndicalist, Flynn shared the anarchists' disdain for electoral politics to achieve meaningful social change. She saw how the potential for democracy in the United States was corrupted by capitalism, but she didn't conclude that democratic states were necessarily an impossibility. She remained steadfast in her commitment to Connolly's vision of a workers' republic, which she hoped would eventually be realized in Ireland. Here in the United States, she championed the democratic ideals expressed in the Declaration of Independence and the Constitution and worked to expose and redress contradictions between those ideals and the often repressive policies of government agencies and actors, while simultaneously working to abolish capitalism through direct economic action. Moreover, unlike the Galleanisti, she opposed the use of violence as a revolutionary tactic. Whatever their philosophical differences, however, Flynn struggled arm-in-arm with her anarchist comrades in the IWW during the free speech fights as well as strikes in Lawrence, Paterson, Mesabi, and elsewhere. She counted several anarchists among her social circle and dropped in to visit when they showed up at the New York City office of Carlo Tresca's newspaper, *Il Martello* (The hammer). But she was essentially an outsider not embedded in any anarchist network, thus when Sacco and Vanzetti were arrested, she was completely unaware.

Tresca informed her about the Boston anarchists and their case. At the time she was traveling often to Massachusetts to meet with Marion Emerson of the New England Defense Conference and to speak on behalf of immigrants rounded up during the Palmer Raids and awaiting deportation on Deer Island. Looking back on the case decades later, she noted, "Just before I left New York on one of these trips, Carlo said, 'Elizabetta, there are two Italian comrades in big trouble in Massachusetts. . . . You investigate while you are there and maybe get the Americans to help.'"[26] Together with Emerson, Flynn visited Aldino Felicani, organizer of the

Sacco-Vanzetti Defense Committee, who spoke so little English they had to find an interpreter to understand him. Felicani related details of the case to the women, and Flynn recalled, "For the first time two Americans heard the story of Sacco and Vanzetti."[27]

Convinced that the trial was a frame-up, Flynn threw herself into the campaign to save the two anarchists. In so doing, she became the node connecting the (mostly) Italian Sacco-Vanzetti Defense Committee—and, by extension, the transnational anarchist network in which it was embedded—with the civil liberties movement, organized labor, and other liberal and radical activists in the United States.[28] The defense committee made two requests of Flynn. First, they asked her to find a lawyer who would be willing to take the case. She and Tresca recommended Fred Moore, the IWW lawyer who had represented Flynn during the Spokane free speech fight. Moore decided to make prejudice against the defendants' politics the pivot on which the legal defense turned. Second, the committee asked Flynn to organize the first English-language demonstrations for Sacco and Vanzetti in New York and Boston.[29]

To get a sense of how Boston area audiences responded to Flynn's early speeches on Sacco and Vanzetti, one has only to read the account of Flynn's first address in Bridgewater (the site of the robbery for which Vanzetti had been tried in advance of the trial for the Braintree crimes) penned by journalist John Nicholas Beffel for the Workers' Defense Union. Beffel noted that Flynn's task was not an easy one: "The air was tense as she began to speak. She had come to attack the credibility of Bridgewater witnesses in a criminal trial in which large rewards awaited those who testify satisfactorily. Three police in uniform were on the edge of the crowd; several soldiers were there." As for the audience, he observed, "The crowd was solemn; it betrayed no sign of sympathy for the cause of the defense when Miss Flynn opened her address. But it listened intently; hung on every word." Flynn's speech was informative: "She told the listeners many things they had never known before; how witnesses from their own town had testified to one set of facts at the preliminary hearing against Vanzetti and then testified to a different set of facts at the trial." But it was her talent for humor, in this case pointing out the absurdity and craven opportunism of the forces arrayed against Sacco and Vanzetti, that ultimately won over the crowd. As Beffel described, "Presently the crowd became a friendly audience. It laughed when Miss Flynn told of Maynard Freeman Shaw, the Bridgewater high school boy who 'identified' Vanzetti, and who said he knew the shot-gun bandit was a foreigner 'by the way he ran.' And the crowd laughed again, uproariously, when the speaker mentioned that Chief Steward had lost the most important piece of evidence in the case—the memorandum containing the number of the bandit's automobile." Her speech transformed listeners from skeptics into supporters, so that "when Miss Flynn concluded, there were cries of 'Come again!' and the audience gave $19 to help the defense."[30]

Nearly thirty years later, Flynn herself observed, "The agitation among the New England and New York workers for Sacco and Vanzetti began as a small spark at first. But it eventually spread around the world."[31] She deserves credit for transforming that spark into a global conflagration. In October 1920, she visited Sacco in the Dedham prison along with Mary Heaton Vorse, who wrote an article on the case for *The World Tomorrow*, a Christian Socialist magazine. She also met with Sacco's wife, Rosina, and with Vanzetti, who was held in a different prison. With Vorse's assistance, Flynn worked to secure an endorsement from both the Massachusetts branch of the ACLU and the national office, which identified Sacco and Vanzetti as "industrial prisoners," a special category for individuals wrongfully convicted of criminal offenses by interests opposed to organized labor and radicals. Upon her return to New York, Flynn presented the case to delegates of the WDU. The organization voted to endorse the case and produced an English-language press release to introduce Sacco and Vanzetti to American audiences. The WDU also sent a $100 contribution to the defense committee, the first from outside the Italian community. Flynn oversaw publication of the first English-language pamphlet, *Are They Doomed? The Sacco-Vanzetti Case and the Grim Forces behind It*, written by Art Shields, illustrated by Robert Minor, and distributed by the WDU. She traveled around the United States giving speeches and passing the hat for much-needed funds to augment contributions from anarchists worldwide.[32]

Fundraising among workers was not an easy task because of unemployment, political repression, and competing causes, but Flynn was adamant that the "seriousness and menace" of the Sacco-Vanzetti case warranted financial support even from cash-strapped unions. Nor was the WDU's defense work limited to the United States. In 1920, WDU journalist Eugene Lyons traveled to Europe, where he succeeded in generating substantial interest among Italians and thus contributed to the growing international movement on behalf of the two anarchists. Flynn's longtime ally James Larkin rallied supporters in Dublin after his deportation from the United States in 1923.[33]

Flynn's early involvement in the defense campaign and her success in convincing the Massachusetts and national ACLU to endorse the case laid the foundation for the massive outpouring of support that followed. The themes articulated in the WDU's early communications about the underlying causes that led to the arrest and imprisonment of two immigrant radicals—particularly the overlap of class politics and ethnic/racial intolerance, what we might call today an intersectional analysis—reverberated in the defense campaign for the next seven years. Even after the WDU dissolved, Flynn continued to advocate on behalf of "the boys," as she affectionately called them. When Fred Moore had a falling out with his clients, she negotiated their parting of ways. Around the time that Moore departed the case, Flynn joined the board of the American Fund for Public Service, also known as the Garland Fund, a philanthropic foundation established by Charles Garland with a $1 million inheritance from his father, a wealthy stockbroker.[34] As secretary of the Garland Fund, Flynn was able to secure money to pay a new attorney, William Thompson, and with direction from Roger Baldwin she presided over reorganization of the defense committee along lines favored by Thompson. Despite her best efforts and the work of two teams of lawyers and countless activists, Judge Webster Thayer passed the death sentence on Sacco and Vanzetti in April of 1927. Amid protests that touched every part of the globe, the two were executed in the electric chair just after midnight on August 23, 1927.

Antifascism

Among the international figures who advocated for the release of Sacco and Vanzetti was the fascist dictator Benito Mussolini. Mussolini's father was an anarchist, and he himself had been a socialist in his youth. By 1914, his politics veered sharply to the right, and he turned against his former socialist comrades and supported Italy's entrance into the war. After the Bolshevik Revolution, he was an ardent anti-Communist. His October 1922 seizure of power was the climax of a bloody campaign of intimidation and repression against labor organizations, Socialists, anarchists, and Communists. Italian rallies for Sacco and Vanzetti frequently devolved into skirmishes in the larger "civil war" that was tearing apart Italian society: anarchists and Socialists combined exhortations on behalf of the two imprisoned Italians with screeds against Fascism while Mussolini's Blackshirt squads counterdemonstrated and threatened violent retaliation. However, unlike radicals in Italy whom his Blackshirts beat and killed with impunity on a regular basis, Mussolini saw political value in defending the lives of the two prisoners in Massachusetts. By standing up for Sacco and Vanzetti, he cast himself on the global stage as a defender of italianità and a protector of Italians abroad who were targets of ethnic prejudice.[35]

From the March on Rome until the 1935 invasion of Ethiopia, the American response to Fascism was generally quite positive. Il Duce, embodiment of the emerging stereotype of the romantic, exotic, alien, and vigorous Latin man, received rave reviews in highbrow publications like the *New York Times*, the *Saturday Evening Post*, and *Fortune*, and he boasted a coterie of admirers in and outside government, including the U.S. ambassador to Italy, Richard Washburn Child; the national commander of the American Legion, Alvin Owsley; muckraking journalist Ida Tarbell; actors Mary Pickford and Douglas Fairbanks; and humorist Will Rogers. In part, this positive response can be explained as a product of the widespread belief that Italians were a childlike and unruly people who would only benefit from the imposition of law and order, even if it was dished out with a heavy hand. (And really, implied many admirers of Il Duce, how heavy could the hand of such a dashing figure be?) That "law and order" meant persecution of radicals, increasingly Communists, was even better. In the minds of American authorities, any leader who beat back the threat of an international Bolshevik revolution was all right.[36]

Italian American business and professional elites also proved receptive to the siren song of Fascism, as did working-class Italian Americans. Some members of the immigrant community undoubtedly embraced Fascism's political goals. But for others, the reaction was more about culture and identity than politics. Mussolini's rise to power activated a nostalgia for Roman glory and offered Italian immigrants and their children redemption from feelings of inferiority that inevitably resulted from systemic ethnic and class discrimination. Fascist policymakers exploited the marginalization of Italian immigrants and nurtured nationalism and ethnic pride to create a lobby for Italian interests abroad.[37] In 1923, Italian Americans organized the Fascist League of North America (FLNA). Blackshirts made their first public appearance in New York on July 4, 1923. Three months later, they celebrated the first anniversary of the March on Rome at Carnegie Hall. Between 1925 and 1928, Italian Americans established fifteen Fascist organizations scattered throughout Manhattan, Brooklyn, and the Bronx as well as Providence and Boston. The New York fascio, called Benito Mussolini, even boasted a ladies' auxiliary named for Queen Margherita.[38] Italian American newspapers gushed with pride over Mussolini's achievements. Organizations like the Dante Alighieri Society and the Sons of Italy also touted an openly pro-Fascist line. Even Italian American priests welcomed Fascism with appeals to italianità. Their efforts were condoned by the hierarchy of the American Catholic Church, which saw Fascism as a bulwark against Godless Communism.[39]

In the 1920s, the only real antifascist resistance in the United States came from members of Italian radical movements. Flynn explained, "With the rise of Mussolini, whom Carlo and others here had known as a Socialist in Italy, then the leader of fascism—a violent, brutal, and anti-democratic, ultra-nationalist movement directed against Socialists, trade unionists, and aliens—a united Italian anti-fascist movement emerged in this country. It was of wide proportions and embraced all political faiths."[40] She played an active part in the early antifascist resistance. In February 1923, Tresca founded the Comitato Generale di Difesa Contro Il Fascismo (General Defense Committee against Fascism) to unify the far Left of the Italian radical movement into a single antifascist organization. The organization constituted the vanguard of antifascist activity in 1923 and 1924. Flynn was the only woman and the only non-Italian among its leadership.[41] In April 1923, a coalition of trade unionists, Socialists, syndicalists, anarchists and Communists joined forces in the Anti-Fascist Alliance of North America (AFANA).

Members of the Comitato Generale and AFANA fought the Blackshirts with deeds as well as words. They broke up Fascist rallies, rumbled in the streets, and issued antifascist polemics in the pages of newspapers like Tresca's *Il Martello* and Frank Bellanca's *Il Nuovo Mondo* (The new world). For their part, Italian American Fascists claimed to be fighting "subversives," by which they meant atheists, internationalists, free lovers, and Communists. Often, they instigated riots and street fights to cast aspersions on antifascists as disturbers of the peace and thugs.[42] American authorities, fixated on beating the "Reds," bought into the Fascist narrative that equated antifascism with subversion. They refused to see that by fighting Fascism, Italian radicals were defending democracy.

Flynn understood the divisive impact of Fascism on Italians in the United States. In a letter to Sacco and Vanzetti's attorney, Fred Moore, she described how "the question of the Faschisti [sic] is tearing every Italian lodge and colony wide-open." On one side were Italian immigrant radicals, who feared for the lives of family members and comrades back home, hundreds of whom were being killed "brutally and publicly." On the other were pro-Fascist Italian immigrants who applauded "the executions of Sacco and Vanzetti's in Italy." "This is no exaggeration," she added to underscore the point, "it is serious!"[43] But Flynn's response to Fascism went far beyond hand-wringing. She was the first American outside of Italian immigrant radical circles to see that Fascism was not merely an

Italian problem but an existential threat to democracy. Her grasp of the antidemocratic values and practices of Fascism is yet another example of her visionary internationalist outlook and approach to activism.

Like her Italian American comrades, Flynn linked the struggle against Fascism in Italy with a defense of democracy in the United States and around the world.[44] While on a speaking tour for Sacco and Vanzetti in New England just days after the one-year anniversary of the March on Rome, she addressed an antifascist meeting organized by anarchists at Garibaldi Hall in Providence. She was the only woman and the only English speaker on the program (the others spoke in Italian). Fortunately for the historical record, agents from the Bureau of Investigation attended the meeting and transcribed much of what she said. In her speech, Flynn acknowledged Fascism as a product of global capitalism. She urged Italian and English-speaking workers to join hands in fellowship and affirm their shared opposition "to the spirit of Fascism in this country or anywhere in the world." In closing, she took a swipe at Mussolini and his antidemocratic politics, noting, "If the Italians had one fair chance at a fair election the Fascisti would go into the political ash heap."[45]

For the next few years, Flynn continued to monitor Fascist activities in the United States and to press organized labor into action against the threat that Fascism posed to democracy and thus to working-class movements. In June 1923, she presided over the first antifascist conference of labor unions, held at Webster Hall in New York City. Sidney Hillman and Morris Sigman, presidents of the Amalgamated Clothing Workers of America and the International Ladies' Garment Workers' Union, respectively, both of which had a large Italian membership, were among the invited speakers.[46] She organized and addressed antifascist meetings throughout the mid-Atlantic and New England. When she spoke, she often drew parallels between the Fascisti's persecution of labor activists in Italy and the American Legion's hyperpatriotism and xenophobia or the Ku Klux Klan's reign of terror over African Americans.[47]

As a U.S.-born American citizen, Flynn did not have to fear that her antifascism would incite retribution by either U.S. officials or Italian Fascist authorities. Many Italian American antifascists had to conceal their views to escape such retribution. Under surveillance by Italian consulates and the Bureau of Investigation, Italian American antifascist radicals risked having their homes searched, losing their jobs, having their Italian citizenship revoked and their Italian property confiscated, and psychological and physical intimidation of friends and relatives in Italy.[48] In contrast, Flynn openly baited Mussolini with quips like "We don't need black shirts in this country, because we have white sheets," disparaging references to his government as "the castor oil regime," and provocative titles for her talks, such as "Mussolini's Finger in America's Pie."[49]

The incident that pushed the antifascist movement into high gear was the kidnapping and murder of Giacomo Matteotti, member of the Italian Chamber of Deputies. Matteotti had delivered a two-hour speech to the chamber in which he accused Mussolini of electoral fraud and denounced Fascist violence. In retaliation, the "bravest voice in Italy," as Flynn called him, was killed on June 10, 1924.[50] Two months later, his body was found in Riano, a town just north of Rome. His murder caused an uproar in Italy, and when the investigation led to Mussolini's inner circle, speculation abounded whether Il Duce himself had ordered the murder. The killing of Matteotti might have toppled Mussolini, had not the leaders of the reformist opposition opted to boycott the Chamber of Deputies rather than move decisively against the regime. Mussolini strengthened his grip on power by taking responsibility for the killing, throwing a number of subordinates under the bus, and making a deal with economic and political elites to stave off a Communist threat by cooperating with the military to crush opposition. The result was a wave of repressive legislation that created a totalitarian state and left Mussolini with an even firmer grip on power.[51]

News of Matteotti's murder rocked antifascists worldwide. Flynn later reflected that it was "shockingly similar to the murder of Karl Liebnicht and Rosa Luxemburg," German communist leaders assassinated by right-wing paramilitary troops in 1919.[52] Italian antifascists in the United States responded immediately with rallies in Chicago, Philadelphia, Boston, and New York. Flynn spoke at the New York rally. She told an audience of twenty-five thousand that Matteotti was killed because he was about to uncover scandals in the Fascist government, which "would have made the Teapot Dome scandals look sick."[53] The militancy of Italian American antifascists increased in response to the Matteotti assassination. Opponents of the regime feuded bitterly with pro-Fascists in the Italian American press, lodged attacks on pro-Fascist organizations, such as the Sons of Italy, Dante Alighieri Society, Italian Chamber of Commerce, and Fascist League of North America. Pro- and antifascists raided one another's meetings and regularly broke into fisticuffs at ceremonial events on Columbus Day, Garibaldi Day, the anniversary of the March on Rome, and even actor Rudolph Valentino's funeral. Moderate Italian Americans criticized violence perpetrated by militant antifascists as the work of communists, anarchists, socialists, IWWs, and "parlor radicals" who were attempting to foist their politics on the rest of the community. The *New York Times* equated the two sides and decried the behavior of both.[54] As long as Fascism was confined to Italy, it was of little concern to American intellectuals and political leaders. They would not begin to see the true nature of the Fascist threat until the rise of Nazism in Germany.

Among the most vehement and unsparing critics of Mussolini in the United States was Carlo Tresca. Not surprisingly, he was a prime target of Fascist retribution. Italian ambassador Gelasio Caetani di Sermoneta regularly complained to the State Department about Tresca's harangues in *Il Martello*, alleging that they were part of a Communist conspiracy orchestrated by Moscow to destroy Italy's good name. The State Department was only too willing to tamp down Tresca's activities, but they could not appear to move against him on orders from a foreign government. Instead, on August 14, 1923, U.S. marshals raided the office of *Il Martello* and arrested him for violating indecency laws by publishing a two-line advertisement for birth control in his paper. Sensing the gravity of the situation, Flynn traveled to Washington, D.C., and prevailed upon U.S. congressman and future mayor of New York Fiorello La Guardia to join Tresca's legal team.[55] Tresca was tried and convicted in November of 1923. His sentence of one year and a day in the Atlanta Federal Penitentiary was the harshest ever handed down for an indecency conviction. LaGuardia filed an appeal, to no avail. Tresca entered prison in January of 1925.

While Tresca was behind bars, his Italian comrades formed a defense committee to agitate and raise funds on his behalf. His American allies pulled out all the stops to get him released. Flynn and birth control advocate Margaret Sanger orchestrated a letter-writing campaign targeting Attorney General Harlan F. Stone and President Calvin Coolidge. Baldwin filed a petition for a commutation with the attorney general. Journalist friends, including Heywood Broun, Robert Morse Lovett, and H. L. Mencken, published articles that roasted the U.S. government as a tool of Mussolini's dictatorship. The campaign was successful, and President Coolidge commuted his sentence to a term of four months of imprisonment. He was released on May 7, 1925.[56]

Flynn was not present when Tresca received a hero's welcome at the *Il Martello* benefit held at Tammany Hall on May 23, 1925. He had ended their thirteen-year affair sometime in April. The pain of their breakup was intensified when she found out Tresca had had an affair with her younger sister, Sabina (Bina). The affair resulted in the birth of a son, Peter, although whether Flynn knew about the child at this time is debatable. Tresca had sent Bina to stay with his family in Italy to hide the pregnancy from the rest of the Flynn family, especially Flynn's mother, Annie, who was still reeling from the recent revelation that her husband had another wife and daughter in Boston, a transgression for which she kicked him out of the house. Fearing for her safety after Mussolini seized power, Bina fled Italy and returned to the United States. After struggling to care for the baby (Peter) as a single mother, she sent him to a boarding home for infants and then placed him in foster care.[57] Flynn, her sister, and Tresca had shared an apartment between 1923 and 1925, when Tresca was sent to prison. The realization that she had unwittingly been party to a ménage à trois with the love of her life and her youngest sister must have left her feeling humiliated, betrayed, and terribly heartbroken. She left her son Buster in the care of her family and spent the rest of the year living alone and licking her wounds, first in the summer house on Staten Island she had shared with Tresca and Buster in happier times and then in an apartment she found for herself in Greenwich Village.[58] She returned to her work in early 1926.

Twenty Years of Labor Activism

The year 1926 marked two decades of labor activism for Flynn. Mary Heaton Vorse noted the occasion with a profile of her in the *Nation*.[59] Her allies in the movement observed the anniversary with a gala in her honor at the Yorkville Casino in Manhattan on February 14, 1926. The event was sponsored by the League for Mutual Aid, an organization founded in 1920 by Flynn, Roger Baldwin, and anarchist Harry Kelly, to provide loans to individuals affiliated with labor and libertarian causes. The gathering of three hundred was notable as a rare display of unity on the Left. "For the first time since the rise of bolshevism," quipped a writer for the Universal Service News Bureau, "the hatchets are temporarily buried today in the divided camps of American radicals."[60] Left-wing Federated Press correspondent Esther Lowell described the event as "most unique—a united front that could hardly be duplicated by another person."[61] She was right. The list of those who attended or sent tributes to Flynn for her twenty years' service to the movement reads like a who's who of bright lights among liberals and radicals: AFL President William Green, Amalgamated Clothing Workers Union President Sidney Hillman, International Ladies' Garment Workers' Union President Morris Sigman, attorney Clarence Darrow, anarchist Emma Goldman, Socialist Victor Berger, Communist James P. Cannon, labor poet and former IWW organizer Arturo Giovannitti, Harvard lawyer Felix Frankfurter, Christian Socialist and writer Vida

Scudder, NAACP President James Weldon Johnson, Unitarian minister and pacifist John Haynes Holmes, and imprisoned anarchist Bartolomeo Vanzetti.[62] No transcript of Flynn's speech at the event exists, but Esther Lowell offered a summary that gives a sense not only of what Flynn said but also of how her allies saw her, still, at this point—good-looking, feisty, embedded in family but not domestic, and a true movement activist who valued solidarity above personal gain:

> Flynn herself was the main speaker, still a dark-haired, good-looking woman with 20 or twice 20 years more for activity. She gave several possible reasons for her presence in the labor movement—her fighting Irish blood inherited from Paddy the Rebel, her good parents (both of whom were present, as well as her son, now a giant five inches taller than she), etc. She said she had no regrets for her life and withal had had much fun. She held the assemblage not a tribute to her personality but to the labor movement. She expressed her pleasure at having "all here as my friends in spite of our differences of opinion."[63]

A month after the gala, Flynn was back on the front lines of the class struggle, this time in Passaic, New Jersey. The first massive industrial strike in the United States led by Communists, the Passaic strike of sixteen thousand immigrant wool workers—half of them women—was instigated by a reduction of hours by Passaic's largest mill, Botany, followed by a 10 percent pay cut in the fall of 1925. The only union in Passaic was the United Textile Workers of America (UTW), an AFL union of skilled workers. When UTW president Thomas MacMahon failed to act decisively, the Workers (Communist) Party sent twenty-five-year-old Albert Weisbord, a Harvard Law School graduate turned communist silk weaver, to Passaic. Weisbord established the United Front Committee of Textile Workers, a de facto union organizing committee, to fight the wage cuts with a strike. He was joined by several other young, inexperienced, but dedicated organizers from the Young Communist League of New York. Flynn, acting on behalf of the Garland Fund, recruited Mary Heaton Vorse to work as publicity director for the strike, and she joined Vorse in Passaic on March 3, 1926. Flynn gave speeches to raise money for the strike fund and, assisted by Ella Reeve "Mother" Bloor, organized the distribution of food to children of the strikers.

Flynn's presence in Passaic recalled the militant IWW strikes of Lawrence and Paterson a decade earlier, and the Passaic strikers employed many of the same tactics used in these earlier struggles, including the

FIGURE 6. Elizabeth Gurley Flynn demonstrating how to use a gas mask to striking workers in Passaic, New Jersey, 1926.
Credit: American Labor Museum / Botto House National Landmark

moving picket line and the exodus of the children. Passaic police likewise used tactics honed during earlier clashes with workers: closing meeting halls, breaking picket lines, beating strikers with clubs, spraying with fire hoses, and shooting with guns as well as a new weapon developed in World War I: tear gas. The strikers' exploits and police retaliation were chronicled in the *Labor Defender*, publication of the recently organized International Labor Defense (ILD).[64]

In her Wobbly days, Flynn would have been the heart and soul of a strike like Passaic, an inspirational symbol of working-class defiance as well as a key player in decision-making about strategy and tactics. In 1926, no longer a member of the IWW but not yet a Communist, she played a less central role. When in August of 1926, after seven months of bitter struggle, the Communist leadership decided to cede control of the strike to the AFL-affiliated UTW, she was not consulted. As part of the deal to transfer leadership from Weisbord to MacMahon, the UTW president requested that Flynn leave Passaic to demonstrate that the strike was officially in AFL hands. The other organizers with whom she'd worked—including Robert Minor, who had illustrated pamphlets for the

Sacco-Vanzetti defense campaign, Lena Chernenko of the Amalgamated Clothing Workers Union, and Alfred Wagenecht, national secretary of the Communist Labor Party—were sad to see her go and sent her off with a farewell dinner and a gift. In a letter she wrote to Mary Heaton Vorse in September 1926, Flynn expressed warm feelings for the organizers and compassion for the strikers, especially the mothers: "I was deeply touched. It helps to heal my wounds. But the life and heart is out of everything, and everyone from outside is waiting for the end to leave as soon as they can too and the poor people to get to work. The mothers are harassed because they need shoes and clothes for the children to go to school. The strike is dead, Mary. The sooner it can be ended with as much dignity and honor, the better. I couldn't bear to go there anymore and I am greatly relieved that MacMahon spared me the agony."[65]

The wounds that needed healing were the betrayal by Tresca and her sister, Bina, and a more recent betrayal by Weisbord, with whom she'd been having an affair during the Passaic strike. While he was involved with Flynn, Weisbord was also involved with Vera Buch, an old flame and recent graduate of Hunter College, whom he would eventually marry. The realization that she was unintentionally involved in yet another love triangle was painful for Flynn. She gave Weisbord an ultimatum, and he chose Buch. In her letter to Vorse, she confessed the pain of this recent heartbreak, so close on the heels of the previous one: "I am terribly hurt, Mary dear. Life pummels me pretty badly."[66]

Although Flynn's personal travails knocked her down emotionally, they did not knock her out of the struggle. She continued to fight for civil liberties for labor activists in the United States and around the globe, to protect immigrant activists from deportation, and to support organizing among Black workers. In May 1926, she spoke against the deportation of "illegal" Italian immigrant labor activists on the grounds that sending them back to Italy meant certain death at the hands of the Fascisti. In September, she addressed a meeting in Harlem to protest the arrest of Afro-Caribbean tenant rights and anti–police brutality activist Richard B. Moore for speaking in front of the Lafayette Theater without a permit in support of striking motion picture operators. The following month, she organized a protest of a U.S. government–sponsored reception for Queen Marie of Romania, "whose government [was] holding 2,500 political prisoners in jail and [had] ruthlessly suppressed all freedom of speech, press, and assembly." In early November, she addressed a meeting of the Brotherhood of Sleeping Car Porters in Harlem on behalf of the ILD, sharing the stage again with A. Philip Randolph. According to a report of her speech in the *New York Amsterdam News,* Flynn was "unusually forceful" in her manner of speaking and the audience could "feel her sincerity." She insisted to listeners, "The Negro must take an interest only in himself to forge ahead" and praised the brotherhood as a step toward the building of power for Black workers: "Only when they gain this power can they meet the white man on his own grounds and demand equality in labor."[67]

The International Labor Defense

It was during this period that Flynn was named national chair of the International Labor Defense. Founded in 1925, the ILD was the outgrowth of a meeting in the Soviet Union between the national chair of the Communist Party of the United States (CPUSA), James P. Cannon, and former Wobbly organizer William "Big Bill" Haywood, who had remained in the Soviet Union since he jumped bail after his conviction under the Espionage Act.[68] With the Workers' Defense Union no longer in existence, the ILD became the most important organization fighting for the rights of radical labor activists. Like its WDU predecessor, membership included liberals and radicals of various stripes (although the Communist Party openly dominated its board until 1937), and assistance was provided on a strictly nonpartisan, nonideological basis. Additionally, like the WDU, the ILD was internationalist in its outlook (as well as its name) and unafraid to breach the color line that divided U.S. society by defending Black workers. In its early years, the ILD dove headlong into the campaign to save Sacco and Vanzetti and took up the cause of Mooney and Billings, who still languished in prison over a decade after their conviction. Its signature campaign was the movement to free the "Scottsboro Boys," nine young Black men from Alabama convicted of raping two women on a train.[69]

Essentially, the ILD was the Workers' Defense Union on steroids: larger, more tightly organized, and embedded in the global network of the Communist Party. Its agenda was ambitious. The organization fought for the release of class-war prisoners and the repeal of criminal syndicalist and sedition laws; advocated for foreign-born workers; provided legal assistance for workers persecuted by bosses for their activities in the class struggle; publicized antilabor initiatives around the globe; offered material support to prisoners and their families; challenged the system of labor frame-ups; defended freedom of speech, press, and assembly for workers; fought for the right of workers to form unions; and protested the persecution and lynching of Black workers.[70] As the most recognized and revered labor radical in the civil liberties movement, founder and head of the Workers' Defense Union, and a skilled builder of alliances across ideological lines, Flynn was the perfect choice to chair the ILD.

The ILD's board voted unanimously to install Flynn as national chair at their second annual convention. Her comments at the convention echoed those she had made in the early days of the WDU. "It is not only the leaders and well known fighters that are being defended by the I.L.D.," she noted, approvingly, "but the obscure unknown worker, mostly likely belonging to some organization too reactionary, or no organization, that now feels secure that his case will be taken care of just as promptly and efficiently as that of a well-known fighter."[71] Her commitment to advocacy on behalf of all labor activists, not just those with influential networks or name recognition, remained steadfast.

Flynn's reputation as a champion of workers and her gifts for public speaking and fundraising were valuable assets for the ILD. In November 1926, the organization sent her on a trip out West to speak on the "Persecution of Strikers at Passaic." Among the cities on her full itinerary were Pittsburgh, Chicago, Denver, Trinidad (Colorado), Los Angeles, San Francisco, Oakland, and San Jose. Her return trip, a route that was to include stops in Minneapolis, St. Paul, Rochester (Minnesota), Ironwood (Michigan), Winnipeg, Gary, and Madison, was scheduled to begin December 26, 1926.[72] That leg of the trip was canceled. Flynn had begun to feel sick on the train west of Chicago; she was exhausted by the time she reached San Francisco. Joe Ettor, her former Wobbly comrade who was now a wine merchant in California, was heading to Washington State and volunteered to drive Flynn to her next stop, Portland, Oregon, where she could rest at the home of another ally from her Wobbly days, Marie Equi.[73]

Respite in Portland

It was a difficult time for Flynn. She missed her family and comrades in and around New York. "I seem as far away as if I were in a different world," she wrote from Portland to Vorse, but she needed time to recuperate body and soul before making the journey home: "I fear I am getting old—the trip does not thrill me as expected. I had too many emotional shocks in the last few years. They have left me tired and empty way inside myself."[74] When Tresca learned of her illness and depression, he telegrammed Equi to urge that Flynn "should give up immediately and stay under [her] care even for months." Tresca also informed Equi that he would provide a weekly allowance for Buster and pay Flynn's mother's rent. Should she wish to return, Tresca had a job as director of the American Department of the Anti-Fascist Alliance waiting for her.[75]

In the size of her personality and the strength of her political convictions, Equi—an out lesbian, pacifist, free speech fighter, labor activist, anti-imperialist, and doctor who dedicated her practice to serving the working-class community in Portland, including providing safe and affordable abortions for women who needed them—was a match for Flynn.[76] Convicted under the Sedition Act for a speech she gave in opposition to World War I, she served ten months in San Quentin Prison, an experience that forever compromised her health, if not her spirit. As chair of the WDU, Flynn had advocated on behalf of Equi. When Flynn arrived physically ill and emotionally exhausted in Portland, Equi returned the favor and saw to it that Flynn got the medical attention she needed.

Flynn's illness originated with an impacted tooth. The tooth had become infected, and the infection had spread throughout Flynn's body, including her heart. No doubt, the many stressful situations she'd endured over the past few years, including the betrayal by her sister, breakups with two men, the frustrating end to her work in Passaic, and the lengthy campaign to save Sacco and Vanzetti, had weakened her immune system and left her vulnerable physically as well as emotionally. In an era before the discovery of antibiotics, this kind of systemic infection was seriously debilitating and dangerous. Flynn was sick for several weeks, and she remained under Equi's care until she returned to New York in the fall of 1927. The *Labor Defender* enthusiastically welcomed back the woman they called a "pioneer in the labor defense movement" and reported that she had been reelected national chair in absentia at the ILD's third annual convention. Flynn's return to labor defense work was eagerly anticipated: "The gratifying recuperation of Elizabeth Flynn is an assurance that she will soon be found in the active swing of the movement for labor's freedom from which she is inseparable."[77]

Flynn was not soon back in the active swing of labor defense work. In December 1927, Equi's daughter Mary contacted Flynn and reported that her mother was seriously ill. After settling her own mother and Buster in an apartment in Brooklyn, Flynn returned to Portland to care for the friend who had nursed her back to health. While she was there, her own mental and physical health declined again. For a while, she withdrew from contact with anyone except Buster and her mother.[78] She found it difficult to parent her son from a distance. "He is a good enough boy from all conventional standards," she explained to Vorse when she was feeling well enough to write to her friend. "[He] doesn't drink, smoke, run around with girls, etc. I guess he's a reaction from my own wild youth." However, her family made decisions about Buster that contradicted Flynn's wishes: "They sent him off to the University of Michigan, tho' where they expect to get the necessary funds to see him through is beyond me. And they do not seem to realize the importance of him getting a job and paying his own way through. So I've been quite upset by it all."[79] While she was with Equi in Portland, Flynn stepped down from the board of the Garland Fund and resigned as chair of the International Labor Defense. Her resignation letter to the ILD suggests she was suffering from depression as well as physical illness. "It is now almost two years that I have been a figurehead chairman of the ILD due to my ill health and there are no present prospects of a reversal of health," she wrote. "I am unwilling to continue in that position. Give it to some active and *useful* person. No present prospects of returning East. Decision final. Carry on, or get out is my slogan."[80] In that moment, Flynn may have felt as if her political career was over.

Flynn returned to New York to visit her mother and siblings in August 1929. The interdependence that tied her to Equi troubled her family and friends. Her family also worried that Equi's lesbianism would damage Flynn's reputation.[81] They urged her to stay in New York, but she found the political situation, particularly the factional rivalries within the communist movement, chaotic and unappealing. "Such a mess! I'm glad to be out of it all," she confided to Vorse in early 1930. Flynn returned to Portland several months later.[82] In total, she spent the better part of seven years with Equi. At one point, she was convinced Equi was dying, and she wrote to Eleanor Roosevelt asking the First Lady to visit her friend.[83] Roosevelt did not respond. Equi eventually recovered and lived until 1952.

Years later, Flynn admitted in a letter to her sister Kathie, "[Equi] was not the easiest person to get along with, she had a high temper from her Irish-Italian origin, but she had a brilliant mind, a progressive spirit, had been in prison for her opposition to World War I, and I admired her a great deal." Flynn was also grateful for the opportunity to rest and, while the nation was in the throes of an economic depression and she was unemployed, for the free medical care and creature comforts that life with the well-to-do Equi afforded: "The cleaning, laundry and other household chores were done for us. Much of our food she ordered from fancy groceries and restaurants. I read a great deal—history, science, the classics, medical books, even the Bible."[84] Historians and activists have speculated on whether the relationship between Flynn and Equi was an erotic one. Some have tried to quell rumors of a love affair by noting that Flynn resented having been kept in a situation resembling captivity.[85]

Whatever the nature of their intimacy, notes Equi's biographer, one thing is clear: the two women bonded through their shared experience of the hazards of activist life.[86]

Flynn eventually left Portland for San Francisco at the urging of Bina, with whom she had reconciled over the affair with Tresca, and Bina's second husband, Romolo Bobba. She returned to New York in the summer of 1936. Her brother, Tom, the youngest of the siblings and the only boy, had committed suicide at the age of forty-two. Her mother's grave illness was another factor that motivated her decision to return east, as was a desire to spend more time with Buster.[87] In addition to feeling the tug of family responsibilities, Flynn had recovered her energy and enthusiasm for activism. Since the onset of the Depression, she had watched from the sidelines as the unemployed mobilized for relief, housewives staged boycotts and demonstrations, and strikes broke out around the country. She recalled, "Naturally, my heart and mind, although I was ill, were deeply involved in the current political problems of the people, the menace of Fascism in Europe, the great struggles of the unemployed led by Communists . . . and later the new unions which were present during the New Deal of President Roosevelt."[88] Capitalism seemed on its last legs, revolution was in the air, and Flynn was eager to be back in the struggle.

In the months after her arrival in New York, Flynn reconnected with members of the activist community that had been so central to her life and well-being at cocktail parties, dinners, and commemorative events.[89] She renewed her work for political prisoners with an appeal for contributions to the Christmas drive for the Prisoners' Relief Fund of the ILD.[90] She also jumped back into the New York–based antifascist movement, speaking at a rally against Mussolini's invasion of Ethiopia organized by the Italian Anti-Fascist Committee. "Famous Woman Leader Fights against Fascism" was the headline that announced her return to antifascist activism. It was followed by "Elizabeth Gurley Flynn Recalls the Old Days as She Prepares to Aid Italian Anti-Fascist Meeting at Mecca Hall on Sunday."[91] Gone were the comparisons with Joan of Arc. Now forty-six years old, Flynn was no longer an upstart firebrand. Instead of youthful good looks and moxie, her years of struggle in the labor movement made her special.

Flynn Joins the Communist Party

In February 1937, over the objections of her sisters and Carlo Tresca as well as old friends—some dating back to her Wobbly days, like Joseph

Ettor, Arturo Giovannitti, and Mary Heaton Vorse—Flynn joined the CPUSA. She had originally applied in 1926 on the recommendation of then party secretary Charles Ruthenberg, but she later observed, "It didn't take."[92] Given her comments to Vorse about her discomfort with the chaotic state of the communist movement in the late 1920s, she may simply have changed her mind.

In 1926, when Flynn allegedly first applied for membership, the party was a small organization rife with factional splits and personality clashes, which ultimately led to the expulsion of two of its four key leaders: James Cannon, founder of the ILD and supporter of Leon Trotsky, who was himself expelled from the Communist Party of the Soviet Union (CPSU); and Jay Lovestone, who later went on to become a vehement anti-Communist working with the AFL and the CIA. Ruthenberg died in Moscow in 1927. Only William Z. Foster remained. Foster shared leadership of the party with William Weinstone and Earl Browder until Browder assumed sole leadership in 1932. From 1928 to 1935, Communists adhered to a "third-period" analysis, which predicted that contradictions in economic conditions would lead to the final crisis of capitalism, accompanied by an acceleration of the "radicalization" of the working class in opposition to capitalist rule. The Great Depression seemed to validate this analysis. Communists threw themselves into organizing workers and the unemployed as the vanguard of a revolutionary movement to overthrow capitalism and establish a farmers' and workers' government. Their efforts to transform the party into a mass organization failed, in large part because the economic crisis—an abstract concept that was experienced by actual human beings as hunger, poverty, and the threat of unemployment—weakened, rather than strengthened, working-class militancy.[93] Instead of revolution, the social unrest that followed the onset of the depression in the United States ushered in the New Deal.

Throughout most of his first term of office Communist leaders vilified President Roosevelt as a demagogue and criticized the New Deal as a bait and switch engineered by finance capital to derail worker militancy and inch the United States toward fascism. The party's policy toward FDR and the New Deal shifted after the Seventh Congress of the Comintern (Communist International), held in Moscow in the summer of 1935. Georgi Dimitrov, general secretary of the Executive Committee of the Comintern, delivered the keynote speech, called "The United Front against War and Fascism," in which he maintained that a bourgeois democratic regime was substantially different from a bourgeois fascist one and the real impulse to fascism was coming from the reactionary forces of capital attacking Roosevelt and his policies. Dimitrov's speech marked the official beginning of the Popular Front, a broad alliance of Communist, socialist, and liberal organizations to defend bourgeois democracy against a common fascist threat.[94]

Flynn responded enthusiastically to Dimitrov's speech at the Seventh Congress, which she read in the Communist paper the *Daily Worker* while she was recuperating in Oregon: "This speech made a deep impression on me.... It is an elegant and dramatic appeal to fight fascism.... It is addressed to Communists especially, and other progressive people elsewhere, to put aside all immediate partisan and sectarian interests or differences or ultimate political aims to fight fascism." The Communist leader's emphasis on antifascism appealed to her and led her to conclude, "Here is where I belong. As soon as I am well I will again apply to the Communist Party."[95]

Flynn's enthusiasm for joining the party over the objections of friends and family is understandable. Dimitrov's speech gave the CPUSA a green light to reconcile itself to U.S. liberalism, and in so doing, play a key role in the economic, political, and cultural upheavals that transformed U.S. society in the 1930s. An opponent of violence as a political tactic, Flynn would have felt comfortable with the party's retreat from armed revolution as a stated goal. As Mark Naison explains, "Dispensing with revolutionary rhetoric, the party leadership wrapped itself in the mantle of militant populism, devoting its energies to building trade unions, mobilizing support for New Deal legislation, and trying to awaken popular vigilance to the dangers of fascism."[96] The party's "energies" were considerable. Communists were the worker bees of organizing campaigns. Their willingness to grind it out, combined with experience, tactical acumen, and networks of legal defense organizations, ethnic associations, and community groups, made them essential allies in campaigns like building the Congress of Industrial Organizations (CIO), the labor federation that organized workers in industrial unions in the United States and Canada, founded as an alternative to the AFL in 1935.[97] Flynn joined the party during the storied sit-down strike against General Motors, which transformed the United Auto Workers (UAW) into one of the CIO's most powerful unions.

It was at an antifascist rally that Flynn made her first official appearance as a member of the party. In April 1937 she spoke at a meeting in New York City to honor members of the Abraham Lincoln Brigade, the U.S. volunteers who had gone to Spain to help defend the democratically elected government from fascist general Francisco Franco, whose attempted military coup was being supported by the fascist governments of Italy and

Germany.[98] She continued to advocate for the antifascist defenders of the Spanish Republic throughout the war.[99] In her *Daily Worker* column after the German invasion of Austria Flynn highlighted the evils of Nazism for women and noted "Is it any wonder that heroic Spanish women cry 'Death before Fascism!' We too must cry 'Death to Fascism!'"[100] Support for the beleaguered Spanish Republic was the focal point of a broader, multiethnic, interracial antifascist mobilization on the part of the CPUSA that included opposition to Mussolini's campaign against Ethiopia, the Japanese invasion of China, and Hitler's repressive regime in Germany. Since 1922 Flynn had been warning that fascism was a danger to democracy worldwide, and it must have been no consolation for her to see that her warning had been accurate.

U.S. Communists were used to being outsiders and it was a heady experience to find themselves now valued allies by union leaders and politicians. This would not have been Flynn's experience. Prior to joining the party, she enjoyed friendships and cordial working relationships with several prominent liberal politicians, lawyers, artists, writers, and activists. She even had the ear of the president of the United States when she needed it, as illustrated by her letter to Joseph Tumulty, Woodrow Wilson's private secretary, regarding her arrest under the Espionage Act, which resulted in the suspension of her case in 1918. She would have felt very comfortable in an organization that was seen as a center of practical activism and a valued partner in liberal-radical cooperative endeavors. The party's embrace of U.S. democratic traditions and the language of Republicanism would also have sat well with her. In 1938, when Earl Browder credited Communists with carrying forward the legacy of the United States' revolutionary past by declaring "Communism is twentieth-century Americanism," he spoke a language of Americanism that she had been speaking since her early days as a soapbox orator in the IWW free speech fights.[101] Indeed, Flynn's connection to the IWW and her legacy of labor and free speech activism made her the embodiment of a distinctly American radical tradition and a valuable symbol of the CPUSA's link to that tradition.

The Popular Front period was the high-water mark of Communist popularity and influence in the United States. Membership grew from an average of about ten thousand members to fifty-five thousand members by the end of the decade. But popularity and strategic alliances did not necessarily translate into approval. Communists could not surmount the pervasive antiradicalism of the U.S. labor movement or U.S. society at large. For all their efforts to build the CIO, Communist organizers

FIGURE 7. Elizabeth Gurley Flynn with fellow Communist Party members (from left) Carl Ross, Gil Green, James Ford, Charles Krumbein, Earl Browder (with a copy of *The People's Front*), Alexander Trachtenberg, and Israel Amter, 1938. Credit: Photo appears courtesy of *People's World*

were never fully accepted by the organization. Instead, Fraser Ottanelli observes, "Recruited when needed and closely watched at all times, the moment they finished organizing or gained a following they were quickly transferred or more often summarily dismissed."[102]

Those who harbored anti-Communist views, including a number of liberal intellectuals, found confirmation in news of the Moscow Trials, a series of show trials that charged members of the Bolshevik Old Guard with a variety of offenses, including conspiring to kill Joseph Stalin, between 1936 and 1938. All the defendants confessed to their "guilt," and were executed. The Moscow Trials were part of a purge of nearly every participant in the 1917 Revolution. The impact of the show trials and subsequent purges on perceptions of the CPUSA was blunted by conflicting news reports (Pulitzer Prize–winning journalist Walter Duranty wrote articles defending the trials for the *New Republic*) and by simple refusal to believe that Stalin could carry out such horrible acts. The party defended the trials as legitimate. Those who doubted kept their reservations to themselves and stood loyal to the Soviet Union, the most antifascist country in the world.[103] Flynn was among those who saw what they wanted to see; she spoke in defense of the party line on the Moscow Trials. But for many, faith in the antifascism of the Soviet Union was dealt a mortal blow with the signing of the Nazi-Soviet Pact on August 23, 1939.

Antifascism had been the core of the Communist Party's policies since 1934. Announcement of the change in Soviet foreign policy just five months after the fall of the Spanish Republic completely shocked the leadership of the CPUSA and left members reeling. On top of their own feelings of dismay and confusion, Communists had to face criticism from family, friends, and co-workers. Flynn's dissonance must have been extraordinary. Since Mussolini's seizure of power in 1922, she had been an outspoken antifascist; now as a highly visible member of a hierarchical organization that demanded discipline and conformity to official policy, she was expected to efface her own political commitments to justify an agreement between Stalin and Hitler.[104] And justify it she did. Although up to now her expertise lay more in labor and civil liberties issues than foreign affairs, when asked—or heckled—about the pact, she explained it as a necessary tactic to protect Russia, the only home to socialism in the world, a justification that wore thin after the partition of Poland by Germany and the Soviet Union followed by the Soviet invasion of Finland.[105] Like others among the party faithful, Flynn maintained that the war was not a fight against fascism but a contest between competing English and German imperialisms and urged a policy of nonintervention by the United States.[106]

In the face of rebuke by friends and allies outside the party, Flynn maintained that her political commitments had not changed. In September 1939, while on a speaking tour for the party, she found herself at the Fay Hotel in Virginia, Minnesota, where she had stayed when she was a Wobbly. "Being here in this same old hotel, where you still walk up two flights of stairs I was bound to remember our experiences here together," she wrote to Mary Heaton Vorse. "Here I am, still at it, barnstorming for the CP and struggling for free speech, as ever. In three weeks I've had two meetings broken up, two disturbed violently and here the City Council refused the auditorium. I feel as if the pages are turning back and we are fast approaching 1917 again. But with a better outlook."[107] It was a hard sell. In a December 1939 column for the *Daily Worker*, Flynn described bumping into an Italian labor leader with whom she had worked on the Sacco-Vanzetti case: "He was apparently pleased to see me, greeted me cordially, inquired as to my health and activities. I said, 'I am speaking as usual.' He said with a pleasant smile, 'For what?' But when I said 'For the Communist Party' his face changed and he actually looked scared. 'Oh heil Hitler!' he said sneeringly and abruptly left." She was insulted by the comment and calmed herself by recalling that Eugene Debs had been called "pro-German" for opposing U.S. entry into the war in 1917.[108]

Communists were not the only ones affected by the announcement of the Nazi-Soviet Pact. Roger Baldwin, who was walking the beach on Martha's Vineyard when he heard about the agreement, called it "the biggest shock of my life."[109] Baldwin had shared the Communists' initial distrust of Roosevelt, whom he believed was too tied to business interests, and the New Deal as a dangerous increase in the power of the federal government. His fear that an enlarged federal government would inevitably entail greater limitations on free speech dissipated as liberal civil libertarians gained a foothold in New Deal agencies and threw their support behind a number of ACLU initiatives, including pardoning the remaining World War I Espionage and Sedition Act victims and pulling back from deportation of immigrant radicals.[110]

Baldwin's realization that a government administered by liberals could be a useful tool for protecting First Amendment rights coincided with the rise of the Popular Front. An enthusiastic participant in Popular Front coalition politics, Baldwin helped organize numerous Front organizations, including the American Committee for the Protection of the Foreign Born, the Consumers National Federation, and the North American Committee to Aid Spanish Democracy. The national ACLU gained increased visibility as a result of cooperating with the International Labor Defense on important civil liberties legal cases, including the Scottsboro case, as well as the DeJonge case, in which the Supreme Court ruled that Oregon's criminal syndicalism law, used to convict Communist Dirk DeJonge for speaking at an outdoor meeting in support of striking longshoreman, violated the due process clause of the Fourteenth Amendment, and the Herndon case, in which the court decided that the insurrection law under which Angelo Herndon, a Black Communist attempting to organize Black and white workers in Georgia, had been convicted violated the First Amendment. Baldwin was inspired by the Popular Front's vision of a mass civil rights-civil liberties movement to expand the ACLU's network of affiliates.[111]

Tensions in the ACLU

These two political currents—New Deal liberalism and Popular Frontism—were reflected in the composition of the ACLU's leadership. Among the New Deal liberals were John Haynes Holmes, Morris Ernst, and Roger Riis. The Popular Front group included Harry Ward, Mary Van Kleeck,

Robert Dunn, Abraham Isserman, Nathan Greene, and Elizabeth Gurley Flynn. There was tension between them. The latter group held to the ACLU's original commitment to free speech as a necessary tool for working-class organizing and activism in the struggle for economic justice in a hostile political environment, while the former was nudging the ACLU in a new direction toward free speech as a value-neutral right that could be invoked by capital as well as labor. The new approach was born of a string of successful court cases and increased popular support for civil liberties under the Roosevelt administration and reflected confidence that the new liberal order would remain in force indefinitely.

Tension between members of the board was not confined to their respective approaches to civil liberties. The New Deal liberals were openly and increasingly anti-Communist. Baldwin tried to manage the tension for a while with mixed results. An ACLU statement issued in March 1937 illustrates an effort to recast the organization's relationship to labor activism without venturing into the anti-Communist camp: "It cannot be too strongly stated that the union is a 'united front' of persons of varied political and economic views who could not possibly agree on any program except defense of civil rights. The union has no political or economic direction whatever; no connection directly with any political party or economic movement; and no bias except to protect orderly and peaceful progress through the exercise of American political rights."[112] It was a far cry from "The cause we now serve is Labor," the informal mission statement of the fledgling ACLU. At the same time, the statement was clearly in line with Popular Front thinking in that it made antifascism a core value and refrained from criticism of the Soviet Union, despite the revelations of the Moscow Trials: "It is said that the defenders of civil liberty condemn Fascism but do not equally condemn Communism. When the term 'Fascism' is used in such a sense, it is to describe the repressive measures characteristic of Fascism, and shared by forces everywhere sympathetic with its objectives. If Communists engaged in such repressive tactics in the United States, we would condemn them equally. The record shows that American Communists do not. We use the words 'Fascism' and 'Communism' only in reference to American conditions."[113]

Two disagreements illustrate the fissure that had opened between the two sides of the ACLU board. One was disagreement over the sit-down strike. The sit-down emerged as a tactic when workers at the Firestone Tire & Rubber Company in Akron, Ohio, used it to protest the one-week (without pay) suspension of a worker, Clayton Dicks, for allegedly beating up a nonunion man. Their protest succeeded in getting Dicks reinstated and the tactic spread. In February 1936, the Goodyear Tire & Rubber Company discharged 137 tire builders for staging a sit-down. A strike ensued that closed the entire Akron plant and succeeded in getting the 137 sit-downers reinstated. By the end of May, Goodyear reported nineteen sit-downs in its Akron plants.[114] Arguably, the most storied sit-down strike was in Flint, Michigan where UAW members occupied the Fisher Body Plant #1 after learning that General Motors was planning to close it. The strike, which began on December 30, 1936, lasted until February 11, 1937, when GM and the UAW signed an agreement that recognized the union as the exclusive bargaining representative for the company's employees.[115]

Although sit-down strikers in the United States did not attempt to seize control of the factories like workers did in Europe, the success of the tactic and the sense of efficacy and self-determination that came with it suggested a shift in the balance of power between employees and employers that many conservatives as well as liberals would have found troubling, especially given that key players, like UAW field organizer Wyndham Mortimer, who led the organizing drive at Flint, were Communists. After avoiding the issue for over a year it became clear to Baldwin that a statement from the ACLU clarifying its position on the tactic was in order.[116]

The statement that resulted was not a clarification. On the one hand, it noted that some in the ACLU saw the sit-down as a "simple issue of trespass involving only property rights, with which the American Civil Liberties Union is not concerned." This was followed by a "contrary view" (to which Flynn subscribed), which held that because sit-down strikers claimed they were not sitting on company property but on their jobs (that is, they were asserting a property right to their jobs), the sit-down "[raised] debatable questions in a field in which public policy [was] yet to be determined." To complicate matters further, the statement also included an objection raised by Arthur Garfield Hays (although he was not named) that sounded like a contemporary right-to-work argument: "The sit-down tactic enables a minority of workers to deny rights to a majority and ... in a public service industry a small minority may cripple service essential to a whole community." After affirming the ACLU's commitment to "the process of discussion and negotiation as against coercion and violence" the statement closed with an assurance: "The Civil Liberties Union will act only to keep open the channels of organization and negotiation, to maintain intact the right to strike and in particular cases to protest and take action against unnecessary force or violence, by whomever employed."[117]

Members of the national committee who weighed in on the statement were divided in their responses. Some were fine with it.[118] A number of supporters of the sit-down felt the statement did not go far enough in supporting the tactic.[119] Opponents decried the sit-down as a danger to law and order and some threatened to resign from the ACLU if the statement were published.[120] And others found that it said almost nothing substantive in an effort to appease both sides.[121] In that vein, Oswald Garrison Villard, who voted in favor, called the statement "Reasonably well-balanced, a pleasant sit-down on the fence!"[122]

Flynn's response to the sit-down statement was not so cheery. "I vote no," she wrote on the top of the letter she penned to fellow board members. No doubt, she was aware of the radical potential of the sit-down, but she refrained from making that point. Her reasoning instead entailed a defense of the right of all workers to strike, including those in the public sector, which was not covered by the National Labor Relations Act (NLRA):

> I do not concur in Paragraph #2 on Page #2 of our proposed statement on sit-down strikes. "The right of a majority" is involved just as definitely in a strike of any group of highly skilled (craft) key workers, who can cripple an industry by hitting a nerve center, as well as in a sit-down strike. We have never taken a stand against strikes per se, either of minorities in public service or that "may cripple service essential to a whole community." Therefore why raise this question solely in relation to the sitdown strikes? To carry this argument to its logical conclusion, we would oppose all strikes in public services, R.R., elevators, powerhouses, at sea, etc.
>
> The C.O.s [conscientious objectors] in wartime were a minority group, who were accused of attempting to cripple service essential to the whole community. Did we see more clearly in our younger days in the A.C.L.U.?[123]

Her question at the end of the letter is an indication of her sense that the organization was losing its way. That sense would only grow stronger over the next two years.

In the end, the ACLU did not endorse the sit-down, although it did decry the use of force to remove strikers and oppose legislation designed to regulate unions and strike tactics. In 1939, property rights won out over workplace democracy when the Supreme Court decided in *NLRB v. Fansteel* that the sit-down strike was a form of trespass and workers could be fired for engaging in a sit-down, even if their actions were provoked by an employer violation of the NLRA.[124] Meanwhile, the tension between ACLU board members remained. Disagreement surfaced again in a contest that pitted Ford Motor Company against the National Labor Relations Board (NLRB) over whether the state could lawfully restrict employer speech, including the circulation of antiunion propaganda during a union organizing drive at Ford Motor Company.

Henry Ford treated his workers terribly. He paid below-industry-average wages; hired, fired, and promoted without regard to seniority; regularly employed the speedup and refused to allow workers to take a break; forced workers to eat lunch in silence; and engaged in bullying and constant surveillance. Not surprisingly, Ford hated unions, which he called corrupt rackets, and vowed that his factories would never be unionized. UAW president Walter Reuther aimed to prove otherwise. The struggle that ensued was bitter and violent. In May 1937, UAW organizers, including Reuther, were brutally beaten by Ford's internal security service under the direction of Harry Bennett while they were attempting to leaflet workers at the Rouge River factory complex in Dearborn, Michigan, an episode known as the "Battle of the Overpass."[125] The UAW appealed to the NLRB, which determined that the assaults were deliberately planned and carried out to crush a union organizing drive. In addition, the NLRB issued a "cease and desist order" directing Ford to stop circulating antiunion literature, which it regarded as "open and active hostility." In essence, the NLRB found that because of the context—an unequal power relationship between unorganized Ford employees and their employer and a history of violent intimidation—Ford's antiunion screeds infringed on workers' right to organize a union "of their own choosing" and thus violated the Wagner Act.[126]

The ACLU's Committee on Labor's Rights issued a majority decision that endorsed the NLRB's finding. The minority, including Holmes and Riis, voiced concerns that the ACLU was venturing into dangerous territory by endorsing restrictions on employer speech. In a letter to board president Harry Ward after a particularly acrimonious meeting, Holmes voiced his concern that some board members, including and especially Flynn, were using the issue of free speech as a tool to wage class warfare.

> In view of certain trends now strong among us, it might be well for us to change the name of the American Civil Liberties Union to the "National Association for the Advancement of Labor"—that is, if present trends are to continue. I believe that there are certain members of our Board who are not fundamentally interested in civil liberties at all, but only in the question as to how the advocacy of civil liberties may now be used for

the benefit of labor in the current struggle. Very significant was the reference yesterday afternoon to the class struggle in relation to the Majority Report. That Marxian doctrine of the class struggle has no more place in the deliberations and decisions of the Union than the Christian doctrine of the immaculate conception."[127]

Ward, who was part of the majority that found in favor of the NLRB, assured Holmes that the differences among board members reflected honest disagreement about the relationship between the rights of labor to organize and the rights of employers to oppose organization: "In my judgement, the basis for agreement lies in our decision that both rights stop where persuasion ends and coercion begins."[128] Holmes was not convinced. There were members on the board, he insisted, "who do not believe in civil liberties on the basis of principle." Instead, they believe in civil liberties for the advancement of labor and the revolution "and when, or if, this is achieved, they will drop civil liberties as promptly as they were dropped in Russia." Holmes feared the presence of members who would use civil liberties as a revolutionary tactic put the ACLU's work in peril, but lest he himself seem to violate the principle of free speech, he assured Ward, "I am not asking for any excommunications or purges, least of all am I pleading for the abrogation of free thought and speech inside our own Board." Instead, members whose commitment was to labor before free speech should resign "as a sheer matter of self-respect and integrity."[129]

Whereas Holmes believed the ACLU was haunted by the specter of Communism, Riis warned of slouching toward fascism. Noting a parallel between the chilling potential of the NLRB decision and efforts to stifle expression in Nazi Germany, he cautioned "we can't bend the civil liberties to serve any purpose except that of freedom of thought and freedom of expression."[130] In a *Reader's Digest* article published a few months later, Riis sounded the alarm against Communist and Nazi dictatorships and implied that board members who sided with the NLRB, especially Flynn, had allied themselves with the former by advocating censorship of capital to advance the cause of labor.[131]

On the suggestion of Arthur Garfield Hays, the ACLU walked back from its original majority report to endorse a both/and position. Hays advised the ACLU to support the main thrust of the NLRB's cease and desist order while opposing those parts that restricted noncoercive speech. This way, the ACLU could support Ford's right to free speech while opposing any communication that threatened individual workers. Hays's logic undergirded the ACLU's memo to the NLRB seeking clarification of the part of the order that addressed Ford's expression of opinion.[132]

The claims by Holmes and Riis that members of the ACLU were looking to make an unholy alliance with labor and thereby move the organization away from its historic commitment to unfettered free speech were, of course, untrue. The organization was founded to fight for the rights of conscientious objectors and radical labor activists targeted by wartime repressive laws; that the fledgling ACLU should defend employers' rights as well would have been regarded as a preposterous idea. It was not until the second half of the 1920s that the ACLU recognized religious freedom, censorship, and civil rights as the purview of a civil liberties organization. For her part, Flynn had not changed course since she first stood on a soapbox and challenged an ordinance against street speaking by labor organizers in Missoula, Montana in 1909. Although her commitment to free expression was expansive, embracing everything from disseminating birth control information to organizing against imperialist regimes, it had never been rooted in abstract principles or a commitment to individual rights. On the contrary, she had always approached free speech and assembly as tools that ordinary people needed for their collective struggle against the powerful forces arrayed against them. Whereas the ACLU was increasingly inclined to defend free speech as *the* most important civil liberty, a hallmark of a democratic society, Flynn continued to view it as a means to human freedom, not an end.

The conflict that animated the ACLU leadership's deliberations about the sit-down strike and the NLRB decision regarding Ford and the UAW was not simply a matter of different approaches to civil liberties. The ACLU was caught up in its own Red Scare. Several board members were rabidly anti-Communist: Norman Thomas, Margaret DeSilver, John Haynes Holmes, Morris Ernst, and Roger Riis. Their anti-Communism was stoked by the formation of the House Un-American Activities Committee (HUAC), chaired by Martin Dies (D-Tex.), in May 1938.[133] During early hearings of the Dies Committee, witnesses identified the ACLU as a Communist front organization.[134] Dies then declared the ACLU "integral" to Communist front organizations in a nationwide radio broadcast.[135] In response to these and other allegations, the ACLU prepared affidavits denying its association with the CPUSA. In one of the affidavits, the ACLU emphasized that only one Communist, Elizabeth Gurley Flynn, sat on either the national committee or the Board of Directors. The affidavit also stressed that the number of ACLU cases involving Communists had dropped sharply in recent years and that on several recent occasions, the organization had opposed the CPUSA.

The Dies Committee's relentless campaign against Left-based subversion enhanced its popularity, thus shielding it from efforts by critics, including the ACLU, to make a case against reauthorization.[136] Frustrated in their effort to beat the Dies Committee in its efforts to ferret out Communists, a few ACLU board members decided to join it. On October 22, 1939, Morris Ernst met with Dies, allegedly to discuss Ernst's idea for legislation requiring political organizations to register with the federal government. The next day, Dies announced that his committee had found no evidence to substantiate the charge that the ACLU was a Communist front organization.[137] A few weeks later, ACLU board chair Harry Ward was called to answer questions about another Communist front organization: the American League for Peace and Democracy. To shield the ACLU from an assault by Dies, a few days before Ward's testimony Ernst and Hays met with Dies and some of his staffers at the congressman's office and again at a cocktail party. They were successful. During Ward's testimony, Dies brushed aside questions about the ACLU being a Communist organization.[138]

The reprieve that Dies granted had not come without a cost. Since Hitler's rise to power anti-Communists had been claiming that the Soviet Union was as much an enemy of freedom as Nazi Germany. These claims could be swept under the rug of antifascism until the Nazi-Soviet Pact of 1939. That agreement drew Baldwin into the anti-Communist camp and transformed tensions between the two factions on the board into what Cletus Daniels calls "the bitterest internecine struggle in the ACLU's history."[139]

On February 5, 1940, the ACLU board voted to approve a resolution that identified communism as a totalitarian ideology on par with fascism and barred members of organizations affiliated with either movement from serving on a governing body of the organization. The "Communazi" resolution read, in part, "The Board of Directors and the National Committee of the American Civil Liberties Union . . . hold it inappropriate for any person to serve on the governing committees of the Union or on its staff, who is a member of any political organization which supports totalitarian dictatorship in any country, or who by his public declarations indicates his support of such a principle." In the category of organizations supporting dictatorships the resolution included "organizations in the United States supporting the totalitarian governments of the Soviet Union and of the Fascist and Nazi Countries (such as the Communist Party, the German American Bund and others); as well as native organizations with obvious anti-democratic objectives or practices."[140]

Communist Purge in the ACLU

As Flynn was the only openly CPUSA member on the board, the resolution targeted her. In 1939, with full knowledge of her party membership on the part of other board members, she had been elected unanimously to a second three-year term of office. If the resolution was intended to bully her into resigning before her term expired (recall Holmes's comment in his letter to Ward that anyone with a specious commitment to civil liberties should resign from the board "as a sheer matter of self-respect and integrity"), it failed. Flynn threw down the gauntlet in the pages of the *Daily Worker*. "Communists are not quitters in a fight," she declared. "It has been said that it is 'inappropriate' for Communists to remain on the Civil Liberties board. My answer is that I deem it most appropriate for a Communist to remain there and to fight for civil liberties within the ACLU itself." If the ACLU wanted her out, they would have to expel her.[141]

The resolution provoked heated controversy within the ACLU. The California, Chicago, and Massachusetts affiliates sought to have it rescinded. Others criticized it as a political test incompatible with the organization's principles. Some pointed out that it said nothing about Catholics who claimed to be following church policy by supporting fascist regimes in Italy and Spain.[142] ACLU board president Harry F. Ward resigned in protest. In his resignation letter, Ward chastised board members who supported the resolution for "attempting to create an orthodoxy in civil liberties, and stranger still, an orthodoxy in political judgement upon events outside the United States."[143] John Haynes Holmes was elected to replace Ward. Soon after taking office, Holmes described Flynn as "a symbol of difficulties" and demanded her resignation by March 25 (the date set for the hearing on her expulsion) as "the only logical and decent action possible" in light of articles she had written about the board's effort to remove her in the *Daily Worker* and another Communist publication, the *New Masses*.[144]

Flynn responded to the resolution and Holmes's request for her resignation in a lengthy statement addressed to the board. In it, she challenged the validity of the resolution and the procedure established for her trial and requested inclusion in the trial record of documents that demonstrate the resolution as a change in ACLU policy. She also pointed out a false statement by Roger Baldwin, who claimed the board had "never originally elected nor appointed Communist Party members to our guiding committees," when the ACLU had knowingly welcomed CPUSA members

William Z. Foster, Anna Rochester, and herself. She charged Holmes too with lying when he accused her of sabotaging the board's work. In answer to the charge that her commitment to civil liberties was not rooted in principle and would crumble with the establishment of a Soviet state, she referred to the NLRB's Ford decision: "Dr. Holmes 'holy crusade' attitude is far more objectionable when it leads him to attack the National Labor Relations Board in its administration of an Act which protects labor's civil rights and right to collectively bargain, and to defend Henry Ford's 'right' to intimidate his employees under the guise of free speech than any hypothetical future attitude could possibly be."[145]

In answer to the charge that her presence on the board was injurious to the ACLU's reputation, Flynn charged that Ernst had done more to harm the organization by "playing with the Dies Committee." She was insulted by the resolution, and she indicated as much in no uncertain terms: "I object to being placed in the same category with Fascists and Nazis and the CP with the Bund, K.K.K., etc." She pointed out that the Soviet Union was a more democratic place than either Germany or Italy, and that the vast majority of people in the USSR enjoyed greater civil liberties than the people of the British Empire, most notably India, South Africa, and Ireland, but the ACLU resolution said nothing about colonial oppression.[146]

Flynn returned the board's insult in her article in the *Daily Worker* (her article in the *New Masses* was an expository piece that laid out her arguments against her removal).[147] After having served twenty years with the ACLU, she explained, certain members of the board expected her to stand aside gracefully when her presence was no longer appropriate: "When, unladylike, I refused, they brought charges against me and I am slated for expulsion." Her wit sharp as ever, she proceeded to skewer the interpersonal politics of respectability being used to paper over the harsh truth of what was being done to her: "Of course they are all very sorry; I will be a 'distinct loss'; there is nothing personal in the matter; they all love me very much; it's such a shame it has to be Elizabeth; her record in fighting for civil rights is unassailable; it's a most embarrassing procedure and deep regrets are in order! I feel like an unwanted wife sent to Reno after all these protestations of affection, except that I don't expect any alimony will be forthcoming."[148]

She hit her target. Members of the board were incensed.[149] They were also worried about public opinion as well as the opinion of ACLU affiliates around the country. After reassuring Baldwin that opinion was on their side, Holmes stated Flynn had thrown down the gauntlet in the

Daily Worker piece and the board could not back down without surrendering advantage to the Communists.

> There was much talk, you may remember, to the effect that we must not make Miss Flynn a martyr, as this would give the Communist Party such a magnificent talking point. But what about making Miss Flynn a victor? It strikes me that that will give the Communists an even better talking point. I don't relish the prospect of her going forth as a martyr on this forthcoming lecture trip of hers, but I can swallow it a darned sight better than the prospect of her going forth as a victor in the fight, a reborn Joan of Arc, flaunting us and taunting us with the charge that we took a stand and then didn't dare go through with it when we faced a Communist who had the nerve to call our bluff.[150]

Holmes's fury over her mockery of the ACLU in a Communist newspaper made him dig in his heels and motivated his demand for Flynn's resignation. He had to wait for satisfaction. Flynn's trial was postponed for six weeks when her son Fred took seriously ill.

On May 7, 1940, the ACLU board, armed with the controversial resolution, met at the City Club of New York on West Fifty-Fifth Street to decide whether to expel Flynn on grounds that her membership in the CPUSA disqualified her from serving on the governing body of the civil liberties organization. The charge against Flynn was brought by board member Dorothy Dunbar Bromley, a Scripps-Howard journalist. Baldwin chose Bromley because he thought it would look better to have a woman initiate the expulsion proceedings. The ensuing debate lasted over six hours. Transcripts of the meeting, which were not publicly available until nearly thirty years later, reveal a defiant Flynn, undaunted by the accusations against her, unassailable in her defense of her near half-century record on civil liberties, and unafraid to call out the hypocrisy of her accusers. Her statement at the trial drew upon the statement she had submitted to the board in March.

> I object to a "loyalty oath"; to penalizing opinion; to the injection of issues or attitudes on foreign governments and policies; to the abandonment of the honored traditional position of the ACLU and to the substitution of political orthodoxy for the political heterodoxy which distinguished our Board. The demand for my resignation is an attempt to force a minority to conform to the political view of the majority or get out. I refuse to resign because I will not be a party to saving the face of this anti-civil

liberties majority nor to whitewashing their red-baiting. I am appealing to the real ACLU elements against such a demand. If this trial occurred elsewhere, it would be a case for the ACLU to defend! This charge violates every principle we fought for in the past. Unless the ACLU returns to its original position, its future record is likely to disgrace its past. I have a moral duty as a charter member of the ACLU, to fight against this danger and to maintain my status.[151]

The strength of Flynn's response is all the more remarkable when considered in light of the personal circumstances surrounding the proceedings: she was facing betrayal by people with whom she had struggled arm-in-arm for decades just two months after losing her only child to cancer at the age of twenty-nine. Buster's death had come less than two years after the death of Flynn's own mother, Annie.

After her testimony, Flynn was asked to leave the meeting. Deliberations continued until just after 2:00 a.m. the next morning. The vote was tied 9–9, but presiding officer John Haynes Holmes broke the tie and voted to expel. Norman Thomas, who had also declared himself averse to expelling anyone from the board on account of political opinions but who was clearly still smarting from factional disputes between the Socialist Party and the CPUSA and from the realization that Communists had eclipsed Socialists as the dominant force among U.S. Left politics, had also voted in favor.[152] Adding insult to injury, when the meeting adjourned, no one bothered to call Flynn back and inform her of the outcome. She found out at an informal meeting afterward with a group of board members at the nearby Algonquin Hotel. Her expulsion was not official until the national committee weighed in. After months of conflict and several defections from the ACLU, the committee decided to uphold Flynn's removal by one vote.

Flynn's articles in the *Daily Worker* and *New Masses*, her response to Holmes's demand for her resignation, and her testimony at the trial indicate that she saw her expulsion as capitulation to red-baiting. Those who opposed the ACLU resolution and the outcome of the trial agreed. Not surprisingly, Baldwin and Holmes claimed otherwise. In their accounts, the 1940 resolution and trial were unfortunate but necessary steps to break the logjam that had paralyzed the board. In her history of the ACLU, Laura Weinrib endorses their view. She reasons from conflict over the Ford case to conclude that Baldwin, Holmes, and other board members who supported the resolution and voted to expel Flynn were not pulling back from their commitment to defending the rights of Communists.

Instead, they were affirming their commitment to "a streamlined civil libertarianism that was impervious to inequalities in the marketplace of ideas."[153]

Neither Riis's comments in the *Reader's Digest* nor Holmes's intense reaction to Flynn's article in the *Daily Worker* support this claim. Nor does it hold up under scrutiny of the trial transcript. Flynn's questioners admitted that she had never once obstructed the organization's work in any way. In fact, the major obstruction seems to have been disagreement about whether Communists should be able to serve on the board. Moreover, disagreement over what approach to civil liberties the ACLU should take, including whether an employer may lawfully claim a right to free speech under the Constitution during a union organizing drive or otherwise, was tangential to the main line of questioning. Instead, the trial focused on whether Flynn endorsed the policies of a totalitarian state—that is, the Soviet Union, and whether her allegiance to the program of the CPUSA subjected her to control by the Soviet Union and thus conflicted with her ability to adhere to the program of the ACLU and uphold the First Amendment.

The ACLU resolution that resulted in Flynn's ouster from the organization has been called a turning point in the alliance between liberals and radicals, but it was much more than that. The ACLU's actions had profound implications for the political landscape of the United States. Similar resolutions were passed by trade unions, youth groups, and civic organizations around the country. The practices and ethical standing of the ACLU's leaders and the organization itself were seriously compromised. After a meeting with J. Edgar Hoover in 1941, Baldwin convinced himself that the FBI director was a friend of civil liberties whose views on labor and the Left had mellowed. He subsequently withdrew a piece he had written for the *New Republic* on the harmful effects of Hoover's red-baiting. In his memoir, published in 1945, Ernst included a chapter on his friendship with Hoover in which he criticized liberals for not taking into account Hoover's full record on civil liberties before attacking him. Ernst had sent the chapter to Hoover for suggestions and edits before publishing it.[154] The ACLU national office began a policy of checking with Hoover on whether various individuals were members of the Communist Party. Its own willingness to capitulate to red-baiting by purging its ranks rendered hollow the ACLU's criticism of other organizations for doing the same. It is no stretch to say that the ACLU resolution of 1940 and the purging of Flynn from the board fueled anti-Communist hysteria and helped lay the groundwork for the second Red Scare and McCarthyism by giving the liberal seal of approval to the doctrine of "guilt by association."[155] If the ACLU could persecute its own founding members for no reason other than their political associations, who or what was there to stop the FBI or McCarthy? The implications for Flynn were equally profound. For the first time in her life, she was an outsider to the movement for civil liberties that she had done so much to build and sustain.

CHAPTER 5

From the Little Red Scare to the Big Red Scare

> We Communists will fight for our Party.
> We will never give up or give in.
> —Elizabeth Gurley Flynn

IN A 1939 May Day article she penned for the *New Masses*, Elizabeth Gurley Flynn brimmed with optimism about the prospect of a socialist America: "Last year I spoke to the Amalgamated [Clothing Workers of America] and at a big park gathering in Pittsburgh; in the Steel Workers Organizing Committee Hall at McKeesport, to the miners in California, Pa. This year I'm off to Southern Illinois, among the miners there. I ask you, could a person want happier, more colorful, more adventuresome and inspiring May Days than I have had? East and West, North and South, 'mine eyes have seen the glory' of labor's coming of age in America." Looking ahead, Flynn predicted a triumphant future. "'*I expect to live to see socialism in my country*,' in the memorial words of Lenin. That will be the best May Day of all!"[1]

A Rising Tide of Anti-Communism

The timing of her choice to become a Communist buoyed Flynn's faith in the inevitability of socialism. She officially joined the CPUSA at a moment when Communists enjoyed a measure of acceptance—even popularity—unprecedented in the history of either the party or the United States. One reason from the party's perspective was its embrace of Popular Front politics, which entailed downplaying its revolutionary rhetoric in favor of emphasis on broad alliances, labor advocacy, support for New Deal policies, and commitment to antifascism. Another reason was the relative tolerance of federal authorities during this period. As M. J. Heale points out, however, even in the 1930s, "American Communists were not safe from everyone." City and state government officials as well as businesses, patriotic societies, veterans groups, and xenophobic and racist organizations were openly hostile to Communists, while trade unions, churches, and educational institutions looked for ways to distance themselves from the so-called red menace.[2] Flynn had a taste of open hostility in November 1938. While she was addressing an audience of miners and their families, including a dozen young children, at a meeting hall in a mining camp in Adena, Ohio, thugs broke a window and tossed a canister of tear gas into the building.[3] The experience left her temporarily shaken, but it did not diminish her faith in the working classes and the appeal of socialism.

The tear gas incident in Ohio occurred as anti-Communism began to intensify at the federal level. Conservative backlash against the New Deal along with a wartime national security imperative encouraged a climate of political intolerance that historians have called a "little Red Scare."[4] After President Roosevelt's failed 1937 effort to "pack" the Supreme Court congressional conservatives created an oppositional bloc of Southern Democrats and rural Republicans. As panic about Communists, fascists, Nazis, and foreigners mounted, Congress passed the Foreign Agents Registration Act, which mandated that all organizations "subject to foreign control" register with the attorney general. For the November 1938 elections, the conservative coalition used the investigations into subversive and un-American activities by the newly formed Dies Committee to target New Deal candidates. Their efforts proved successful. Democrats lost seats in both the Senate and the House, and Republicans took control of Congress. In the summer of 1939, the powerful conservative coalition passed the Act to Prevent Pernicious Political Activities, also known as the Hatch Act, which prohibited federal employees from engaging in political activity or belonging to any organization that advocated for the overthrow of the U.S. government.

The signing of the Nazi-Soviet Pact intensified the perceived need for the federal government to crack down on subversive activities by Communists as well as fascists. It makes a tidy argument to characterize the conflation of Communists and fascists as a reasonable consequence of the pact, but the origin of the trend predates it. Newspapers began making comparisons between Stalin and Hitler as early as 1934.[5] In 1936, Roosevelt met secretly with J. Edgar Hoover at the White House and ordered a surveillance program to determine how the activities of right- and left-wing organizations might affect the political and economic life of the country.[6] A number of liberal antifascists were openly anti-Communist before the Nazi-Soviet Pact, including, as we have seen, members of the ACLU Executive Committee but also prominent progressive Democratic politicians like New York Congressman Emmanuel Celler, an outspoken civil liberties advocate, and California Congressman Jerry Voorhis, architect of the Foreign Agents Registration Act, known also as the Voorhis Act. To many emergent anti-Communists, the Nazi-Soviet Pact merely confirmed their beliefs about similarities between Hitler and Stalin and the respective ideologies the two men embodied. Communists unwittingly contributed to the growing movement for political repression by chastising the ACLU for defending Nazi free speech and arguing that the German American Bund was an agent of the German government, thus mirroring claims their adversaries were making about their own party.[7]

The Smith Act

In May 1940, Roosevelt authorized the FBI to use electronic surveillance against suspected subversives, which overrode a 1937 Supreme Court decision that outlawed wiretapping.[8] A month later, Congress passed HR 5138, the Alien Registration Act, otherwise known as the Smith Act after its principal author, Congressman Howard Smith, a Democrat from Virginia. Composed of various bills that Congress had voted down between 1935 and 1938, the "omnibus gag bill," as the ACLU called the Smith Act, married criminal syndicalism with immigration restriction. The Smith Act would prove an indispensable weapon in the federal government's crusade against the CPUSA during the postwar Red Scare. In 1939 and 1940, it was simply one of many undemocratic bills under consideration by Congress.

Hearings on HR 5138 before a subcommittee of the House judiciary committee began four months before the signing of the Nazi-Soviet Pact, on April 12, 1939. No representative from the CPUSA testified personally against the bill. Among those who did speak against it were Osmond Fraenkel, general counsel for the ACLU, and Ralph Emerson, an anti-Communist and legislative representative of the Maritime Union, a CIO affiliate. The American Committee for the Protection of the Foreign Born, a Popular Front organization founded by Roger Baldwin, registered its opposition in writing. After debate and revisions, including removal of a provision for detention camps for aliens who were to be deported but whose home countries would or could not take them because of the wartime situation, the bill came before a subcommittee of the Senate Judiciary Committee a little over a week after Flynn's ACLU trial, on May 17, 1940. More debate ensued, but by this time, the bill was virtually unstoppable. It was reported to the Senate Judiciary Committee and then to the full Senate. A conference committee reconciled the House and Senate versions, and the bill went to the House floor for a final vote on June 22, 1940. The only member of the House of Representatives to speak against it on the House floor was Vito Marcantonio, American Labor Party congressman from New York, and head of the International Labor Defense.[9] The bill passed by a vote of 382 to 4. Thus, Congress enacted the first peacetime sedition law since the Alien and Sedition Acts of 1798.

HR 5138 required registration and fingerprinting of all adult noncitizen residents and made it a crime

- to speak, or to publish, edit, or circulate printed matter with the intent to impair or influence "the loyalty, morale, or discipline of the military or naval forces of the United States";
- to "advocate, abet, advise, or teach" the overthrow of the U.S. government by force; and
- to organize or be a member of a group devoted to such advocacy.[10]

Proponents of the Smith bill rationalized it as an effort to protect the United States from "fifth column" subversives, spies, and saboteurs. The phrase "fifth column" originated during the Spanish Civil War. General Emilio Mola, one of the leaders of the fascist coup that started the war, allegedly announced that while four columns of his troops marched toward Madrid, the city would fall to a fifth column (*quinta columna*) ready to strike from within. Mola used the term to describe his fascist supporters inside Madrid. The expression caught on to refer to an internal enemy that threatened to undermine the state, usually to benefit a foreign interest. A 1938 FBI report of a German spy ring based in New York and led by a Nazi agent, Guenther Gustav Rumrich, stoked fears of a Nazi "fifth column" in the United States, but Americans tagged Communists as well as fascists as a potential "fifth column" threat. The difficulty of defining fascism with any precision, Rebecca Hill points out, facilitated easy conflation with other "subversive" movements. Further confusing the matter, the president and his New Deal allies, along with their conservative opponents in Congress, used the labels "fascist" and "communist" to vilify one another as part of an un-American "fifth column."[11]

Vito Marcantonio continued to speak against the Smith Act after its passage.[12] As president of the International Labor Defense, he led an unsuccessful campaign to have the law repealed. The *Daily Worker* and the *New Masses* reported opposition to the bill by the ILD, the ACLU, the American Committee for the Protection of the Foreign Born, as well as Italian, Greek, and Spanish organizations that advocated for the rights of immigrants, and a number of social workers.[13] Communists also voiced their own criticisms of the bill in their publications. An article in the June 20, 1939, *Daily Worker* titled "An Un-American Bill" called it "one of the weirdest and most dangerous bills ever to face an American Congress." Of great concern was the bill's language, which was "so vague as to be a blanket warrant for seizure of anybody the Dies gang doesn't happen to like.... It would strangle political liberties."[14] Communist critics of the bill chose their language carefully to emphasize that the allegation of revolutionary intent was just that: an allegation, not a fact. As a July 1939 article in the *Daily Worker* put it, "The bill, with some original measures stricken out, now demands the deportation of all aliens who have been members, for no matter how short a time or how far in the past, of any group *allegedly* [emphasis mine] advocating the overthrow of the government by force."[15] Another *Daily Worker* article recast the party as a progressive, rather than revolutionary, organization akin to a labor union or fraternal organization: "This language [against organizing or helping to organize groups that advocate overthrow of the U.S. government] is so sweeping that it might be held to bar membership in the Communist Party or even in any number of labor and fraternal organizations with progressive aims."[16]

The general substance of the criticism—that the Smith Act was anti-labor, anti-immigrant, antithetical to civil liberties, a throwback to the eighteenth-century Alien and Sedition Acts, and un-American—remained consistent as the proposed legislation wended its way through Congress and landed on Roosevelt's desk.[17] Before the Nazi-Soviet Pact, Communists attacked the bill as a fascist measure. They heaped criticism on Senator Robert Rice Reynolds, a Democrat from North Carolina and a co-sponsor of the legislation, calling him "an open admirer of Nazi barbarism and an unofficial spokesman of Hitler in the Senate" who had smoothed the way to the bill's passage with xenophobic screeds on the radio.[18] Communists also warned that the provision for compulsory fingerprinting of immigrants made possible the deportation of antifascist refugees, some to certain death.[19] After the Nazi-Soviet Pact, the frame shifted to reflect the party's changed orientation to the war—from an antifascist struggle to an imperialist competition—and to President Roosevelt, whom they now depicted as a tool of Wall Street, bent on plunging the country into war for the sake of empire and capital. In January 1940, Gale Thorne, writing for the *New Masses*, illustrated the party's retreat from antifascist rhetoric in its criticism. Thorne predicted that Congress would enact the Smith bill "in the supercharged atmosphere which [had] tensed the country since France and England actively engaged in the European war."[20] In a May 28, 1940, article, the *Daily Worker* noted, "'Fifth Column' hysteria swept both houses of Congress today and included in its destructive sweep the civil liberties of the American people and the rights of organized labor as well as the welfare of the foreign born." Reflecting the party's recently developed antagonism toward Roosevelt, the paper claimed that unanimous approval by the Senate Judiciary Committee of the Smith bill (already passed by the House) was a "direct consequence of the President's 'national defense' program."[21]

Flynn undoubtedly shared her comrades' concerns about the Smith Act. Her experiences defending herself and other labor activists arrested and charged under the Espionage Act during and after World War I would have made her well aware of the feeding frenzy the new law would likely unleash against immigrant labor organizers and radical Left-based movements and organizations. In February 1941, Congress debated yet another troubling piece of legislation, HR 3, also known as the Hobbs "Concentration Camp" Bill. The bill reintroduced a provision that had been stripped from the Smith Act: the detention of deportable immigrants—without hearings or due process—who could not be returned to their home country because of international conditions.[22] In an article she wrote for the *New Masses* titled "Tom Paine Was an Alien Too," Flynn attacked the bill as a reversal of the nation's long tradition of political asylum: "What a shameful travesty on the great traditions of America—a haven for the oppressed, a political asylum. The Statue of Liberty symbolizes this."[23] The Hobbs Bill left immigrants who had come to the United States to escape Fascism in Europe vulnerable to deportation. Flynn pointed out the deleterious effect the bill would have on antifascist refugees who had been targeted for their politics and urged that they instead be treated as dignitaries: "Political asylum should be given gladly to people who come here 'illegally,' to escape fascist oppression. To plan a wholesale deportation of these people is cruel and inhuman. We should receive them as honored guests like Lafayette, Pulaski, Kosciusko, and VonSteuben."[24] The bill did not pass.

Flynn's opposition to the Hobbs Bill reveals the extent to which antifascism was in her bones. Although debate on the bill occurred during the "imperialist war" phase, she did not retreat from the rhetoric of antifascism in her criticism. Despite whatever pressure she might have felt to conform, she remained a steadfast and vocal ally of comrades threatened with deportation back to fascist countries.

Yet despite her long-standing commitment to civil liberties and to defending the rights of immigrants and refugees, there is no evidence that Flynn spoke out against the Smith Act during its congressional hearings; nor did she object when it was used to squash the party's Trotskyist rivals in 1941. The first Smith Act indictments targeted thirty-nine members of the Socialist Workers Party (SWP) in Minnesota, fifteen of whom also belonged to Teamsters Local 544. Included among them was James Cannon, whom Flynn knew from her Wobbly days and with whom she had worked in the ILD. The indictments stemmed from the SWP's outspoken opposition to the war, but also from rank-and-file opposition to Local 544's Trotskyist-dominated leadership.[25] As Donna Haverty-Stack has documented, informants within the Teamsters aided the FBI in its investigations of the SWP.[26]

During the trial and appeals process, the defense argued for application of the "clear and present danger" test to federal restrictions on free speech. The prosecution challenged this argument, claiming its mandate was merely to prove a conspiracy to advocate violent overthrow of the government. Their challenge prevailed, which set the bar for seditious speech pretty low. The case against the Trotskyists rested primarily on evidence from books and other print publications: Marxist classics and SWP pamphlets and periodicals, which were alleged to constitute proof of conspiracy to commit the crimes with which the defendants were charged.[27] The defendants seized an opportunity to provide their own take on these works and present their ideas to a larger public. Their propaganda strategy had mixed results. The jury found eighteen defendants guilty but recommended leniency in sentencing. The defendants received sentences of twelve to sixteen months; Grace Carlson, the only woman, served her time at the Alderson Federal Industrial Institute for Women, where, ironically, Flynn herself would be sent after her own Smith Act conviction a decade later.

The facile standard for proving seditious speech, the spurious nature of the evidence against the Trotskyists, the outcome of the trial, and the Supreme Court's refusal (three times!) to review the conviction of the eighteen should have raised alarms among Flynn and her comrades. They did not. Communists should also have been concerned that collusion between anti-Communist members of the Teamsters and the FBI had enabled the attack against the Trotskyists. They were not. Instead, articles in the *Daily Worker* accused the Trotskyists of using protests against the federal government's involvement in union affairs as a shield for their "disruptive and disreputable record in Local 544."[28]

Free Earl Browder!

Flynn spent much of the Nazi-Soviet Pact era working to get CPUSA General Secretary Earl Browder released from prison. The fight to free Browder, in many ways a classic labor defense campaign, was a familiar endeavor. Flynn had been doing this kind of work in one form or another since she was a teenager working alongside James Connolly to free imprisoned Western Federation of Miners leaders Moyer, Haywood, and Pettibone in 1907. Over three decades later, she drew on her years of experience and utilized her considerable talents as an organizer, speaker, writer, and fundraiser on behalf of Browder. She also brought name recognition and popularity in and outside the party to the campaign. In an interview conducted sometime in the early 1970s, Dorothy Healy, another of the few women to rise to a leadership position within the party, who enjoyed a warm relationship with Flynn, reflected on Flynn's unique position among party leaders and her popularity among workers.

> Elizabeth enjoyed a very positive reputation in the Party.... She moved directly into the top leadership. She didn't need to adopt that fierce demeanor that was required of other women who were battling their way up the top of the hierarchy. She was genuinely concerned about people in a way that most Party leaders were not.... She was very effective in the role of a public face for the Party, as well as a link with the historic past of the Wobblies, the "Bread and Roses" strike in Lawrence, and the free speech fight in Spokane. She had a remarkable ability to speak in plain language before a large audience and establish immediate rapport.[29]

Browder's case was one of several crises during which Flynn represented the party to its members and mainstream Americans. The case began in September 1939. While testifying before the Dies Committee, he admitted that in the past he had traveled with passports obtained under assumed names. To appease anti-Communists, Roosevelt had Browder arrested a month later. Authorities could not charge him for assuming a false identity because the statute of limitations had passed; instead, they indicted him for having failed to mention these earlier applications when he applied to renew his passport under his own name in 1937.[30] The court set bail at $10,000—a very high sum, given the relatively harmless nature of the charge against Browder. To make matters worse for Browder and his comrades, bonding companies refused to post bail for him, even though the party offered adequate security.[31] Browder's arrest raised an alarm among Communists who saw it as part of a campaign to destroy the party. For a while, it seemed as if they were right. Browder's indictment was followed by indictments against CPUSA Treasurer William Weiner and foreign editor of the *Daily Worker* Harry Gannes. Weiner was found guilty and sentenced to two years in prison, but his sentence was suspended due to a life-threatening heart ailment.[32] Gannes died of a brain tumor before his trial. The arrests did not end there. In fall 1939 and spring 1940, the Dies Committee raided offices of the party and Communist front organizations in Washington, D.C., Pittsburgh, Baltimore, and Philadelphia. In February 1940, FBI agents raided party offices in Detroit and Milwaukee and arrested twelve people for having signed up as volunteers for the Abraham Lincoln Brigade, but the case was dropped by Attorney General Robert Jackson after liberals protested.[33]

Political repression of Communists occurred at the state and local levels as well. In Alabama, suspected Communists were arrested without warrant, detained without charge, and subjected to interrogation and intimidation.[34] Communists in California and Iowa were arrested. The New York City Board of Elections cited minor technicalities to invalidate nominating petitions of four CP candidates for city council. Communist candidates were knocked off the ballot in Ohio and Illinois as well. In June 1940, the *Pittsburgh Press* doxed signers of a petition to get Communist candidates on the November ballot by publishing their names and addresses in the paper, subjecting them to harassment and loss of employment. Those whose names appeared were given the opportunity to recant or to claim their signatures had been illegally obtained, which many did out of fear. Thirty-one people were then tried for having illegally obtained signatures on petitions for Communist Party candidates.[35]

Fearful that the federal government was moving to outlaw the party—a not unfounded fear, as the French government had banned the French Communist Party soon after the signing of the Nazi-Soviet Pact—Communist leaders created a shadow organization and sent a number of members underground.[36] To their enemies, this tactic, like the about-face on Roosevelt and the "imperialist war" rhetoric that followed the Nazi-Soviet Pact, confirmed suspicions that the party was a secretive, duplicitous organization.[37]

Flynn was not among those chosen to go underground; had she been, it is unimaginable that she would have agreed to do so. Instead, during this moment of crisis, she remained openly, proudly, and, one might say, defiantly associated with the party—the public face of American Communism. She volunteered to fill Browder's speaking engagements when he was deplatformed while awaiting trial. She also took a leading role in the campaign to get Browder released from prison and to defend any other Communists targeted in this wave of repression. Together with Robert Minor, with whom she had worked on the campaign to free Sacco and Vanzetti in the 1920s, she co-chaired the Defense Committee for Civil Rights for Communists (DCCRC).[38]

Within twenty-four hours of its founding, the DCCRC raised over $2,000 for a bail fund. The initial response heartened Flynn, who said, "It shows that Americans won't be intimidated by this campaign of persecution. The reactionaries won't get away with their move to stop all bail for Communists."[39] Seeing that bonding companies refused to work with them, the committee's goal was to raise $100,000, most of it in the form of loans to the committee, enough money to defray legal defense expenses for any Communist who faced arrest.[40] Flynn herself made a $25 donation to the campaign, part of the balance of her son's pension from the International Workers Order (IWO), a Communist-affiliated mutual aid society, which she had used to pay his funeral expenses. Fred had not been a member of the CPUSA, his mother pointed out in the letter to co-chair Minor that accompanied her donation, but he "was so keenly interested in the safety of the labor movement" that he had been the first to move that his lodge of the IWO support Browder's bail fund. "I know of no better way to express my gratitude to MY Party," she wrote, "for its great kindness and sympathy to me during the period of his sickness and after his death than to make this wholly inadequate contribution to its defense, in his name." She also donated $10 to the defense fund of the Furriers Union as a token of her "deep appreciation that the last blood given to Fred was from a member of this union, Ludwig Schneider."[41]

Flynn's contributions illustrate the deep sense of community and solidarity she felt with fellow party members. As Jodi Dean explains, comrades share a relationship of solidarity borne of being on the same side of a political struggle: "Comrades are those you can count on. You share enough of a common ideology, enough of a commitment to common principles and goals, to do more than one-off actions. Together you can fight the long fight."[42] On the first anniversary of Fred's death, Flynn wrote a memorial for the *Daily Worker* in which she expressed her gratitude for the community that had carried her through her devastating loss: "In sorrowful memory of my dearly beloved son, Fred Flynn, who died one year ago on March 29th, 1940, and with grateful appreciation to all comrades and friends who comforted me then and sustain me now. To you, dear son, the night. To us, the fight. I will do my best for both of us, Fred."[43] Her words are those of a mother grieving for the loss of her child and a political activist drawing strength and sustenance from the bonds of comradeship.

Civil Rights for Communists

Defense work was indeed a long fight. In January 1940, Flynn wrote to her old friend Mary Heaton Vorse about the Browder campaign, "My present activities are like turning back the hands of the clock twenty years!"[44] Notwithstanding its familiar feeling, the DCCRC was a departure from the kind of labor defense work that Flynn had done in the 1910s and 1920s in two significant ways. Use of the phrase "civil rights" in the committee's name points to the first difference. Historically, radicals launched a labor defense campaign when they perceived a government entity had overreached and denied an activist's (or activists') rights—to free speech, press, assembly, counsel, or a fair trial—in an effort to tamp down working-class militancy. In pamphlets, flyers, and speeches, organizers typically framed the campaign as a defense of these constitutionally guaranteed rights for the accused. The phrase "civil liberties" became common in labor defense rhetoric after World War I. That the Workers' Defense Union was an affiliate of the Civil Liberties Bureau and, later, the ACLU, illustrates the close connection between labor defense and civil liberties work in the first decades of the twentieth century.

By the early 1930s, with the Scottsboro case, the language of defense campaigns had begun to shift. As they did with Sacco and Vanzetti, Communists claimed the young Black men were class-war prisoners, but in addition to claims about defending the civil liberties of the accused, Communists championed the cause of "civil rights" for Blacks. The shift reflected an awareness that, although all members of the working class suffered exploitation, some were also singled out for discrimination because of their membership in a reviled racialized minority group. This argument was a mainstay of propaganda for the Scottsboro defendants. According to the League of Struggle for Negro Rights (LSNR), organized by the CPUSA to work for self-determination for the Black Belt region of the South and headed by Langston Hughes, the Scottsboro case "lays bare the fact that the barbarous oppression of the Negroes is a link in the chain of American capitalist exploitation and plunder of the entire working class."[45] In 1933, according to Robin D. G. Kelley, Alabama Communists made the right of free speech and assembly "a campaign priority articulated as a basic right denied all working people."[46] The same year, the LSNR issued a pamphlet that contained a "Bill of Civil Rights for the Negro People: Against Discrimination by Reason of Nationality or Color, or of So-Called 'Race.'" The bill was presented by the "Free the Scottsboro Boys Marchers" to the U.S. president and Congress. It laid out a comprehensive list of demands, including voting rights; the right to serve on a jury; the right to education; desegregation of the U.S. military, transportation, hotels, restaurants, and cultural institutions; employment rights; housing rights; and the right to run for and hold elected office.[47] The league's aim was nothing less than immediate and "complete economic, social, and political equality" for Blacks.[48] With the advent of the Popular Front, Communists pulled back from the militant rhetoric of Black self-determination to concentrate on civil rights and employment discrimination as unifying issues in the Black community and a basis for common ground with white liberals.[49]

In the hostile climate of growing anti-Communism that followed the Nazi-Soviet Pact, Communists began to see themselves not only as champions of an economically exploited and—particularly in the case of Blacks—racially oppressed working class, but also as victims of political prejudice. Members of the party, they claimed, faced discrimination because they belonged to a hated political minority. This move dovetailed with the emergence of civil rights law in the 1940s.[50] It reflected the realization that capitalism was not confined to the purely economic realm. Rather, capitalism shaped culture by constituting race relations and shaped politics by circumscribing the field of permitted political activity. Thus whereas liberal interpretations of civil rights ultimately would focus exclusively on discrimination rooted in racial prejudice without considering the political economy of race relations, Communists had a more expansive view that acknowledged racism as a feature of capitalist society and also recognized the existence of political discrimination, especially against those whose politics involved a challenge to capitalism. These differing interpretations are yet another sign of the split between liberals and radicals that would continue to grow in subsequent decades.

Since World War I and her leadership of the Workers' Defense Union, Flynn had been calling for the United States to acknowledge the existence of political discrimination and to grant political prisoner status to those who suffered it because of their labor activism. She fought for this recognition for the most marginalized individuals even when she herself was not in any immediate danger. Now, in the context of growing anti-Communism, her embrace of the idea of civil rights for Communists was not simply a strategy for self-preservation but a continuation of the kind of work she had been doing since 1918. However, her conception of political minorities whose rights were wrongfully abridged by the state was not neutral. Fascists were excluded.

Flynn popularized the idea of civil rights for Communists in her speeches and writings. A December 1939 article that she published in the *Communist*, the party's theoretical magazine, is illustrative. Titled "Defend the Civil Rights of Communists," it warned that the party's very existence was at stake: "The Defense Committee for Civil Rights for Communists, consisting of Robert Minor and myself, are authorized to receive contributions for the defense of the legal existence of the Communist Party under the Bill of Rights."[51] Flynn chose her words judiciously. Calling attention to the constitutionality of the party, Flynn pushed back against the idea that Communism was a foreign ideology and affirmed the identity of Communists in the United States as legitimate political actors.

The Nazi-Soviet Pact framed Flynn's rhetoric on this issue. Communists were under attack because of their opposition to the "imperialist war," she claimed, and only the party could protect labor and the American people from a full-on attack by Wall Street. According to Flynn, Browder's indictment and subsequent deplatforming at Harvard and Princeton, the revival of criminal syndicalism laws, the arrest of Communists in Iowa, and other such developments were "evidences of an organized attack, which, if not checked now, will be directed, before long, against the democratic rights of labor and the entire people."[52] But Flynn did not always describe anti-Communism in such dire terms. She understood that relentless crisis rhetoric could leave people feeling overwhelmed and defeated and so she often used humor to raise spirits or strip adversaries of their power. This situation was no exception. When she addressed the subject of anonymous donations to the bail fund in the *Sunday Worker*, for example, her Irish wit was in evidence. "Many people do not care to give their names; others cannot afford to do so with Mr. Dies sniffing around and their jobs at stake. So our lists sound like the roll call of the Irish Sweepstake [a lottery established by the Irish Free State in 1930 to finance hospitals]! We have 'friends,' 'comrades,' and 'sympathizers' galore. We have John Jones and Tom Paine!"[53]

The second difference between the DCCRC and past labor defense campaigns that Flynn had led was the composition of the committee and the tone of the appeals. From 1918 to 1926, when she headed the Workers' Defense Union and worked closely with the Sacco-Vanzetti Defense Committee, Flynn successfully built coalitions among liberals and radicals of various ideological stripes. She brought together individuals from organizations across the liberal-left spectrum on committees and in conferences. She carefully avoided divisive political positions in speeches, pamphlets, and articles. Her goal was always to portray defendants in the most sympathetic light and build the widest possible base of support. Her ability to unite otherwise antagonistic individuals and organizations into a unified campaign to defend unjustly arrested labor activists made her a key figure in the liberal-radical alliance that was central to the civil liberties movement in the years after World War I. By the end of the 1930s, however, the steady rise of liberal anti-Communism and the Nazi-Soviet Pact had torn that alliance asunder. The DCCRC was run entirely by Communists, and its appeals were directed to party members.

Things got worse during the Nazi-Soviet Pact, when what had previously been a strength of Flynn's was no longer a viable approach. Where she once championed the cause of ideological diversity in a labor defense campaign, Flynn now depicted ideological uniformity as an asset. In an interview conducted by Art Shields for the *Daily Worker* while she was recovering at home from influenza, she noted approvingly that the Communist Party had raised every cent of the $56,000 currently in the bail fund: "All the publicity came from the *Daily Worker* and other Party papers. The workers and professional people who came into my office at 799 Broadway with loans of $100, $1,000, $50 and ten dollars got their inspiration from the *Daily Worker*."[54] In contrast, she recalled the ideological diversity of defense campaigns she worked on in the post–World War I years as a liability: "Defense committees used to get up fancy stationery embossed with the names of well-to-do liberals. Sometimes these liberals wanted to weaken our class appeal. Today there is no such pressure on our defense committee. It is directed by the Communist Party. The Communist Party set the committee up to defend its leaders and to give the class reasons behind the Department of Justice's attack on civil rights."[55] The article appeared a few weeks before the ACLU passed its Communazi resolution and five months before Flynn's expulsion from the ACLU Executive Board. Perhaps she was simply rationalizing a bad situation. But it is also possible she was expressing convictions born of the growing rift between herself and her erstwhile liberal allies.

While Browder awaited trial, Flynn spoke on civil rights and civil liberties for Communists, including at colleges and universities, such as

Swarthmore, City College of New York, Temple University, and Cornell.[56] Although her college and university appearances were not without controversy, her student audiences typically responded with enthusiasm. Years later, she was remembered as something of a legend for her ability to pack an auditorium with students and members of the local community, many of whom had heard her before and wanted to hear her again. "The Q and A was the best part," recalled Bob Lewis, president of the Young Communist League at Cornell in 1940 and 1941. "She was able to deal with any question asked." Lewis noted Flynn's wit, warmth, openness, and ability to socialize into the wee hours of the morning, usually outlasting her student hosts, as well as her irrepressible Irishness: "She taught us a lot of Irish liberation songs. She was sure Irish."[57]

Flynn accompanied Browder to the Federal Court in New York for his preliminary hearing on December 3, 1939. She recorded the event in a notebook and noted, in a passage she subsequently annotated and underlined in red ink, that Browder's court date coincided with the ACLU policy meeting that began the organization's anti-Communist stand.[58] Browder's trial opened in New York City on January 17, 1940. Five days later, the jury found him guilty and he received an unusually harsh sentence of four years in prison and a fine of $2,000.[59] Worse, months later, the DOJ moved to begin deportation hearings against Browder's wife Raissa, who was born in Russia but had become a U.S. citizen and had three American-born children with Browder.[60] The Immigration Department continued to harass her with the threat of deportation for over a decade, even when she was dying of cancer.

In late April 1940, just three weeks after she buried her son, Flynn attended a two-day civil rights conference in Washington, D.C., Also in attendance were delegates from a variety of organizations, including the League of Women Voters, American Newspaper Guild, League of Women Shoppers, and the Industrial Union Council.[61] In her speech at the conference, Flynn once again championed the cause of civil rights for Communists. She compared attacks against party members with repression of the IWW, the left wing of the Socialist Party, pacifists, and militant trade unionists during "the first imperialist war." In both cases, she argued, opposition to the war was the "causative factor." What made the present moment worse than the Palmer Raids were the subtle and insidious tactics deployed by the Dies Committee and the FBI—including decapitating the Communist Party, bleeding it dry financially, hamstringing its activities, and blacklisting its members in the industry. Never one to waste an opportunity to flay her opponents verbally, she attacked the

ACLU for its newfound "class consciousness," no doubt a thinly veiled reference to the controversy among board members over whether to support the sit-down strike and their divergent views of the Ford case with the NLRB, and she accused the group of becoming an "open shop" organization. When she finished, the audience responded with thunderous applause.[62] Conference attendees passed numerous resolutions to address discrimination against Blacks, immigrants, labor unions, and Communists. They condemned the antitrust prosecutions of trade unions, the antiunion and red-baiting activities of the ACLU, and the poll tax; demanded passage of the antilynching bill and a civil rights bill for Washington, D.C.; sought the abolition of the Dies Committee; and demanded that the DOJ cease colluding with state and local governments against "progressive Americans."[63]

Two months later, Flynn attended the Conference on Constitutional Liberties, held at the National Press Club Auditorium in Washington, D.C. She was one of the featured speakers on a panel, "Rights of Minority Groups." Also on the panel were Max Yergan, president of the National Negro Congress (successor to the League of Struggle for Negro Rights), and C. Fayette Taylor of the American Committee for Democracy and Intellectual Freedom, an antifascist organization of scientists founded by Franz Boas in 1938.[64] The conference launched the National Federation for Constitutional Liberties, an organization that fought for the protection of the rights of minority political parties and for civil rights for Blacks, labor activists, and Communists.[65] Flynn was neither an officer nor a member of the federation's executive committee, but that did not stop critics from seeing the newly formed organization as an attempt by Communists to compete with the ACLU as payback for having expelled her. Roger Baldwin dismissed such concerns among the ACLU's local affiliates, noting, "As a clearing-house for trade-union and left-wing groups active in civil liberties, the federation is performing a function quite different from that of the Civil Liberties Union."[66] In 1946, the National Federation merged with the International Labor Defense and the National Negro Congress to become the Civil Rights Congress. Anti-Communists at the state and federal level used the presence of Flynn, "a high ranking member of the National Committee of the Communist Party," at the federation's founding to prove that it was a Communist front organization.[67]

Browder's case came before the Supreme Court in January 1941. A month later, in *Browder v. United States*, the court unanimously upheld his conviction. He entered the Atlanta Federal Penitentiary on March 26, 1941. This time, Communists did not go underground. Instead, with an air of insouciance, they launched a recruitment drive to bring thousands of new members into the party in honor of Browder's birthday (May 20).[68] They also demanded that President Roosevelt release him. Flynn was unsparing in her criticism of "the squire of Hyde Park" as she referred to Roosevelt. In an article she wrote for Browder's birthday, she compared the U.S. president to Adolf Hitler, who had imprisoned Ernst Thaelmann, secretary of the Communist Party of Germany: "The pattern of Adolf Hitler has become a blueprint for American capitalism, as it became in France and under the same guise—preparing to fight Hitler."[69] She likened Browder to the iconic antiwar activist Eugene Debs but noted that whereas Wilson had Debs imprisoned for political speech, Roosevelt had Browder imprisoned on a technical charge (passport fraud) as cover for his real motive: to silence criticism of his plan to save American capitalism through war profiteering. Even as she criticized Roosevelt, Flynn displayed her unrelenting commitment to antifascism. She claimed that Browder's advocacy of socialism over capitalism made him a true antifascist because "fascism is the last foul spawn of capitalism."[70] Flynn correctly saw Browder's case as part of a growing campaign to narrow the range of acceptable political opinion in the United States: "The Communist Party," she observed, "is the acid test of the right of any minority party to challenge the Siamese-twin party system, which, Janus-faced, shouts for war today."[71]

And then, once again, everything changed. On June 21, 1941, Germany invaded the Soviet Union, thus nullifying the Nazi-Soviet Pact and bringing antifascism back to the visible center of Communist activism. Efforts to secure Browder's release took on a new urgency in the changed situation and the party's about-face on the war necessitated a new approach. On August 18, 1941, a headline in the *Daily Worker* announced the formation of the Citizens' Committee to Free Earl Browder. Tom Mooney chaired the committee; Elizabeth Gurley Flynn was its secretary. The two were legends in the field of labor defense and their leadership of the committee linked the campaign to free Browder with historic labor defense campaigns like those for Mooney himself; Moyer, Haywood, and Pettibone; Ettor and Giovannitti; Eugene Debs; and Sacco and Vanzetti. However, Mooney's role as committee chair was purely symbolic. He lived in San Francisco (the committee's headquarters were in New York) and was in very poor health from having served twenty-two years in prison. A month after the committee's formation, the two legends came together when Flynn traveled to Saint Luke's Hospital in San Francisco to "consult" with Mooney.[72] He died two months before Browder's release. After Mooney's death, Flynn pulled no punches when she described the

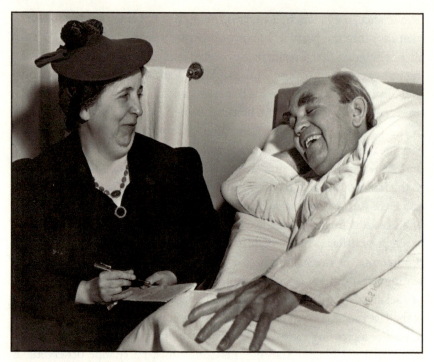

FIGURE 8. Elizabeth Gurley Flynn and Tom Mooney, 1941.
Credit: Courtesy Labor Archives and Research Center, San Francisco State University

herculean effort her longtime comrade had made to work on Browder's behalf, noting, "He came out from under an oxygen tent, after a major operation last summer, to accept the chairmanship."[73]

The campaign to free Earl Browder was now Flynn's major concern. Her comments on the formation of the Citizens' Committee exemplify how the party's changed orientation to the war manifested in the rhetoric of the campaign: "It is a sad state of affairs that in our present deadly struggle with Hitlerism, and when all that is beautiful and good and promising in life is at stake, America's pioneer antifascist should be kept behind prison bars."[74] To counter the image of Communists as agents of a foreign power, an essential task now that the fate of the Soviet Union was at stake, the committee represented Browder as quintessentially American. The pamphlet that Flynn wrote, *Earl Browder: The Man from Kansas*, could not have been more explicit: "If anyone is entitled to be called an American, it is Earl Browder. Oblong shaped Kansas is the central state of these United States. His birthplace, Wichita, comes pretty close to being the exact center of the country."[75]

The December 7, 1941, Japanese attack on Pearl Harbor, which made the United States and the Soviet Union allies in the struggle against fascism, further intensified efforts to secure Browder's release. The Browder committee organized a petition drive, collected statements from individuals, and encouraged resolutions from unions and other sympathetic organizations urging executive clemency. On December 19, 1941, Vito Marcantonio, along with committee members Louis Weinstock and William Albertson, presented the petitions, letters, and resolutions to Attorney General Francis Biddle, to no avail. Additional petitions, statements, and resolutions likewise failed. Communists would not be the ones to secure Browder's release.

Flynn possessed an extraordinary amount of energy, but the stress of her activist life and personal tragedy took its toll once again, as it had throughout her career, and she became seriously ill in the midst of the Browder campaign. The day after Pearl Harbor she was taken to New York's Beth Israel Hospital for surgery, her second operation in as many years (she had had surgery to remove a tumor in June 1940).[76] Three weeks later, she went to the Jersey Shore to recuperate from what she described as an illness that had left her "too weak for a life of activity." As she explained to readers of her *Daily Worker* column, "I carry out my major political assignment to get well and be able to get back to work again, by walking in the sun, resting, sleeping, eating, watching the breakers, and breathing deep of the ozone, of which there is plenty hereabouts."[77] Although she would not return to her normal level of activity until spring, Flynn took to the airwaves to make the case for Browder's release just four days after she published the *Daily Worker* column. She delivered radio addresses on the station WHOM for Lincoln's birthday (February 12), Washington's birthday (February 22), and one other occasion in March.[78]

With Josephine Truslow Adams, an artist and member of the Citizens Committee to Free Earl Browder, as an intermediary, Flynn requested an audience with Eleanor Roosevelt to plead Browder's case. The First Lady declined, noting that an appeal from Flynn would carry "no weight" because she was a Communist.[79] Flynn and Browder believed that Adams had privileged access to the president when in fact she had lied about her relationship with both Franklin and Eleanor Roosevelt. Even so, it is worth noting the contrast between Flynn's ability to secure a meeting with Woodrow Wilson's private secretary, Joseph Tumulty, to lobby (albeit unsuccessfully) for a stay of execution for imprisoned fellow Wobbly Joe Hill in 1915 and Eleanor Roosevelt's flat dismissal of her as a legitimate voice on behalf of fellow Communist Earl Browder because of her membership in the CPUSA.

When her strength returned, Flynn was back on the circuit advocating for Browder's release. In March 1942 alone, she spoke at rallies in Chicago, East St. Louis, Detroit, Cleveland, Washington, D.C., Boston, Newark, and Buffalo.[80] On March 28, she attended the National Free Browder Congress, attended by over 700 union members, as well as several elected officials, clergy, and academics. Among the organizations invited to send a representative to the Congress was the ACLU. John Haynes Holmes declined the invitation on behalf of the organization, but he noted that the ACLU would act "in its own way for the same end."[81] In fact, the ACLU had been actively working to secure executive clemency for Browder since at least September 1941. Members of the board saw no violation of civil liberties in the prosecution of Browder, but they did see political prejudice in the excessive sentence imposed upon him.[82] As Roger Baldwin observed to an unsympathetic Morris Ernst, Browder's sentence of four years—two years on each of two counts—"I assure you from a very careful examination of the records is the longest sentence for a similar offense in the entire history of passport cases."[83]

Baldwin appealed to the ACLU's membership for official and personal letters in support of Browder's application for executive clemency.[84] He believed the ACLU had "a serious responsibility" in the case because he and other members were the only ones who could handle "the delicate negotiations" required to secure Browder's release.[85] As part of those delicate negotiations, Baldwin, along with Holmes and Hays, wrote directly to President Roosevelt, urging "that no American citizen should be discriminated against for his political views whatever their character."[86] Baldwin also put pressure on Francis Biddle to raise the matter of clemency with Roosevelt.[87] In the past, Flynn would have acted as a liaison between the ACLU and the party in these behind-the-scenes negotiations to free Browder. Now the role fell to Robert Minor, whom Browder had appointed as his temporary replacement as head of the CPUSA.

May 20, 1942, Earl Browder's fifty-first birthday, was to be his second birthday in prison. His comrades planned to mark the occasion with a rally at Madison Square Garden featuring speeches by Flynn, W. E. B. Du Bois, Vito Marcantonio, Max Yergan, and others. They canceled the rally at the last minute when Roosevelt commuted Browder's sentence in the interest of "national unity" and he was released on May 16, 1942. Upon Browder's release, Flynn and Warren Billings, who had replaced Mooney as head of the Free Browder committee, issued the following statement: "This act of simple justice will meet with the approval of the overwhelming majority of the American people who will see in it a further step in the direction of strengthening our national unity for victory over the bestial fascist forces of Hitler and Hirohito."[88] It is debatable whether "the overwhelming majority of the American people" actually did approve of FDR's action. The Soviet Union's resolute stand against the German invasion, the United States' entry into the war, and Roosevelt's embrace of Stalin as a military ally made Browder's release a matter of political expedience. Although the collapse of the Nazi-Soviet Pact, which had officially reoriented Communists back to antifascism and support for Roosevelt, likely greased the wheels of sympathy for Browder it did not necessarily translate into sympathy for the CPUSA.[89]

After Browder's release, Flynn dedicated her prodigious energy to the war effort. As she had in the past, she saw the advance of fascism as a threat to the existence of the Soviet Union and to democracy itself, and she reveled in the U.S.–Soviet alliance. So did her comrades. Browder's birthday rally was rescheduled from May to a weeknight just before the Fourth of July to reaffirm the party's ties to American political traditions. Communists greeted their leader at Madison Square Garden with tears, cheers, applause, and a rousing rendition of the classic labor song "Solidarity Forever." Flynn sang "at the top of her voice."[90]

Allies in the Fight against Fascism

Now that the United States and the Soviet Union were allies in the fight against fascism (a development that Flynn surely greeted with a sigh of relief), Communists sought to reclaim some of the trust they had lost with the Nazi-Soviet Pact. An icon of the American labor movement and the party's most popular speaker, Flynn played a critical role in this effort. She traveled the circuit recruiting members and rallying support for the war. In speeches and articles for the *Daily Worker* she addressed her favorite audiences: coal miners and the Irish. She exhorted miners to vote against authorizing John L. Lewis, president of the United Mine Workers of America, to call a coal strike because it would cripple the war effort.[91] She called upon the Irish and Irish Americans to stand with the Allies against Hitler, despite their deep-seated animosity toward England.[92] The role suited her well and she performed it with verve.

In her efforts to rally support for the war, Flynn connected with working people. As she traveled around the country, she kept a diary in which she recorded brief vignettes of the men and women she met in various cities and towns. Among them were an ex-waiter from Philadelphia, now a soldier, who played in the choir at home and "hoped all the cathedrals in

Italy and Germany would not be bombed because he [wanted] so much to see them"; a plainly dressed, middle-aged woman with glasses "who stood at a counter in the 5 and 10¢ store in Pittsburgh and laboriously tested a youth on a world map, undoubtedly the places her son had written to her about"; two soldiers—privates—in a New York restaurant who "talked about poetry all the time during their meal"; and a Black miner in West Virginia who told her the following story about a Black woman going to work in the big house: "A white lady came out and waved to her, 'don't come up—we've got measles, diphtheria and chicken pox here!' 'Oh, that's all right,' the Negro woman said, 'we had all that down here last week!'"[93] She recorded the small details of her encounters with great care. For Flynn, "the working class" was not an abstract concept from Marxist theory but a community of human beings, each possessed of dignity and individuality and deserving of respect.

Working people connected with Flynn because she was interested in them, but also because they were interested in her. Unlike many other party leaders, she had practically grown up in the public eye, and her long years as an activist had made her a familiar figure. Moreover, because she was a woman, her personal life was considered fair game for public discussion. And she did not seem to mind. On the contrary, as previously illustrated, at times she deliberately blurred the public-private distinction to her advantage—when she faced imprisonment for violating the Espionage Act, for example. As a result, people knew about her family and the pivotal moments in her personal life: pregnancy, the birth of her son Fred, her failed marriage to Jack Jones, her passionate romance with Carlo Tresca, Fred's tragic death in the midst of her break with the ACLU. As she continued to mourn her son, the struggle against fascism seemed at times to deepen her sense of loss. She shared her feelings publicly. On the second anniversary of Fred's death, she wrote, "If my son were alive today I am sure he would be one of our American armed forces fighting for the freedom of the peoples of the world. It is an added sorrow to my loss of a friend, companion, and dear son, that an active valiant young fighter was so prematurely cut down in death."[94]

Just months after this painful anniversary Flynn suffered more personal tragedy. Her sister, Bina, with whom she had reunited after the betrayal of Bina's affair and child with Carlo Tresca, died of a longtime illness at age forty-four on December 10, 1942. January 1943 was an even crueler month. On January 10, a mobster killed Tresca on a Manhattan street corner. A week later, Flynn's father died in Boston. As tragedy often does, these losses drew Flynn closer to her surviving family members. She and her sister Kathie, a retired schoolteacher, and Kathie's daughter, Frances Onipede, moved from the Bronx to an apartment in Manhattan near Flynn's office, where they shared a loving and, according to Frances, "respectable" household.[95] As the proximity between home and office suggests, Flynn's personal life was never completely separate from her political work. In her diary from the 1940s, which is packed with descriptions of places she visited and people she met while recruiting for the party, she noted the personal significance of March 29: "This is always the saddest day in the year for me—the day I lost my dear son Fred. I'd give my life gladly to see him once again, to talk to him a little while. I try to work for both of us."[96] In 1945, as she faced another painful anniversary of Fred's death, Flynn published a memorial "in deepest sympathy with all other mothers whose sons have died that freedom may live."[97]

Women's Issues

Because she was a woman, party leaders frequently tasked Flynn with seeing to "women's issues." During the war, her energy was directed toward getting women behind the war effort and getting labor unions to be more inclusive of women and more attentive to the needs of women workers. She attended women's meetings and wrote numerous articles and pamphlets, including a popular *Daily Worker* column "Sister Kathie Says," in which she explored a variety of issues, including the bobbysoxer craze for Frank Sinatra, in the form of an often humorous dialogue with her younger sister.[98] In her study of women's activism in the CPUSA, Kate Weigand considers Flynn's wartime writings on women, along with articles in the *Daily Worker*, as "evidence for Communists continuing commitment to women's equality."[99]

As part of her efforts to enlist women in the struggle against fascism, Flynn consistently spoke and wrote about the unique forms of oppression and exploitation experienced by Black women and the dangers of Jim Crow to democracy.[100] That she did so is not surprising. She had been an outspoken ally of Black labor activists since World War I, and she had been calling attention to white supremacy as a type of American fascism since her attacks on the KKK in the early 1920s. Her involvement in the party and the friendships she made with Black Communists like Claudia Jones deepened her understanding of racism and her commitment to fighting against it. By the 1940s her understanding of the struggle for women's rights had matured to the point where she recognized that race as well as gender shaped women's experiences. A 1943 pamphlet she authored, *Women in the War*, is illustrative: "Eternal vigilance is the price of democracy. The best resolutions and declarations of principle must be put in practice or they are empty words, 'full of sound and fury—signifying nothing.' The doubly shameful and un-American discrimination against Negro women, as Negroes and as women, is widespread. It demands the most emphatic protest by women's organizations, by trade unions, and by government agencies."[101] Flynn saw clearly that racism and sexism were intertwined threats to democracy and impediments to the war effort.

> "Jim Crow" is a provocative agent of Hitler and Hirohito—whispering to people whose patience and long suffering quietude is nearing the breaking point, "You see—this is a 'white man's war'!" Lynchings, poll tax, frameups, enforced unemployment through discrimination segregation, insults are not good food for democracy. Race hatred cuts at the deepest roots of real Americanism, endangering our country. Our government and our unions must take a firm, uncompromising stand against "Jim Crow." Let us white women follow the admirable example set by the Ford Women's Auxiliary in fighting for the rights of our Negro sisters to work at all jobs and professions for equal pay. Every gate and door must be open for them. Help them cast aside the apron and cap of domestic service and put on the coveralls of the shop![102]

Her prescription for opening wartime industries and unions to full participation by women was comprehensive. She offered a list of "the vital needs of American women workers to help win the war":

1. Equal opportunity to work for all women (Negro and white) at all occupations.
2. Adequate training for jobs, under government and union supervision.
3. Equal pay for equal work.
4. Safe and sanitary shop conditions.
5. Equal membership, protection by, and participation in labor unions.
6. Childcare centers with federal funds and supervision.
7. Adequate modern housing.[103]

Sadly, more than eighty years after Flynn proposed this list, the items on it have yet to be realized for a significant number of working women.

The end of the war expanded the scope of Flynn's involvement in the struggle for women's rights in yet another way. In November 1945, she attended the founding meeting of the Women's International Democratic Federation (WIDF) in Paris. Although she had been an internationalist and actively supported global labor and anticolonial movements since her teenage years, it was her first trip outside North America. Founded by members of the PCF (French Communist Party) who had played a crucial role in the Resistance, the WIDF was an international women's rights organization dedicated to antifascism, world peace, child welfare, and the status of women.[104] It supported women's anticolonial struggles around the globe.[105] Flynn was named chair of the organization. At the Paris conference, she met a number of Communist women leaders: Marie-Claude Vaillant-Couturier, a survivor of the Auschwitz and Ravensbrück Nazi death camps one of the founders of the WIDF; Dolores Ibarruri (La Pasionaria), now secretary general of the Communist Party of Spain; Ana Pauker, unofficial head of the Romanian Communist Party and soon to become the world's first female foreign minister; and Nina Popova, head of the Antifascist Committee of Soviet Women.[106] What a thrill it must have been for her to meet these formidable female comrades and not to be the "exceptional" woman in a room filled with men. And what a thrill it must have been for them to meet Flynn. Her trip also included a brief sojourn in England, where she attended a session of the British Communist Party Congress.[107] The trip was momentous not simply because it was Flynn's first visit to Europe and because she was now directly involved in the international women's rights movement. She was also the first of several U.S. Communists to meet with comrades in other parties after the war.[108] The opinions exchanged at such meetings, according to Joseph Starobin, figured heavily in vital party decisions in the United States at a time of uncertainty for the international Communist movement.[109]

In addition to her position as chair of the WIDF, Flynn served on the national committee of its U.S. affiliate, the Congress of American Women (CAW). She also chaired the party's Women's Commission. Although the formation of these organizations indicated a growing awareness of the importance of women's issues, they carried little prestige among the male-dominated leadership of the party who still tended to view sexism as a personal matter best addressed through individual actions rather than a deep structural problem that required radical changes in social policy. Along with other white and Black Communist women, Flynn saw the fight against women's oppression in its myriad forms as an integral component of the larger struggle to overturn capitalism. Like many

Communist women, she resisted the "feminist" label because of its white, nationalist, bourgeois connotations.[110] Her heart was in the labor movement, and she did not want to be pigeonholed into working exclusively on "women's issues." As Annette Rubinstein observed, Flynn "wanted to work with miners."[111]

Reorganizing the CPUSA

The end of the war also entailed a significant and painful process of reorganization for the CPUSA, which had been initiated by Earl Browder in 1944. Buoyed by his interpretation of the December 1943 meeting of Stalin, Roosevelt, and Churchill at Teheran to coordinate military strategy against Germany and Japan and convinced that the postwar era would be one of continued friendly relations among the wartime allies, Browder sought to deepen and extend the party's commitment to Popular Front politics within a distinctly American context. Encouraged by Stalin's disbanding of the Comintern a year earlier, Browder reorganized the CPUSA and reconstituted it as the Communist Political Association (CPA), a nonrevolutionary organization that would seek cooperation with enlightened capitalists, liberals, and mainstream labor organizations and work within the two-party system (rather than run its own candidates) to support New Deal policies and ensure peace and prosperity.[112] As Fraser Ottanelli explains, Browder believed that Communists would be valued players in the U.S. political scene if they adapted the strategy that had worked so well for them in the late 1930s to the emerging postwar order.[113] One sign of his conviction that Communists would be respectable political actors was the disbanding of the Defense Committee for Civil Rights for Communists in January 1944.[114] Such a committee was deemed unnecessary in an environment in which Communists saw themselves not as a reviled minority but as valued political associates.

Flynn supported Browder and the CPA. In a February 1944 letter to him, she optimistically predicted that the announcement of the name change and formal adoption of the "new perspectives" would bolster the party's popularity and "increase tremendously" the number of new members.[115] Browder's rival, William Z. Foster, was critical of Browder's action, as were a few other comrades, but their criticism was muted because the founding of the CPA was assumed to have the support of Soviet Communists. This assumption proved false.

In April 1945, Jacques Duclos published an article in the French Communist theoretical journal *Cahiers du Communisme* in which he denounced the liquidation of the CPUSA. Stunned by this harsh criticism, several leaders of the U.S. party correctly interpreted the Duclos article as a directive from Moscow and sought to reverse course. Flynn remained supportive of Browder—as did Robert Minor, Roy Hudson, and Benjamin Davis.[116] As the controversy was heating up, she shared the stage with Browder at a CPA recruitment event in Cleveland Ohio—the last time he spoke to a public audience as a Communist in good standing.[117] But when he dug his heels in and refused to consider altering course, she joined others at a meeting of the CPA national committee in voting to revoke Browder's executive power and transfer it to a group headed by William Z. Foster. She leveled an attack on Browder and Minor in her speech at the meeting that was subsequently published in *Political Affairs*, the revamped and renamed magazine formerly known as *The Communist*. It was not the first time she demonstrated willingness to sever a relationship with a political ally when his ideas came under attack. In 1924, during the campaign to save Sacco and Vanzetti, she facilitated removal of longtime friend and ally Fred Moore from the legal team because his tactics had alienated the defendants and the Italian anarchists on the defense committee.

Flynn's speech against Browder is interesting for what it reveals—or conceals—about her self-perception as a leader. She admitted to having had "an inferiority complex" in her relationship with both Browder and Foster because she did not come up through the ranks of the party. She also admitted to having misunderstood the nature of Communist leadership as requiring complete acquiescence on account of her prior experience as a Wobbly agitator.

> I suppose this inferiority feeling was partly due to the fact that I came into the Communist movement late in life and late in my labor experience. All my background in the I.W.W. was different from the approach to work and the concepts of leadership in the Communist movement. I tried very hard to learn how to work as a Communist and how to work under this conception of leadership. I can tell you frankly it wasn't easy, because I went to Plenums where I was revolted by the repetition of acquiescence of everything Comrade Browder had said, in speeches prepared before he had made his speech, and I said to myself, "Elizabeth, there is just something wrong with you. After all, these comrades are all experienced, they have long years in the Communist movement, you were always engaged in struggles of a mass character as an agitator, and you are just not on the beam. You will have to learn to work this way. This is the proper attitude toward leadership."[118]

Was she dissembling when she claimed she did not challenge Browder on the CPA, despite reservations, because she did not think it was possible for a good party member to disagree? Perhaps. If so, it would not be the first time she bent the truth in service to a larger goal. In her 1918 letter to Woodrow Wilson seeking clemency after she had been arrested for violating the Espionage Act, Flynn dismissed her reputation as a labor agitator and antiwar radical, claiming instead that she was only acting as any good mother would act in a time of war. She also disavowed membership in the IWW, another false claim, in spirit if not in letter. By her own admission years later, she ceased to be a Wobbly only when she cast her first vote, for New York City mayoral candidate Fiorello LaGuardia, on November 2, 1937.[119]

As she spoke, Flynn continued to reflect on her insecurities as a party leader: "I cannot understand why I am never afraid to go out and talk to a group of miners or steelworkers or workers anywhere in the country, and why I was afraid of our own National Board and the National Committee." A factor that Flynn did not mention, but one that surely shaped her self-perception, whatever the veracity of her claims in this speech, is the tendency of her male comrades to underestimate her intelligence and political acumen. Despite her years of experience as a labor activist, her pioneering work in civil liberties, and her talent for establishing rapport with working people, other prominent party members regarded her as a lightweight. Joseph Starobin described her as "one of the most distinguished (though least sophisticated) Party leaders." Rosalyn Fraad Baxandall claims that most of the party's leadership did not take Flynn seriously as a leader because she was neither a theorist nor a bureaucrat: "Her talent and interest were not in directing or running organizations, but in organizing, agitating, and infusing others with militance."[120]

Flynn vowed to bring the same fearlessness she felt in front of working-class audiences into party meetings, should she be elected to the new national committee: "I promise you that there will never be another meeting of the National Committee that Elizabeth Gurley Flynn doesn't speak her mind on any subject either because she has differences or can make a contribution."[121] As it turned out, she was true to her word, at least as much as it was possible for any party leader to speak her mind. Fellow party member and Spanish Civil War veteran Steve Nelson recalled Flynn's flexibility—in comparison to the hardliners in party leadership positions—on matters of party policy, especially after World War II.[122]

Her public denunciation of Browder was not enough to atone for Flynn's sin in supporting the dissolution of the party in 1944. In preparation for the emergency convention to reestablish the CPUSA that was scheduled for the following month, she presented herself to a group of national committee members and trade union affiliates to demonstrate her bona fides. This "ritual cleansing" was undoubtedly humiliating, but because she was seen as having been a supporter of Browder, she had to perform it if she hoped to keep her position in the party. That she would subject herself to such treatment might be hard to understand, but Flynn's personal identity and social networks, as well as her political commitments, were tied up with being a member of the party. In this she was not unique. For a Communist, to be outside the party was to be nothing.

She passed the test, although she later expressed resentment.[123] When the convention met, she voted with the majority to dissolve the CPA, reconstitute the CPUSA, and install Foster as its head (Browder was the lone dissenting vote). At the same meeting, Flynn was elected to the national committee and national board (the new name for the political committee) of the reconstituted Communist Party of the United States. Minor, Hudson, and Ford were removed from leadership positions. Browder was expelled from the party at the meeting of the national committee in February 1946.[124]

The leadership of the party may not have appreciated Flynn, but those outside its ranks certainly did. As Communists attempted to find their footing yet again, Flynn's reputation as an icon of the U.S. labor movement and her rapport with working-class people made her once again the public face of the party. Now firmly in her fifties, she was no longer a precocious firebrand, but a stout woman of a certain age. Whereas her youth, beauty, and quick wit once disarmed critics, her grandmotherly appearance now rendered her innocuous in the eyes of some observers. One Nebraska newspaper called her a "plump, mild mannered woman."[125] Yet although the Rebel Girl was no longer a girl, she was still recognized by many as a leading figure on the Left, "one of the foremost women of the Party in this country."[126]

Flynn spent much of 1946 traveling to major industrial centers of the United States to recruit for the reconstituted CPUSA. She authored a pamphlet, *Meet the Communists*, in which she presented Communism as a global antifascist, anti-imperialist, anticapitalist, antimonopoly movement whose U.S. component was working to fend off challenges to the New Deal waged by big business with the complicity of the Truman administration. She included appeals to women, young people, military veterans, and Black Americans. Her aim was to dispel the notion that Communists were a foreign menace and present them as typical Americans: "Who are we—the Communists of America? We are Americans—native born and immigrants; we speak all languages; we are of all religions; of all colors; men and women; young and old. We are miners, steel, railroad, electrical, textile, office workers, trade unionists, farmers, veterans, professionals, housewives, students. We are a cross section of America—folks just like you. Communists are not hermits or highbrows—we like baseball, go to the movies, fish, work in the garden, relish a good Sunday dinner, like nice clothes, enjoy a joke, play with the children—are normal human beings."[127] This passage suggests that, despite her disavowal of him, Flynn was conflicted about what had happened to Browder. Even though she had publicly attacked him, she still held on to his ideas about the importance of defending the New Deal and the compatibility of Communism with Americanism. Had he still belonged to the party, Browder no doubt would have approved.

Meet the Communists was serialized in Flynn's *Daily Worker* column. She also wrote several articles that demystified the party for new members and other interested parties by describing its origins, leadership structure, the format of its meetings, and even its office space.[128] She was quite successful at signing up new members, and her talent did not go unnoticed by her comrades. As the recruitment campaign neared its conclusion and she focused her efforts on her hometown, the *Daily Worker* celebrated her as "an internationalist to the core, but a New Yorker nonetheless" and the party's "ace recruiter."[129] In addition to recruitment events, Flynn attended meetings of the CAW, as well as women's conferences and labor conferences in various locations.[130] The CPUSA had renewed its commitment to addressing the problem of racism, a commitment that had lagged during the Popular Front period and the war, and Flynn was deeply involved in this work as well.[131] She spoke out against police brutality and lynching, advocated for fair housing, sharing the stage with legendary folk singer Lead Belly at an event in Harlem.[132] In April, she attended the Civil Rights Congress in Washington, D.C. The gathering was organized by "patriotic Americans," as the *Daily Worker* described them, who were "tired of seeing democracy getting kicked around" by men such as John Rankin (D-Miss.), a vocal anti-Semite and anti-Black racist, who had proposed the amendment that made the House Committee on Un-American Activities a permanent body.[133]

Now that the war was over, Flynn was eager to return to her first love: labor agitation. In May 1946, she spoke at a meeting in Salt Lake City and remarked that her life as a free speech advocate had become "comparatively tame" when measured against her days with the IWW before

World War I: "Certain basic civil rights have become so well established by now that the battle need not be fought all over again every time one steps onto a lecture stand. After 40 years in the labor movement I can see signs of great progress." Among the signs she identified were the right to organize and the right of collective bargaining, both of which had been codified into law with passage of the NLRA in 1937. She saw the postwar upsurge in strikes as a "natural outgrowth" of the war: "It stands to reason that after so many unions kept their 'no strike' pledges during the war, we were due for a siege of labor troubles when postwar demands for better working conditions were not met." Flynn also assured her audience that the Communist Party was "much healthier" than it had been a year ago—with strongholds in New York, California, the Pacific Northwest, Illinois, and Michigan—and that the party was positioned to use its considerable leverage at the ballot box: "We now have candidates on the Arizona and Michigan ballots and hope to pull a strong minority vote in many other states, although we may swing to the support of a good labor man of either majority party in some instances."[134]

In July 1946, Flynn urged Communists to resume the storied tradition of soapbox speaking at open-air meetings on city streets, which had been so effective in the past, noting, "It is on the streets that we reach the people."[135] Two months later, for the observance of the twenty-seventh birthday of the CPUSA, she shared her reasons for being a party member in the *Sunday Worker*. Her article, "Why Am I a Communist?" presumably a question she was frequently asked, traced the origins of Flynn's politics to her childhood spent in "bleak poverty" among "proletarian communities" in the textile towns of New England and the South Bronx. The material conditions she observed and experienced firsthand instilled in her both a hatred of the rich and a desire to see poverty, misery, and worry abolished from the lives of workers. She became a Communist because the party, she said, "fulfills all the aspirations for socialism I dedicated myself to 40 years ago, which are now much nearer achievement. It is the party of the advance guard of the working class, whose freedom is its goal. It carries forward all the best militant traditions of the American labor movement."[136]

Here again, Flynn presented the party as an institution deeply rooted in U.S. labor history and, at the same time, part of an international working-class movement: "It is the champion of international working class solidarity, indispensable for peace and against international fascist reaction. It gives life a purpose—to build a free world."[137] To this formulation she added the idea of membership in the party as a vocation. Her optimism would shortly prove misplaced, but she had reason to feel positive at the time. External signs indicated that Communists were at the peak of their influence: Their speakers drew mass crowds to rallies and the party met its goal of recruiting twenty thousand new members.[138] Yet things were beginning to fall apart.

Red Scare Rising

Although she wanted to focus on labor agitation, forces beyond her control soon pulled Flynn back to defense work. Despite her optimistic predictions for the future, on March 11, 1947, Secretary of Labor Lewis Schwellenbach floated a proposal to outlaw the Communist Party. Predictably, his proposal provoked an outcry from Communists. The national committee immediately organized a drive for $250,000 to cover the expenses of a major public relations campaign consisting of newspaper advertisements, radio broadcasts, speeches, pamphlets, and letters that would pierce the "iron curtain" of media controlled by the Chamber of Commerce and the National Association of Manufacturers, whom they derided as "architects of an American form of fascism." The campaign was announced with a full-page ad in the *Daily Worker* that posed the question "WHAT IS DEMOCRACY WORTH TO YOU?" in boldface type.[139]

In addition to its appropriation of Winston Churchill's "iron curtain" phrase, which became a staple of anti-Communist rhetoric almost immediately after he uttered the words in a March 1946 speech, the ad called upon Communists and their allies to defend the Constitution from the "clear and present danger" posed by Schwellenbach's plan, the same language used by Supreme Court Justice Oliver Wendell Holmes in *Schenck v. the United States* to determine in what circumstances limits can be placed upon free speech.[140] Benjamin Davis and Pete Cacchione co-chaired the fund. Elizabeth Gurley Flynn was treasurer. In the next day's *Daily Worker* Flynn expressed her determination to fight back against red-baiting and she invited readers to do the same: "We Communists will fight for our Party. We will never give up or give in. Let every Party member show the enemies of democracy our devotion to our Party in piling up this fund. In fighting for our Party, we fight against the first open step of our country into fascism. We expect and welcome support from all non-Communists who are anti-fascists and defenders of the Bill of Rights."[141]

Over the next several days donors to the fund sent Flynn their answers to the question "What is democracy worth to you?" along with their contributions. Their responses illustrate the personal connection that people felt with Flynn as well as their various reasons for supporting the party.

Among those who responded were two older women from Connecticut who pledged to sell their war bonds and send the money to Flynn: "You ask what is democracy worth to us? What was it worth to our founding fathers? They pledged, their lives, their fortunes, their sacred honor." A Black worker who donated twelve dollars responded, "As a Negro interested in the broadening of democracy to include my people, I feel that any attempt to outlaw the Communist Party would jeopardize our struggle for national liberation."[142] The Fighting Fund, as it was called, received just shy of $125,000 in contributions in one week. By April 6 the fund had exceeded its goal.[143]

Despite an intense public relations effort on the part of Communists, the hits did not stop coming. Shortly after Schwellenbach made his proposal, President Truman issued Executive Order 9383, which required a loyalty oath of all civil service employees. The order also authorized the establishment of a Loyalty Review Board (LRB) with the power to advise all federal agencies in making loyalty determinations. On what basis would the LRB make its determinations? From the listing of subversive organizations the DOJ was directed to provide the LRB and that the LRB would disseminate to all departments and agencies.[144] At the same time, Senator Robert Taft (R-Ohio) and Representative Fred Hartley (R-N.J.) introduced legislation that would significantly reverse the gains labor had made under the NLRA. Among other things, the Taft-Hartley Act authorized "right-to-work" laws, made it easier for employers to union bust during an organizing drive, and banned secondary strikes. Most troubling for Communists was Section 9H, which required unions that wished to utilize National Labor Relations Board procedures for determining a collective bargaining unit to file non-Communist affidavits. Truman vetoed the Taft-Hartley Act on grounds that it would involve the federal government in matters where it did not belong and erode relations between employers and employees, but Congress overrode his veto.[145]

Toward the end of November Communists held another Civil Rights Congress, this time at Hull House in Chicago, with the expressed aim of revoking the loyalty oath for federal employees and abolishing the House Committee on Un-American Activities chaired by J. Parnell Thomas (R-N.J.). Under Thomas's leadership, the committee had summoned suspected Communists working in the Hollywood film industry to appear for questioning. Ten of the witnesses refused to answer the committee's questions, an act of defiance for which the "Hollywood Ten," as they became known, were charged with contempt of Congress and blacklisted from the industry.[146] The 336 delegates who attended the meeting also pledged to work for laws against lynching, the poll tax, racial discrimination and segregation, and anti-Semitism, and to protect immigrants and cooperate with labor for the repeal of Taft-Hartley. Introduced as "a representative of the most persecuted Party," Flynn denounced attacks upon Communists as antidemocratic and antilabor: "It is under the Hitler techniques of red baiting that the attacks against labor and the political rights of the people generally are carried out," she said.[147] In her report on the gathering, she endorsed the determined vision of Harry Ward, honorary chair of the Civil Rights Congress, who proclaimed "This is the Stalingrad of American freedom. From here we will not retreat a single inch further but will advance to hurl the enemy to defeat."[148]

At first, it appeared that labor unions were united in refusing to sign Taft-Hartley affidavits. By autumn 1947, however, they capitulated to Section 9H, thus formally endorsing anti-Communism within the labor movement. The expulsion of eleven Communist-led unions from the CIO that resulted from Taft-Hartley severed the party's most important institutional connection with workers. Things turned from bad to worse in 1948, when Communists supported Henry Wallace's presidential campaign on a third-party line. Flynn had predicted a positive outcome. "Leap year 1948 is off to a good start," she observed in her *Daily Worker* column, "with Henry Wallace saying 'yes' to the American people, in announcing Monday from Chicago, 'I shall run as an independent candidate for President of the US in 1948.'"[149] She could not have been more mistaken. Forced to choose between throwing their support behind the newly formed Progressive Party and FDR's former vice president or continuing to support Truman, who had vetoed Taft-Hartley, and the Democratic Party—in other words, choosing between the CPUSA and their respective unions—many Communist union members opted for the latter. The decision to back Wallace also cost Communists the support of liberals, many of whom they had lost with the announcement of the Nazi-Soviet Pact and worked hard to win back during the war. The weakening of ties with union members and loss of support from liberals combined with the Progressive Party's defeat showed the folly of this strategy and left Communists further isolated, their reputation for exceptional political acumen in tatters.[150]

Flynn's response to these developments was, as always, to continue fighting the good fight. In 1947 alone, with the exception of February when she was sick with bronchitis, she spoke in Massachusetts, New Hampshire, Connecticut, Rhode Island, Pennsylvania, Ohio, Wisconsin, Minnesota, Michigan, West Virginia, North Carolina, and all around New York City to raise money for the Fighting Fund and recruit new members for the party. She also went to Washington, D.C., to testify along with Benjamin Davis on behalf of Gerhardt Eisler, a German Communist who was arrested and charged with misrepresenting his Communist affiliation on his immigration application.[151] In her *Daily Worker* column, she railed against the DOJ's list of subversive organizations and urged readers to petition Congress to abolish the House Committee on Un-American Activities.[152] According to Flynn, the current uptick in political repression was comparable to the first Red Scare. As it did in the post–World War I era, she predicted that a working-class alliance would soon emerge "to defend the Constitution and the Bill of Rights for all" thus enabling Communists to triumph over their adversaries.[153] In a display of confidence that was as admirable as it would turn out to be unfounded, especially after the Wallace debacle, she claimed, "The forces of reaction are weaker today than they were then ... because the forces of the progressive people are far stronger today."[154]

In August 1947, while Flynn waited to address an audience of workers at the Winchester Arms Factory in New Haven Connecticut, the song "Which Side Are You On" played over a speaker that had been set up by her comrades. Another speaker on top of the building that had been installed by the company blasted discordant music to drown out the song and Flynn's speech. Flynn wrote about the incident for the *Daily Worker* and noted that she had been unperturbed by the sonic interference. On the contrary, she insisted the event was a success because she had connected with Black and white members of the audience: "I felt very happy. We belong—we Communists. Down on the ground, in and outside the factory, among the tired, hot, sweaty workers, pouring out for a few minutes respite, we belong. We speak their language. We know their needs. They will listen to us." She was confident that in the struggle for working-class loyalty, Communists would prevail.[155]

The New Haven incident was one of many efforts to shut down Communist meetings. For over forty years Flynn had dealt with efforts to silence her, and she was not cowed.[156] However, her resilience would soon be put severely to the test. On January 19, 1948, Claudia Jones—an immigrant from Trinidad, member of the National Committee of the Communist Party, and executive secretary of the Women's Commission—was arrested, charged with plotting to overthrow the government, and held for deportation. The arrest of Jones, whom she called "my closest co-worker," aroused Flynn's indignation. She had defended many people targeted by the federal government for repression, but no incident evoked as visceral an emotional response from her as this one.

Flynn lambasted Truman for "spouting windy phrases on the civil rights of Negro people" while turning a blind eye to the assault on Claudia Jones and compared the case with the "deportations delirium" of the 1920s. Jones's health (she had contracted tuberculosis when she was sixteen years old) and complete unfamiliarity with the country to which she would be returned were particular causes of concern for Flynn, and she deplored that her comrade had been targeted: "I have known of many deportation cases in the last 40 years, but this time the Department of Justice has struck an all-time immoral low."[157] At a meeting in Harlem Flynn pledged to the assembled audience that her comrades would fight for Jones's release: "I promise you that the Communist Party will give Claudia Jones its maximum support."[158] True to her word, Flynn published in the *Daily Worker*, organized and addressed meetings, and spoke on the radio to advocate for her young comrade's defense.[159] Jones was eventually released.

Flynn's commitment to the struggle for racial equality was used as a weapon by anti-Communists. In July 1948 she, Henry Winston, and Alexander Bittelman, respectively secretaries of the National Negro Commission and the Jewish Commission of the Communist Party, were criticized for deliberately fostering tension between and among racial groups. The criticism came from Rabbi Benjamin Schultz, executive director of the American Jewish League Against Communism, who wrote a letter to President Truman asking him to investigate the activities of the three.[160]

The most crippling blow, however, had come earlier in the month. On July 20, 1948, twelve leaders of the Communist Party, including Chairman William Z. Foster and General Secretary Eugene Dennis, were arrested and charged under the Smith Act. As she had many times before, Flynn moved quickly to head the defense committee. The second postwar Red Scare was in full throttle, and she was once again leading the fight against political repression and suppression of civil liberties. However, whereas during the previous Red Scare she could call upon a wide network of allies in and out of government, in this fight Communists were largely on their own.

CHAPTER 6

The Smith Act Trials of Communists in New York

> My body can be incarcerated, but my thoughts will be free.
> —Elizabeth Gurley Flynn

NINETEEN FORTY-EIGHT WAS not a good year for Communists in the United States. The year began with an effort by James B. Maloney of the Veterans of Foreign Wars (VFW) to ban Crown Heights (Brooklyn) Communists from using a school building to hold a meeting at which Elizabeth Gurley Flynn and others were to speak against the Truman Doctrine and the Marshall Plan.[1] On the surface, there was nothing unusual about this particular event. In most of her speeches during the early postwar period, Flynn had been sharply critical of U.S. foreign policy and castigated Truman for risking war with the Soviet Union to protect and promote the interests of American capitalists.[2] As tensions between the United States and the Soviet Union mounted, however, so too did efforts to restrict the First Amendment rights of Communists.

In September 1947, three months after the announcement of the Marshall Plan, representatives of the CPSU and the parties of several European states met and formed the Communist Information Bureau (Cominform) to coordinate strategy in response to Truman's latest initiative, which they attacked as an attempt to use material resources to extend U.S. political influence in Western Europe. Formation of the Cominform made it easier for U.S. anti-Communists to characterize members of the CPUSA as tools of the Russians and enemies, not just of the state, but of civil society as well. Maloney did just that in Brooklyn, accusing Crown Heights Communists of being under the control of Soviet Communists and of advocating force and violence, as well as free love and the destruction of the family.

In its petition to the court, the CPUSA denied Maloney's allegation that it was affiliated with the CPSU and affirmed its status as a legal political entity that did not advocate force and violence. Maloney's effort failed, but not because Judge L. Barron Hill was sympathetic to the party. On the contrary, he had a decidedly negative view of Communists, but he was not convinced they posed a danger serious enough to warrant curtailment of their First Amendment rights. In his ruling, which upheld the Board of Education's legal right to grant a permit to Communists for use of a building, Hill referred to Communism as "the cancer of our body politic" that could not be "cured" by restricting access to public meeting spaces.[3]

Although she decried Judge Hill's red-baiting comments, Flynn, with her characteristic optimism, saw the incident as a victory for the party, which it was, in a way. In a *Daily Worker* column titled "Crown Heights Wins a Free Speech Fight," she wrote, "The publicity brought many strangers who for the first time saw Communists in the flesh, heard their views, and were able to judge for themselves their validity. They appeared well impressed. Congratulations to Crown Heights on a good job well done."[4] Flynn's claim that non-Communists in the Crown Heights audience were "well impressed" now appears misplaced optimism, but we can excuse her for that error. She was a leading figure in a political organization at the peak of its postwar power in terms of membership and influence within the labor movement. Moreover, the key role that the Soviet Union had played in defeating fascism and the postwar dynamism of European communist parties—the very things that stoked fears of a Soviet takeover among anti-Communists in the United States—certainly made her feel like she was part of a powerful global movement that heralded an era of international working-class solidarity and the ultimate triumph of socialism over capitalism. In short, her personal inclination and position within the party did not allow her to see or admit that the success of the Crown Heights "free speech fight" was less a victory for the CPUSA than a portent of repression to come.

The Noose Tightens

As 1948 continued, events outside the United States had implications for Flynn and her comrades that would be increasingly difficult to shrug off. In February, Communists seized power in Czechoslovakia. That same month, Flynn made a speaking tour that took her to Florida. When she stopped in Miami to make an appeal for funds for the defense of Claudia

Jones and two other comrades who faced possible deportation, Alexander Bittelman and John Williamson, she was besieged by reporters. "It was all very like a silly movie," she observed in her *Daily Worker* column, written from Chicago, another stop on her trip. "Newsboys shouted out on the streets 'Communists Take Over Miami Beach.' A 15-minute radio account of our meeting was picked up later by Walter Winchell to vent his spleen on a local labor leader he claimed was at the meeting, and who was not present."

But there was nothing silly about what happened, and Flynn knew it. She described trying to distract photographers so they did not take pictures of locals who came to her talks for fear that they would be blacklisted and lose their jobs. She also described how anti-Communists in the national Transport Workers Union (TWU) demanded that local leader Charles Smolikoff be expelled for having had coffee with her—sending international TWU President Mike Quill from New York to Miami to investigate the matter—and how hooded Klansmen had terrorized Smolikoff's wife and children.[5]

As usual, efforts to intimidate Flynn were ineffective. She continued to travel and speak for the defense of Jones, Bittelman, and Williamson. She also advocated for Rosa Lee Ingram, a Black woman in Georgia who, along with two of her children, faced execution for killing a white man in self-defense while he was raping her.[6] And she did the same for Constance Harmon, a Camden, New Jersey, Black woman whose husband, James, was arrested, held incommunicado for twenty-five days, and died while in police custody, all without explanation. Flynn used the Harmon case as an opportunity to accuse Truman and Eleanor Roosevelt of hypocrisy: "Page Mr. Truman and his Civil Rights Committee. What about 'force and violence?' Page Mrs. Roosevelt and her Human Rights Committee of the UN. Mrs. Constance Harmon wants to know: 'What happened to my husband?'" She also seized an opportunity to puncture Northern superiority about racism, writing, "It's Camden, Georgia, Mississippi, Harlem—there is no Mason and Dixon line on violence."[7]

Flynn was not merely playing politics with these cases. She was deeply invested in the fight for Black liberation; indeed, she considered it one of her most important commitments. It was, in part, an expression of her Irish American identity. Throughout her career, Flynn professed admiration for the Irish men and women who struggled to liberate their nation from England's imperial rule and build a more just society along socialist principles. In a 1948 *Daily Worker* column that she wrote for St. Patrick's Day Flynn reflected on her ethnic identity. "One is not responsible for being of any group, therefore one claims no personal credit. But I am proud of my heritage, the fighting traditions of my rebel ancestors and the freedom-loving spirit they expressed in their native land." She also praised Irish Americans who had contributed to the American Revolution, the Civil War, westward expansion, and building the U.S. labor movement while she heaped scorn on xenophobic and red-baiting Irish Americans, whom she labeled "crass vulgar careerists" and "ignoramuses."[8]

Flynn believed that the painful history of the Irish and Irish Americans should suffuse members of her ethnic group with empathy for the sufferings of others: "Irish Americans should naturally be progressive, should never be guilty of race prejudice or political baiting, from which their forebears in Ireland and their immigrant parents suffered so deeply." Her antiracist politics were not only a product of her ethnic identity; they also stemmed from the political movement to which she had dedicated herself. "We Irish-Americans, who are Communists," she wrote, "feel confident that we are truly carrying forward the historical traditions of the Irish."[9] To be Irish American, in other words, was not enough. One had to be an Irish American *and* a Communist to embody the true spirit of the Irish freedom struggle. Whatever their ethnicity, however, Flynn insisted that all Communists should dedicate themselves to the struggle for Black liberation: "Let us never fail to keep faith with the Negro people—on big or small issues. It is one of our major responsibilities as Communists in the USA—land of Jim Crow and 'force and violence' against Negroes."[10]

Throughout the spring, developments in Eastern Europe—most notably, rising tensions between Stalin and Josip Broz Tito, president of Yugoslavia, which resulted in the expulsion of Yugoslavia from the Cominform in June 1948—heightened perceptions in the United States that the Soviet Union was bent on global domination and muted arguments from anyone outside the CPUSA that American imperialism was driving the Cold War. As this drama unfolded, a proposed law to facilitate surveillance of the CPUSA made its way through the U.S. Congress. Described as an effort to combat "a world communist movement" that aimed "to establish a communist totalitarian dictatorship in all the countries of the world through the medium of a single world-wide communist political organization," the Subversive Activities Control Act—popularly known as the Mundt-Nixon Bill after its principal sponsors, Representatives Karl E. Mundt (R-S.D.) and Richard Nixon (R-Calif.)—would have required all members of the CPUSA and their alleged front organizations to register with the attorney general.

On May 19, 1948, the bill passed the House—despite opposition from Vito Marcantonio—by a vote of 319–58. At hearings held by the Senate Judiciary Committee days later, William Z. Foster, Paul Robeson, and Henry Wallace spoke against the bill. While the bill was being debated, Communists distributed leaflets warning of its dire implications.[11] Communist women conducted letter-writing campaigns and held demonstrations against Mundt-Nixon. Flynn reported that one group of Bronx Communist women registered their opposition with a "baby carriage parade."[12] On June 2, as many as five thousand people marched in Washington to protest Mundt-Nixon and press for civil rights legislation; the next evening, Paul Robeson and others spoke against the bill before a crowd of 1,000 people at the Manhattan Center in New York.[13]

Flynn proffered her own criticism of the Mundt-Nixon Bill in her *Daily Worker* column. Her comments were vehement and visceral: "It is the death of democracy. Fascism will not come in America through a man on horseback dramatically riding down Pennsylvania Ave., although they have their generals ready, too." Instead, the Mundt-Nixon Bill "would legalize Hitler's 'Big Lie' by declaring by law what cannot be proved in any court of law by evidence—that Communists are 'a criminal conspiracy.' This bill is not just another step towards Fascism. This is it, the last step into Fascism."[14] If passed, Flynn argued, the bill would kill advocacy for all progressive causes "such as all democratic rights for labor and the Negro people," under the banner of anti-Communism. She urged an alliance of Communists and liberal anti-Communists in defense of constitutional liberties "unless the latter are willing to destroy their own rights in order to deprive Communists of theirs."[15] Her comments illustrate the "fascism is coming" mentality of postwar Communists, and although we may be tempted to dismiss the reaction as excessive (which, in part, it was), we should not dismiss the grain of powerful truth that Flynn expressed: Anti-Communism *did* (and still does) provide cover for efforts to squelch working-class political movements.

The Mundt-Nixon Bill eventually died in the Senate. Meanwhile, the impulse to destroy the Communist Party remained very much alive—and popular. On June 2, 1948, Mundt, who had made a bid for the Senate seat in his district, handily won his primary. Nixon, who had cross-filed as a candidate in his district, won both major party primaries. The two men would go on to win seats in the Senate and House, respectively, by a substantial margin in the general election.

First-String Smith Act Indictments

In the midst of the campaign season on July 20, 1948, a week after Democrats had nominated Harry Truman and right before the convention at which the Progressive Party would nominate Henry Wallace, twelve FBI agents burst into CPUSA headquarters in New York City and arrested five party leaders: William Z. Foster, Eugene Dennis, John Williamson, Henry Winston, and Jack Stachel. Soon after, federal agents arrested Benjamin J. Davis Jr., Carl Winter, John Gates, Irving Potash, Robert G. Thompson, Gil Green, and Gus Hall. Flynn, who had been elected to the party's national committee after the initial FBI roundup, was the only Communist leader not arrested. Indictments in *The United States of America v. Eugene Dennis, et al.*, or the Dennis case as it came to be called, charged the defendants with having violated the Smith Act. Looking back on the case, Flynn observed with humor and not a little bit of sarcasm, "As the only woman member of the Board I felt quite embarrassed and at a loss to explain why I was not arrested with my co-workers. I felt discriminated against by Uncle Sam!"[16] She would soon discover a reason why she had not been included among the group. In the meantime, as she always did when the civil liberties of comrades were under attack, she sprang into action.

The arrests pulled Flynn back into defense work. Throughout the pretrial period and the ten-month duration of the trial, she stressed four themes about the Dennis case:

- Trying Communists as criminals was a politically motivated tactic designed to tamp down working-class discontent.
- Communists were exemplary Americans—advocates for, not enemies of, the people.
- The real enemies of the people were greedy capitalists.
- Persecution of Communists posed a mortal danger to civil liberties and was a harbinger of Fascism.

In her first *Daily Worker* column about the case, published between the two series of arrests, Flynn came out swinging. The indictments had not taken party leaders by surprise, she noted, and Communists would not surrender without a fight. For younger comrades who might not have knowledge of how political repression worked in the United States, she put the current campaign in historical context: "Such charges usually happen during great labor struggles or in a war atmosphere, which is certainly thickening rapidly in our country." Flynn noted how in the heated atmosphere of World War I, "Socialist Party leaders, Debs, Kate Richards O'Hare, Victor Berger, were similarly charged under the Espionage Act of 1917. Over 100 IWW leaders and organizers, engaged in an eight-hour campaign, were similarly tried before Judge Landis in Chicago, in 1918." She urged workers not to panic at "the legalistic sound of this frame-up charge," which was no more truthful than past efforts to frame Tom Mooney, Bill Haywood, or Sacco and Vanzetti.[17]

Like the federal government's effort to destroy the IWW thirty years earlier, the Smith Act indictments relied on conspiracy doctrine, which meant that party leaders were not charged with having committed an overt unlawful act. Instead, the indictment charged party leaders with having conspired to overthrow the government by force and violence when they disbanded the Communist Political Association and reconstituted the CPUSA in 1945. If convicted, the defendants faced prison terms of ten years (the law was later amended to stipulate a prison term of five years) and $10,000 fines. "The indictment covers only the period from April 1, 1945," Flynn noted sardonically in the *Daily Worker*. "Contradictorily, the inference is that we were lawful for 26 years from 1919 to 1945." She insisted that ordinary Americans would easily see by its timing (the summer of an election year) and the lack of specific charges ("it is all in the realm of political ideas and organization") that the case was a political, rather than criminal, matter. Flynn exuded certainty in the *Daily Worker* that any present attempt to outlaw the advocacy of socialism would be no more successful than past attempts to outlaw the theory that the earth is round and orbits the sun. At the same time, she warned of dire consequences should the prosecution succeed in nullifying the civil liberties of Communists: "We want no martyrs. We must fight to vindicate our rights to advocate views, or the darkness of fascism falls on our country."[18]

Flynn was right about the Smith Act indictments against Communist leaders being politically motivated, just not in the way she imagined. Originally, she suggested the indictments were staged as part of an electoral campaign strategy. In their platform, adopted a week before the arrests, Democrats had attempted to frame the party and Truman as vigorously ferreting out subversives while simultaneously protecting civil liberties—a delicate balancing act, to say the least.[19] After Truman won the election, the trial was not called off and Flynn realized the Smith Act prosecutions were not simply political theater staged by Democrats to ensure a Truman victory, but she still insisted the president was behind them.[20] As Ellen Schrecker has noted, however, there is no evidence that

Truman was consulted while J. Edgar Hoover and his minions at the FBI prepared their case. The Smith Act trial was theater on a much grander scale and Hoover, not Truman, directed the show.²¹

Before the end of World War II, Hoover had decided to take the Communist Party to court. The tactic was part of a larger strategy to "prove" that Communism posed an existential threat to U.S. national security so great that it necessitated denying Communists protections normally afforded by the Constitution. Thus freed from the constraints of civil liberties, FBI leaders and zealous anti-Communist politicians could surveil, harass, and prosecute members, ex-members, and alleged members of the party with minimal cause or justification. In other words, the Smith Act indictments were a key component of Hoover's plan to destroy the Communist Party and the Communist movement in the United States.²²

Although repression of Communists was popular, the indictments were not met with universal acclaim. The last of their remaining liberal allies had largely deserted them because of the Progressive Party debacle, but several organizations, most of them Communist controlled, along with a few prominent individuals outside the party, voiced opposition. Among those who did were the Civil Rights Congress, National Lawyers Guild, American Veterans Committee, American Labor Party, Communists in the CIO, Progressive Party, ACLU, Los Angeles County Democratic Central Committee, Max Weber, Arthur Garfield Hays, Norman Thomas, and Henry Wallace. Notable among organizations that opposed the indictments was the Socialist Workers Party, the Trotskyist organization whose members had been prosecuted for violating the Smith Act—while Communists looked on approvingly—in 1941.²³

Ironically, it was Flynn's own comrades who were slow to join the fight against the Smith Act indictments. She found it appalling that almost no one raised the issue of a defense campaign at the party's fourteenth annual convention in August 1948. Defense work was not the sole purview of lawyers, she insisted in a speech she gave at the convention: "This is our Party. These are our leaders. No one else will defend them unless we do." Earlier, Foster had warned that transforming itself into a defense organization would destroy the CPUSA, citing as evidence the example of the General Defense Committee of the IWW, which devoured the union during World War I. His comment bothered Flynn because it depicted defense work as a drag on the party rather than a necessary response to political repression, and she publicly dissented. "But comrades," she enjoined, "this does not mean that we, as a Communist Party, farm out the defense of our Party, and forget it, while we go about as usual." Instead, citing Tom

Mooney, Sacco and Vanzetti, the Scottsboro Boys, and Angelo Herndon as precedents, she urged party members to draw on their legendary capacity for organizing in defense of the civil rights of others and forge the mass movement necessary to ensure the same for their own leaders: "Let us not hesitate to speak boldly to demand *our* civil rights. When our rights cease to exist—all rights of the people come to an end."[24]

As she had done in previous labor defense campaigns, Flynn invoked the rhetoric of Americanism to justify her call to action on behalf of the CPUSA in its current moment of crisis: "We are Americans. We have inalienable rights. Let us never forget this." As they had so often done when defending the rights of others, Communists must now defend their rights by taking the Dennis case from the court of law to the court of public opinion: "We must make the trial court a mighty tribunal of the people, so that the accused become the accusers and the enemies of the people find themselves on trial before the larger court of American public opinion."[25]

Although she still sounded like the East Side Joan of Arc, Flynn's August 1948 speech reveals the extent to which her years in the CPUSA had isolated her from other political movements and prevented her from gauging the opinions of mainstream Americans. During the Popular Front period, Communists could effectively appeal to their own members as well as those outside the party. By the time of the Dennis case, however, given the rising tide of anti-Communism in just about every segment of U.S. society, and the resentment that onetime allies among liberals, labor, and the Democratic Party had for the CPUSA, it was an impossible task for Communists to generate propaganda that roused masses of people in sympathy with their embattled leadership.

Additionally, the Americanism that suffused her rhetoric belied the extent to which Flynn's political point of reference was increasingly global. A proposal she offered in the speech is illustrative: "Let us popularize our leaders—like Thorez, Togliatti, who, when they walk down the street are greeted by workers by their first names; and are known and loved by millions."[26] Here, Flynn suggested that William Z. Foster could become as familiar and beloved in the United States as Maurice Thorez and Palmiro Togliatti, leaders of the French and Italian Communist Parties, respectively, were in their own countries. This idea was a hard sell. Foster lacked the political acumen and charisma of Thorez and Togliatti. Moreover, because France and Italy had active wartime antifascist resistance movements in which Communists played an essential and visible role, the two Communist leaders were national heroes, and the parties they led played an important part in rebuilding their respective nations after the war. In contrast, Foster, and by extension the CPUSA, could not lay claim to such a political legacy. Flynn's vision was more a revelation of her own desires than a plausible goal. To put it bluntly, she had become myopic to the point of self-delusion.

In addition to her columns in the *Daily Worker*, Flynn wrote a number of pamphlets to arouse interest in the Dennis case and raise money for the defense campaign. Her first, *The Twelve and You*, appeared in September 1948. (It was also excerpted in the *Daily Worker*.) The pamphlet presented a scathing critique of inequality and violence in the United States. At the time of publication, the U.S. economy was on the brink of a recession, and Flynn urged readers to see political repression as a tool used by powerful business interests to quell unrest in response to rising prices and falling wages.

> Ask yourself a few questions. Are you going to get low prices by putting some guys in jail? Who—the food profiteers or the Communists? Are you going to get a house by putting some guys in jail? Who—the real estate profiteers or the Communists? Where does all the red baiting come from? Who pulls out the old red herring every time you ask for a raise in pay? The Steel Trust and other big bosses shout: "Tools of the Communists!" You want a sirloin steak or a couple of lamb chops? The Beef Trust bellows: "Dupes of the Communists!" You want a house with a bathroom? "Communist agents!" roar the Real Estate interests. When will you get wise to all this ballyhoo?[27]

Flynn sketched a history of violence against working people in the United States, from the 1911 Triangle Shirtwaist Factory fire in New York to the 1937 Memorial Day Massacre in Chicago, and railed against "the deaths of 17,000 workers in preventable industrial accidents in 1947." She also decried the lynching of five thousand Black Americans since 1882, police violence against Blacks in the North as well as the South, and efforts by the KKK to deprive Black citizens of their right to vote. With a series of rhetorical questions, Flynn encouraged readers to consider who really was to blame for the "force and violence" that threatened U.S. society: "Are the Communists responsible for this appalling waste of human life? Do they own the mines and factories, hire guards, ignore safety regulations and make widows, orphans, and cripples?" The real enemy was not Communists, she insisted, but the capitalist system: "The hands of the rich are stained with blood. They are guilty of murder underground, on the picket line, in the darkness of night."²⁸ Drawing upon her long years of activism, Flynn highlighted the one-sided nature of political trials in the United States: "I've seen pickets and strike leaders arrested by the hundreds and innocent workers framed up, like Tom Mooney and Sacco and Vanzetti, like Eugene Debs and Joe Hill," she wrote, "but I have yet to see a mine owner, mob leader, trigger happy copper, strike-breaking thug, vigilante or gunman, punished for crimes against the people. I hope to live that long, dear reader."²⁹

Although she did not know the exact nature of the forces behind the Smith Act prosecutions, Flynn understood that powerful enemies had arrayed against her comrades. She interpreted the indictments as further evidence of the party's position that "fascism is coming to America" and explained the situation in the direst language available to her. She was not the only one to do so. In a speech he gave at Madison Square Garden, Eugene Dennis drew similarities between the Smith Act indictments of CPUSA leaders and Hitler placing blame for the Reichstag fire on Georgi Dimitrov to justify his decree outlawing the German Communist Party in 1933. Flynn repeated the analogy to evoke fear and outrage about where the current anti-Communist campaign in the United States was headed: "The Hitler big lie leads to—the prison, the concentration camps, the fiery furnaces."³⁰

It was intense rhetoric designed to convey extreme urgency, but it was a message without an audience outside the circle of committed Communists. Even Flynn, with her considerable experience creating labor defense appeals that cut across ideological lines to rouse the masses, could not make the message stick. Most Americans at the time likely did not remember—or if they remembered, did not care—about the Reichstag fire of 1933. Nor did they see fascism as a threat to U.S. national security. Why would they? The Nazis had been decisively defeated in the war and the United States was helping to rebuild a humbled Germany through the Marshall Plan. It was the Soviet quest for world domination—real or imagined—that now struck fear into American hearts, and the Smith Act indictments fed upon and intensified that fear.

Yet even as she presented a grim vision of capitalist America, Flynn also expressed her unwavering faith "in the ultimate justice of the American people, when the fog of the present hysteria rolls away." Although they were reviled in the present, Flynn insisted the Communists on trial would one day be honored along with pioneers in the movements for public education, labor unions, and women's suffrage. Rightly so, she claimed, because the Smith Act defendants were not common criminals plotting to use "force and violence" against democratic institutions, but exemplary Americans bound to the cause of working-class emancipation: war veterans, labor organizers, civil rights leaders, public officials, advocates for the unemployed, family men, fathers, and grandfathers.[31]

Flynn wrote another pamphlet, specifically for female readers, which was distributed with a letter of endorsement by Anita Whitney. *An Appeal to Women* presented a more cautious approach than the combative posture she had adopted when the indictments were first announced. Instead of calling for a classic labor defense, in which Communists would take their case directly to the public, Flynn urged supporters to write letters to President Truman demanding that the indictments be quashed.[32] This explicitly gendered appeal drew upon social relationships and domestic concerns rather than political arguments. Flynn referred to the defendants as friends as well as comrades: "good, clean-living, honest men . . . who can laugh at a joke, sing a song to a child, enjoy a movie with their wives" but also "terribly serious about peace, security, freedom, happiness for their children, and yours." After reassuring readers that her friends were not criminals, had not disgraced their country, and were not a threat to peace, Flynn explained why she had written a special message to women: "Women are closely associated with the home, the family. The things Communists fight for are close to the hearts of women. It isn't only my twelve men friends I want to tell you about. Their wives and mothers suffer from their arrests and thought of long prison terms for those they know to be loving sons and husbands, devoted fathers, good citizens, high-minded human beings."[33] It is not clear whom this "Communists are just like you and me" message was designed to persuade. Those who would be open to it already agreed.

The bulk of Flynn's writings from this period present the views of a determined optimist or, as Rosalyn Fraad Baxandall described her, "a believer in people and in America."[34] A January 1949 *Daily Worker* column, for example, recounted the story of Mrs. Leah Adler Benemovsky, a garment worker and Miami Beach resident, who had been arrested for attending a meeting that Flynn held in that city the year before. She was cited for contempt and sentenced to ninety days in prison when she refused under questioning to admit whether she was a Communist. Despite efforts to charge her under Florida's "criminal Communism and Fascism law," Benemovsky was acquitted by the Florida Supreme Court in a 5–2 decision. The ruling established the legality of the Communist Party in Florida and, Flynn noted, affirmed that one's political views were a private matter not subject to judicial interference: "If they think the issue through, regardless of prejudice, the majority of Americans will agree with this wholeheartedly."[35] Although it says good things about her, this expression of faith in the open-mindedness of Americans is yet another example of how Flynn did not take full account of the fear and mistrust of Communists that increasingly pervaded U.S. politics, culture, and society.

The Dennis Case

On January 17, 1949, the trial of "the Twelve" officially began with an encounter in front of the Foley Square courthouse that saw five hundred New York City police officers—the largest police contingent ever massed in front of a courthouse at the start of a trial in New York—aligned against approximately four hundred protestors. Pickets outside the courthouse would continue throughout the trial, although the band of protestors was usually small—about a dozen members of the Civil Rights Congress. The five-person legal team for the defendants was led by Harry Sacher and Abraham Isserman, both of whom had been identified as Communists by witnesses before the HUAC. Another of the defense attorneys was George Crockett, the first Black attorney to be employed in a legal capacity by the U.S. Department of Labor. A sixth attorney and the only woman, Mary Kaufman, a New York–based civil liberties lawyer, acted as staff counsel. They faced off against a five-person team of government lawyers led by U.S. Attorney John McGohey. The primary adversary of the defendants and their legal counsel, however, was presiding judge Harold Medina. A relatively recent Democratic appointee to the bench, Medina possessed great intelligence and legal acumen, but also a big ego, an aggressive demeanor, thin skin, and a sharp tongue. Throughout the proceedings, he clashed openly with the defense lawyers.[36]

At the start of the trial, Flynn, along with Simon Gerson and William Norman, established a provisional leadership group for the party. The group immediately set about raising desperately needed money with a goal of $100,000 in fifteen days. The defense fund was managed by the Civil Rights Congress. To encourage contributions a quota was established for states that had large party memberships. Flynn nurtured competition to be the first state to meet the quota. In an urgent appeal to readers of the *Daily Worker*, she co-opted the pejorative expression used by anti-Communists to refer to financial support provided to the CPUSA by the Soviet Union and implored comrades, "You are our 'Moscow Gold.'"[37] To encourage contributions she offered an image of popular support for the defendants that harkened back to an earlier era: "Masses are reading and talking about the trial. Organizations are demanding the indictments be dismissed. Millions were raised to defend Mooney, Haywood, Sacco and Vanzetti. Millions were involved in the mass organizations. Locals gave from their treasuries. Workers gave in shops. Defend the Communist leaders on trial! Support today's class war heroes! Smash frame-up in 1948! Stop thought control in the U.S.A.!"[38]

Flynn's image did not align with the present reality on the ground. Despite her legendary ability to forge alliances among disparate groups, her appeals did not resonate with audiences outside the CPUSA and its most stalwart band of allies. Rather than acknowledge the uphill battle of a labor defense campaign when the defendants were so enormously unpopular, Flynn expressed frustration at the lackluster effort on the part of those inside the party, especially her younger comrades, who seemed not to understand "the enormous amounts of money required for the legal defense and the prodigious organized efforts needed for mass agitation, publicity, etc."[39] To energize the defense campaign, she organized a "spark plug" committee, officially known as the Communist Committee for the Defense of the Twelve.[40] But the spark failed to ignite a fire and the fundraising drive sputtered along. Within months, the defense was in debt.[41]

Appeals to highlight the obvious danger to civil liberties posed by the Smith Act had fallen flat. For one thing, the party's enthusiastic support for the prosecution of their Trotskyist rivals under the same law just a few years earlier suggested to many observers that Communists only cared about civil liberties for themselves. Critics like journalist Henry Lee Moon, public relations director for the NAACP, highlighted what he saw as Communists' hypocrisy on the issue of civil liberties in the prominent Black newspaper the *New York Age*: "Ironically, the Communists, who now seek support on the grounds that all dissident elements are threatened by the Smith Act, lifted not a single finger to aid the Trotskyists whose leaders were tried and convicted under the same act in 1944." According to Moon, the party's unwavering devotion to Stalin had trumped its members' loyalty to civil liberties during the earlier trial of the Trotskyists: "Not only did they fail then to see the danger to their own party and refuse to aid the indicted followers of Leon Trotsky; they also sought to prevent believers in civil liberties from coming to the defense of accused anti-Stalin Communists."[42]

In the broader Cold War climate, it is difficult to imagine how Flynn might have succeeded in generating support for her comrades in an atmosphere in which Communists were increasingly feared and despised for their apparent unwavering devotion to Stalin. Much of that fear and loathing was stoked in the United States by politicians, government agencies, and the press, but developments abroad also fueled anti-Communism at home. After the Soviet-sponsored coup in Czechoslovakia, the Truman administration seized an opportunity to create an alliance of countries in North America and Western Europe with the aim of halting further Soviet expansion into Europe. Communist parties throughout the world criticized the move as a form of imperialist aggression against the Soviet Union. In late February 1949, just weeks before the official creation of the alliance, now known as the North Atlantic Treaty Organization (NATO), Maurice Thorez, head of the Communist Party of France, made a shocking declaration: Should the Red Army enter France in response to an act of aggression against the Soviet Union by U.S.-allied nations, French Communists would not fight against the Soviets. Italian Communist Party head Palmiro Togliatti issued a similar declaration days later. Heads of the communist parties of Germany and England followed with similar statements. So too did CPUSA leaders Eugene Dennis and William Z. Foster. American Communists, they proclaimed, would oppose "an unjust, aggressive, imperialist war" and would work "with all democratic forces" to end that war.[43] An unidentified spokesperson for the party insisted that the statement was not issued "on orders from Moscow." The full text was published in the *Daily Worker*.

Harkening back to the "imperial war" position that Communists adopted after the Nazi-Soviet Pact, the statement was, in part, a proclamation of solidarity with comrades in Western Europe who would feel the immediate effects of a war on the continent: "French and Italian sovereignty and independence are threatened today solely by Wall Street's schemes of world domination as expressed in the Marshall Plan and the proposed Atlantic war alliance." Foster and Dennis went further, however, and indicated that U.S. Communists would oppose any act of aggression against the Soviet Union as a form of imperialist aggression: "If, despite the efforts of the peace forces of America and the world, Wall Street should succeed in plunging the world into war, we would oppose it as an unjust, aggressive, imperialist war, as an undemocratic and an anti-Socialist war, destructive of the deepest interests of the American people and all humanity." Coming just days before the start of their trial, the statement presented a view of growing tensions between the United States and the Soviet Union that many interpreted as unabashedly pro-Soviet, which further confirmed public suspicions about the loyalty of Communists. When asked what he thought of the announcement by Dennis and

Foster, President Truman reportedly responded, "I have no comment on the statements by traitors."[44]

While Flynn struggled to launch a broad-based campaign in the increasingly hostile court of public opinion, attorneys for the defense inside the courthouse at Foley Square attempted to secure a postponement of the trial. First, they alleged bias on the part of the grand jury that issued the indictments. They also requested a delay until public opinion had moderated. When Medina dismissed these efforts, defense counsel sought postponement until an ailing Foster was healthy enough to stand trial. In response, Judge Medina moved to sever Foster's case from that of the other defendants. Thus "the Twelve" became "the Eleven." Finally, the defense alleged discrimination in the jury selection process, arguing that Blacks, ethnic and religious minorities, and the poor were systematically excluded while the rich were overrepresented. When they failed to prove willful and deliberate exclusion of any identifiable group, Medina overruled the challenge and announced the trial proper would begin the following Monday, March 7, 1949.[45]

From the beginning, a lack of evidence that the defendants had acted or plotted to overthrow the government, coupled with the fact that Communists had explicitly disavowed any desire or intent to do so in multiple public forums, hampered the case against the CPUSA leaders.[46] Unable to prove incitement or revolutionary deeds or plots, prosecutors used the conspiracy provision of the Smith Act against the Eleven. The successful prosecution of Trotskyists under the act provided a model for how to get around the evidentiary hurdle. As they had done with the Trotskyists of the Socialist Workers Party 1941, prosecutors in the Dennis case alleged that Communist leaders' commitment to overthrow the U.S. government by force and violence was inherent in the party's adherence to and teaching of the doctrines of Marx and Lenin. Their case rested on the argument that after dissolving the CPUSA in 1944 and abandoning a program of violent revolution in favor of a peaceful, democratic approach to establishing socialism in the United States, the defendants reconstituted the party in order to overthrow democratic institutions in a manner consistent with Marxist-Leninist ideas.[47] Michael Belknap explains that although technically, the CPUSA and the alleged conspiracy on the part of Communist leaders to overthrow the government were distinct, the real defendant in the Dennis case was not the party's leadership but the party itself: "For if that organization was not what the government claimed, planning to establish it could not possibly constitute a violation of the Smith Act."[48]

To prove its case that basic Communist doctrine mandated revolutionary violence, the prosecution submitted copious amounts of printed matter, including incendiary passages from the works of Marx, Lenin, Stalin, and other Communist propagandists. They argued that teaching such revolutionary doctrine, as the party did in its schools, was expressly forbidden under the Smith Act. Primary witnesses for the prosecution were FBI informants (or as Flynn and her comrades called them, "stool pigeons") and a handful of ex-Communists, including Louis Budenz. A former publicity director for the ACLU and former Communist—he had been managing editor of the *Daily Worker*—Budenz laid claim to substantial credibility with the jury. His testimony was the vehicle for inserting the most lurid passages from CPUSA literature into the record. He also explained that Communist leaders who disavowed revolutionary intent were merely using Aesopian language—that is, cryptic or allegorical language designed to avoid censorship when presenting subversive ideas.[49]

Not surprisingly, Flynn was critical of Budenz. In another pamphlet she wrote about the case, "Stool-Pigeon," she accused him of perjury for his accusation that Communists used Aesopian language. It was true that revolutionary writers like Lenin used caution in their writing to avoid censorship by the Czar, she observed, but that fact had no bearing on the present conduct of members of the CPUSA: "When they meant Russia and the Czar, they said 'Japan' and 'the Mikado,' and everybody understood. So what? What has that to do with the U.S.A. in 1949?" As she often did in the face of political repression, Flynn used Irish-inspired examples to highlight the absurdity of the situation. She noted that Irish literature often uses symbolic language: "'Dark Rosaleen' means Ireland, and 'Spanish wine will give you hope!' referred to aid and arms expected from Spain. So every time the Irish say 'wine' do they mean 'guns?' When I write about the Easter Uprising of 1916 in Ireland, is it a directive to take over the nearest post office, run up revolutionary flags, and declare a Workers' Republic, as my revered friend James Connolly and his comrades did? Of course not." Despite her dismissive tone, Flynn understood that charging Communists with using "Aesopian language" to hide their true intentions had serious implications for the case. It put Communists in a double bind by denying them access to any language with which to defend themselves: if they embraced revolutionary Marxist-Leninist rhetoric, they were clearly guilty of conspiracy to overthrow the government by force and violence; if they disavowed such rhetoric, they were necessarily lying and therefore guilty of the same.[50]

Defense attorneys challenged the government's case and questioned the admissibility of the books and articles that were introduced because of their age and lack of relevance to the CPUSA's current program. Judge Medina overruled each of their objections. As the trial wore on, Medina and the defense counsel clashed on an almost daily basis. Dennis, who had asked the court if he could dismiss his attorney and represent himself, used his time on the stand to vindicate Communism from the attacks leveled against it. His performance did not endear him or his comrades to the judge. Medina jailed five of the defendants—Gates, Winston, Hall, Green, and Winter—for contempt. Three of the five were charged with disruptive behavior. The other two—Gates and Winter—were charged with failing to answer a question the government posed. Both had refused to answer questions that asked them to identify other party members by name.

As the trial progressed, Flynn traveled around the United States to speak on behalf of her comrades and used her *Daily Worker* column to report on the progress of the fundraising campaign and encourage participation by readers. She also reported on egregious examples of red-baiting and openly expressed anti-Communism by government officials that posed a threat to the civil liberties of the defendants and, by extension, all other Americans. In August, she lambasted Truman's recent appointee to the Supreme Court Tom C. Clark for publishing an article in *Look* magazine, "Why the Communists Won't Scare Us Any More," which, in addition to Clark's boast that the trial cost the federal government $1,000,000, included FBI pictures of the defendants (Dennis, Foster, Stachel, Winston, Williamson, and Davis). Flynn called the piece "a stink bomb" that violated the presumption of innocence of men still before a jury.[51]

Still critical of Browder (she voted to turn down his application for readmission to the party in 1948), Flynn opined, "[The party's leadership has been] singled out for the most vicious attack today and the vengeance of the ruling class directed against them" because "they successfully broke with Browder's revisionism, which would have emasculated our party of its revolutionary socialist objective, taken us out of the class struggle and isolated us from the working class."[52] Although she continued to claim that the CPUSA was a quintessentially American organization with deep historic ties to the American labor movement, it was increasingly obvious that as she and her comrades were more and more isolated in the United States, Flynn drew inspiration and support primarily from communist parties and comrades abroad. For the thirtieth anniversary of the CPUSA, she wrote, "The cables from Communist Parties from all over the world (with China and, of all places, Ireland, on the first page [of the *Daily Worker*]) gives one great pride in our American party and the role it has today."[53]

In late summer, the defense tried to turn things around after reports that one of the jurors, Russell Janney, had delivered a blistering anti-Communist speech in Macon, Georgia, in February and, more recently, had discussed the trial at length with a young reporter, Carol Nathenson. In response to these reports, Crockett submitted a detailed affidavit and moved for a mistrial.[54] Flynn used Janney's indiscretions to inspire the defense campaign. Despite a barrage of letters, petitions, delegations to New York organized under the auspices of the Civil Rights Congress, and endorsements by leaders of CIO-affiliated unions and the American Labor Party, Judge Medina denied the defense motions.[55]

Just days after the Janney revelations, a riot broke out in Peekskill, New York, when Paul Robeson attempted to perform at an open-air concert to raise funds for the Civil Rights Congress and the defense of the Communists on trial. Earlier in the spring, Robeson was harshly criticized for reportedly having said that Blacks in the United States would not support a war started by American imperialists.[56] Before he arrived in Peekskill, a mob that had been riled up by anti-Communist members of the American Legion and the Veterans of Foreign Wars attacked members of the audience with baseball bats and rocks, seriously injuring thirteen people, and lynched Robeson in effigy. Because of the violence, the concert was suspended. Robeson was invited back to perform a week later. That day, another mob of five hundred anti-Communist veterans accompanied by brass bands attempted to ruin the concert by drowning out Robeson's performance. When a security force comprising members of the Furriers and National Maritime Unions confronted them, the mob backed down. After the event, however, they attacked, stoning buses, overturning cars, and beating concertgoers, including children. In a heated exchange afterward among members of the House of Representatives, two congressmen, John E. Rankin of Mississippi and Edward Cox of Georgia (both Democrats), blamed the violence on Robeson and the Communists.[57] The violence and the reaction from Congress illustrated how far anti-Communists were willing to go in their attacks against the party and anyone who supported it.

How different it must have felt when Flynn arrived in Paris on September 18. She was there for a week—"Such a short time!" she wrote in her *Daily Worker* column—to attend the birthday celebration of Marcel Cachin, editor of *L'Humanité*, the daily newspaper of the French

FIGURE 9. Elizabeth Gurley Flynn and Paul Robeson (no date). Credit: Photo appears courtesy of *People's World*

Communist Party. The trip was like a breath of fresh air: "I have certainly accumulated a myriad of inspiring impressions and I feel as if it is much longer and I am in another world." While in Paris, Flynn mingled with Marie-Claude Valliant Couturier, secretary of the WIDF, as well as Italian, Spanish, Chinese, Russian, Czechoslovakian, Belgian, Romanian, Hungarian, and Indian comrades. In contrast to the increasing political isolation she was experiencing at home, she found the environment in Paris quite welcoming: "There is an aura of warmth, of comradeship, that makes you feel like one of the family." The difference between French and American public memory of the war also struck her. In Paris, Flynn noted, "memories of war and the cruel traitorous actions of the Vichy government, are deep and cannot be erased." French sympathy and feeling for the people of the Soviet Union, born of gratitude for the latter's role in defeating the Nazis, was reflected in the Parisian cityscape: "A station in their subway (Metro) is 'Stalingrad.' A street is 'Rue Leningrad.'"[58]

On September 23, 1949, while Flynn was in Paris championing the cause of peace along with Communists from around the globe, President Truman announced that the Soviets had successfully built and detonated an atomic bomb.[59] Eight days later, Chinese Communist leader Mao Zedong declared the creation of the People's Republic of China. These events, which heightened fears that Communists aimed for worldwide domination, did not bode well for the outcome of the case. One week after Mao's announcement, on October 7, the defense began its closing statements. The prosecution followed on October 12. In her *Daily Worker* column that day, Flynn expressed faith not only that the defendants would be exonerated but also that former New York City Councilman Benjamin Davis would successfully stand for reelection. For once, however, she seemed aware of the odds stacked against her comrades: "Maybe I'm an optimist with little cause." Nevertheless, she held to the party's official position that the outcome of the trial was a bellwether for fascism in the United States: "This is a fateful week. All over the world people by the millions are awaiting word of 'the 12.'" Although Foster had not been tried, she included him among the defendants: "'Does America go fascist?' they ask anxiously."[60]

Verdict and Appeal

The following day, Judge Medina issued a charge to the jury that lasted two hours. After deliberating for two days, the jury found all the defendants guilty. Medina sentenced ten of the eleven party leaders to five years in prison in addition to a $10,000 maximum fine for all. Thompson received a three-year sentence in recognition of his Distinguished Service Cross, a military award he had won during World War II. Medina denied all appeals for bail. (After some wrangling, bail was eventually granted.) Still Medina had not finished. After he had passed sentence and sent home the jury, he charged the defense attorneys with criminal contempt of court for attempting to delay the case as a tactical strategy and attempting to provoke the judge or impair his health to achieve a mistrial. He issued prison sentences of thirty days to six months. At its conclusion, *Life* magazine called the trial the "longest, most noisy, most controversial in US history."[61]

In a widely publicized interview with the press after the jury's decision had been announced, Flynn once again expressed the conviction shared among many American Communists at the time that the United States teetered on the brink of fascism and called the verdict "a Hitler-like decision." She also persisted in seeing Truman as the driving force behind the trial: "In its attempt to start war with Russia, the administration is trying to outlaw the Communist Party because it represents a large segment of the population, which is for peace." As she had done before in numerous labor defense campaigns, Flynn strategized for ways to appeal to the broadest audience possible: "We must make tremendous efforts now to appeal our case to the larger jury and the final court of judgement—to the American people. This will require meetings, leaflets, radio broadcasts, literature, tours of speakers, ads in newspapers, etc."[62] She believed that a well-coordinated, energetic campaign would succeed in convincing the American people that her comrades had been unjustly targeted for their political beliefs and enlist their support for the defense. "Millions will rally in our cause," she asserted confidently.[63]

At the same time, Flynn recognized that the defense campaign was hobbled by a bail restriction imposed upon the defendants by the U.S. attorney for the Southern District of New York, Irving Saypol, whom she described with admirable alliteration as a "pint-sized peanut politician."[64] The restriction limited their ability to travel beyond the Southern District, which extends only to the city limits of Albany. Consequently, Green, Hall, and Winter had to obtain a court order to be granted permission to return home to their families. Thompson and Gates had to secure permission to return to Queens nightly. Defendants who lived in Manhattan were not even allowed to travel to Brooklyn without special permission. In her *Daily Worker* column, Flynn explained that the restriction, designed to limit the party's ability to organize nationwide speaking tours for the Eleven, violated the defendants' civil liberties: "This constitutes in fact 'protective custody' and not freedom on bail, as it is usually practiced in the U.S.A. It is a violation of Article 8 of the Bill of Rights, which guarantees 'protection against excessive bail and punishments.'"[65] In another article published in *Political Affairs*, she asked "How can we build a mass movement, how can we raise the defense funds needed, if the defendants cannot participate?"[66]

It was not just the civil liberties implications of the bail restriction, nor its effect on the defense campaign, that troubled Flynn. She was genuinely concerned for the families of the defendants. Perhaps recalling her own son Fred's reaction as a child upon seeing her when she returned home from a speaking tour, she described in detail in her *Daily Worker* column the scene at party headquarters in New York when children were united with their fathers after the latter had posted bail: "Little Genie stood by the elevator with tears on his cheeks waiting for his dad," and "Little Larry sat up from a sleep, looked at his father who had been in Jail since June 3, stretched out his arms and cried, 'Daddy!'"[67]

Given the array of repressive forces arrayed against Communists, it is not hard to understand why Flynn would have believed that the United States was tilting dangerously close to fascism. She was right to note similarities between the Smith Act trial and repression of Communists in fascist regimes in the 1930s. She clearly understood that the legality of a political party and the freedom of its leaders was at stake, as was "the future liberty of not only 12,000 persons immediately threatened, but of 12 times 12 million Americans."[68] She correctly recognized how the charge of criminal contempt that Medina had made against counsel for the defense and the prison sentences he imposed would empower other judges to threaten or enact punitive measures, including disbarment, for any lawyer who undertook the defense of a client with politically unpopular views and thus jeopardize the right of an attorney to represent their client adequately and the right of a defendant to be properly represented. She did not exaggerate when she claimed that the fight to defend the Eleven—along with the struggle to defeat the Mundt-Nixon Bill, repeal the Smith Act and the Taft-Hartley Act, and the campaign against nuclear war—were component parts of a large-scale defense of the Bill of Rights.[69] Where she made her mistake was in assuming that masses of people outside the party would share this point of view and feel compelled to defend the rights of Communists.

She was not the only Communist to err this way. The party's lawyers knew that chances for an acquittal were slim to none, so leaders pinned their hopes on a classic labor defense campaign to rouse the masses and pressure the government to drop the prosecutions. This strategy had worked in the Scottsboro case of the 1930s, saving nine young Black men from execution on false allegations of rape. As Ellen Schrecker observes, however, "the Cold War was not the Popular Front and a federal courtroom in New York City had more legitimacy than one in the Jim Crow black belt of Alabama. Moreover, by 1949 Communism was so unpopular that even a decorous appeal to civil liberties would have been futile."[70]

Flynn's memory of successful labor defense campaigns extended even further back than the 1930s. So too did that of some of her comrades. One reader of the *Daily Worker* offered a vivid and humorous account of Flynn's almost uncanny ability to fundraise among diverse audiences in a letter to the editor, published in April 1950:

> In the old days, that beautiful daughter of the American labor movement, Elizabeth Gurley Flynn, used to be without doubt the world's most moving and irresistible collection speaker at mass meetings. The largest halls in New York would resound with her eloquence and a voice that might have put La Duse and Bernhardt to shame.
>
> When she had succeeded in wringing the last penny from every pocket, with her thunderous appeals, she would read off the list of contributors: "South Slavs, $50! Italian Section, $30! Finnish Federation $100!" And so on down the line. And invariably, she would wind up with a loud query: "But where in hell are the Irish?" And, before she was done, an Irish contribution would be forthcoming from somewhere, somehow.[71]

Despite her past successes and best efforts to make comparisons with the present, Eugene Dennis was not a charismatic and revered leader like Eugene Debs (despite Flynn's claim of "remarkable parallels" between the two men) and the Eleven were not like Sacco and Vanzetti or other of labor's martyrs from previous campaigns.[72] There would be no large-scale, politically diverse, working-class agitation for their freedom.

While Flynn tried unsuccessfully to rouse Americans in sympathy with beleaguered Communists, the defendants appealed the verdict. Counsel filed briefs arguing that the jury challenge was not a delay tactic, the trial had been improperly conducted, and Judge Medina had exhibited bias and engaged in misconduct. In addition to these procedural claims, they filed a brief arguing the trial was political and intended to punish speech and thought rather than conduct. The ACLU also filed a brief arguing that the Smith Act violated the First Amendment.[73] On June 21, 1950, a three-judge panel for the U.S. Court of Appeals for the Second Circuit began hearing oral arguments. The final day for hearing arguments was June 23, 1950. Two days later, the army of the Democratic People's Republic of Korea marched south across the thirty-eighth parallel into the United States–supported Republic of Korea. President Truman ordered U.S. forces to Korea on June 27. The next day, North Korean forces captured the South Korean capital of Seoul.

Although they occurred almost seven thousand miles away, developments in Korea influenced the judges' deliberations in New York. The appeal was denied on August 1, 1950. Judge Learned Hand, known as a defender of civil liberties because of his efforts to prevent the postmaster general from suppressing *The Masses*, a socialist magazine of art and politics, during World War I, wrote the opinion. In it, he argued that given the current political situation, in cases where the defendants were Communists, the clear and present danger standard was met if the prosecution demonstrated intent plus conspiracy to advocate violent overthrow of the government. In other words, Communists' relationship to the Soviet Union, not Marxist-Leninist doctrine, made them dangerous.[74]

After Judge Hand issued the opinion, the Eleven appealed to the Supreme Court. Meanwhile, Congress debated the Internal Securities Act, otherwise known as the McCarran Act after its principal sponsor, Senator Patrick McCarran (D-Nev.). The act required that associations determined to be Communist by the federal government register with the government and submit information about membership, finances, and activities.[75] Both houses of Congress passed it, but Truman vetoed the act because of the danger it posed to freedom of speech and the Bill of Rights on September 22, 1950. Within two days, both the Senate and the House had voted overwhelmingly to override his veto. Flynn and her comrades called it a "monstrous" piece of legislation—on par with the Alien and Sedition Acts and the Fugitive Slave Law—that trampled on the Bill of Rights.[76]

While Congress institutionalized domestic fears of communism by "continually beating the drum of anti-Communism" in its policy deliberations, the press played its part by relentlessly covering issues related to Communism and subversive activities, thus priming Americans to see the defendants as guilty even before a verdict had been reached. Kevin Baron points out that from 1946 to 1952, there were over 110,000 mentions of these topics in the *Washington Post* and the *New York Times* alone.[77] Rather than creating martyrs for the cause of civil liberties, the Dennis case and those that followed it confirmed a belief many Americans had been coaxed into embracing: that Communists were duplicitous agents of a foreign power bent on destroying the United States.

The international scene also continued to fuel hostility to Communists at home. By the end of September, a combined U.S./U.N. force in Korea, led by General Douglas McArthur, retook the city of Seoul. McArthur then crossed the thirty-eighth parallel and continued to send his troops farther and farther north toward the Yalu River, the border between China and Korea. He was convinced the Chinese would not fight, despite repeated warnings from Mao Zedong that the Chinese would not tolerate U.N. troops near their border and that the war would be over by Christmas. He was wrong on both counts. The Chinese attacked, and Seoul once again fell to Communist forces on January 4, 1951. The U.S./U.N. forces would not retake Seoul until March. Truman relieved McArthur of his command a few weeks later on April 11, 1951.

As the Korean conflict continued, taking thousands of lives in the process, the Supreme Court rendered its decision on the Smith Act convictions. On June 4, 1951, in *Dennis v. the United States*, the court upheld the verdict by a vote of six to two and found that the law did not violate the Constitution. In his opinion of the court, Chief Justice Frederick Vinson, a Truman appointee, argued that government has an interest in limiting speech when faced with the threat of overthrow by force and violence. Like Learned Hand, he justified government action against the defendants with the clear and present danger standard, and like Hand, he located the clear and present danger in the escalating tensions of the Cold War.

> The mere fact that from the period 1945 to 1948 petitioners' activities did not result in an attempt to overthrow the Government by force and violence is of course no answer to the fact that there was a group that was ready to make the attempt. The formation by petitioners of such a highly organized conspiracy, with rigidly disciplined members subject to call when the leaders, these petitioners, felt that the time had come for action, coupled with the inflammable nature of world conditions, similar uprisings in other countries, and the touch-and-go nature of our relations with countries with whom petitioners were in the very least ideologically attuned, convince us that their convictions were justified on this score. And this analysis disposes of the contention that a conspiracy to advocate, as distinguished from the advocacy itself, cannot be constitutionally restrained, because it comprises only the preparation. It is the existence of the conspiracy which creates the danger. . . . If the ingredients of the reaction are present, we cannot bind the Government to wait until the catalyst is added.[78]

Now that the Smith Act verdict had been given the imprimatur of the highest court in the land, there was no stopping the federal government's crusade to rid the United States of the so-called Communist menace.

Flynn, sensing the urgency of the situation, called the Supreme Court's decision a direct assault on the First Amendment and urged mass action to demand another review of the Dennis trial and of the Smith Act itself. Her plan, which she outlined in the *Daily Worker*, demanded only a commitment to the Bill of Rights and against jailing ideas. "Don't be sectarian as to whom you approach," she urged her comrades; everyone—"pro-Communists, anti-Communists, and those that are neutral to Communists"—shared a common interest in the Bill of Rights and in keeping the United States off the road to fascism. Flynn also questioned the authority of the Supreme Court and the legitimacy of judicial review. With her own take on Winston Churchill's phrase, she called for defenders of free speech to "break through the paper curtain."[79]

Second-String Smith Act Indictments, a.k.a. the Flynn Case

On the morning of June 20, 1951, sixteen days after the court announced its decision in the Dennis case, three FBI agents knocked on the door of the apartment on East Twelfth Street in Manhattan that Flynn shared with her sister Kathie and Kathie's school-age daughter, Frances. Flynn described how, when the knock came, Kathie, who had been cooking breakfast, opened the door and screamed "indignantly" as "three FBI agents, two men and a woman, roughly pushed their way past her" with a warrant for Flynn's arrest. She was being charged with having violated the Smith Act. Flynn had a gift for keeping her cool in a difficult situation, and this one was no exception, although the same seems not to have been the case for the female FBI agent. "I dressed in the presence of the jittery young woman who came uninvited into my bedroom," she recalled. "I was allowed time for one cup of coffee. I tried to reassure my family in parting, 'Don't worry. This is a long range proposition.'" She was right. The ordeal would not be over until six years later when she was released from prison and free of parole restrictions.[80]

The "raiding party," as Flynn called the arresting agents, escorted her to FBI headquarters located in the federal courthouse at Foley Square in Manhattan. There, she was registered and fingerprinted along with fifteen other comrades: Marion Bachrach, Isidore Begun, Alexander Bittelman, George Blake Charney, Betty Gannett, Simon W. Gerson, V. J. Jerome, Arnold Johnson, Claudia Jones, Albert Lannon, Jacob Mindel, Pettis Perry, Alexander Trachtenberg, Louis Weinstock, and William Weinstone. A frail and ailing Israel Amter, then over seventy years old, was released in the custody of a lawyer. The group of "second string Communists," as they were identified by the press, was then taken to a courtroom where they were arraigned and had bail set. The label initially bothered Flynn: as a member of the party's national committee, she felt she was anything but "second string." During the course of the trial she realized that she had been purposely left out of the first case and held over for the second to link two groups of defendants who were charged with the same alleged conspiracy.[81] Recent changes to federal law—namely, a new conspiracy section of the U.S. code and the McCarran Act of 1950—meant that mere membership in the CPUSA was insufficient evidence of conspiracy and mandated proof of an overt act to further any alleged conspiracy was necessary.[82] Flynn's alleged overt act was her participation in a meeting at the Riverside Plaza hotel on August 2, 1948. She scoffed at the flimsy nature of these allegations, calling the overt acts "fig leaves" to hide the "nakedness" of the Smith Act.[83]

Three other women were indicted along with Flynn: Claudia Jones, also a member of the national committee; Marion Bachrach; and Betty Gannett. After their arraignment, the four women were moved to the Women's House of Detention at 10 Greenwich Avenue in Manhattan, where they waited for bail to be posted. "It had a swanky sounding address," Flynn later noted, and it was the same prison where Ethel Rosenberg was kept until she was removed shortly before their arrival and subsequently taken to Sing Sing Prison, where she would be executed three years later for espionage on the basis of perjured testimony by her own brother.[84]

The Civil Rights Congress posted bail for Flynn, Jones, Gannett, and eleven other defendants (bail for Marion Bachrach and one other defendant was posted by family members). When trustees of the bail fund refused to provide the names of people who had loaned money to it, they were jailed for contempt of court, bail bonds from the fund were canceled, and Flynn and the other thirteen defendants were ordered back to jail. She referred to this series of events as "the ugly face of fascism in the U.S.A."[85] The bail issue was a direct violation of the defendants' constitutional rights, and Flynn contacted Roger Baldwin to enlist help from the ACLU. Baldwin regretted that he was out of town and unable to help, but he encouraged her to contact Patrick Malin in the New York office. Malin too declined to intervene. It would not be the last time she would be disappointed by her former civil liberties allies.[86]

The two comrades who had been released established a committee to raise new bail. "It was a lengthy and tedious procedure," according to Flynn. Those who offered bail were required to take the witness stand and swear that the money was theirs. Flynn's "excessively high bail" of $25,000 was put up by her friend and comrade Grace Hutchins, whom she described as "an elderly woman of courage and integrity."[87] It was not until November that the Supreme Court ended the practice of excessive bail with its ruling in *Stack v. Boyle*.[88]

While the bail ordeal for the second-string defendants was unfolding, the party's leadership grappled with the question of how to keep the

FIGURE 10. Elizabeth Gurley Flynn with (clockwise, from top left) Marian Bachrach, Claudie Jones, and Betty Gannett en route to the Women's House of Detention, 1951.
Credit: AP Photo

organization functioning in the face of government repression. Foster, who believed that war between the United States and the Soviet Union and the outlawing of the CPUSA were inevitable, argued that comrades who had been convicted should skip bail and go into hiding, where they would operate as part of a clandestine structure for the party. The National Board split on the question. Flynn, whose preference was always to stand and fight, insisted that going underground was unnecessary and all the convicted should report to serve their sentences so as not to feed the image that Communists were engaged in illegal activities. The result was a compromise. On July 4, seven out of the eleven first-string comrades went to prison while four others—Henry Winston, Gil Green, Gus Hall, and Bob Thompson—went underground to the chagrin of the Civil Rights Congress, which forfeited $80,000 in bail.[89] About three weeks later, federal agents arrested fifteen Communists in California. The following month, August 1951, saw a flurry of arrests: six in Maryland; six in Pennsylvania, including Spanish Civil War veteran Steve Nelson; and seven in Hawaii. Gus Hall was captured and extradited from Mexico in October. Although she had disagreed with the decision to send him underground, Flynn never aired her disagreement in public. Instead, she criticized the U.S. State Department for violating Hall's right to political asylum.[90]

Throughout the pretrial ordeal, Flynn was the face of party leadership for regular members. While she was out on bail, she continued to write her *Daily Worker* column where she explored the civil liberties implications of the Smith Act and urged her readers to fight for repeal of the law. She provided regular updates about the progress of her own case and relayed news about the arrests of comrades around the country. Never one to be caught up in abstractions or bogged down by the minutiae of the legal system, she offered moving accounts of how the government's prosecution of Communists affected whole families, particularly wives and children. She urged readers not to forget the Dennis defendants who languished in prison and encouraged them to send cards and letters. She also insisted that members of the party not lose sight of its larger program and continue to work for peace, civil rights, and economic security for all.[91] Flynn herself tried to remain focused on the party's campaign for peace. Along with Pettis Perry and Claudia Jones, she petitioned for permission to meet with Secretary of State Dean Acheson to discuss the party's proposal for a peaceful solution to the Korean conflict. It was a bold request coming from defendants in a conspiracy trial, and it showed Flynn's trademark moxie. Not surprisingly, the judge denied it.[92]

Self-Defense Campaign

As she did during the Dennis trial, Flynn assumed leadership of the defense campaign for herself and her New York comrades, this time as chair of the Self Defense Committee of the 17 Victims of the Smith Act, founded on August 26, 1951. As she and Marion Bachrach explained in the committee's first letter to would-be supporters, "Our self defense is the defense of civil liberty itself."[93] The number of defendants decreased after first Israel Amter and then Marion Bachrach were severed from the trial (Bachrach to undergo an operation for cancer), leaving fifteen defendants in the Flynn case, as it came to be called. That hers was the name chosen to identify the case "did not mitigate [her] indignation against the whole legal chicanery," Flynn noted wryly.[94] The sheer number of arrests, however, soon called for a larger scale approach to fundraising for expenses that had increased exponentially. On October 12, the party mailed 125,000 posters with a photo of the New York defendants announcing an appeal for $250 thousand for the defense of all Eastern Smith Act cases. At the same time, California Communists announced a $150 thousand appeal for defendants in West Coast and Rocky Mountain states. In addition to covering legal expenses for Communists under indictment, these campaigns aimed to arouse a national movement against the Smith Act. In pursuit of the latter aim, Communists called for monthly mass meetings and even went so far as to produce and sell "Repeal the Smith Act" Christmas seals.[95]

As always, Flynn's family supported her during a time of crisis. In January 1952, Kathie wrote a letter summarizing her sister Elizabeth's forty-five-year-long activism for unorganized and underpaid workers, the rights of women, full equality for Black Americans, and civil liberties, during which time, Kathie noted, "even in the most redbaiting papers, there [had] never been a report 'of advocacy of the violent overthrow of government' on her part." Kathie mailed the letter to three hundred prominent Americans, calling upon recipients to join or contribute to a defense committee and speak out against the Smith Act.[96] Despite these various efforts, however, an ecumenical movement against the Smith Act failed to materialize. Only one mass meeting occurred between October 1951 and April 1952.

The bail ordeal was just the first obstacle that confronted Flynn and her co-defendants. Defense counsel in the Dennis case had been sentenced to prison for contempt of court, and two of the attorneys faced disbarment from federal court (Abraham Isserman would be disbarred for two years and Harry Shacker for life). These harsh penalties coupled with an atmosphere of intense anti-Communism made it nearly impossible for the Foley Square defendants to find attorneys willing to represent them. Over two hundred attorneys turned down Flynn and her comrades.[97] "In the main the replies were courteous," she noted. "A few were curt, but all declined to help us."[98] Among those who courteously declined were Harold Ickes, a lawyer as well as FDR's secretary of the interior for thirteen years, and Arthur Garfield Hays, whom Flynn had known since the two were actively involved in civil liberties campaigns in the 1920s. Ickes, who was "concerned as a lawyer" and "disturbed as a citizen" by the Smith Act cases, felt he was too old to accept the challenge (he was seventy-six and would, in fact, die a year later). Hays told Flynn that he was "sorely tempted to join" but could not do so because of the "irreparable harm" his involvement in the defense of Communists would do to the work of the ACLU. His refusal, yet another reminder of how the organization she had helped bring into existence had turned its back on her to protect its reputation, must have stung.[99]

As the trial approached, Flynn and her comrades explained their situation to Judge Sylvester J. Ryan. The lawyers that Ryan initially attempted to appoint were all either too busy, too ill, too expensive, or—when they found out that the evidence comprised primarily books about politics, economics, and history, which they would have to read—too lazy. The next round of lawyers he approached were criminal defense attorneys, a number of whom were publicly connected to grafters and smugglers. Finally, the defendants found an acceptable lawyer willing to take their case: Frank Serri, a Brooklyn-based attorney and officer of the National Lawyers Guild. He was soon joined by Mary Kaufman, who had been part of the defense team for the Dennis case; James Wright, a Black attorney based in Washington, D.C.; and John McTernan, a California civil liberties lawyer who had formerly worked for the NLRB. Yale Law Professor Thomas Emerson would join the defense team near the end of the year.[100]

One obstacle that defendants in the Flynn case did not have to confront was a blatantly hostile judge. Instead, they faced newly appointed Judge Edward S. Dimock, who was, according to Flynn, "in every possible way different" from Harold Medina. Dimock shocked observers who had come to see an indictment under the Smith Act as a de facto conviction when he ordered the direct acquittal of Simon Gerson and Isidore Begun for lack of evidence, thus reducing the number of defendants to thirteen. Flynn recalled, "He was calm, reasonable, and courteous to lawyers and defendants. We were granted the presumption of innocence. He created a relaxed court atmosphere, allowing one defendant with ulcers to have milk brought in regularly." Flynn was ecumenical in her approach to friendship, and over the course of the trial, she grew fond of Dimock. When she was legally required to remain within the Southern District of New York, he granted her exceptions to travel to Philadelphia to address a meeting of the Freedom of the Press association and to the Atlanta Federal Penitentiary with counsel to consult with Gene Dennis after the testimony of former Communist Louis Budenz. "I cannot speak for all my co-defendants," she later observed, "but I have a kindly feeling for 'our little judge.'" After the trial, she remained in touch with Dimock, and when her prison memoir was published, she sent him an autographed copy.[101]

The Trial

The trial opened on March 31, 1952. As the defendants were now otherwise engaged, the newly formed Citizens Emergency Defense Conference took over responsibility for raising funds and publicity, including publication of a biweekly trial report. This time around, there were no demonstrations in front of the courthouse. As with the first trial, proceedings began with a jury challenge by the defendants that lasted three weeks. The second trial was a repeat of the previous one in other ways. As Flynn explained, "The charge against us was practically identical—'conspiracy to teach and advocate,' etc. The government witnesses were the same informers and stool pigeons [including Louis Budenz with allegations of Aesopian language], posing as experts. The so-called 'evidence' was the same, books by Marx, Engels, Lenin, Stalin, and a few American writers." She noted the tedium of the trial. Volumes of written material were "trundled into court daily by an FBI agent, in a cart like a baby carriage. Long and unintelligible quotes, torn out of context, were read to a bored and uncomprehending jury."[102] After a while, even the press got bored.

As far as Flynn was concerned, the case was a repeat performance in one other respect. Although ostensibly she and her comrades were the defendants, the real entity on trial was the CPUSA. Consequently, much of the evidence had little or nothing to do with any of the men and women in the dock. However much Flynn liked Judge Dimock, he was similar to his counterparts in other Smith Act cases in that he was deaf to pleas of insufficient or irrelevant evidence. He was also unmoved by the argument that Cold War attitudes made it impossible for Communists to get a fair trial. The latter argument certainly had merit. During the Flynn case, the Senate Internal Security Committee issued a pamphlet claiming the CPUSA aimed to overthrow the government by force and violence and held hearings on Communist infiltration of the United Nations in the same building as Dimock's courtroom.[103]

Constitutional law had interested Flynn since her early days as a free speech fighter, and over the years she had acted as her own counsel when she was on trial. This time was no different. Her co-defendant Pettis Perry also represented himself. To combat the idea that Communists were agents of a foreign power, Richard O. Boyer, public relations director for the defense campaign, exploited the symbolism of their respective gender and race in an effort to root the party in the history of progressive U.S. social movements. Boyer likened the two comrades to Elizabeth Cady Stanton and Frederick Douglass, noting that a white woman and a Black man had not jointly represented a public case of such significance since Stanton and Douglass "acted together a hundred years ago to fight for women's rights and the abolition of slavery."[104]

Flynn delivered her opening statement on April 24, 1952. Four months shy of her sixty-second birthday, no longer a girl, although still a rebel with decades of experience charming hostile audiences, she chose her words carefully. Her task was to ingratiate herself to the jury, humanize herself and her co-defendants, and destigmatize the party. Given the intensity of feelings against Communists at the time, there was practically no chance she would succeed.

At the outset, Flynn announced her intention to inform the jury about "what the Communist Party of the U.S.A. really stands for, what it advocates, what its day-to-day activities are, and what are its ultimate aims" in "simple, non-technical language." She acknowledged that members of the jury might never have seen or met an actual Communist before and might find their ideas "new and strange." She asked not for agreement but for open-mindedness when confronted with "the sensational tales of stool-pigeons and planted agents" who served as witnesses for the government.[105]

After thus framing her objectives, she introduced herself to the jury. As always, she began by claiming her Irish American identity: "I am an American of Irish descent. My father, Thomas Flynn, was born in Maine. My mother, Anne Gurley, was born in Galway, Ireland. I was born in Concord, New Hampshire, 62 years ago." She went on to describe her labor lineage by noting, "My father, grandfather, and all my uncles were members of labor unions." Flynn located the origins of her own politics in the feminist, socialist, antiracist, anti-imperialist politics of her parents, her exposure at a young age to writings of Marx and Engels, and the poverty and discrimination she witnessed and experienced firsthand. She traced her career as an advocate for working people from middle school in the Bronx—where, at the age of twelve, she won a silver medal in a debate on the resolution "Should the Government own the mines?"—to organizing for the IWW in her teens and twenties, to her efforts to save Sacco and Vanzetti as head of the Workers' Defense Union and a founding member of the ACLU, to her application for membership in the Communist Party after reading Georgi Dimitrov's speech calling for a united front against fascism in 1935.[106]

In the rest of her statement, Flynn combined a defense of the party and Marxist-Leninist theories with a classic civil liberties argument: "We will prove to you that it is not we who flaunt the Constitution and the Bill of Rights, but that it has always been done by the employing class. We will prove that we are fighting here for our constitutional and democratic rights, not to advocate force and violence, but to expose and stop its use against the people. We will demonstrate that in fighting for our rights, we believe we are defending the constitutional rights of all Americans.

We believe we are acting as good Americans."[107] The Bill of Rights grants everyone the freedom to advocate their views, Flynn pointed out, but since Communists' ideas were on trial, she and her comrades had "a sacred duty to [themselves] and to [their] Party to adequately defend them from any slander or distortion." This duty to defend the party and its principles was a First Amendment right afforded to her and her co-defendants as American citizens: "We contend that Americans have a right to speak their minds out on any subject. We Communists have a right to defend socialism or the evolution of the capitalist system and economy and of the private ownership of the means of life of all the people."[108]

Flynn's defense of the party and of Marxist-Leninist ideas was largely boilerplate language. The CPUSA was not under control of a foreign power. Communists did not advocate force and violence. The transition to socialism would come if, and only if, the people wanted it, which, of course, she believed they did. In other words, Americans had a right to be Communists, and if left to their own devices, they would almost certainly exercise that right. Force and violence would come into play only if capitalist profiteers attempted to thwart the will of the people.

Things got interesting when Flynn addressed the party's electoral fortunes. The CPUSA, she asserted, was a legitimate political party that had nominated candidates for all public offices, including that of president. Communist candidates, among them herself and several of her co-defendants, had won a substantially high number of votes. If the CPUSA and other third parties had not been hampered by electoral restrictions and barred from the ballot in various states, they would have won even more votes and elected candidates to more offices, including Congress. As proof, she turned to the international scene. Without stopping to acknowledge differences between political circumstances in the United States and elsewhere, she pointed out that Communists held office in the parliaments of all major nonfascist countries in the world. "This," Flynn insisted, "is the arena where political views belong, in the marketplace of public discussion, to be passed upon solely by the electorate of our country."[109]

Flynn made this argument several times in her statement. Each time, she justified her claim with the "marketplace of ideas" concept. The idea, which originated with John Stuart Mill, was introduced into American free speech rhetoric by Supreme Court Justice Oliver Wendell Holmes in his dissent from a majority ruling in *Abrams v. the United States*, which upheld the conviction of an anarchist under the Espionage Act in 1919. It rested on an analogy between the free flow of ideas in a democratic society and the free flow of goods in a market economy. That Flynn would use a concept that had migrated from legal discourse to public discourse was unremarkable. That a Communist would defend her party's right to advocate for socialism with a concept that depended for its meaning on a capitalist free market analogy is ironic, almost tragically so. It suggests the extent to which the logic of capitalism had pervaded U.S. society and constrained possibilities for articulating alternatives, even among those who were dedicated to subverting the system. The days when Flynn and other Wobblies climbed atop street corner soapboxes in Missoula, Montana, and exercised their right to speak for the abolition of wage labor in defiance of the law were long gone.

As part of her effort to educate the jury about the activities and aims of the CPUSA, Flynn spoke at some length about her advocacy for women's issues. Her comments reveal the extent to which her thinking had become more sophisticated because of her friendship with Claudia Jones: "My comrade, Claudia Jones, a defendant here, is the executive secretary [of the national committee]. We have worked together, spoken together, written, and helped organize women for full equality, both politically and economically, for the building of movements for peace, consumers' councils, parent-teachers' organizations, for the unity of Negro and white women, and to overcome the exploitation of Negro women as workers, as women, as Negroes."[110]

Here, Flynn referred to the "triple jeopardy" thesis—the idea that working-class Black women face exploitation because of class, race, and gender. She first wrote about the "threefold bond of oppression" in which Black women were caught in an essay for the theoretical journal *Political Affairs* to mark International Women's Day in 1948. At the time, party members were tying themselves in knots over allegations of "white chauvinism," but Flynn's commitment to the struggle for Black liberation was unquestioned. Her way of thinking about the complex reality of Black women's lives in the United States was rare among white women in the late 1940s and early 1950s. In 1981, Angela Davis, who praised Flynn for her perspective on class, race, and gender, noted that the "triple jeopardy" analysis "was later proposed by Black women who sought to influence the early stages of the contemporary Women's Liberation movement."[111]

The day after Flynn delivered her opening statement, Judge Dimock barred the defendants from discussing their trial in public. His order prevented Flynn from referring to the proceedings in her *Daily Worker* column or speaking about the case at meetings or other fundraising events. Although she was now unable to advocate for herself or her co-defendants, the order did not prevent Flynn from discussing other Smith Act cases. She continued to campaign for her jailed comrades, whom she referred to as "political prisoners," highlighting the poor treatment and deplorable conditions they experienced in prison. She also promoted the party's amnesty movement for the Dennis defendants, which was launched on May Day 1952.[112] On May 29, Dimock lifted the "gag order," as it was called, for all the defendants but Flynn and Perry.

Subversive Activities Control Board Testimony

During the trial, Flynn was called on to testify before the Subversive Activities Control Board. Established in November 1950 and operating under authority of the McCarran Act, the board was tasked with identifying "Communist-action" or "Communist-front" organizations and ordering the registration of such organizations with the DOJ. Its hearings had been held in Washington, but they were moved to New York, where Flynn appeared before a two-member panel for three days. Her testimony was sought to help the board determine whether the CPUSA was a Soviet-controlled organization participating in a worldwide Communist movement and thus required to register.

In preparation for the hearings, Flynn wrote to Jacques Duclos, secretary of the Communist Party of France and author of the article that had precipitated the dissolution of the CPA in 1945. She asked him to submit an affidavit to support the party's argument that it was not under the control of a foreign power. The affidavit was to state that Duclos had never given the CPUSA orders or directives but that he simply "wrote an article in a French Party magazine which was directed to the membership of the Communist Party of France which [the CPUSA was] entirely free to draw conclusions from, if [they] so desired."[113] Duclos acceded to the request with a sworn statement that his 1945 article "expressed the point of view of a member of the French Communist Party and cannot be considered as constituting either an order or a directive to American Communists, who [were] solely responsible for determining their political direction and activities."[114] Flynn's overture was clever but also disingenuous. Whether his article was intended as a directive to dissolve the CPA was by now a moot point. When it was published, numerous party leaders, including Flynn herself, interpreted it as such.

In her testimony to the panel, Flynn insisted the party had received neither directions, instructions, nor financial aid from the Soviet Union since she joined the national committee in 1938. She also testified that relations between the CPUSA and the Comintern had ceased when the former disaffiliated with the latter in 1940. In addition, she stated that she had never advocated the overthrow of the U.S. government by force and violence and that the party did not advocate sabotage or espionage to fulfill its aims. In a throwback to the first Red Scare, when she had been arrested for violating the Espionage Act, Flynn was questioned about her authorship of the pamphlet *Sabotage*, published during her Wobbly period in 1914. She dismissed the pamphlet as "extreme infantile leftism."[115] Highlights of the exchange between Flynn and her interlocutors appeared in the *Daily Worker*.

To show that Flynn's antiracism and anti-imperialism had not been mandated by the Soviet Union, Vito Marcantonio, attorney for the party, asked her if her parents had discussed racial discrimination and imperialism with her. In reply, Flynn described how her parents had fought discrimination against Irish Americans and all forms of British imperialism. She also spoke about her father's opposition to the Spanish-American War and the annexation of the Philippines. The panel permitted her to discuss her early years as a socialist, but she was not allowed to testify about her long and varied experience with civil liberties and labor defense campaigns. When asked, "To whom do you owe allegiance?" she responded, "I owe allegiance to the American people." Of course, being herself, she could not resist the impulse to inject her signature brand of witty repartee into the proceedings. "Do you owe allegiance to any foreign power?" she was asked. "No foreign power at all. But I admit I have a soft spot for Ireland."[116] The comment went over well among European Irish radicals, prompting the London-based Connolly Association to praise Flynn as "one of the greatest living Irish Americans" and to call for telegrams and letters of protest to American embassies demanding that she and her co-defendants be released.[117]

The Fight Drags On

Such witty exchanges aside, Flynn and her co-defendants struggled through the remainder of 1952. The resources required to fund bail for comrades around the country, educational and publicity materials, attorneys, and other expenses associated with litigation for multiple defendants left the party constantly appealing for money. The unpopularity of their cause meant that Communists could not count on a wide base of financial support. Donations came in, some of them accompanied by fond recollections of Flynn leading a free speech fight or strike or speaking at a mass meeting, but not nearly as many or as often as needed. At one point, Flynn noted that the defense campaign needed to raise "about six times as much money per day" as they were currently raising.[118] By mid-June 1952, the campaign was in debt. Throughout the trial, Flynn and others complained that mainstream papers refused to acknowledge press releases from the defense committee or consider any point of view that might have pierced the veil of pervasive anti-Communism that marked the moment. Increasingly, they were shut off from other ways of taking their case beyond the confines of the party to working-class New Yorkers. Flynn reported on violence that erupted when gangs of thugs broke up street meetings in Manhattan and Queens while police stood by and did nothing.[119] The situation for Communists did not improve in the fall of 1952. In September, during a presidential campaign rife with allegations that Democrats were soft on Communism, government agents rounded up comrades in Michigan, Missouri, Washington, Oregon, and Illinois. President Truman touted the roundups as key to a national campaign against subversion.[120]

On October 3, 1952, Flynn, the only defendant to testify, took the witness stand, where she was questioned by defense attorney Mary Kaufman. The process of direct and cross-examination lasted an exhausting eight weeks. Initially, few observers came to hear her testimony. During the appeals process, Flynn recalled that throughout the ordeal she saw no representative of the ACLU appear as an observer "to see if due process was served or to help [them in their] struggle against a stacked jury system." She was not surprised: "How can they, when they assert they believe the lies peddled in these trials?" In fact, she laid responsibility for the Smith Act trials at the feet of the organization: "When and if the prison door closes on me and I serve a three-year sentence on a Smith Act thought control conviction, it is the logical conclusion of my expulsion from the ACLU fourteen years ago. How could they defend me today against the very charges they themselves made then?"[121]

Joseph North also reflected on the lack of observers in the courthouse for the trial, and especially for Flynn's testimony, in the *Daily Worker*: "You look at the long empty benches in the press box, at the sparse rows of spectators. And you think: These are truths that should echo across the nation." He continued, with palpable frustration, "You have an impulse, when the day's session is ended, to go out on the street corners and shout to New Yorkers, 'Come fill these benches: listen to the men and women whose truths will keep you out of the tin shacks of Hooverville.' You want to shout, 'Gurley Flynn is on the stand fellow Americans.'"[122]

Unfortunately, the fellow Americans to which North wanted to shout were being subjected to a barrage of negative reporting about Flynn during the trial. Not all of it concerned her political views. Newspaper accounts referred to her rather unflatteringly as a "big, fat slob" who should be pushing "a hefty, useful mop in prison"; "Red Liz"; "a war horse of radical agitation"; "the 'first lady' of American Communism"; and "an old Communist Party battle-axe."[123] It must have been difficult to read such unflattering descriptions of herself. Of course, she had the support of fellow Communists in the United States as well as a few individuals whom she had known since before she joined the party, including Catholic Worker movement founder Dorothy Day, who attended the trial periodically, ACLU board member John Codman, and social reformer Mary Dreier.[124] Solidarity from comrades in Paris, London, Dublin, Belfast, and elsewhere outside the United States surely buoyed her as well.[125]

Among fellow Communists, reactions to Flynn's testimony were mixed. According to some, she made a noble effort, but she struggled to answer questions about theoretical doctrine, events around the reconstitution of the CPA as the CPUSA, and the relationship between the party and the *Daily Worker*.[126] Others praised Flynn's performance, especially her courageous refusal to identify Communists who were not already Smith Act defendants when asked to do so by the prosecution. The Fifth Amendment did not apply to voluntary witnesses, and for her refusal, Judge Dimock charged Flynn with contempt of court and sentenced her to two sentences of thirty days in the House of Detention, which he allowed her to serve concurrently. Before a large audience that had come to hear her defend her choice to withhold the identity of her comrades, Flynn thundered that for her to name Communists would discredit her Irish ancestry as well as her long years in the labor movement and subject innocent people to the risk of losing their jobs, surveillance by the FBI, and legal prosecution. Claudia Jones wrote admiringly of Flynn's principled position, "It was a day for our history books. It was a day that will live. Made memorable by the words and actions of a proud woman, a Communist woman defending the traditions of her Irish ancestors, the working class, the Negro people and all who cherish peace, democracy, brotherhood."[127]

Flynn spent most of December being transported to and from the Foley Square courthouse and the Women's House of Detention. She was released on January 4, 1953. That same day, the defense opened its final plea to the jury. Flynn presented the text of a written interview with Joseph Stalin by James Reston, diplomatic correspondent of the *New York Times*, published on Christmas Day 1952.¹²⁸ In response to four questions posed by the *Times* reporter, Stalin expressed belief that the United States and the Soviet Union could live peacefully together and indicated a favorable disposition toward the idea of meeting with incoming president Eisenhower as well as a willingness to cooperate in a new diplomatic initiative to end the Korean War. He also stated his belief that the cause of world strife lay in the Cold War policies of the Western powers. In presenting the text, Flynn aimed to refute Judge Dimock's ruling that the existence of the Soviet Union under Communist leadership and the activities of communist parties throughout the world—as evidenced by events in China, Tibet, Korea, Malaya, Indochina, and Berlin—constituted a "clear and present danger" of inevitable war, which was a necessary precondition for conviction by a jury under the Smith Act.¹²⁹

On January 6, Flynn delivered her summation speech. Although she promised to be brief, the text of her speech is thirty-four typed pages and reflects considerable effort on her part, all the more so because she had spent the previous thirty days in prison, or as she put it, she had been "under certain disabilities" in her preparations. In her speech, Flynn rooted the origins of the CPUSA in the history of socialism in the United States, refuted allegations of conspiracy, challenged the nature and relevance of the evidence, exposed nefarious motives of witnesses for the prosecution, championed the Bill of Rights, warned of the dangers of creeping fascism, and called for an acquittal for herself and her comrades.¹³⁰

Verdict and Appeal Redux

Deliberations began on January 15, 1953. Six days later, the jury found the defendants guilty. Flynn was sentenced to three years in prison and fined six thousand dollars. Bail was set at $25 thousand. In a move that surprised everyone, Judge Dimock offered to withhold sentencing, giving Flynn and her co-defendants the option of exile to the Soviet Union instead. Flynn quipped that the offer "was comparable to asking a Christian if he wanted to go to heaven right away" and refused, stating that she and her comrades had "no desire to enjoy the fruits of socialism in a land where [they] did not work for it." Upon receiving her sentence, she remarked, "My body can be incarcerated, but my thoughts will be free."¹³¹

The defense immediately began preparations for an appeal, and Flynn contributed to that effort. She also returned to her role as the face of the party by speaking against the Smith Act at New York City rallies held within the boundaries of the Southern District and contributing regularly again to the *Daily Worker* (she had taken a leave from her column while she testified during the trial). She wrote and spoke on a variety of issues, including the importance of the right to travel, which was denied her while her case was under appeal; the threat to civil liberties posed by the Subversive Activities Control Board order that the CPUSA and its leadership, as well as twelve Communist front organizations, register with the federal government under the McCarran Act; the danger of the Goldwater-Rhodes Bill, a proposed law that would strip Communist-led unions of collective bargaining rights; the harsh treatment of political prisoners in the United States, including first-string defendant Robert Thompson, who had been apprehended at his underground hiding place in California, arrested, and sent to the Atlanta Penitentiary; and the execution of the Rosenbergs.[132]

As was her style throughout her career, Flynn explained even the most arcane concepts in clear and accessible language without patronizing her audience. The result was an engaging mix of politics and opinion that occasionally included details about her personal life. She was forthcoming, for example, about her need to "to get rid of excess poundage" in order to "banish arthritis." She also announced that she had begun writing her autobiography and invited readers "of the older generation" to share recollections of when they first heard her speak or any labor struggles they were in together as well as photos or documents that might help jog her memory about long-ago events.[133] Her column presented a humane face for the party at a time when comrades were dealing with the stress of external repression by turning against one another and looking to expel members for any number of so-called political or personal transgressions, ranging from "Browderism" and "left deviationism" to homosexuality and "white chauvinism."[134] Flynn, who typically did her best to avoid internecine squabbles, threaded the needle by encouraging vigilance among party members to root out "stoolpigeons" while cautioning against "witchhunts."[135]

The fighting spirit that Flynn displayed in her writing inspired journalists and Smith Act defendants around the country to champion the Bill of Rights and mount their own challenges to the federal government's campaign against the CPUSA.[136] Behind the scenes, however, she remained frustrated by comrades who were not in jail or under indictment and were using Foster's warning at the 1948 convention to dismiss the importance of defense work. She shared her frustration with the lingering popularity of Foster's admonition in a letter to Steve Nelson, with whom she shared a warm friendship: "How can we build an amnesty movement or defend the legal existence of our Party if 'defense' becomes something to be warned against?" She also noted how those who dismissed the need for defense work and showed no concern for the toll that being on trial took from defendants changed their minds once they found themselves targeted by an indictment: "I have to laugh up my sleeve when folks who talked like that get arrested themselves and overnight change their viewpoint. Dialectics!" Ever mindful of the party's leadership structure, she thought Foster should clarify his point and thus clear up the matter.[137]

Her own fight against the Smith Act took a great toll on Flynn's mental and physical health. Because her *Daily Worker* column was so popular with readers, she was pressured to continue writing it even while she was trying to complete her book manuscript, not to mention shouldering the stressful burden of defense work and facing an increasingly likely prison sentence. She periodically escaped the pressure and the hectic pace of New York City for "a quiet restful place"—that is, Wappingers Falls, a town near Poughkeepsie. There, she confessed in a letter to Mary Kaufman (who was by now a dear friend as well as legal counsel for the defense), she could at least partially recover from "the complete mental and physical exhaustion which overwhelmed [her]."[138] It is no wonder she felt a need to relax. As reported by her physician, Flynn's blood pressure at the time was 180/110, a sign that she was entering hypertensive crisis, a potentially life-threatening situation—often accompanied by shortness of breath, chest pains, and heart palpitations—that could cause permanent organ damage.[139]

The appellate brief for defendants in the Flynn case was filed in November 1953. The appeal was based on three grounds: lack of evidence linking any of the defendants to a specific intent to overthrow the U.S. government by force and violence; lack of evidence demonstrating "clear and present danger" of overthrow of the U.S. government by the defendants; and prejudicial testimony with no connection to the defendants along with prejudice on the part of jury members. On January 7, 1954, while the brief was wending its way through the legal system, Dwight Eisenhower delivered his second State of the Union address to Congress. In the speech, he identified the "world Communist conspiracy" as the greatest threat to American freedom and the freedom of other people around the globe. He also referred to the Smith Act trials, stating, "The subversive character of the Communist Party in the United States has been clearly demonstrated in many ways, including court proceedings." According to Eisenhower, membership in the CPUSA was "akin to treason" and demonstrated lack of allegiance to the United States. He therefore called for legislation to strip Smith Act violators of citizenship.[140] In such a political climate, the appeal had no chance of success.

Arguments for the appeal began May 10, 1954. They lasted six weeks. Meanwhile, the situation continued to deteriorate for Communists. On June 4, eight comrades were arrested in Connecticut. In August, Communists were arrested in Colorado and Utah. That same month, President Eisenhower signed into law the Communist Control Act, which amended the McCarran Act to outlaw the CPUSA and criminalize support for the party or "Communist-action" (front) groups. A week later, Eisenhower signed the Expatriation Act, which fulfilled his State of the Union request of Congress by providing for the automatic loss of U.S. citizenship for anyone convicted of rebellion and insurrection, seditious conspiracy, and advocating overthrow of the government by force and violence in the manner proscribed by the Smith Act.[141]

Always a fighter, Flynn refused to be cowed into submission by the federal government's latest efforts to crush the CPUSA. Nor would she ever consider going underground and working clandestinely. Instead, she led a series of highly visible initiatives as part of the party's "Fight Back" movement. During the summer of 1954, while Congress was debating the Communist Control Act and the Repatriation Act, she announced the party's intention to file a petition with the U.S. Court of Appeals to reopen hearings of the Subversive Activities Control Board so that it could present new evidence challenging the credibility of three of the government's main witnesses. She also assembled a team of mostly young adult volunteers and made a run for Congress as an independent candidate in the Twenty-Fourth Congressional District of New York. The campaign was intended as a message that Communists did not consider themselves outlawed and were determined to exercise their political rights. Against all odds, Flynn's group of volunteers, which called itself the People's Rights Party, collected four thousand signatures on her petitions, thus earning her a spot on the ballot. She then led the party's effort to charge the federal government with tax harassment after the Internal Revenue Board issued over twenty subpoenas to various individuals requiring them to turn over financial records.[142] These initiatives highlight Flynn's steadfast political commitments and her determination not to surrender easily or quietly.

The appellate court upheld the verdict in the Flynn case in late October. In fact, appellate courts would affirm every conviction that came before them after the Dennis case. The Flynn defendants then appealed their conviction to the Supreme Court, but the court declined to hear their case. On January 11, 1955, Flynn, Claudia Jones, and Betty Gannett were remanded once again to the Women's House of Detention. A little less than two weeks later, the trio boarded a bus to the Alderson Federal Industrial Institute for Women.

The same day that Flynn arrived at Alderson, her sister Kathie gave an interview to reporter Virginia Gardner, who had written a series on the personal lives of the Rosenbergs for the *Daily Worker*, which was then compiled into a book. As she typically did, Kathie spoke of her sister's years of activism in the labor movement, free speech fights, and defense campaigns. She also provided a glimpse of the "ordinary things" that occupied Elizabeth between speeches and meetings: her love of gardening, flair for cooking and sewing, willingness to do odd jobs around the house, and quasi-compulsive tendency to put things in order. Intimate as well as political, the image that Kathie presented was far from that of the treasonous radical seeking to overthrow the U.S. government by force and violence (it was also far from the truth—Flynn was not fond of the domestic arts). The piece struck its most touching note, however, when Kathie described going home to their shared apartment after her sister was remanded to prison. She turned on all the lights in Elizabeth's front room, went in, and made herself look at "her empty chair, her empty desk." She recalled, "My daughter came over and said, 'We saw all the lights blazing from the street.' 'Yes,' I said. 'I have to see the emptiness and get used to it.'"[143]

Not long after Flynn and her comrades arrived at Alderson, the defense filed a motion for a new trial based on the confession of Henry Matusow, a former Communist and paid FBI informer who testified at the trial and then admitted that he had perjured himself and retracted his testimony. A month later, the Supreme Court again declined to hear their case. In April, Judge Dimock denied the motion for a new trial based on the Matusow confession for all of the second-string defendants except Alexander Trachtenberg and George Charney.[144] Appeals for the Flynn case were now exhausted.

For the first time in a lifetime of skirmishes with the law, Elizabeth Gurley Flynn would not snatch victory from the jaws of defeat. Almost sixty-five years old, overweight, and not in the best health, she faced a lengthy prison term. Still, her fighting spirit did not desert her. While she was behind bars and after her release, she continued to champion the rights of working-class activists to hold and express ideas and to organize for collective action without fear of repression.

CHAPTER 7

The Struggle Continues
Flynn's Final Years

> Let me say, here and now, blunt and plain, no one and nobody can take my country away from me at the ebb of my life.
> —Elizabeth Gurley Flynn

THE ALDERSON FEDERAL Industrial Institute for Women, located in a picturesque mountainous region in southeastern West Virginia, first opened its doors in 1927. It was the brainchild of Assistant Attorney General Mabel Willebrandt, who had proposed the idea of a women's federal prison in the early 1920s. Intended as a place of regulation and reform rather than punishment, Alderson, as it became known, was modeled after a boarding school, with fourteen cottages arranged in a horseshoe pattern, each with its own kitchen. There was no barbed wire, and there were no armed guards. Most inmates were there for minor offenses related to drug and alcohol use.[1]

Flynn took comfort in the natural beauty that surrounded Alderson. "The scenery is lovely," she told her sister Kathie in a letter she wrote soon after her arrival on a cold January day, "and the quiet is a blessed relief. There is a light covering of snow on the hills. Spring should be beautiful."[2] Yet despite the beautiful rural setting and the lack of barbed wire, Alderson was nonetheless a prison. In her memoir of her Alderson experience, Flynn recalled, "The turning of a key on the outside of the door is a weird sensation to which one never became accustomed. One felt like a trapped animal in a cage."[3] In addition to the psychological difficulty of physical confinement, Flynn struggled with noise during the day, including the "cowboy music" she was forced to endure, physical discomfort from arthritis in her knee, a dearth of intellectual conversation, lack of male company, and an unquenchable thirst for news from the outside. She dearly missed family, friends, comrades, her cat, her daily routines, and the movement.

Unlike many of her comrades who found themselves doubting the course of American Communism or seriously questioning fundamental premises of the party while they were in prison or underground, Flynn's political faith was not shaken by whatever isolation and loneliness she may have experienced at Alderson.[4] The seismic changes that were beginning to manifest in U.S. popular culture gave her pause: she puzzled over the popularity of Elvis; lamented the changing literary preferences of college students, particularly their fondness for poet (and, as she noted, fascist sympathizer) Ezra Pound; decried the wearing of slacks by women, which she dismissed as a "fad"; and criticized the ACLU for expanding the purview of its work to include defense of the right to distribute pornography. At the same time, she welcomed the rise of a new generation and expressed hope that younger people would be open to the wisdom that she and others with years of "experience" might have to offer. What she did not question was the political trajectory of her life or her party.

The "Politicals"

Flynn saw herself as a political prisoner, and that identity steeled her commitment to the CPUSA. (Surveillance of her while she was at Alderson suggests that Hoover and the FBI saw Flynn as a political prisoner as well.) She had been fighting for the recognition of political prisoners in the United States since her days with the Workers' Defense Union in the aftermath of World War I. If the federal government refused to afford her the official status of a political prisoner during the Cold War, no matter; she bestowed it upon herself: "Come what may, *I was a political prisoner* and proud of it, at one with some of the noblest of humanity, who had suffered for conscience's sake."[5] Rather than accept the label of "criminal" imposed on her by the Smith Act, she rewrote herself, Claudia Jones, Betty Gannett, and, by extension, all Communists as idealists whose only crime was holding their country up to its own promise. She identified the Puerto Rican nationalists in Alderson as political prisoners for the same reason.

Being a Communist political prisoner meant that Flynn, Jones, and Gannett suffered discrimination at the hands of some of the prison guards—and Jones, of course, suffered discrimination for her race, as did the Black prison guards—but it had its advantages. Whereas most of the women received few if any letters and were penniless or sent at most a couple of dollars from home, the "politicals," as she called them, got visitors as well as letters and always had funds on hand. The money was donated mostly by the Families Committee of Smith Act Victims, an organization of wives and family members of Communists who were arrested under the law headed by Peggy Dennis, the wife of Gene Dennis. It was against the rules to give money away or to buy things from the commissary for the other prisoners, but the politicals regularly did so. Their sharing amounted to a type of mutual aid, a time-honored enactment of solidarity and resistance among the working classes.

The profile of Alderson's prison population will not surprise twenty-first century readers: mostly poor and working class (as Flynn noted, "no rich women were to be found at Alderson"), majority Black and Spanish speaking, many from abusive backgrounds, some suffering from mental illness and/or drug addiction.[6] Inmates and guards were racially segregated when the prison was founded, and the situation had not changed by the time Flynn, Jones, and Gannett arrived. Jones was assigned to a segregated "colored cottage." After the Supreme Court declared segregation unconstitutional in its 1954 decision in *Brown v. Board of Education*, Alderson was tasked with integrating its prison houses. Officials relied on Flynn, Jones, Gannett, and Dorothy Rose Blumberg, another Communist who was serving three years at Alderson for a Baltimore Smith Act conviction, to help with integration, which "amused and flattered" the women.[7] Although she and her comrades could not eradicate the structural racism that pervaded Alderson, their interventions and educational efforts helped build trust and improve relationships among white, Black, and Latina inmates.

Publishing While in Prison

While she was at Alderson, Flynn's manuscript of the first half of her autobiography was prepared for publication by the periodical *Masses & Mainstream*. Prison regulations prohibited her from editing the manuscript, so she asked her sister Kathie and friend Muriel Symington for help. In August 1955, *Masses & Mainstream* published an excerpt of the forthcoming work, which they titled "An Irish-American Childhood." The book itself was published in November 1955.[8] Its title, *I Speak My Own Piece*, referred to a comment that teenage Flynn had made to a theater producer who had proposed that she act on the stage. She had not chosen it, and the next edition was retitled *The Rebel Girl* to reflect her preference. Flynn was not happy with the book. Years later, in a letter to Al Richmond, she confessed that she thought herself a fool for allowing "party discipline" to pull her away from writing to raise defense funds. She "got chopped into jail" before she could finalize the manuscript, and she observed, as a result, "[The book was] unfinished and full of errors, which makes me sick to contemplate."[9]

Obviously, Flynn could not attend any events to celebrate publication of her autobiography, but that did not stop her comrades from organizing one. On May 4, 1956—Mother's Day—the Families Committee of Smith Act Victims honored her and the publication of *I Speak My Own Piece* with music, dramatic readings of excerpts from the book, and tributes from friends and allies. Kathie Flynn was the featured speaker at the event. Among those who penned tributes were comrades William Patterson and Ben Davis as well as Flynn's allies from before she joined the party, including Scott Nearing and Roger Baldwin. Never one to miss an opportunity to distance himself from Communists, Baldwin qualified his tribute by pointing out that he and Flynn had "parted company long ago over her political views."[10]

Her autobiography was not the only thing that Flynn published while she was at Alderson. In an ironic turn, prison authorities invited her to compose a "patriotic article" for publication in the July 4 issue of the 1956 *Alderson Eagle*, the prison's magazine. The offer gave her a chance to make a case for the revolutionary origins of the United States and the centrality of democratic rights to the national project, all of which she had been doing throughout her activist career, so of course she accepted.

In the article, Flynn included a brief historical sketch of how the Declaration of Independence came into existence and who signed it as well as a summary of its contents. She also noted the declaration's significance for anticolonial/anti-imperial movements around the world as well as efforts to expand democracy at home. The section listing grievances against King George III, she noted, has "echoed in similar declarations by people of the Philippines, Puerto Rico, Viet-Nam, Algeria, Ireland, and many others." In the United States, the declaration's "clarion call for the rights of men" was amplified in the Emancipation Proclamation "declaring the slaves forever free" and in the Nineteenth Amendment to the U.S. Constitution, which granted suffrage to women. She claimed the Bill of Rights as "a logical conclusion of the Declaration of Independence" and urged every American to read both documents annually on the Fourth of July to "refresh our memories of their immortal words, to cherish our democratic traditions and to practice them in life." Flynn concluded the article by listing not the amendments that comprise the Bill of Rights but the Four Freedoms, which then President Franklin Roosevelt had presented in a speech to Congress in 1941:

1. Freedom of Speech and Expression
2. Freedom of Religion
3. Freedom from Want
4. Freedom from Fear[11]

While she could not take the opportunity to promote a socialist America, with this list Flynn could—and did—connect the nation's eighteenth-century revolutionary tradition with the New Deal and the working-class militancy of the 1930s.

Her willingness to pen and publish an article to mark a holiday celebrating independence and freedom while she was in prison for holding "dangerous" political beliefs illustrates that Flynn was not one to dwell on the negative even in the most difficult circumstances. To make best use of her time at Alderson, she committed herself to losing weight ("I feel ashamed when the scale registers 248!" she confided to Kathie), a challenge given the "excellent and plentiful" food that was available, and to keeping busy by sewing (her job assignment), reading both fiction and nonfiction, writing poetry, organizing her thoughts in preparation for the second volume of her autobiography, getting to know fellow prisoners, and reading/writing letters.[12] She eagerly looked forward to visits from her sister, who came on the last day of the month and stayed overnight to visit again on the first day of the following month, which made the trip from New York City to West Virginia a bit less arduous.

During the twenty-eight months she spent in prison, Flynn corresponded regularly with Kathie, nephew Peter Martin (the son of Tresca and her sister Sabina), friends Symington and Clemens France, and attorneys John Abt and Mary Kaufman, who also made occasional visits to Alderson. Prison regulations permitted her to write three letters per week to her designated correspondents (these did not include her attorneys), and while she wrote often to Kathie, she rotated among the other recipients. Letter-writing provided Flynn a way to maintain personal connections with friends and family, keep apprised of legal issues pertaining to her case and those of other Smith Act defendants, and receive information about political developments at home and abroad, which, because she was prohibited from receiving the *Daily Worker*, she read about in publications like the *New York Herald Tribune*, the *Nation*, the *New York Times*, and *Time*.

Khrushchev's Speech and the Dennis Report

The factionalism that had disturbed Flynn so much during the party's contentious era in the 1920s resurfaced while she was at Alderson as a battle over the future of the CPUSA erupted among her comrades. She followed as best she could from afar. The first skirmish was over the party's relationship to Stalin. It began in response to reports of a four-hour speech that Nikita Khrushchev delivered to a closed session of CPSU delegates at the party's twentieth congress on February 29, 1956. Khrushchev was said to have detailed Stalin's abuse of power from the purges of the 1930s—during which 70 percent of Central Committee members elected at the Seventeenth Congress, many of whom had joined the party before the Revolution or during the Civil War, were arrested and shot—until his death in 1953. He allegedly used the phrase "cult of the individual" to explain how Stalin had come to dominate the party at the expense of internal democracy.

In contrast to their counterparts among many communist parties around the globe, when leaders of the CPUSA heard reports of the secret speech, they did not dismiss the reports as capitalist lies. On the contrary, after a period of stunned silence, a debate of sorts about Stalin's virtues and vices erupted in the *Daily Worker*.[13] Foreign editor Joseph Clark reported that an East German Communist leader had identified Stalin as the source of the "cult of the individual." The next day, Alan Max, managing editor of the paper, wrote an editorial in which he criticized American Communists for having gone overboard in defending the idea of Stalin's infallibility, opposing arguments that civil liberties were not fully respected in the Soviet Union, and discouraging any critical discussion about Soviet culture.[14] Foster followed up with a rejoinder in which he warned against rushing to judgment about Stalin's mistakes, given the severe trials and struggles of the Soviet people, which had required a high degree of centralization and strong discipline to surmount. Unable to resist an opportunity to cast aspersions on his formal rival, he chastised members of the CPUSA for having come perilously close to investing too much power in the hands of one of their own leaders—namely, "the renegade Browder."[15]

Flynn learned of the secret speech and the debate in the *Daily Worker* from the *New York Times*. She did not flinch at the idea of reevaluating Stalin. Instead, in a letter to Muriel Symington, she praised the CPSU for an "impressive example of self-criticism." Like Foster, she thought it prudent to hold off judgment until all the facts were known, however she did try to put her own gloss on the speech: "I imagine 'cult of the individual' is an awkward translation and 'hero worship' is what is implied. The great man theory is incompatible with modern scientific historical analysis is what they are really saying, and correctly, I believe."[16] In fact, Flynn believed there were too many so-called great men trying to run the world, and she was frustrated at their unwillingness to step down, get out of the way, and turn the ship over to a younger generation. She referred explicitly to political leaders like Churchill, but she was likely thinking of leaders of the Communist Party as well.

The next skirmish concerned the overall direction of the CPUSA. It happened at an enlarged meeting of the national committee (the first such meeting in five years) held in late April 1956. The meeting was attended by several party leaders convicted in the first New York Smith Act Trial who had completed their prison terms and those who had reemerged after serving time "underground" as well as dozens of district level organizers and trade union activists. Steve Nelson chaired. Recently released from the Atlanta Penitentiary, General Secretary Gene Dennis dropped a bomb when he issued a report evaluating party policy since the fall of Browder. The report, which had been vetted and approved by members of the national committee in advance, was an unprecedented act of self-criticism by American Communists.

Dennis's report criticized the party's leadership for misreading the economic and political situation at home and abroad and, as a result, making flawed policy decisions and egregious tactical errors. The assumption that a third world war was inevitable had led the party to sacrifice all other concerns to foreign policy considerations. Belief in an imminent fascist takeover of the United States had motivated the decision to send party members underground, which hurt those who were subject to that decision. The party's flawed analysis of economic data had led to the false conclusion that economic crises were imminent in the mid and late 1940s and the erroneous prediction of a major economic depression in 1955–1956. These blunders, Dennis concluded, exemplified a long-standing tendency to apply the experiences of other communist parties and the science of Marxism in "a mechanical and doctrinaire fashion," which fueled the claim among their enemies that Communists in the United States were "foreign agents." He proposed the idea of replacing the CPUSA with a "united, mass party of socialism" with a broader doctrinal basis and members that included pro-Socialist Americans who did not identify as Communists.[17] Although he focused primarily on errors made by the party during the last ten years, Dennis implicitly vindicated Earl Browder and his program to transform the CPUSA into a more collaborative and American-oriented organization. Not surprisingly, William Z. Foster, who was at the national committee meeting, vehemently opposed the report.

At the same meeting, national committee members received a letter from a British comrade containing a synopsis of Khrushchev's "secret speech." Secondhand reports and rumors, even if they were deemed credible, had not prepared party stalwarts for the substance of Khrushchev's revelations. Those who heard the details at the national committee meeting were shocked and horrified—some to the point of tears. As Steve Nelson recalled, "You might prove that one guy was a rascal. Perhaps you could prove this about two or even a dozen, but 70 percent of the Central Committee? This was a massacre."[18] Many decided that the relationship between the Soviet and American parties had been ill conceived and that Marxism-Leninism had ceased to function, at least among the leadership of the CPUSA, as a dynamic and flexible system and instead had degenerated to the point where it meant simply whatever Stalin said. It was time, they concluded, for American Communists to think for themselves.

Flynn did not learn the actual content of the Khrushchev speech until it was made public after the State Department released an edited version on June 4, 1956. She initially read only excerpts, and they left her feeling disquieted. "I write of one thing and my mind is on the other—the Khrushchev speech," she told Kathie in one of her weekly letters in early June. "It's quite ghastly—hard to understand."[19] A week later, after she had read the edited version in the *Times*, framed by a front-page article that blared, "Dead Dictator Painted as Savage, Half-Mad, and Power-Crazed," she still struggled to understand: "Comment is difficult, not knowing if there was more, if this is a correct and accurate translation, etc." Unlike Communists at the gut-wrenching national committee meeting, Flynn was not learning of Stalin's crimes from a trusted source in the company of longtime comrades. She was isolated, with no alternative sources of information for corroboration and, since Claudia Jones had been released in October 1955, no one with whom to process the news, and she found the situation "terribly disturbing." She seems not to have known that the *Daily Worker* had printed the speech, the only Communist newspaper in the world to do so, nor did she know about the intense and unprecedented debate among her comrades that was happening in the pages of that newspaper. What she did know was that in the already fraught atmosphere of the Cold War, Khrushchev's revelations had "furnished a field day for all reactionaries, social democrats, and others who hate the Soviet Union."[20]

Once the shock abated, however, Flynn was characteristically upbeat. As she wrote to Clemens France, rather than fret about something she could not know or understand with any certainty, she would refrain from judgment until she was able to read and discuss the situation from all angles. In the meantime, she said, "Socialism will survive, and people will live, fall in love, marry, have children, educate new generations, and advance along the path of human progress. In this serene confidence I will pass my 300 odd days I have still to go here."[21]

Serenity would prove difficult to maintain given everything that was happening in the world and in the CPUSA. In response to the Khrushchev revelations, thousands left the party during the summer of 1956.[22] It is unclear whether Flynn knew about the mass exodus, but she was aware of high-profile members who left because of the attention they received from the press. Acclaimed novelist Howard Fast was one well-known Communist whose decision to quit the party made national news. Fast expressed his horror at Khrushchev's revelations about Stalin in the *Daily Worker*. He called the speech "a shameful and awful document . . . that itemizes a record of barbarism and paranoic blood lust that will be a lasting and shameful memory to civilized man." Although he praised the Soviet Union for achievements that in his mind transcended Stalin, such as the defeat of Nazism, Fast regretted that he had not criticized the USSR as he had the United States. Fast's apology did little to mollify the editors of *Time*, who opined, "Such breast-beating had a hollow sound when matched against the agonies of anti-Communists and ex-Communists who have for years tried to warn the world against Communism, only to be smeared by slaves like Fast."[23]

Fast's comments infuriated Flynn. "The arrogance and effrontery of it, in the face of world tragedy, is offensive," she wrote to Clemens France. "Breast beating and 'mea culpa' from one as insignificant as he is in the working class movement are out of place." Her comment contained an interesting mix of elitism and populism. That Fast was both insignificant and an intellectual among the working classes sparked her outrage. It would not be the last time that anti-intellectualism surfaced in her defense of the party.[24]

Joseph Starobin was another former member of the party—he had left in 1954—whom Flynn took to task for his criticism of the CPUSA. Starobin had been foreign editor of the *Daily Worker* from 1945 to 1954. In 1951, he went underground at the party's suggestion and traveled widely throughout Latin America, France, China, and Indochina. His travels were the basis of two books: *Eyewitness in Indochina* (1954) and *Paris to*

Peking (1955). In August 1956, the *Nation* published a letter from Starobin in which he declared, "It is clear that the American Communists do not have what it takes to generate a Socialist revival." He acknowledged party members as "honorable casualties of a fierce assault," but also noted that Communists had disabled themselves by trying to meet the assault with a flawed analysis of the United States and the world in the postwar era that had been shaped by "how the party was formed and the premises on which it functioned, even in its best days." Starobin pondered what form a future socialist movement might take in the United States but could not imagine it, and he laid part of the blame at the feet of liberals and progressives, who had marginalized Marxists and who refused even to recognize a Marxist perspective in the political spectrum: "My own experience is that it is easier to have personal and intellectual contact with conservatives than with liberals."[25]

In her correspondence with Muriel Symington, Flynn offered harsh criticism of Starobin for his letter to the *Nation*. She called it "astonishing" and "shocking." Moreover, she accused Starobin of passing judgment without the benefit of firsthand experience: "Everything is our fault, no realization of the difficulties we have endured since 1948 especially. Of course, he was out of the country most of the time, so passing judgement comes easily." As with her criticism of Howard Fast, Flynn's reaction to Starobin revealed a distaste for intellectuals. She noted that "breast beating" was far more common among "intellectuals" like Starobin than among "working class folks."[26]

Not all visible critics of the party's past practices earned Flynn's ire. She was much more favorably disposed to working-class Gene Dennis and heartily approved of his report to the national committee. In fact, she noticed an important similarity between Dennis's report and her own trial testimony. "I often wonder if in the rush of life in N.Y. Gene ever had a chance to read the testimony in our trial?" she mused in a letter to Kathie. "I hope so—especially my famous colloquies with Judge Dimock, which were under considerable fire at the time you will recall. Now I see in the statement exactly what I said then in my testimony (last paragraph) 'To attain Socialism by constitutional, peaceful means.' I don't want to blow up the importance of this except that it substantiates Gene's remarks today and incidentally gives me a lot of personal satisfaction."[27]

To her male comrades who saw her as lacking in theoretical sophistication, here was proof that she understood how the party might achieve its goals in the political terrain of the United States better than they did. In another letter to Muriel Symington, Flynn gushed about Dennis's

FIGURE 11. Elizabeth Gurley Flynn and Eugene Dennis, 1951.
Credit: Photo appears courtesy of *People's World*

reaction to the Khrushchev speech: "I'm really proud of my friends, especially Gene, who really has become big international news. He speaks plainly and forcefully and I agree with his words that there must be further explanation of how and why it happened and for so long."[28] In 1929, Dennis had fled the United States and spent six years in the Soviet Union to avoid being arrested under California's criminal syndicalism law. When he came under fire after Khrushchev detailed Stalin's purges for not having spoken out, Flynn defended him, insisting that he had no control over events that had happened while he was in Russia.[29]

The Draft Resolution

Members of the national committee scheduled the party's sixteenth national convention for February 1957. In advance of that meeting, the first in seven years, a group of mostly younger Communists who shared a sense that the party needed to reform, although they could not agree on a unified program to achieve that goal, prepared a remarkable document for discussion. The Draft Resolution, as it was called, presented a more radical critique than the Dennis report. It rooted the CPUSA's problems not in events of the past ten years but in bad habits that had been around as long as the party itself. The resolution charged American Communists with accepting interpretations of Marxist theory provided by other parties rather than interpreting Marx for themselves, neglecting to examine and reappraise Marxist theory "in the light of ever-changing reality," and subordinating the U.S. party to communist parties in other countries, even when the views of Marxists in those other countries "did not correspond to American conditions." To address these faults, it challenged the CPUSA to embrace "equality and independence" in "the mutual discussion and resolution of common problems" and to engage in "comradely criticism" of the policies and practices of Communists in other countries.[30]

The resolution also offered an unprecedented criticism of Lenin's principles of democratic centralism and monolithic unity by finding fault with the party's organizational structure and communication practices. The CPUSA was excessively "bureaucratic," which discouraged participation of the membership in policy discussions, and its habit of imposing disciplinary actions on dissenters "further inhibited expressions of disagreement." To make the party more responsive to its members, the resolution called for creation of "channels for freedom of discussion, dissent and criticism within the framework of carrying out the majority will." Finally, it endorsed a more collaborative approach to building socialism in the United States. The assumption that other socialist organizations would eventually find their way into the CPUSA was incorrect and should be replaced by "serious and painstaking efforts to assist in the eventual development of the broadest possible unity of all socialist-minded elements."[31]

The Draft Resolution was published in *Political Affairs* in September 1956. Members were invited to debate it, which they did in subsequent issues of the same publication. Foster, who had voted for the resolution with qualifications but then changed his vote to oppose it, expressed his reservations in a lengthy article published in the journal the following month.[32] As the conflict heated up, Dennis, who had initially been at the forefront of the campaign to reform the party, began to waver. In the weeks and months that followed, John Gates, a Spanish Civil War veteran who had been a Browder supporter during World War II, emerged as the resolution's most outspoken advocate.[33]

Flynn approved of the Draft Resolution. She explained to Muriel Symington in October 1956, "The present statement, which is very good, is an effort to now correct mistakes in policy, trade unions and otherwise." In the same letter, she was critical of journalist I. F. Stone—another breast-beating "intellectual"—for being not altogether fair in his discussion of those mistakes. With regard to the party's alleged sectarianism, she noted that despite their missteps (here she was referring to the party's treatment of Trotskyists prosecuted under the Smith Act), Communists had defended many non-Communists among the Left, including Sacco and Vanzetti and Tom Mooney. Critics of the CPUSA like Stone and others, she lamented, repeatedly failed to notice the party's laudable contributions, especially to the labor movement: "No one ever seems to total up the contributions our people made to originally building up the CIO, only to be dumped when they were no longer needed as pioneer organizers, so that others could get all the fat, well-paid jobs."[34]

Hungary

Ten days after she penned her letter to Muriel Symington, Flynn's faith was shaken again. On October 25 and again on November 4, 1956, Soviet troops invaded Hungary to squelch a popular uprising that had been initiated by university students and was supported by Communist leader and reformer Imre Nagy. Protestors demanded free elections, an impartial legal system, private ownership of farmland, removal of Soviet troops, and a withdrawal from the Warsaw Pact. The uprising had been inspired, in part, by Khrushchev's secret speech, in which he announced a new policy of de-Stalinization that would favor diplomacy, rather than force, when dealing with other nations.

Flynn's initial reaction was disbelief. Events in Hungary were "probably and purposely exaggerated," she wrote to Kathie. She was convinced the news was propaganda designed to inflame anti-Communism during election season in the United States: "One can always expect some outrageous slander and gossip, especially about us, just before an election."[35] News of the Soviet Union's violent incursion into Hungary bled more members from the Communist Party and drew those who remained into increasingly bitter disagreement. In a meeting of the national committee, Gates and at least eight other members voted to condemn the October invasion. Dennis and Davis abstained from taking a position. Foster was absent. (He would later call the first Soviet invasion a "grim necessity" to keep Hungary within the Communist bloc.) The committee could not decide whether to condemn the November invasion and finally settled on an agreement "neither to condemn nor condone." This dissembling frustrated Gates. Over the protest of several members of the committee, the

Daily Worker took the remarkable step of publishing an editorial written by Gates criticizing the Soviet action of November 4. As with the Khrushchev speech, it was the only Communist newspaper in the world to do so. The editorial asserted, "The action of the Soviet troops in Hungary does not advance but retards the development of socialism because socialism cannot be imposed on a country by force."[36]

Flynn, who would have seen a report about the *Daily Worker* editorial in the *New York Times*, soon realized that news about Hungary was not simply a trumped up story for Cold War propaganda purposes. She admitted to Clemens France that the Soviet invasion was "regrettable." At the same time, because she did not once again have "all the facts," she refused to pass judgment. She thought the debate among her comrades was healthy, but she chose her words very carefully in her correspondence so that nothing she wrote could be used as evidence that she was on one side or another. In a reference to the *Daily Worker* editorial, she observed, "Maybe what happened does not 'retard,' but I doubt if it helps." She also expressed openness to the suggestion that Soviet troops had entered Hungary in response to "imperialist intervention" on the part of the United States and other capitalist countries to steer discontent into a full-blown counterrevolution.[37]

Isolation from the party had the unintended effect of broadening Flynn's intellectual and political horizons. She read voraciously—literature, history, philosophy, science, economics, and business. As she learned about economic and technological developments, she saw opportunities for the CPUSA to reorient itself from international concerns toward a more U.S.-centered model: "Twelve years now after the war and no postwar depression, no slump, more employment today than even Henry Wallace's 'Utopia,'" she observed to Kathie in January 1957. "60 million jobs demanded—new industries, tremendous scientific research projects, etc. It needs a Karl Marx to analyze the new trends of capitalism. Our people should be thinking about all this rather than worrying all the time about whether the S.U. is right or wrong." Additionally, she wanted the party to pay attention to "high prices and the drought problem of the S.W., the 'poor year' of the desperate textile industry, the farmers' problems, and the slump in auto production and sales."[38] Her observations were a gentle admonition to the party to show more concern for the United States than the Soviet Union or Hungary, in theory as well as practice.

Meanwhile, disagreement over Hungary among party members became so intense that the sixteenth national convention steered away from the issue to avoid total disintegration. Instead, discussion centered on the Draft Resolution. Foster spoke in opposition to it. To reprise his role as spoiler from a dozen years earlier, French Communist leader Jacques Duclos sent a letter attacking the resolution as "revisionist."[39] It was to no avail. The convention adopted the Draft Resolution with minor revisions. Delegates also voted to abolish the posts of chairman and general secretary, thus issuing a rebuke to Foster and Dennis, who currently occupied them, while also skirting the issue of who would guide the party on its new course. Every other national leader was reelected. A proposal to transform the party into a political association also passed, but action on the proposal was tabled. Although it looked like the reformist wing of the party had won, no substantive changes in structure or policy were implemented after the convention. The failure to achieve their goals combined with revulsion at the Soviet invasion led more members to leave the party. Al Richmond, a member of the California party who stayed until 1972 and who attended the sixteenth convention, offered a poignant reflection on the personal cost of losing one's comrades: "These were not the transient associations of youth; these had been enduring parts of one's life and hence of one's self. And now there was a feeling of ineffable loss."[40] Flynn would soon feel the loss. Among those who left the party at this time was her dear friend, Steve Nelson. In his autobiography, Nelson recalled the kindness that Flynn showed him during this difficult period: "I had worked with some of these people for decades. . . . Of all the National Board members, only Elizabeth Gurley Flynn came at that time to talk to me about my decision."[41]

She's on the Inside!

In her letters from Alderson, Flynn repeatedly insisted that she did not have enough information to make an informed opinion about controversial issues and events. Kathie assisted her in projecting a neutral image. When asked, "Which side is Elizabeth on?" Kathie replied, "She's on the inside!" Despite her claims of neutrality, as conflict over the direction of the CPUSA intensified, it was not hard to determine which side Flynn was on. She embraced what she saw as the middle ground between the extremes of Foster and Gates. Her letter to Muriel Symington praised those who attended the national convention for having had the courage "to honestly face one's mistakes, to note where one has failed, and to try to chart a better course to achieve the American road to Socialism." To Clemens France, she wrote that she was satisfied with the results of the convention: "The critics range from those who would have us commit suicide (dissolve, disappear, etc.) to those who, like yourself, want us to continue as in the past, only more so. The happy medium is what is now attempted."[42]

Flynn adamantly opposed dissolving the party and replacing it with a political association. She had been burned once by "Browderism," and this time she would have nothing to do with it. Yet she realized the party needed to change to meet the demands of a changing world. As she had already indicated several times, she welcomed the ascendance of a new generation of leaders. However, unlike many of her comrades who sought to reform the party and reinvigorate its membership, she did not believe the CPUSA had been functioning essentially as an adjunct of the CPSU since its founding. Flynn was fiercely protective of the Soviet Union and proud of its accomplishments, but she cherished the American socialist tradition that she had done so much to build and nurture. Narratives of the history of socialism in the United States that began with the Russian Revolution frustrated her. She saw the CPUSA as a distinctly American organization and chastised France and others like him for failing to appreciate it as such: "We have a good record which goes back to the deep indigenous roots of the American socialist experiment, which you dismiss as 'pre-Socialist,' I fear. All socialist history is not in the last 40 years exclusively, nor is it confined to 2 places [the Soviet Union and China]."[43] In short, Flynn simply did not buy the argument that socialism had been imported to the United States. How could she when her own personal history proved otherwise? The long history of socialism in the United States, she believed, was a wellspring of inspiration for those who wished to steer the party into the future.

Freedom

Flynn's release date was set for May 25, 1957. Her three-year sentence (minus statutory time for good behavior) had been originally set to end April 25, but she had to remain at Alderson another thirty days while the federal government examined her assets and determined her ability (or lack thereof) to pay the $6,000 fine that had been levied against her. "Since I have no $6000, nor six thousand cents, for that matter," she explained to Clemons France, "I sign an affidavit here so stating and am released on May 25th." As the date approached, Flynn reflected on what she wanted to do once she was free. She wanted to retire from legal defense work and fundraising. She wanted to see a few good movies, get acquainted with television, get busy on her book. She longed for "little old N.Y.," especially her own home. She wanted to slow down and to expand her circle beyond people who agree with her. She did *not* want to become involved in "endless discussion" about controversial topics pertaining to the CPUSA.[44] Alas, most of these wishes would remain unfulfilled.

Her last few letters from prison reveal Flynn's remarkable psychological resilience. After twenty-eight months at Alderson, she was unbowed. Events around the world had shaken but not broken her political faith. She remained a proud member of the CPUSA and a stalwart American. In her final letter to Clemens France, Flynn reflected on her prison experience and the personal insight she gained from having borne it with equanimity: "All the years I dealt with labor defense cases I used to ask myself if I could take a prison sentence, if it ever became necessary. It seemed so terrible, in anticipation. One's imagination conjures up much worse than the reality." Yet she had faced her fear: "Now that it is nearly over I am at least satisfied that I could and did take it, in spite of age and viewpoint. My health is excellent and I have had a lot of time for reading and reflection. . . . I do not feel any sense of martyrdom or sacrifice."[45]

So strong was Flynn's belief in the rightness of her cause and the ultimate goodness of ordinary Americans, she speculated that like the Salem witches, she might be exonerated in a few generations.[46] The strength of Flynn's beliefs was evident in her last letter from prison to Muriel Symington. Flynn revealed that she had meant to write her friend a poem but was never able to finish it to her satisfaction. It was to be called "My Country." After sketching a few stanzas, she summarized the theme: "Let me say, here and now, blunt and plain, no one and nobody can take my country away from me at the ebb of my life." It was a powerful statement about Flynn's relationship to the United States. She was a Communist *and* an American, and the two identities were indivisible. As if to underscore the point, she quickly added, "I'll be writing to rival Whitman if I keep it up!"[47]

An entourage greeted Flynn when she walked through the gates of Alderson to freedom. Her sister Kathie, attorney John Abt, physician Marcus Goldman, and comrade Marion Bachrach, all of whom had traveled from New York to meet her, received warm hugs. Bachrach, whose case had been severed from that of the other Smith Act defendants because of illness (she had cancer), wrote a moving account of the reunion for the *Daily Worker*. She noted that the "beautiful and slender" Flynn who walked out of prison bore little resemblance to a picture that had recently appeared in the *Worker* article announcing her release. The picture gave Flynn a laugh, but her first look at the *Worker* brought tears to her eyes. Bachrach described a quintessential Elizabeth Gurley Flynn: "Her first questions were about people—all the dear comrades, and especially those recently released and the others still with long terms to serve. She wanted to know too about her neighbors on the Lower East Side, the Italian grocer around the corner, the waiter in her favorite restaurant." She was also curious to know about changes in industry, including how the rise of automation was affecting workers. Although she enjoyed the beautiful scenery during the drive through the Shenandoah Mountains, Bachrach reported that Flynn's eyes "really lit up" when her car passed through the first industrial community. "Her one disappointment was there were no coal towns on our route," wrote Bachrach. After having spent several months listening to the rumble of coal cars as they made their way through Alderson, she "was hungry for the site of a real live coal miner or steel worker."[48]

Upon her return home to New York City, Flynn, who was on parole for forty-two days, reported to a parole officer. On the advice of Mary Kaufman, she also reported to the local Social Security office. Like most people who leave prison, she had no income (she could not draw a salary from the party) and she needed money to restart her life. She received a lump sum of more than $1,000 for the time she had been at Alderson, which she set aside for Kathie to use for a trip to visit her daughter Frances, who was now married and living in Nigeria, and thereafter a check of $90 per month, of which $10 went toward the fine she had incurred when she was convicted.[49] A week after her release, comrades Louis Weinstock and Alexander Bittelman were also released from prison, which meant that all of the Communists convicted in the Second Smith Act trials were now free. Of the other Smith Act defendants, three who had jumped bail and either surrendered or were captured and given contempt sentences in addition to their original terms remained behind bars: Bob Thompson, Gil Green, and Henry Winston. A fourth, Irving Potash, who had been voluntarily deported to Poland in 1955, was serving a prison term after being arrested when he returned to the United States.

Choosing Sides

Flynn spent the next few weeks resting; reconnecting with family, friends, comrades, and her cat; and catching up on all she had missed while she was in prison, especially the controversies that had riven the party. During her time at Alderson, she had tried to position herself as occupying a middle ground between extremes, but when an organization is debating whether to implement radical changes in structure and policies, a decision not to support those changes is effectively an endorsement of the status quo. Summer 1957 was a contentious one for the party, as disagreements over the proposal for forming a political association grew more and more heated. As the summer wore on, Flynn would find herself at odds with the reformers. She knew the party had to change to survive. At the same time, her life's work for socialism made it impossible for her to agree that the CPUSA had been unmoored from American culture and politics from its inception. Her bruising experience with the last proposal to transform the party into a political association kept her from endorsing yet another effort to remake the party into something else. Like Gene Dennis, her "moderate" position would ultimately align her with Foster.

While Flynn was recuperating, Communists received some good news about the HUAC and the Smith Act. On June 17, the Supreme Court announced its decision in *Watkins v. United States*. When questioned by the HUAC, John Watkins, a labor organizer, had refused to give information about individuals who had left the CPUSA, arguing that the question was beyond the authority of the committee. In a six-to-one vote, the court agreed that the committee did not have unlimited power to investigate the lives of American citizens, and therefore the question about former CPUSA members was a violation of the due process clause of the Fifth Amendment. The same day, in *Yates v. United States*, a case that sought to determine whether the conviction of leaders of the Communist Party in California violated the First Amendment, the court reversed the convictions in another six-to-one decision. Justice John Marshall Harlan, writing for the majority, addressed the distinction between "advocacy of doctrine" and "advocacy of action."[50] His opinion required that prosecutors in Smith Act cases prove that the accused advocated illegal conduct, not mere abstract doctrine. Because the government could not meet this burden, the charges against all defendants in *Yates* were dismissed. Notably, all the *Yates* opinions avoided mention of the clear and present danger. The Yates decision effectively ended Smith Act prosecution of Communists in the United States. Predictably, it came under fire from President Eisenhower and J. Edgar Hoover for hampering efforts to eradicate the CPUSA. Communists called the decision evidence of "America's potential return to sanity."[51]

Flynn and others among the CPUSA leadership interpreted the Supreme Court decisions as evidence that the Cold War was beginning to thaw, and Communists should seize the opportunity to rebuild their base. The question was, how best to move forward? Flynn gave her answer at her first post-Alderson public appearance—a "Bill of Rights Rally" to celebrate the recent release of Smith Act prisoners at Carnegie Hall on July 24. Ever mindful of her popularity, organizers gave Flynn top billing among a triumvirate of speakers that included Pettis Perry and Robert Thompson, who had been ordered free on bail a day before the *Watkins* and *Yates* decisions. In a display of party unity, Gates and Dennis, who were by now on opposite sides, greeted the recently released defendants. When Flynn stood up to speak, she received a standing ovation. It brought tears to her eyes. When she spoke, her position in the disagreements that were racking the party was clear. She stressed the need to recruit new members in what she saw as a changing political landscape: "youth, Negroes, Labor, all the groups we were identified with in the past." In an implicit answer to the charge that the CPUSA had been unduly influenced by issues and events outside the United States since its inception, she admonished those in attendance never to sell short the history of the Communist Party and reminded everyone that the history of socialism in the United States predated the Bolshevik Revolution by at least a decade: "I was here in 1907 when Jack London spoke in this hall—in 1907, and don't laugh because after all, there did take place a socialist revolution 10 years later—and he was speaking of the Socialist Revolution."[52] If anyone doubted where she stood on the future of Communism in the United States before the rally, it was now obvious. As she had done in the earlier contest with Browder, Flynn sided with Foster. Not from personal affinity—as Dorothy Healy has noted, Flynn was very critical of Foster and not at all taken in by the "glamour of his historic past as a union organizer."[53] Her decision was a pragmatic one: she wanted to be a part of the one remaining organization that dedicated itself, although perhaps by now in name only, to the struggle for working-class emancipation.

In late August, Flynn announced that she was running for New York City Council in the Twenty-Fourth Manhattan District.[54] The idea had been suggested to her by Ben Davis and Albert Blumberg, another Smith Act defendant who had been convicted in 1956 and, while his appeal was pending, had charges against him dropped after the *Yates* decision. Campaign volunteers immediately set about collecting the three thousand signatures needed to qualify her as an independent candidate under the designation of the People's Rights Party. By running for office, Flynn was sending a message to anti-Communists that their efforts to destroy the party and cow its members into submission had not succeeded and that Americans supported the rights of Communists to share their views in the political arena.[55] At the same time, she was sending a message to

Gates and others who had been arguing to dissolve the CPUSA that they were wrong to claim it was not a political party in the traditional American sense of endorsing policy goals and supporting candidates for elected office in pursuit of those goals. Foster echoed this message in a call for volunteers to the campaign in a *Daily Worker* article that appeared after the resignation of foreign editor Joe Clark, who had been a longtime member of the party and a supporter of Gates.[56] The campaign also sent a message to the Trotskyists, who were fielding candidates for office, including one who was running for mayor. By refusing an offer to collaborate on getting signatures, the Flynn campaign rejected the idea of a pan-Socialist alliance. The CP State Committee of New York went so far as to declare a vote for any candidate of the Socialist Workers Party as support for counterrevolution.[57]

Flynn was still the party's most popular member, and as had happened so often in the past, others drew encouragement from her fighting spirit. The example of an older woman who canvassed for Flynn and shared her experience in a letter to the *Daily Worker*, published under the name Jeannie with the Light Gray Hair, is illustrative. "Jeannie" described herself as a person of modest means who had been a lifelong socialist. Her experience canvassing for Flynn had deepened her love for the people, reinforced her desire for Socialism, and restored her faith in the Communist Party. She longed to see the CPUSA become the kind of party that the oppressed believed it to be: "a party of socialism and of socialist people, a party that is a preview of the future, where people of all races, creeds, and color meet in harmony, where debate is friendly and dissenters are not treated as traitors, a party not torn with factional strife, but one where fraternalism prevails." At the conclusion of her letter, she offered a recommendation: "If you want to feel the way I do, go canvassing for signatures for Elizabeth Gurley Flynn." Flynn clearly had not lost her ability to motivate and inspire others.[58]

On September 24, 1957, the *Daily Worker* issued a front-page announcement that Flynn had gathered 3,725 signatures for her independent candidacy (the eventual count would exceed 4,000). Once she was assured a place on the ballot, Flynn's campaign kicked into high gear with a grueling seven-day-a-week schedule of canvassing and rallies that lasted until Election Day.[59] So much for slowing down after her release from Alderson! A detailed description of her wide ranging platform, which was distributed to voters, included the following items: democracy in housing, a better education system for youth, better transportation facilities, improved hospital services, provision of childcare services, creation of parks and recreation facilities, improved sanitation, expanded public markets, and protection of civil liberties, especially for teachers and other public employees.[60] It was nothing short of a call to bring socialism to the city.

Flynn's campaign received extensive coverage in the *Daily Worker*, including a photo essay that showed her returning to Strauss Square (formerly Rutgers Square) near East Broadway in Manhattan, where she had made her first street corner speech in 1906.[61] The campaign distributed one hundred thousand flyers, held thirty outdoor rallies, and presented three radio broadcasts and two one-minute radio announcements. Flynn managed to secure a spot at a League of Women Voters candidates meeting, but she was banned from addressing an audience of students at the City College of New York (CCNY).[62]

Despite these intensive efforts, Flynn garnered just 710 votes, approximately 1 percent of the roughly 70,000 votes cast. In terms of numbers, the campaign was a cataclysmic failure. Her supporters did not see it that way. Campaign manager Arnold Johnson told the *New York Times* that getting Flynn on the ballot was "an important victory for civil liberties." In a postmortem published in *Political Affairs*, campaign co-chair Evelyn Wiener seized an opportunity to declare victory against both anti-Communists in New York and around the United States and proponents of reform within the party. "In the person of Comrade Flynn," she wrote, taking a swipe at both groups, "we see the lie to the foreign-agent charge; we see also the answer to those within our ranks, who in the past period seem to have forgotten the deep roots in American life and struggle that the Communist Party has planted—roots which will once again bear fruit as the struggle to overcome the isolation of the Party goes further and deeper." Wiener took to task those who opposed Flynn's candidacy because it hindered developing unity movements or because they did not think the party could play a role as an independent force in the campaign for having "displayed strong liquidation tendencies" and doubting "the capacity of [their] weakened organization to collect the necessary 3,000 signatures."[63] Her willingness to run for office had made Flynn a useful tool for Foster and other hardline opponents of reform.

With her city council campaign behind her, the longed-for opportunity to retire from defense work and immerse herself in writing the second half of her autobiography still eluded Flynn. Instead, she was as busy as ever with party responsibilities. She oversaw a Christmas amnesty campaign—which, when it failed, became a July 4 amnesty campaign—for imprisoned comrades Green, Winston, and Potash.[64] To generate interest in the amnesty drive and help the party bolster its membership, she went on a tour of the Midwest, where she spoke about the Constitution and civil liberties. Flynn's reports from the circuit were upbeat, sometimes to the point where they seem divorced from reality. She noted, for example, that a large and enthusiastic audience attended her talk in Cleveland, where she spoke in defense of Ohio comrades who had been indicted for not signing non-Communist affidavits mandated by the Taft-Hartley Act. She also observed that excitement about Sputnik, the Soviet-launched first artificial space satellite, had greatly increased interest among local workers in the Soviet Union and socialism.[65] It is hard to imagine great concern for Communists who violated Taft-Hartley, harder still to imagine that a satellite could mitigate years of anti-Communist propaganda and generate good will for the entity that most Americans by now considered a mortal enemy of the United States.

To further her aim of recruiting young people for the party, Detroit Communists set up a Committee for Teen Agers to Meet Elizabeth Gurley Flynn, which invited teens to chat with a "celebrity" of the labor movement.[66] The goal of connecting with young people was frustrated, in Milwaukee at least, when authorities canceled Flynn's speaking engagement at Milwaukee-Downer College. She was then invited by a student organization to speak at the University of Wisconsin–Milwaukee, but the provost canceled that event, ostensibly because the students had not filed paperwork correctly. The Wisconsin chapter of the ACLU protested the ban, but nothing seems to have come from the protest.[67] Universities were not the only entities to refuse Flynn access to a platform because of her political views. An event in her honor sponsored by the Washington, D.C., Freedom of the Press Committee had to be canceled because the organizers were unable to hire a hall for a Communist speaker.[68]

The *Daily Worker* Is Disbanded

While Flynn worked to defend civil liberties for Communists and recruit new members for the party, the battle over the future of the CPUSA continued unabated. In December 1957, over the strenuous objections of Gates, members of the national committee voted to disband the *Daily Worker* and replace it with a weekly paper. Members of the national committee were also divided on whether to endorse the "Declaration of Twelve Communist and Workers Parties," signed by leaders of the communist parties of socialist nations (with the exception of Yugoslavia) who had met in Moscow to mark the fortieth anniversary of the Russian Revolution in November 1957. Gates, Dorothy Healy, and other reformers supported a statement that lauded the declaration as "an important expression of unity among these 12 parties of the Socialist countries, a unity achieved through fraternal discussions and the mutual exchange of views," but also warned that it should not stymie the CPUSA's efforts to chart its own course, as embodied in the resolution approved at the American Party's sixteenth national convention. The statement passed, although Flynn, along with Ben Davis, Gene Dennis, and Robert Thompson, opposed it. Foster, who had suffered a stroke in October 1957, was not present for the vote.[69] The national membership, however, voted it down.

The same issue of *Political Affairs* that carried the statement about the Declaration of Twelve Communist Parties also ran a lengthy piece by Foster, "The Party Crisis and the Way Out, Part II." As the title suggests, it was the second of two articles. (Part I appeared in the previous issue.) In the articles, Foster restated arguments he had made at the sixteenth national convention, defending the policies of the CPUSA, resisting claims that the movement needed more grounding in the mainstream of American life, and opposing any effort to transform the party into a political association.[70] The timing and placement of the pieces amounted to a significant counterattack on the reform program.

Convinced that none of the changes prescribed by the resolution would be implemented and outraged by the suspension of the *Daily Worker*, Gates resigned from the party in early January 1958. Flynn could not resist the opportunity to discredit her former comrade publicly. After Gates appeared in a television interview with journalist Mike Wallace, she wrote a column for the *Worker* (the paper's name had been changed to reflect its once-weekly circulation) in which she viciously attacked him for resigning from the paper and leaving the party. Gates, she noted, was "a stranger, drained of personality, incapable of fight-back, lacking in courage, allowing himself to be made into a punching bag."[71]

Flynn wrote a widely quoted eulogy of sorts for the *Daily Worker* that was published in the last issue. In it she praised the "valiant efforts" of the "heroic working-class paper" during more than three decades and pledged herself to a united effort among "Party and non-Party friends" to rebuild the paper into an "agitator, an educator, and an organizer" for the socialist movement. She had harsh words for those who had left the party: "We cannot allow defectors from our ranks to demoralize or demobilize us. . . . Let us close our ranks as a team. In spite of deserters and calamity howlers, if we give them no heed it can be done." According to Flynn, the time for looking inward was over, and Communists should now turn their attention to problems that beset the American people: unemployment, automation, the threat of war, nuclear weapons, racial segregation and discrimination, repression of the radical wing of the labor movement. Yet even as she emphasized the need to focus on American issues, Flynn saw the greatest hope for socialism in the United States as coming from the Soviet Union. She projected the awe that she felt for the achievements of the Soviets onto her fellow Americans: "Today, as never before, there is great interest among American workers in socialism, especially since Sputnik rose to the heavens."[72] For the rest of her life, she would see the Soviet Union as a source of inspiration and claim that American workers were growing more interested in socialism, despite a mountain of evidence to the contrary.

Although Flynn was now sixty-seven years old and not in the best of health, she was as busy as ever. In February 1958, she was elected to the party's National Executive Committee, along with Davis, Dennis, and Thompson. As the party limped along, Flynn worked to create a positive image and promote the idea that things would soon turn around. She selected favorable letters to print in the *Worker* and described enthusiastic reactions whenever party members appeared at public events.[73] In spring 1958, Flynn toured California in an effort to recruit for the party and raise money for the *People's World*, the West Coast Communist newspaper. She then made a trip to the Pacific Northwest after which she returned to California. On the way home to New York, she made stops at various cities in the Midwest. Overall, she spent about three months on the road and spoke to over 2,600 people.[74]

Flynn had adored the West since she was a teenage soapboxer organizing for the IWW. She loved California in particular, especially San Francisco, and wished she could retire and move there, but the party needed her in New York. Upon her return from her tour, she wrote a regular column for the *Worker*, titled simply "Elizabeth Gurley Flynn," in which she covered a range of topics, including her recent travels around the United States and recollections of past trips abroad, lynching and other acts of racist violence against Black Americans, voting rights for Black women, and the campaign for the release of Henry Winston and Gil Green, who were still serving prison terms for their Smith Act convictions, as well as Robert Thompson, who had been remanded back to prison.

As she had done from her earliest days as an activist, Flynn did not limit herself to issues that concerned only Americans. Her vision remained international. She wrote about amnesty campaigns for political prisoners in Northern Ireland and Franco's Spain, civil rights activism in England in which dear friend Claudia Jones played a leading role, and the antiapartheid campaign waged by Black working women in South Africa, to name just a few examples.[75] One topic that she did not cover in any substantial way was the U.S. labor movement. For four decades, she had organized and advocated for miners, lumber workers, textile workers, restaurant workers, steel workers, and others who toiled away in various industries. After 1948, the CPUSA was isolated from the labor movement, and Flynn's lifelong ties faded as well. Where once she had been a movement insider, she was now a firsthand expert on labor history.

Sister Kathie also needed Flynn in New York. Toward the end of 1958, Kathie had a serious heart attack. Her convalescence required Elizabeth to take a vacation from party work, and she went with Kathie to Florida in the spring of 1959. The need to look after her sister meant Flynn could not travel for meetings or events for a while, which afforded her time to begin work on her Alderson memoir.[76] She felt strongly about the importance of writing about prison. As a former political prisoner, she believed she had a moral obligation to describe the experience in detail "so that everyone will realize what it is like to be there." Empathy for imprisoned comrades, she hoped, would inspire readers of her column to advocate for their release.[77] When reflecting on the process of writing her Alderson memoir, she expressed a desire to be of service to the women she met while she was in prison: "I feel this is a social responsibility, as a political prisoner, to many women I met there who are friendless, penniless, helpless and hopeless victims of the society in which we live." Flynn's experience had shown her that the U.S. prison system was in dire need of reform. Among the problems that she observed were discrepancies in sentencing; a byzantine parole system; political, racial, and ethnic discrimination; and inadequate preparation for life after release.[78] She would tackle all these issues in her book, although it would be another four years before it would be published. In the meantime, she devoted space in her column to discussions of these and other issues, such as the causes of drug addiction and proposals for treatment, which serving time in prison had brought to her attention.[79]

One Step Forward and . . .

As part of her defense work, Flynn kept an eye on legal developments that affected the fate of Communists. In the summer of 1959, decisions by the Supreme Court drew her ire for two reasons. First, because they upended the *Watkins* decision that had called the authority of the HUAC into question. In *Uphaus v. Wyman*, the court upheld by a vote of five-to-four a New

Hampshire court's decision to hold pacifist Methodist minister Willard Uphaus in contempt for refusing to turn over correspondence he had with speakers at a summer camp he sponsored and a list of names of those who attended the camp.[80] Uphaus had argued that forcing him to produce the information was a violation of his First Amendment rights. He was sentenced to prison for up to one year or until such time as he presented the information. In his majority opinion, Justice Tom C. Clark justified the state's request as a means of its self-preservation. In *Barenblatt v. United States*, the court upheld the conviction of University of Michigan professor Lloyd Barenblatt, who, when he had been called to testify before the HUAC, refused to answer questions about his relationship to the Communist Party. Barenblatt was found in contempt of Congress for failing to cooperate with the committee's investigation and sentenced to six months in prison. In this five-to-four decision, the court ruled that the committee's line of investigation did not violate the First Amendment because it was intended to "aid the legislative process" and protect government interests.[81]

The second reason for Flynn's anger was personal. A former ally in the civil liberties movement, Felix Frankfurter, had sided with the majority in both cases. Flynn had worked with Frankfurter on the campaign to free Sacco and Vanzetti as well as other labor defense cases in the 1920s: "I visited Felix Frankfurter in his study at Cambridge several times, and once at his home to get his advice on legal counsel and procedure. I see no resemblance between this alert minded progressive young man of over 30 years ago and the crotchety, hair splitting old reactionary of today . . . whittling away the Bill of Rights and other constitutional amendments."[82] As she saw it, the once fierce champion of civil liberties was now a traitor to the cause he had served in his younger days.

If the fortunes of Communists took a step backward with the *Uphaus* and *Barenblatt* decisions, Khrushchev's tour of the United States in September 1959 and his series of meetings with Eisenhower suggested that peaceful coexistence between the two superpowers might really be on the horizon. Khrushchev referred to the friendly, informal mood that characterized his meetings with the U.S. president and the period afterward as "the Spirit of Camp David." Inspired by this development, American Communists made "peaceful coexistence" the theme of the party's seventeenth national convention in December 1959. The meeting signaled an official end to the CPUSA's own internal battles as Foster allies officially took control of the party. Delegates elected Gus Hall general secretary. Dennis was elected party chair. Flynn and Claude Lightfoot were elected vice chairs.[83]

To Socialist Lands

Flynn had never been keen on joining the upper echelon of party leadership, and she did so now only out of a sense of duty, but she would not let the office dictate her movements.[84] In late April 1960, she left New York for Copenhagen, where she was one of thirty American women attending the International Women's Assembly commemorating the fiftieth anniversary of International Women's Day. Although there were delegations of women from around the world in attendance, she was most interested in the Soviet women. "There were 30 of them, young and old," she wrote to *Worker* editor James Jackson. "Their clothes, luggage, and general appearance very much like ourselves."[85] In the mythos of the Soviet Union that Flynn and other American Communists embraced, these female comrades had achieved a kind of social, political, and economic parity with men to which American Communist women aspired. She seemed almost starstruck to be in their company. At the close of the assembly, Flynn and Communist women from other nations who had attended flew to Moscow. The trip may or may not have been Flynn's first sojourn in the Soviet Union—Helen Camp has found evidence to suggest that she may have gone there in 1957.[86] Either way, it was the first stop on what would be an eight-month tour of socialist countries. There, she was again starstruck when Khrushchev waved to her during a ceremony held at the mausoleum where Lenin and Stalin were buried. She kept her composure and "waved back, naturally," she told a friend.[87]

Flynn's desire to see socialism in action took her to Romania (where she implicated herself and the CPUSA in developing Sino-Soviet tensions by comments she made in a speech), Czechoslovakia, the German Democratic Republic, and Hungary.[88] In a thinly veiled reference in one of her letters, she told Steve Nelson that she wanted to visit China as well. She must also have told someone else about her plan because an FBI informant passed that information along to the bureau.[89] Her passport was not validated for travel there, and because the FBI was monitoring her movements, it is doubtful that she made the trip unless she found a way to go in secret. In one of the regular reports about her trip that she wrote for readers of the *Worker*, she explained her motivation for the lengthy trip: "When I was young, I had no doubt I would live to see a Socialist America.... But now that I have reached that ripe old age, I am far from certain my early hopes would be realized.... So I decided I must visit other lands, where Socialism has already arrived and is flourishing."[90] She wrote detailed and glowing reports about the culture, industry, agriculture, race and gender relations, and prisons of the places she visited. A flare-up of her arthritis, which necessitated a stay at a sanitarium outside Moscow, also gave her cause to praise Soviet health care.[91] Upon returning home to the United States in December, she rested briefly before embarking on a tour to speak about her travels, generate new members for the party, and raise revenue and subscriptions for the *Worker*. By the end of January 1961, seventy-year-old Flynn was on the road again with her first stop in Chicago.

The red-baiting and repression Flynn had endured since 1948 had clearly taken its toll. For the first time in her life, she seemed not to embrace her American identity. In contrast to Moscow, she found New York "dirty, gloomy, cold, nerve racking."[92] "I am not happy to be back" in the United States, she informed readers of a *Worker* column published while she was at the start of her speaking tour. Flynn was, in her own words, "homesick for Moscow." And why not? As she had explained in one of her letters to Steve Nelson, in comparison to her experience in the United States, "Everyone in the Socialist countries is so comradely and kind."[93] In her *Worker* column, she informed readers that she had been treated as "an honored guest getting the red carpet treatment everywhere." She remarked, "It is quite an experience for an American Communist, I assure you, in contrast to here."[94] It was no doubt difficult to go from being a celebrity to being a pariah. Her readjustment to life in the United States was made even more difficult by the death of beloved comrade Gene Dennis from cancer on January 31, 1961. She returned to New York immediately. At the memorial service for Dennis, Flynn spoke on behalf of the national committee with "a heart filled with grief." She felt the loss in a deeply personal way: "The loss of Gene, who was my closest friend is second only to the death of my son Fred."[95]

First Female Chair

Dennis's death left a hole in the leadership of the party. A March meeting of the national committee resulted in the election of Flynn to the position of national chairman, the post that Dennis had occupied. It was a historic vote because she was the first woman ever elected to that office, and members of the press were on hand to report on the occasion.[96] Attention from the press did not cease after the national committee meeting. For weeks afterward, reporters accosted Flynn when she appeared in public: "My age, sex, long labor record, and now this responsibility seem suddenly to intrigue the press. They also seem determined to picture me of all people as 'a sweet old lady.'" She would have nothing to do with this label: "I told them it sounds like an epitaph."[97]

Flynn's ascension to the chair position has been dismissed by some as symbolic because she did not wield real authority among the men who made decisions about policy. It is true that her male comrades were dismissive of her because of her gender and apparent lack of intellectual sophistication. It is also true that these same comrades frequently leaned upon Flynn to do things she would have preferred not to do and that friends like Marion Bachrach encouraged her to resist being "pushed around."[98] Yet it could also be argued that all of the party's leaders now occupied largely symbolic roles, as the CPUSA was isolated from movements in which it historically had a strong presence. The party no longer played a part in the labor movement, and members were increasingly relegated to behind the scenes in the civil rights movement. Moreover, there was almost no one left to lead. By the end of the 1950s, the party had shrunk to about three thousand members, a twentieth of the size it had been ten years earlier.[99]

Flynn resumed her speaking tour after Dennis's memorial. Although they were hardly unbiased, her talks nonetheless gave Americans a rare opportunity to hear from someone who had actually been behind the Iron Curtain. She shared her experiences with audiences in Philadelphia, Detroit, Seattle, Portland, San Francisco, Los Angeles, and other locales. The trip was not an altogether positive one. In the Pacific Northwest, she was frustrated by hecklers who disrupted meetings and by those who recorded what she said and later took quotes out of context. "We are not arranging meetings for the convenience of Red Baiters," she opined in her *Worker* column. To remedy the problem, she suggested that organizers of meetings charge an admission fee and prohibit unauthorized recording of speeches.[100] It was the first time in her long speaking career that Flynn admitted her adversaries had gotten under her skin. Her spirits improved when she arrived in her beloved San Francisco and then in Los Angeles, where she held a two-hour press conference that was attended by more than thirty reporters from newspapers, radio, and television. The reporters, who had been drawn by the novelty of a woman heading a political party, were treated to Flynn's characteristic wit. When she was asked about the claims of Robert Welch, founder of the ultraconservative John Birch Society, that former president Eisenhower was a Communist along with some seven thousand Protestant clergy, she replied, "If they are, they haven't been paying their dues."[101]

Fighting the McCarran Act

The following month, reporters again flocked to an event at which Flynn was present. This time, they came to witness party leaders sign forms to register the CPUSA as a foreign agent. Registration of the party was mandated by the Subversive Activities Control Board under the McCarran Act, which had been upheld by a June 5 decision of the Supreme Court, *Communist Party of the United States v. Subversive Activities Control Board*. Once again, Felix Frankfurter sided with the majority. In his opinion, Frankfurter stated that the Communist Party was an action group and declared as constitutional the requirement that it register in the interest of national security. The ruling forced a day of reckoning for the CPUSA. Instead of compliance with the law, however, some two dozen representatives of the press heard a defiant Gus Hall, seated between Flynn and Ben Davis, issue an adamant refusal to register the party or its members and pledge to defend the Bill of Rights. In refusing to comply, Hall, Davis, and Flynn were taking a serious risk. Penalties under the McCarran Act were five years imprisonment and a $10,000 fine. During the exchange that followed, reporters asked Hall whether the Bill of Rights should cover the John Birch Society. He responded "No" because the society was out to destroy the Bill of Rights. At this moment, Flynn jumped in and showed why she was such a valuable asset to the party. "The John Birch Society's rights are not being interfered with," she said. Her intervention helped the party avoid the trap of defending its own rights while urging destruction of the rights of its adversaries.[102]

The Supreme Court's decision on the McCarran Act, along with another decision announced the same day that upheld the membership clause of the Smith Act, indicated that the federal government's campaign against the CPUSA was not over. At the same time, promising signs of change in the political climate had become evident. For example, in its coverage, the *New York Times* acknowledged the much-diminished presence of the CPUSA in the labor and civil rights movements and implied the battle between Hoover and the organization had become lopsided. Another article quoted Gus Hall and Harvey O'Connor, chair of the Emergency Civil Liberties Committee, who denounced the court's decisions on the Smith and McCarran acts as attacks on democracy, the Constitution, and American rights. In addition, for the first time since 1947, the *Times* published an ad that was signed by the national committee of the CPUSA. The ad protested the court's decisions and called upon Americans to fight for repeal of the "fascist-like laws."[103] Buoyed by these developments and determined to continue its fight against the McCarran Act in court, lawyers for the CPUSA filed a motion to reconsider the recent decision. In response, the court issued a stay of mandate, which delayed all action under the law until October, when it could hear the motion.

Flynn's stubborn optimism again caused her to interpret small things as signs of big changes. She reveled in what she saw as the press's more favorable stance toward the CPUSA, and she believed the Supreme Court's move to stay the mandate provided much-needed time "to build a real defense movement" in opposition to the McCarran Act.[104] To inform that movement, she wrote a pamphlet, *Freedom Begins at Home*, in which she characterized the law as part of a "fascist threat" to chisel away the constitutional rights of all Americans.[105] In July, she spoke at an "Uphold the Constitution" rally in New York City headlined by Dirk Jan Struik, a mathematics professor at the Massachusetts Institute of Technology (MIT) and avowed Marxist who had been suspended from MIT when he refused to answer more than two hundred questions posed to him by the HUAC after he had been brought before the committee on suspicion of being a Soviet spy. She was also scheduled to participate in a National Assembly for Democratic Rights in New York, to be held two weeks before the Supreme Court convened and decided whether to hold a rehearing on its decision on the McCarran Act, but her appearance was precluded by another tragedy. In September 1961, she lost another longtime comrade when William Z. Foster died in Moscow. Foster, who had been seriously ill for years and had traveled to the Soviet Union for medical treatment, was still under indictment for having violated the Smith Act when he died. At the request of his wife, Flynn traveled to Moscow to lay a wreath on his bier. U.S. Communists would remain "forever true to Foster's spirit," she said at his memorial service. "And we will win. We will win. The world will belong to the workers."[106]

While Flynn was in Moscow, the Supreme Court denied a rehearing on the McCarran Act. "I hope you are not worried by this decision," she wrote to a friend in the United States. "It is just the beginning of a struggle."[107] Her Soviet experience was like a jolt in the arm. She witnessed the Twenty-Second Congress of the CPSU, taped a radio broadcast and a television program, and went to the circus. Once again, the special treatment she received made it hard for Flynn to contemplate returning "to the sidewalks of New York City."[108] From Moscow, she traveled to Stalingrad, which had been renamed Volgograd in 1961, where she paid homage to the heroes who had fought and died there in World War II. Here too, she received VIP treatment in what she called a "beautiful, invincible, Socialist city."[109] She returned home suddenly in November, possibly because her sister Kathie was ill.[110]

If Flynn was "homesick" for Moscow when she returned to the United States this time, she kept her feelings private. Her public posture was once again militant. She had met many people in the Soviet Union who had urged her to "defect," she wrote in a letter published in the *New York Times*, "But it happens that I am an American. I love my native land and feel confident that there are millions of Americans who, whatever their political views, are also horrified at such monstrosities as the McCarran Act." Her spirited comments recalled the feisty Flynn of old. She refused to accept the label of a "foreign agent" and pledged, "[I will] fight for my rights and those of all Americans, rights embedded in our Constitution and Bill of Rights, even as I have consistently fought since I was first arrested in 1909 in Spokane, Wash., in a free speech fight," and she challenged the *Times* and its readers to put aside political differences and join her in the struggle.[111]

Not long after Flynn returned home, she, along with Hall and Davis, received a subpoena to appear before the HUAC in response to the party's refusal to register with the federal government as required by the McCarran Act. Neither she nor Davis appeared. When questioned about their absence by the committee, Hall declared himself the sole leader of the party, a move designed to protect the CPUSA from decapitation. It was a blatant lie, but by now, the image of the party as a secretive sect was so ingrained in U.S. culture and politics that it hardly registered.

Tragedy struck Flynn again in 1962. She was scheduled to begin the year with another speaking tour to raise money for the *Worker*, but the plan was shelved when Kathie's health took a turn for the worse. Kathie died on February 24, 1962. Flynn soon moved from the Twelfth Street apartment near CPUSA headquarters that she and her sister had shared for twenty years to the Chelsea Hotel on Twenty-Third Street, a haven for bohemian artists, intellectuals, and other nonconformists. Flynn was a welcome guest at the Chelsea, which must have eased the pain of her personal loss and increasing political isolation somewhat. Among those who delighted in her presence was the Irish writer Brendan Behan, who stayed at the hotel while he was writing a new book. To express his joy upon meeting her there, Behan picked Flynn up and shouted, "Gurley, you're the only Irish American I know who's worth anything!"[112]

Defending Hall and Davis

The federal government's unrelenting campaign to destroy the Communist Party robbed Flynn of time to grieve for her sister. In mid-March, federal agents arrested Gus Hall and Benjamin Davis for failing to register under the McCarran Act as officers of the CPUSA. For some unknown reason, they decided against arresting Flynn. The party was then hit with a lawsuit claiming that it owed a whopping $500,000 in taxes going back to 1951. It was the first time since the income tax law was passed in 1914 that the federal government levied a tax assessment against a political party, which was precisely the point. By stripping the CPUSA of its tax-exempt status, the government was making a de facto argument that it was not a legitimate political party.[113] The party was not the only entity to be squeezed for money. In early 1960, the Passport Office and the FBI colluded to determine whether the court had imposed any travel restrictions on Flynn while she was paying her $6,000 fine. When it was determined that no such restrictions were in force, Flynn was called to testify at a hearing to answer questions about her assets. In light of her travels outside the country, officials wanted to know whether she could afford to pay more than $10 per month. She called the move "federal harassment."[114] It failed, and her payments remained the same.

As she had always done when comrades were targets of political repression, Flynn sprang into action after the arrest of Hall and Davis to organize and chair their defense committee. Extreme right-wing organizations—most notably the John Birch Society, an anti-Communist group named for a young soldier who had died in a skirmish with Chinese Communists after World War II—were growing rapidly during the Kennedy administration.[115] In her first public statement as chair of the Hall-Davis Defense Committee, Flynn called the McCarran Act "the Bible of the Birch society, House Un-American Activities Committee, the Crusaders, the White Citizens Councils." She warned that the party was only the first target of "ultra-Right bombardment" and that "unnumbered organizations" were next in line for attack: "And that includes about everyone who fights for integration, for academic freedom, for labor's rights and for the right of the human race to survive." Old habits die hard, however, and Flynn could not resist the temptation to use familiar language to describe an all too familiar situation. "The indictments, the subpoenas, the harassments," she pointed out, were "a sorry mess of fascist devices being used to undermine the fundamental rights of the people."[116] Herbert Aptheker, editor of *Political Affairs*, did her one better by calling the McCarran Act

"Hitlerian." To meet the cost of freeing Hall and Davis, the committee pledged to raise $100,000. Given the size of the party's membership and its political isolation, it was a huge hurdle to overcome.[117]

That Flynn would be chairing yet another defense committee at the age of seventy-two is evidence of how shallow the bench had become in the CPUSA. There was simply no one else willing and able to do this work. Not that Flynn complained (publicly, at least). When asked by the *Worker* how she felt about taking on the responsibility, she replied, "It is an honor and I am proud to accept, although I regret the necessity of having to defend my good friends and co-workers against the infamous, unconstitutional and fascist-like McCarran Act." She also found the work a welcome distraction from the loss she felt now that her sister was gone.[118]

Whatever reservations Flynn had about continuing to do defense work were matched by her sense that civil liberties was reemerging as a popular cause in the United States. Flynn wrote enthusiastically to friends about this development: "The interest is tremendous, the support against interference with free speech by students, faculty, trade unions, etc., is strong and the repudiation of the ultra-Right increases daily."[119] Unlike her misguided optimism during the late 1940s and the first two Smith Act trials, this time she was right.

The first organized major opposition to the HUAC had come from college students during hearings of the committee in San Francisco in 1960. Students protested by marching outside City Hall, where the hearings were being held, and lining up in front of doors to gain access to public seats inside the hall. Police responded by turning fire hoses on the protestors and then dragging or throwing them outside. Not surprisingly, Hoover labeled the protests a Communist plot, although the party barely registered a presence on most college campuses. Students also fought back against campus-wide bans on left-wing speakers, like those that had kept Flynn from CCNY during her campaign for city council. In 1961, three thousand students boycotted class at City College to protest a ban on Communist speakers. The same year, a student group at Berkeley sponsored a campus speech by Frank Wilkinson, a Los Angeles housing official who had lost his job and been sentenced to a year in jail for contempt of Congress after he refused to tell the HUAC whether he was a Communist. The students then launched a campaign to abolish the school's ban on subversive speakers. In February 1962, the Student Committee for Constitutional Liberties at Berkeley invited Gus Hall to speak. While right-wing activists protested, a campus advisory board, the *San Francisco Chronicle*, Berkeley City Council, and State Attorney General

Stanley Mosk defended Hall's constitutional right to address the students. In Oregon, the Wilmington College student newspaper called for organized resistance to their school's speaker ban after Ben Davis was prohibited from speaking on campus.[120]

Students also protested the McCarran Act. In April 1962, Davis, an alumnus of Harvard Law School, spoke on the law at a meeting of the Harvard Law Forum.[121] His comments, which were published in pamphlet form by the Hall-Davis Defense Committee with an introduction by Flynn, informed a campus movement against the McCarran Act that emerged when an organization of students and workers known as "Advance" was targeted. Opposition to the McCarran Act was not limited to students. The United Auto Workers and the Amalgamated Clothing Workers passed resolutions calling for an end to prosecutions under the law.[122]

The Passport Denial

While she was fighting on behalf of Hall and Davis, Flynn faced another challenge: her passport was revoked under Section 6 of the McCarran Act in January 1962. When the Supreme Court denied a rehearing on the law, it had activated the passport section. Under this section, it was illegal for any member of the Communist Party to apply for, use, or attempt to use a passport. Flynn refused to comply with the order from the Passport Office to return her passport. Instead, attorney Joseph Forer requested a hearing with a passport official for her and any other party leaders whose passports had also been denied.

Flynn was not the first American to lose her passport because of her political beliefs. Soon after the United States entered World War I, Congress passed what came to be known as the Travel Control Act, a wartime emergency measure that granted broad authority to the president to create laws regulating the entry and exit of citizens and noncitizens. Wilson had requested the law to enforce his ban on "enemy aliens" coming to or leaving the United States. A week after it passed, the State Department renamed the Bureau of Citizenship as the Division of Passport Control. From then on, the State Department claimed absolute discretion over passports as part of its authority over foreign affairs. It retained this discretion even after the war ended, in large part because of the efforts of Ruth Shipley, who was head of the Passport Division from 1926 until 1955. A master bureaucrat, Shipley ran the department like a well-oiled machine, routinely denying a passport to anyone whom she deemed unsuitable to represent the United States abroad. Shipley was also an ardent anti-Communist, and during the Cold War, her office prevented several of Flynn's comrades and allies from leaving the country, including Paul Robeson and W. E. B. Du Bois, who were denied passports for seven and eight years, respectively. Passports were also denied to blacklisted writers, such as Ring Lardner Jr. and Donald Ogden Stewart. After 1952, anyone denied a passport had the right to a hearing, but the State Department retained the right to deny passports for political reasons. To that end, it declared that anyone requesting a hearing had to sign an affidavit swearing that they were not now and never had been a member of the Communist Party.[123]

Section 6 of the McCarran Act, then, was a congressional stamp of approval for the kind of political judgments that Shipley's Passport Division had been issuing for decades. However, those judgments were increasingly called into question in the courts and in academic and public discourse. Those who were denied a passport, along with liberal critics of the Passport Division, and Communists (including Flynn) argued that denial of a passport was a violation of what came to be seen as "the right to travel." In response to a growing number of such claims, the State Department's procedures came under scrutiny. In 1955, for example, the U.S. District Court for D.C. determined that evidence used in passport hearings had to appear on the record. Momentum for recognizing a constitutional right to travel continued to grow. In 1957, the Supreme Court's *Kent v. Dulles* decision, in which the court heard the appeal of artist Rockwell Kent, a socialist whose passport was denied because he refused to sign the affidavit swearing that he was not a Communist, invalidated the Passport Division's regulations.[124] Section 6 of the McCarran Act, however, remained in force. Flynn and her lawyers seized an opportunity to chip away at the law by contesting its limits on what was now seen by many as a constitutional guarantee of freedom of movement.

Flynn's was the first hearing on a passport denial under Section 6. The State Department intended to question her about whether she was a member of the CPUSA on the date of the revocation of her passport and the date of the hearing. Of course, it was a trap. If Flynn admitted to being a Communist, she would be in violation of the McCarran Act and subject to penalties. Forer, her attorney, avoided the trap by making it clear that the issue he intended to pursue at the hearing was not whether Flynn was a Communist, but whether the passport section of the McCarran Act violated the Constitution. He further noted that Flynn might not even attend the hearing, and if she did, she would have nothing to say.[125]

The hearing, which was held in Washington, D.C., began April 24, 1962. James Allen Gash, staff reporter for radio station WNEW appeared as a witness for the government. Flynn did not appear. When the hearing resumed on May 3, Joseph Zoltan, a paid FBI informer, was the government witness. Again, Flynn did not appear. After the hearing, Flynn received a letter from Frances G. Knight, director of the Passport Office, informing her that the examiner had decided against her.[126] Forer then moved to take the case before the Board of Passport Appeals. After a delay of several months, the Appeals Board heard the case and again ruled against Flynn. Forer and John Abt then filed suit on behalf of Flynn with the federal district court. The two also filed a similar suit on behalf of Herbert Aptheker, whose passport had likewise been revoked. In her affidavit, Flynn swore that the purpose of her travel was peaceful. She wished to rest and relax, gather information for her writing, and speak to European audiences "about the activities of the American people, particularly in the labor movement and on the question of peace."[127]

Not long after the initial passport hearing, Flynn embarked on another cross-country tour, stopping for a brief period in Chicago before reaching San Francisco. As she traveled west, her heart leapt when she saw her "beautiful country" from the train, and she felt that it was worth a fight to claim the United States for its people.[128] But she was growing weary of being in the front lines of that fight. She went to San Francisco to finish writing her prison memoir far from the distractions that always pulled her away from her writing when she was in New York. The opportunity to slow down and reflect caused her to see that she no longer wanted nor had the stamina to keep a grueling schedule of speaking at meetings practically around the clock. She did not mind delivering an occasional speech, but she was wistful for the days when she spoke to workers. "I am not retiring from speaking—far from it," she assured readers of her *Worker* column, "but I would really enjoy a chance to agitate, as of old, among workers. I hope from this gentle hint to receive some invitations from working class communities."[129] Her wish was partially fulfilled on her trip home, when she spoke about the Hall-Davis defense campaign at a July 4 picnic in Detroit that was attended by a number of auto workers.[130]

The scope of resistance to the McCarran Act grew in tandem with the number of persons targeted for prosecution by Attorney General Robert Kennedy. In September 1962, the *Worker* reported that Kennedy had given the Subversive Activities Control Board (SACB) names of ten people to investigate to determine whether they were Communists and thus required to register as "foreign agents" under the McCarran Act. The first of the individuals to face the SACB was William Albertson, who handled publicity for the CPUSA. Flynn and the Hall-Davis Defense Committee pledged to advocate for Albertson and anyone whose name appeared on the list.[131] Also on Kennedy's list was Dorothy Healy. Flynn, who in November had left New York once again for a cross-country tour, arrived in California in time for Healy's hearing, which, she noted approvingly, was televised and protested by Quakers and the California ACLU.[132]

As she pondered the twelve individuals targeted for prosecution, Flynn noticed that three of them (Ben Davis, William Patterson, and Roscoe Parker) were Black. She reflected that the federal government failed to defend the rights of Black Americans or to seek justice when Blacks were targets for racial violence, but it did not discriminate when it came to accusing and prosecuting Black political leaders.[133] The list of targets would continue to grow, and Flynn would continue to report for the *Worker* on the attorney general's efforts to snare more Communists even as challenges to the constitutionality of the McCarran Act were still being filed in the courts.[134]

The Right to Travel

Flynn also published articles attacking the McCarran Act in *Political Affairs*.[135] Her piece on the passport section warrants attention because it illustrates how Flynn's defense of free speech had developed from claiming the right of labor activists to speak on street corners and in other public spaces in cities and towns around the United States to defending the right of political dissenters to travel beyond the national borders and, in so doing, share ideas and tactics as part of an international political network. Her writing demonstrates not only a sophisticated understanding of civil liberties in an international context but also an ability to convey that understanding to others in nontechnical language.

Provocatively titled "The Borders Are My Prison," Flynn's article offered a spirited argument against any political litmus test for U.S. citizens who wished to travel abroad: "That I am an American citizen is indubitable. In common with other citizens of the United States, I have the right to expect the Secretary of State to issue a passport in my name, when I request it for purpose of travel. My opinions—and even more, his opinions about my opinions—are quite irrelevant to this right." A passport, Flynn observed, was not an indication that one held acceptable ideas: "The passport serves only to identify me, to make plain my citizenship and to request, formally and as a matter of civilized behavior, that the nations

I may visit receive me with ordinary courtesy." Flynn also noted how the right to travel was bound up with other rights. Freedom of movement, she observed, is necessary to the exercise of basic rights of expatriation, emigration, and asylum as well as scientific research, cultural exchange, and peaceful relations between and among nations.[136]

In her own case, her work as a historian—by which she meant a nonacademic labor and political historian—made travel professionally necessary. Prior to the revocation of her passport, she had lectured to international audiences and conferred with professional colleagues in Europe and Asia (the Soviet Union). She had since been invited to speak at Humboldt University in Berlin and at an international conference of Marxist historians in Dresden. Now she was unable to accept such invitations. The denial of the right to travel was consequently not only a restriction on her freedom of movement; it also limited her scholarly and professional freedom.

With this argument, Flynn offered a defense of what legal scholars now call "transborder speech." As defined by Ronald J. Krotoszynski, transborder speech "involves the exercise of freedom of speech, assembly, association, press and petition across national borders; it relates to the global information flows of people, ideas, knowledge, and argument."[137] Flynn pointed out that by confiscating her passport, federal authorities subjected her to viewpoint and content-based censorship while simultaneously denying those beyond U.S. borders the right to hear her views. Moreover, her treatment established political standards that all American intellectuals must meet before they may be issued a passport, which invited further censorship.[138]

In essence, Flynn claimed that one's intention to cross the national border should not be an occasion to strip one of their constitutional rights. With a nod to the late Zechariah Chafee Jr., renowned legal scholar and her staunch ally in the fight against the Espionage Act, she equated loss of freedom of movement with prison. "To deny a person the right to travel," she observed, "is to imprison one within the borders of the U.S.A." The *Political Affairs* article is a noteworthy example of how Flynn made the issue of civil liberties meaningful and understandable to a general audience. The writing was easy to follow, the arguments were crisp, and her knowledge of the issues at stake was unsurpassed. Much of what she wrote in the article was reproduced and distributed as a pamphlet.[139]

The CPUSA itself stood trial for violating the McCarran Act on December 11, 1962. Party members were predictably—and understandably—outraged.[140] This time, they were not alone. The absurdity and blatant hypocrisy of trying the party was noted even by its Trotskyist rivals, who pointed out in an article in the *Workers World* that the Ku Klux Klan had never been brought to trial nor found itself the specific target of a law: "Unlike the Klan, the Communist Party never horsewhipped anybody. It never tarred and feathered anybody. It never lynched anybody." Nor had the federal government ever attempted to prosecute the people responsible for exploiting workers and creating conditions of grinding poverty or those who brutally repressed anticolonial liberation movements. In an admirable show of unity, the *Workers World* urged its readers to send contributions to the Hall-Davis Defense Committee.[141]

The trial of the party lasted ten hours, and its outcome was not a surprise to anyone. After about a half hour of deliberation, the jury found the CPUSA guilty of not registering as a Communist-action organization with the SACB. The party was fined $120,000. As she often did, Flynn saw a victory of sorts in the trial despite the negative outcome. The question that had been adjudicated, she explained to readers of her *Worker* column, was whether the party had *registered* as a Communist-action organization (the Supreme Court's designation of the CPUSA in *Communist Party of the United States v. Subversive Activities Control Board*), not whether it *was* a Communist-action organization as defined by the law.[142] It was hair splitting, to be sure, but Flynn's underlying point was an important one. The burden of proof was on the federal government to show whether the CPUSA was a Communist organization as defined by the law. The party appealed the decision with briefs filed by attorneys Abt and Forer, and the verdict was eventually overturned.[143]

The Alderson Story

Flynn's prison memoir, *The Alderson Story: My Life as a Political Prisoner*, was published in March 1963. To celebrate the author and the book, a group that called itself the Friends of Elizabeth Gurley Flynn hosted a reception at the Belmont Plaza in New York City on March 29, 1963. Members of the committee that sponsored the book release party included Betty Gannett; Claudia Jones, who was living in England, having been deported there upon her release from Alderson; and Alexander Trachtenberg of International Publishers as well as prominent activists who shared Flynn's commitment to civil liberties. Among the latter group were Warren Billings, a friend from Flynn's Wobbly days who, along with Tom Mooney, had been convicted of the San Francisco Preparedness Day bombing in 1916; John Haynes Holmes, a Unitarian minister who had advocated for her resignation from the ACLU board; Rockwell Kent, an acclaimed artist, and his wife, Sally; and Dorothy Day, founder of the Catholic Worker movement. The event was promptly canceled by the Belmont Plaza when a right-wing political organization, the Nationalist Party, threatened to picket, but an order from the New York State Supreme Court forced the hotel to honor its contract. Greetings and salutations came from around the United States and the world. Such luminaries of the Left as Irish playwright Sean O'Casey and Spanish Communist leader Dolores Ibarruri chimed in, as did comrades from Canada, Mexico, the Soviet Union, and Hungary. Because the CPUSA was part of an international movement, *The Alderson Story* enjoyed global visibility, even if Cold War politics limited its reception in the United States. Dietz Verlag, a publishing house in East Berlin, released a slightly edited version the following year. Flynn sent autographed copies of the English-language version to comrades in Canada, France, England, Russia, and elsewhere.

Arguably, the book's most enthusiastic readers in the United States were progressive social workers, who hailed it as a clarion call for prison reform. Two of them—Jessie Binford and Bertha Reynolds—felt so strongly about its importance they organized the Committee to Bring the Alderson Story to Public Attention. Calling the book "an unusual document from the closed world of a women's prison" and "a living page of history," Binford and Reynolds wrote social workers around the country urging them to put aside their political preconceptions, read this "account of women without a voice to speak for themselves," and be stirred to "more thought and really concerned action." In addition to these motivated social workers, distribution in the United States relied on the party's network and Flynn's numerous and varied personal contacts from a half century of activism.[144]

The Passport Fight Continues

News of Flynn's passport case finally came on July 12, 1963. In *Flynn v. Rusk* (the Flynn and Aptheker cases had been consolidated by order of the court), the three-judge U.S. District Court of the District of Columbia affirmed the constitutionality of Section 6 of the McCarran Act. In their ruling, the judges found that whatever the stated purpose, foreign travel by U.S. Communists posed a danger to the internal security of the United States. A few days later, the judges refused to grant an injunction to prevent Secretary of State Dean Rusk from applying the passport provisions. Flynn and Aptheker appealed the ruling. The ACLU filed an amicus brief, which stated, "It believes this case presents important issues affecting freedom of association and the right to travel."[145]

Flynn expressed her frustration about the decision in a lively *Worker* column, "Why Can't I Go to Ireland?" She noted the warm welcome that President John F. Kennedy had received when he visited the Emerald Isle for four days in late June. Her mother hailed from Galway, her father's people from Mayo, and Flynn lamented that her own "fond hopes" of visiting the land of her ancestors had been dashed by the decision of the U.S. District Court. She mocked the reasoning that informed the decision: "The Government lawyers contended it is necessary 'for the preservation of the government.' How silly can they get?" She also noted the absurdity of keeping her at home, because wherever she traveled and whatever she did, Flynn would act like a Communist: "What shall I act like, a Birchite or a Holy Roller?" As she waited for the Supreme Court to hear on Section 6 of the McCarran Act, Flynn, by her own admission, "ever an optimist," informed readers that she would be brushing up a bit on "Gaelic, family history and the glorious fighting tradition and history of [her] friends—Jim Larkin, James Connolly, and the Skeffingtons—who never gave up in a fight for freedom." She ended the column with a rousing Irish cheer: "Up Galway and Mayo and down McCarthy and McCarran!"[146]

Her dogged determination to convince Americans of the threat to civil liberties posed by the McCarran Act garnered Flynn the reputation of being the leading figure in the fight for the law's repeal.[147] This work, however, came with a personal cost. Flynn spent so much time fighting McCarran, she had no time to finish the second half of her autobiography.[148] Often, the details of all the pending cases against party members left her with little ability to think about much else. She expressed her exasperation about it in a letter to Al Richmond in 1963: "Well, enuf of McCarran—that damned stuff runs out of my ears." She resented the SACB for its continued targeting of party members. In addition to violating civil liberties, she complained to Richmond, the board's actions confined her to a summer of "raising more dough, press releases, etc."[149]

The grind of defense work was not all that bothered Flynn. She was bored by the New York City CPUSA: "With all due respect to my colleagues, I'm a bit tired, fed up in fact, with all our ways here. I almost know what people are going to say, after years of close association." She felt "shackled" in the city, but the party needed her in New York, and so she stayed, albeit unhappily.[150] When she did leave the city for another speaking tour, the response was disappointing. In another letter to Richmond, she described a picnic she had recently attended in Detroit: "good people, devoted to the paper, but few in numbers and on the old side, unfortunately." She had assumed that diminishing support for anti-Communism would lead to a rebound in members for the party. When that did not happen, she speculated that young people were no longer attracted to the kinds of events that the party hosted, like picnics "with little entertainment."[151] The reality was that young people, even those with radical leanings who had allied with the party in its fight against political repression, no longer felt drawn to the CPUSA.

Events outside the United States were partly to blame. As tensions between China and the Soviet Union grew, the CPUSA stood on the Soviet side. The reasons were several. During the Cuban Missile Crisis, American Communists had supported the Soviet Union's removal of missiles as a responsible action that had thwarted an American invasion of the island. In contrast, the Chinese had criticized the removal as "capitulation." In addition, the CPUSA disagreed with Chinese Communists who maintained that the most important global struggle was not between capitalism and socialism but between the developed world and the nations of Asia, Africa, and Latin America. China's attack on the partial nuclear test ban treaty between the United States and the Soviet Union was another point of contention. Finally, the CPUSA disagreed with Chinese Communists about the extent of political repression in the United States—the country was not, American Communists argued, teetering on the brink of fascism—and resented China's characterization of them as puppets of Moscow, an image they were working diligently, if unsuccessfully, to shed.

These tensions spelled an opportunity for young Americans who wanted to embrace ultra-Left politics while at the same time distancing themselves from the Soviet Union. Instead of the CPUSA, many joined Maoist groups. Others who might have become Communists in years past because of the party's commitment to the Black freedom struggle, joined the burgeoning civil rights movement. Those who once might have been organizers for the party in labor unions had nowhere to go but into a labor movement now dominated by bureaucrats and Cold Warriors. As a result, the world of the CPUSA got smaller and smaller even as the noose of political repression around its neck loosened.[152]

Vindication

In early October 1963, Flynn and Aptheker received notice that the Supreme Court would likely hear the appeal their attorneys had filed on the passport case.¹⁵³ A week later, Flynn announced she was taking a six-month break from her *Worker* column. Except for when she was at Alderson, she had been writing a column for the paper regularly since 1939, and by now, she was weary of it. She told readers that she felt the column had become too focused on the McCarran Act, but mostly, she wanted to finish her autobiography and refresh herself with travel outside New York.¹⁵⁴ She had hoped to return to California but decided against the idea because she thought it would suggest that she was merely a figurehead or, worse, that she was retiring. At this time, retirement was not an option for Flynn.¹⁵⁵ She hoped to balance work with her writing, but once again, the party took precedence over her autobiography. In November, as attorneys Abt and Forer argued the appeal of Albertson and Procter, two of the twenty-seven people identified by Attorney General Kennedy as Communists and therefore legally obligated to register with the SACB, Flynn was tasked with raising much-needed funds for the defense campaign. In December, she published the second of two pamphlets on the McCarran Act. That same month, the Supreme Court announced that it would hear the passport case.¹⁵⁶

Oral arguments in *Aptheker v. Secretary of State* (the two cases had been consolidated) were heard by the Supreme Court in April 1964. The case garnered considerable attention. The *New York Times* interviewed both John Abt and Joseph Forer for an article. Abt faulted Section 6 of the McCarran Act as too broad because it covered all Communists whatever their status in the party or purpose in traveling. He noted that Flynn and Aptheker needed passports to go to Europe for travel and study. Forer said the law violated the First Amendment by restricting Communists' right to read, associate, and study, which are purely private activities.¹⁵⁷ The significance of her passport case, waning of anti-Communist fervor, and uptick of interest in radical movements on college campuses led to Flynn being invited as a guest of honor at Lowell House at Harvard University. When she accepted the invitation, she joined an illustrious group that included poet Robert Frost and New York City Mayor Robert Wagner. She spent a pleasant evening dining with her hosts and "wowing" several hundred students afterward.¹⁵⁸ Not long after the Harvard affair, the court issued its ruling. In a 6–3 decision, it found that Section 6 was overly broad and indiscriminate in its restriction of the right to travel because it did not distinguish between active and inactive members or among various possible purposes for traveling. In so doing, Section 6 deprived an individual of liberty without due process of the law in violation of the Fifth Amendment.

After the victory, Flynn filed again for her passport. When her initial passport appeal had been filed, the State Department had ordered new passport applications requiring applicants to respond under oath to the question of whether they are members of the CPUSA.[159] Flynn, who had spent years arguing that travel was a right of all Americans, not a privilege afforded only to those who professed acceptable politics, refused to sign. She attached a note to her application indicating as much: "I am not signing . . . because these sections have been declared unconstitutional by a US Supreme Court decision on June 22, 1964—6–3. Dr. HERBERT APTHEKER and I were the ones who sued DEAN RUSK, Sect. of State, to restore our passports."[160] In her application, she indicated her intention to visit Ireland for the first time, as well as England, Czechoslovakia, Poland, the Soviet Union, and possibly other countries.[161]

Flynn never made it to Ireland. She did return to the Soviet Union. On August 12, 1964, just five days after her seventy-fourth birthday, she sent word from Moscow to comrades in the United States that she would be going to the hospital for two weeks: "They found sugar in my blood and urine—so will try to correct it. Too much birthday I guess. Nothing serious, I hope."[162]

Her condition was indeed serious. On September 5, Flynn died in the Central Clinic of the Soviet Health Ministry in Moscow from inflammation of the lining of the stomach and intestines, aggravated by a blood clot in the lung. She was honored with a state funeral in Red Square, and a portion of her ashes was buried underneath the Kremlin Wall. The remainder of her ashes were flown to the United States and buried in Chicago's Forest Home Cemetery next to Eugene Dennis, per the instructions in her will, and near Emma Goldman, Lucy Parsons, Big Bill Haywood, and the Haymarket martyrs. A stone bearing this inscription was placed at her gravesite: Elizabeth G. Flynn, 1890–1964, "The Rebel Girl," Fighter for Working-Class Emancipation.

Epilogue

Not long after her death, Flynn's ashes were flown back to New York City, where a memorial service was held in her honor at the Community Church on Thirty-Fifth Street on September 22.[1] Among her numerous friends who were invited to speak was Dorothy Day. Day was in Vermont and could not deliver remarks in person, but she penned a moving tribute that was read at the service by the associate editor of the *Catholic Worker*, Tom Cornell, and printed in the November issue of the paper. In her tribute, titled "Red Roses for Her," Day recalled meeting Flynn for the first time at a rally in New York to raise funds for striking miners on the Mesabi Range in 1916. She noted how Flynn "charmed" the audience into donating their "meager money" for the strikers. Day herself was among those who succumbed and willingly gave of her modest means: "I forsook all prudence and emptied my purse, not even leaving myself car fare to get back to the office." The anecdote was not intended as a purely personal recollection. Day credited the young Flynn's talent for making the stories of workers' struggles meaningful and even urgent to those who might otherwise find them far removed as integral to the development of the IWW and to the broader development of a militant U.S. labor movement. As she put it, "If there had not been an IWW there would have been no CIO." Indeed, Day predicted, "Gurley Flynn's name will be immortal in the labor and radical movements."[2] Flynn has not been forgotten, but anti-Communism has affected the way she has been remembered in the decades since her death.

In April 1976, the ACLU Board of Directors voted to nullify Flynn's 1940 expulsion and posthumously reinstate her. The board expressed regret that Flynn had been deemed guilty by association, which violated a basic ACLU tenet, and had been denied a vote at the "trial," but essentially, their decision stemmed from recognition that it was now safe to be associated with a Communist. As reported in the minutes, "Today we operate in a different climate, where an individual can be a Communist and a civil libertarian." In fact, the decision to repeal Flynn's expulsion was deemed good for the organization's reputation. Board members believed that it would "signal that the ACLU judges the individual and is not a red-baiting group."³ Of course, that view was not unanimous among members of the board. For example, Paul R. Meyer, attorney and founder of the Oregon ACLU, openly disagreed. Henry Schwarzschild, another prominent civil libertarian, although not a member of the board, applauded Meyer's position. "I do not understand the doctrine that there is some rite of conscience that compels vegetarian societies to have meat-eaters on their policy-making bodies," he wrote in a letter to Meyer. "Why libertarians should have to be on the defense in 1976 about an action against a rationalizer of Stalinist totalitarianism in its heyday is a mystery."⁴ Not every defense of the ACLU's action against Flynn was so pointed. Legal scholar Burt Neuborne characterizes her expulsion as a "pragmatic and principled act." Had the ACLU not expelled Flynn because of her political views, he argues, the organization would have been vilified as an arm of the Communist Party, and its mission as a "credible and effective defender of constitutional values" would have been seriously compromised. In other words, it was necessary for the ACLU to impugn Flynn's commitment to civil liberties because of her political views to continue its own work in defense of civil liberties.⁵

The ACLU's reversal opened space for recognition of Flynn as a radical labor leader and a civil liberties advocate. Yet the specter of anti-Communism continues to haunt efforts to commemorate her and the important contributions she has made to labor and civil liberties history. On May 1, 2023, activists had a historical marker dedicated to Flynn installed at the site of her childhood home in Concord, New Hampshire. Two weeks after it was unveiled, Republican lawmakers had the marker taken down, arguing that Flynn did not deserve such recognition because she was un-American, a charge they based on her membership in the CPUSA. The marker did not erase this history; it explicitly stated that Flynn was a party member and that she was sent to prison under the "notorious Smith Act." The plaque also identified Flynn as a "nationally renowned labor leader" whose "fiery speeches" earned her the nickname "the Rebel Girl." Yet it also claimed that Flynn worked through the ACLU to advocate for women's rights, particularly suffrage and birth control. That claim is simply not true. Moreover, as the removal of the plaque demonstrates, the reconstruction of Flynn as a feminist, rather than a class warrior, does not mollify anti-Communist critics. The idea that Flynn was primarily a women's rights activist has also seeped into media coverage of the controversy over the plaque. An article about the plaque controversy in the *Washington Post*, for example, bore a headline that refers to Flynn as "feminist, with Communist past." She would be surprised to see herself described this way, even if she espoused many ideas that we think of as feminist. Flynn would also recoil at the subordination of "Communist" to "feminist." From the moment she joined the CPUSA until the day she died, Flynn saw herself as a Communist—no qualifier.[6]

The controversy over Flynn's historical marker in Concord was laid to rest when a judge dismissed the lawsuit that activists brought against the state for having removed it. No doubt, Flynn would be gratified to know that she is still making news and would approve of activists having fought back against ideologues trying to control the content of public speech. Still, it is a shame that the marker has not been replaced. Flynn deserves a greater presence in U.S. historical memory.

Why should we remember Elizabeth Gurley Flynn? She was one of the most exciting and innovative labor leaders the United States has ever had. Her fighting spirit, fearlessness, creativity, and absolute dedication to working-class people and their struggles for a better life offer a wellspring of inspiration for labor organizers today. She was an Irish American radical who fought the law (and sometimes won) to defend civil liberties and civil rights for workers of all races and ethnicities in the United States and supported antifascist, anti-imperialist, and anticolonial movements around the globe, Her lifetime of activism challenges the simplistic image of Irish Americans as bigoted authoritarians and provides a model for how to organize across divides that are often difficult to bridge. She was a woman who championed working women's issues, displayed warmth and compassion for others, enjoyed close ties with her family, bore a son whom she loved, had close female friendships and a likely lesbian affair, and suffered heartbreak but who also left her son in the care of others for extended periods and craved the company of men sometimes more than that of her own sex. In other words, she lived life on her own terms, at least as much as it was possible for a woman of her era to do so, and having done so, she complicates our idea of what makes a "good" feminist. Finally, she was a socialist who despised capitalism but embraced Americanism and ardently defended the U.S. Constitution, even at the cost of her own personal liberty. Often, she was more faithful to American ideals than those who vilified her as un-American. In short, she was a rebel. And what a rebel she was.

ACKNOWLEDGMENTS

I FIRST ENCOUNTERED ELIZABETH Gurley Flynn in 1976. I was a teenager, and my mom gave me a copy of *Life* magazine's bicentennial issue, which contained a special report entitled "Remarkable American Women." Flynn, a working-class, Irish American radical, caught my eye. Years later, when I was a graduate student in rhetoric at the University of Maryland–College Park, my professor and advisor Martha Watson assigned Flynn's speech "The Truth about the Paterson Strike" to our public address class. That second encounter sealed the deal. I was won over by Flynn's intelligence, moxie, and sense of humor. Thanks to my mom for introducing me to Flynn, and to Martha and another professor, Robert Gaines, for encouraging me to present an analysis of her speech as part of the department's colloquium series. Little did I know that my work on Flynn would continue in one way or another for three decades.

Like so many scholars of American radicalism, my research for this book brought me to the Tamiment Library at New York University. I am indebted to the many archivists, staff members, and student workers there who have assisted me, either in person or online. Thanks also to archivists and staff at the University of Baltimore Special Collections Department at Langsdale Library who digitized the records of the Workers' Defense Union to make them more accessible. I am also grateful for the assistance of various archivists and staff at the Spokane Public Library's Inland Northwest Special Collections, Missoula Public Library's Tony Veazey Montana Room, University of Montana Library, Paterson Public Library, Smith College Archives Special Collections, Special Collections Research Center at Syracuse University, New York Historical Society, New York Public Library, New York State Archives, Boston Public Library, Mudd Manuscript Library at Princeton University, Walter Reuther Library at Wayne State University, Special Collections at the University of Delaware

Library, Labor Archives and Research Center at San Francisco State University, and American Labor Museum / Botto House National Landmark. To get a sense of what it felt like to speak to a crowd of militant striking immigrant workers, I stood (several times) on the balcony at the Botto House imagining myself an orator facing a crowd of thousands on the lawn on a Sunday afternoon during the Paterson strike of 1913. It's a terrific museum, and I encourage everyone to visit, find a spot that calls to you, and let your imagination transport you back in time.

I started my work on Flynn before the internet was used for academic research; now I cannot imagine doing research without it. I am especially grateful to the administrators of the Internet Archive and the Marxists Internet Archive who make sources that would otherwise be difficult to track down freely available online. The New York Public Library allowed at-home access to the *Daily Worker* and other materials during the COVID-19 pandemic, which enabled me to keep working during that difficult time.

Hofstra University provided support for this project in important ways. Sabbatical leaves afforded me time for research and writing. Grants from the Lawrence Herbert School of Communication and the Hofstra College of Liberal Arts and Sciences helped fund various research trips.

I am grateful to have been invited to speak about Flynn and my work on this book at online events hosted by the Vito Marcantonio Forum in partnership with the Claudia Jones School for Political Education and by the Communist Party of the United States as well as on *All Hail to the Pod*, hosted by Jim Slaven and recorded in Edinburgh, Scotland (birthplace of James Connolly), and the *Irish People* podcast, hosted by Caoimhe Garland and recorded in Belfast. Each of these conversations helped me see Flynn from a different perspective. Shawn Gude invited me to write a piece about Flynn for the online version of *Jacobin* to coincide with the inauguration of Donald Trump in 2017. That piece caught the eye of Peter Mickulas at Rutgers University Press, and a subsequent conversation led to our collaboration. Peter and I have enjoyed a productive relationship and more than a few laughs. I could not imagine an editor I'd rather work with.

A sincere thank you to colleagues who provided support for this project in a variety of ways at various stages. Ron Meyers shared his extensive knowledge of the Spokane free speech fight when I was in town doing research and helped me understand how locals at the time viewed Flynn and her role in the events of 1909. Thoughtful comments from Boston area rhetoricians Greg Goodale, Michele Kennerly, Jamie Landau,

Melanie McNaughton, Chuck Morris, and Tom Nakayama and from participants in the 2011 Boston Immigration and Urban History series at the Massachusetts Historical Society, especially commentator Michael Willrich, strengthened the chapter on free speech fights in Missoula and Spokane. Mari Lee Mifsud provided an opportunity to publish an article on Flynn's free speech activism from the soapbox, an experience that refined my ideas on that subject. Kenyon Zimmer helped clarify my thinking about Flynn's advocacy on behalf of deportees during and after the first Red Scare. The late Silvia Thompson provided me my first glimpse into the world of American Communists and connected me with Bob Lewis, a member of the Young Communist League at Cornell University with whom I had an informative and thoroughly enjoyable conversation that has remained with me ever since. Gary Bono and the editorial board for International Publishers invited me to write the foreword to the reissued edition of Flynn's prison memoir, which deepened my understanding not only of that work but also of Flynn's sense of herself as a political prisoner. Paul Buhle and Norman Markowitz reviewed the manuscript for Rutgers and offered constructive suggestions for revising it. Mike Goldfield read the revised manuscript in record time and provided important feedback in a variety of places.

The late Nunzio Pernicone encouraged me during the early stages of this project, and I am sorry that he did not live to see it completed. His advice that I convey the spirit of my subject without lapsing into hagiography has been my North Star. Thank you, Nunzio.

A chance encounter with Fraser Ottanelli ten years ago changed my life forever. Husband, comrade, and editor par excellence, he has read every chapter several times over the past decade. His sharp eyes, keen intellect, and extensive knowledge of labor and radical history led me to rethink assumptions and strengthen arguments. I am profoundly grateful to him for making this a much better book than it otherwise would have been. And for so much more.

As always, my children and grandchildren fill my heart to overflowing and remind me why the work matters.

Finally, this book is dedicated to my parents, Dominick Trasciatti, son of Italian immigrants and a hardworking union man with a heart of gold, and Ruth Gilboy Trasciatti, the proud Irish American coal miner's daughter and fierce class warrior who introduced me to the Rebel Girl. They died before the book was finished, but I feel like they know and are proud.

NOTES

Introduction

1. In the half century since her death, three major biographical works about Flynn have been published: Rosalyn Fraad Baxandall, *Words on Fire: The Life and Writing of Elizabeth Gurley Flynn* (New Brunswick, N.J.: Rutgers University Press, 1987); Helen Camp, *Iron in Her Soul: Elizabeth Gurley Flynn and the American Left* (Pullman: Washington State University Press, 1995); and Lara Vapnek, *Elizabeth Gurley Flynn: Modern American Revolutionary* (New York: Routledge, 2015).

2. Larry D. Kramer, *The People Themselves: Popular Constitutionalism and Judicial Review* (New York: Oxford University Press, 2004); Larry D. Kramer, "Popular Constitutionalism circa 2004," *California Law Review* 92, no. 4 (July 2004): 959–1011.

3. "Notebook of Autobiographical Events," 1937–1948, 7, Elizabeth Gurley Flynn Collection, box 3, Tamiment Library, New York University (hereafter NYU EGF Papers).

4. Baxandall's *Words on Fire* is an invaluable collection for anyone looking to get a sense of Flynn in her own words.

Chapter 1: Strategizing from the Soapbox

1. Elizabeth Gurley Flynn, *The Rebel Girl: An Autobiography, My First Life (1906–1926)* (New York: International Publishers, 1955), 62; my account of Flynn's early years is from pp. 23–126.

2. "Gossip of Gotham Town," *Rising Son*, October 25, 1906, 3.

3. On soapbox oratory in the early twentieth-century United States, see Mary Anne Trasciatti, "Athens or Anarchy? Soapbox Oratory and the Early Twentieth-Century American City," *Buildings & Landscapes* 20, no. 1 (Spring 2013): 43–68.

4. "Embracing a philosophy of accessibility to all workers as well as low dues and transferable membership," Anne F. Mattina notes, "the IWW represented a

unique opportunity for female activists at the dawn of the twentieth century." See Mattina, "'Yours for Industrial Freedom': Women of the IWW, 1905–1930," *Women's Studies* 43, no. 2 (February 2014): 170.

5. The first and, to date, only international history of the IWW is Peter Cole, David Struthers, and Kenyon Zimmer, eds., *Wobblies of the World: A Global History of the IWW* (London: Pluto Press, 2017).

6. Ahmed White, *Under the Iron Heel: The Wobblies and the Capitalist War against Workers* (Oakland: University of California Press, 2022), 48.

7. Flynn, *Rebel Girl*, 77.

8. "Labor Unions Protest," *Brooklyn Daily Eagle*, February 16, 1907, 8. On the case, see Philip S. Foner, *The Industrial Workers of the World 1905–1917* (New York: International Publishers, 1965), 51–59; and White, *Under the Iron Heel*, 31–32.

9. John Carstairs Matheson to James Connolly, October 14, 1907, National Library of Ireland, https://garms.nli.ie/Record/vtls000619203/StaffViewMARC; Connolly to Matheson, October 28, 1907, National Library of Ireland, https://catalogue.nli.ie/Record/vtls000618319.

10. James Connolly, "Declaration of Principles of the Irish Socialist Federation," January 1908, transcribed by the James Connolly Society of Canada and the United States, https://www.marxists.org/archive/connolly/1908/01/decisf.htm.

11. "An Irish Manifesto," *Montana News*, May 30, 1907, 1.

12. "The New Preamble," *Industrial Union Bulletin*, December 12, 1908, 4.

13. University of Washington, "IWW History Project: IWW Strikes and Free Speech Fights 1905–1920," accessed December 8, 2024, https://depts.washington.edu/iww/strikes.shtml.

14. "Convention of Hoboes," *Freeport Journal-Standard*, September 30, 1908, 2; "New York Joan and Husband Beat Freights All Way to Chicago," *Spokane Press*, October 7, 1908, 2; "Leaders of the Unemployed," *Fargo Forum and Daily Republican*, October 14, 1908, 10; Flynn, *Rebel Girl*, 83–85.

15. J. H. Walsh, "Tactics Adopted at Portland," *Industrial Union Bulletin*, May 18, 1907, 2.

16. R. H. Williams, "Propaganda Leagues," *Industrial Union Bulletin*, December 12, 1908, 2.

17. John Duda, *Wanted! Men to Fill the Jails of Spokane* (Chicago: Charles H. Kerr, 2009), 7.

18. See, for example, Philip S. Foner, *Fellow Workers and Friends: IWW Free Speech Fights as Told by Participants* (Westport, Conn.: Greenwood, 1981); David M. Rabban, "The IWW Free Speech Fights and Popular Conceptions of Free Expression before World War I," *Virginia Law Review* 80, no. 5 (1994): 1055–1158; and David M. Rabban, *Free Speech in Its Forgotten Years, 1870–1920* (Cambridge: Cambridge University Press, 1997), 77–128.

19. Rabban, *Free Speech*, 77–128.

20. A much abridged account of Flynn's leadership of the Missoula, Spokane, and Paterson free speech fights and the importance of women, generally, in these

struggles is Mary Anne Trasciatti, "Sisters on the Soapbox: Elizabeth Gurley Flynn and Her Female Free Speech Allies' Lessons for Contemporary Women Labor Activists," *Humanities* 7, no. 3 (2018), https://doi.org/10.3390/h7030069.

21. Allan James Matthews, *A Guide to Historic Missoula* (Helena: Montana Historical Society Press, 2002), 21–43.

22. Erik Loomis, *Empire of Timber: Labor Unions and the Pacific Northwest Forests* (Cambridge: Cambridge University Press, 2016), 23–30; Michael Goldfield, *The Southern Key: Class, Race, & Radicalism in the 1930s & 1940s* (Oxford: Oxford University Press, 2020), 180–192.

23. Loomis, *Empire of Timber*, 34.

24. Loomis, 34.

25. See, for example, "Samuel Gompers, the Man and His Work," *Daily Missoulian*, September 5, 1909, E1; "What Uncle Sam Is Doing for Labor," *Daily Missoulian*, September 5, 1909, 4; "Labor's Great Day Finds the Garden City Prepared to Entertain Its Guests," *Daily Missoulian*, September 6, 1909, 1; "Labor Day Plans Meet with Success," *Daily Missoulian*, September 7, 1909, 1, 4; and "Well Handled," *Daily Missoulian*, September 7, 1909, 4. On the IWW's reaction to Labor Day festivities in Missoula, see Pete Brown, "IWW and AFL in Missoula Montana," *Industrial Worker*, September 23, 1909, 1.

26. Jon A. Peterson, "The City Beautiful Movement: Forgotten Origins and Lost Meanings," *Journal of Urban History* 2, no. 4 (1976): 415–34; Paul Boyer, *Urban Masses and Moral Order in America* (Cambridge, Mass.: Harvard University Press, 1978), 264. See also William H. Wilson, *The City Beautiful Movement* (Baltimore: Johns Hopkins University Press, 1989).

27. Melvin Dubofsky, "The Origins of Western Working Class Radicalism, 1890–1905," *Labor History* 7, no. 2 (1966): 133–135.

28. "Local History Is Encouraging," *Industrial Worker*, March 25, 1909, 1.

29. Elizabeth Gurley Flynn, "Successful Trip Work of E.G. Flynn," *Industrial Worker*, August 12, 1909, 1.

30. Flynn, *Rebel Girl*, 96.

31. Flynn, "Successful Trip," 1, 3.

32. Elizabeth Gurley Flynn, "IWW Agitation in Missoula, Mont.," *Industrial Worker*, September 16, 1909, 1.

33. Flynn, "IWW Agitation," 1.

34. Flynn, 1.

35. Flynn, 1.

36. Matthews, *Guide to Historic Missoula*, 34–45.

37. Flynn, "IWW Agitation," 1.

38. Flynn. See also "Miserable Slavery in Logging Camps," *Industrial Worker*, August 19, 1909, 1.

39. Silvia Federici, *Caliban and the Witch: Women, the Body and Primitive Accumulation* (New York: Autonomedia, 2004), 135.

40. Federici, 136.

41. David Roediger, *The Wages of Whiteness: Race and the Making of the American Working Class* (London: Verso 1991), 66; David Roediger, "Race, Labor, and Gender in the Languages of Antebellum Social Protest," in *Terms of Labor: Slavery, Serfdom and Free Labor*, ed. Stanley L. Engerman (Stanford: Stanford University Press, 1999), 168–187; and David Roediger, *Colored White: Transcending the Racial Past* (Berkeley: University of California Press, 2002), 108.

42. On the discourse of slavery among Lowell factory women, see Lori Merish, *Archives of Labor: Working-Class Women and Literary Culture in the Antebellum United States* (Durham, N.C.: Duke University Press, 2017), 60–62.

43. Eric Foner, *Free Soil, Free Labor, Free Men: The Ideology of the Republican Party before the Civil War* (Oxford: Oxford University Press, 1995), xxxviii.

44. James Wilson, "Modern Slave Traders," *Industrial Worker*, October 24, 1908, 1.

45. An institutional history of the organization is Edward H. McKinley, *Marching to Glory: The History of the Salvation Army in the United States, 1880–1980* (San Francisco: Harper & Row, 1980).

46. Diane H. Winston, *Red-Hot and Righteous: The Urban Religion of the Salvation Army* (Cambridge, Mass.: Harvard University Press, 1999), 1–2.

47. Flynn, "IWW Agitation," 1.

48. Not surprisingly, critics questioned the allocation of funds and moral integrity of its social welfare programs. For a contemporary example, see C. C. Carstens, "The Salvation Army: A Criticism," *Annals of the American Academy of Political and Social Science* 30, no. 3 (1907): 117–128.

49. Richard Brazier, "The Story of the IWW's 'Little Red Songbook,'" *Labor History* 9, no. 1 (1968): 94.

50. George A. Venn, "The Wobblies and Montana's Garden City," *Montana: The Magazine of Western History* 21, no. 4 (October 1971): 20.

51. "Industrial Workers of the World Are Sent to Jail," *Butte Miner*, October 1, 1909, 3.

52. Paul McIlvenny, "Heckling in Hyde Park: Verbal Audience Participation in Popular Public Discourse," *Language in Society* 25, no. 1 (March 1996): 27–60.

53. "Industrial Workers," 3.

54. Venn, "Wobblies and Montana's Garden," 22.

55. "Free Speech Battle; Fight or Be Choked," *Industrial Worker*, September 30, 1909, 1.

56. Gary Gerstle defines Americanism as a political language that emerged in the second and third decades of the twentieth century and explores its varied working-class dimensions in *Working-Class Americanism: The Politics of Labor in a Textile City, 1914–1960* (Princeton: Princeton University Press, 2002).

57. James R. Barrett, "Americanization from the Bottom Up: Immigration and the Remaking of the Working Class in the United States, 1880–1930," *Journal of American History* 79, no. 3 (December 1992): 996–1020.

58. "Free Speech Battle," 1.

59. "Free Speech Battle," 1.

60. The comradeliness of hobo street life is discussed in Don Mitchell, "Controlling Space, Controlling Scale: Migratory Labour, Free Speech, and Regional Development in the American West," *Journal of Historical Geography* 28, no. 1 (2002): 67.

61. Implications of the logic of masculinist protection are explored in Iris Marion Young, "The Logic of Masculinist Protection: Reflections on the Current Security State," *Signs: Journal of Women in Culture and Society* 29, no. 1 (2003): 1–25.

62. Francis Shor, "Masculine Power and Virile Syndicalism: A Gendered Analysis of the IWW in Australia," *Labour History*, no. 63 (1992): 83–99; and Francis Shor, "'Virile Syndicalism' in Comparative Perspective: A Gender Analysis of the IWW in the United States and Australia," *International Labor and Working Class History*, no. 56 (1999): 65–77.

63. "Gurley Flynn Sends Horrible Story," *Daily Missoulian*, October 6, 1909, 2.

64. See, for example, Sidney L. Harring, "Class Conflict and Suppression of Tramps in Buffalo, 1892–1894," *Law and Society Review* 11, no. 5 (Summer 1977): 873–911; and Mark H. Haller, "Historical Roots of Police Behavior: Chicago, 1890–1925," *Law and Society Review* 10, no. 2 (Winter 1976): 313–314. For an illuminating account of the feudal origins of United States vagrancy laws, see Arthur H. Sherry, "Vagrants, Rogues, and Vagabonds: Old Concepts in Need of Revision," *California Law Review* 48, no. 4 (1960): 557–573.

65. Mitchell, "Controlling Space," 68.

66. Matthew May, "Hobo Orator Union: Class Composition and the Spokane Free Speech Fight of the Industrial Workers of the World," *Quarterly Journal of Speech* 97, no. 2 (2011): 156. For a compelling account of how the transience and mobility of soapbox culture generated new forms of class struggle, see May, *Soapbox Rebellion: The Hobo Orator Union and the Free Speech Fights of the Industrial Workers of the World, 1909–1916* (Tuscaloosa: University of Alabama Press, 2013).

67. "Woman Would Fill City's Prisons," *Daily Missoulian*, October 3, 1909, 10.

68. "Socialists in Trouble," *Great Falls Daily Tribune*, October 5, 1909, 1.

69. F. H. Little, "The Beating of Jones by the Missoula Sheriff," *Industrial Worker*, October 27, 1909, 1.

70. "IWW Orators Thrown into Missoula Dungeon," *Butte Miner*, October 2, 1909, 10.

71. Matthews, *Guide to Historic Missoula*, 39.

72. Duda makes this case about the Spokane free speech fight in *Wanted!*, 3.

73. Flynn, *Rebel Girl*, 102.

74. *Butte Miner*, October 4, 1909, 3.

75. On the production of space and scale by Wobbly free speech fighters in Denver, see Mitchell, "Controlling Space," 63–84.

76. "IWW Leader Arrested as a General Disturber," *Butte Miner*, October 4, 1909, 3.

77. "Woman Organizer among Score Confined in Jail at Missoula," *Anaconda Standard*, October 4, 1909, 5.

78. Though Flynn insists the IWW is a leaderless union. In an article on leadership, she explains, "Every man is a leader—he has a following numbering one.... Men are

often valuable to the IWW. No man is indispensable." See "As to Leaders," *Industrial Worker*, November 10, 1909, 4.

79. "IWW Leader Arrested," 3. On Edith Frenette's Wobbly career, see Heather Mayer, "Edith Frenette: A Transnational Radical Life," in *Wobblies of the World*, 228–236.

80. "Gurley Flynn Sends," 2.

81. "Crowd Is Unruly—Missile Is Thrown," *Anaconda Standard*, October 6, 1909, 1.

82. "The Arrest Almost Precipitated a Riot," *Billings Daily Gazette*, October 7, 1909, 1.

83. "Arrest Thirty," *Great Falls Daily Tribune*, October 7, 1909, 1.

84. Flynn, *Rebel Girl*, 104.

85. Henri LeFebvre, *Writings on Cities*, trans. Eleonore Kofman and Elizabeth Lebas (Oxford: Blackwell, 1996), 34.

86. "Industrial Workers of the World Refuse to Leave Jail Demanding Food and Then a Jury Trial," *Butte Miner*, October 8, 1909, 1.

87. Historical analyses of the cultural force of parades include Susan G. Davis, *Parades and Power: Street Theater in Nineteenth-Century Philadelphia* (Philadelphia: Temple University Press, 1986); Simon P. Newman, *Parades and the Politics of the Street: Festive Culture in the Early American Republic* (Philadelphia: University of Pennsylvania Press, 1987); and Mary Ryan, "The American Parade: Representations of the Nineteenth-Century Social Order," in *The New Cultural History*, ed. Lynn Hunt (Berkeley: University of California Press, 1989), 131–153.

88. "Missoula Officers Make More Arrests," *Anaconda Standard*, October 8, 1909, 1.

89. "Five Hundred Men Asked for by IWW," *Daily Missoulian*, October 9, 1909, 1.

90. Flynn, *Rebel Girl*, 105.

91. Nancy Arlene Driscol Engle argues that respectability is a complex idea shaped by individual interpretations of morality, gender norms, economic interest, and ethnicity. See Nancy Arlene Driscol Engle, "Benefiting a City: Women, Respectability and Reform in Spokane, Washington, 1886–1910" (PhD diss. University of Florida, 2003), ix–xv.

92. Engle, x.

93. "Do You Vote Yea or Nay on Plans to Make Spokane a Beautiful City?," *Spokane Chronicle*, January 2, 1906, 10.

94. Many of the Olmsted recommendations were put into effect, and the firm's report continues to guide park planners. See John Charles Olmsted, *Report of the Board of Park Commissioners, Spokane*, 1908, http://www.historicspokane.org/HeritageTours/olmsted/Olmstead%20Brothers%20Report.pdf.

95. Lucile F. Fargo, *Spokane Story* (New York: Columbia University Press, 1950), 215.

96. Roger Bruns, *Preacher: Billy Sunday and Big-Time American Evangelism* (Champagne: University of Illinois Press, 2002).

97. "Billy Sunday at Spokane," *Kettle River Journal*, January 2, 1909, 3; "He'll Stay," *Spokane Daily Chronicle*, January 16, 1909, 1.

98. Jonathan David Knight, "The Spokane and Fresno Free-Speech Fights of the Industrial Workers of the World, 1909–1911" (master's thesis, Washington State University, 1991), 69.

99. Fargo, *Spokane Story*, 216.

100. Knight, "Spokane and Fresno," 70.

101. Fred W. Heslewood, "Flathead Indians; Flathead Whites," *Industrial Worker*, March 18, 1909, 1.

102. See Brazier, "'Little Red Songbook,'" 93.

103. Knight, "Spokane and Fresno," 63.

104. Joyce Kornbluh, *Rebel Voices: An IWW Anthology* (Chicago: Charles H. Kerr, 1998), 94.

105. "Ordinance no A3890," *City of Spokane Auditor*, vol. M, no. 352, 1908, EW Regional Archives.

106. "Ordinance no A39," *Municipal Code of the City of Spokane Washington* (Spokane, Wash.: Inland Printing, 1903), 64.

107. "Streets Are for All the People," *Spokesman-Review*, March 9, 1909, 4.

108. "Streets Are for All," 4.

109. Carlos Schwantes, *The Pacific Northwest: An Interpretive History*, revised and enlarged ed. (Lincoln: University of Nebraska Press, 1996), 288; Engle, "Benefiting a City," viii.

110. Glen J. Broyles, "The Spokane Free Speech Fight, 1909–1910: A Study of IWW Tactics," *Labor History* 19, no. 2 (Spring 1978): 1; "IWW Sidestep Citizenship Test," *Spokesman-Review*, January 5, 1910, 7; H. Lloyd, "The Foreigner," *Industrial Worker*, January 29, 1910, 4.

111. Knight, "Spokane and Fresno," 66.

112. "Walsh Heads off Violence," *Industrial Union Bulletin*, February 27, 1909, 1.

113. They enjoyed fleeting success with this tactic in Portland, Oregon, when a judge decided that a law against street speaking in the city was unconstitutional; see "Reds Can Now Talk Again," *Industrial Worker*, April 8, 1909, 1.

114. *Industrial Worker*, August 12, 1909, 1.

115. The paper's stance on outdoor oratory is exemplified in "Making the City Beautiful," *Spokesman-Review*, October 29, 1909, 4.

116. Fred W. Heslewood, "Barbarous Spokane," *International Socialist Review* 10 (1910): 705–713; Jack Phelan, "The City Beautiful," *International Socialist Review* 10 (1910): 713.

117. Heslewood, "Barbarous Spokane," 710.

118. Kornbluh, *Rebel Voices*, 25–26.

119. "Judge Mann Declares the New Ordinance Unconstitutional and Releases Thompson, but Declares the Old Ordinance Still in Effect Which Forbids Street Speaking of Any Nature," *Industrial Worker*, November 3, 1909, 1.

120. "Pits Entire Force against IWW," *Spokesman-Review*, November 2, 1909, 1.

121. Elizabeth Gurley Flynn, "Call to Action," *Industrial Worker*, November 10, 1909, 1.

122. "For Right to Stand on a Soapbox and Talk Bitter Industrial War Is Waged in Spokane," *Tacoma Times*, November 19, 1909, 1.

123. "To Raise Free Speech Army," *Industrial Worker*, November 24, 1909, 4.

124. Richard Brazier, "Spokane Free Speech Fight, 1909," in Duda, *Wanted!*, 99.

125. Brazier, 104.

126. Jane Little Botkin, *Frank Little and the IWW: The Blood That Stained an American Family* (Norman: University of Oklahoma Press, 2017), 380n48.

127. Brazier, "'Little Red Songbook,'" 91–105; David A. Carter, "The Industrial Workers of the World and the Rhetoric of Song," *Quarterly Journal of Speech* 66, no. 4 (1980): 365–374.

128. Brazier, "Spokane Free Speech Fight," 99.

129. Brazier, 100.

130. "Free Speech Fight Is on in Spokane," *Industrial Worker*, November 3, 1909, 1; "Blow Dealt to Free Speech in Spokane," *Albuquerque Journal*, November 3, 1909, 2.

131. Heather Mayer, *Beyond the Rebel Girl: Women, Wobblies, Respectability, and the Law in the Pacific Northwest, 1905–1924* (Oregon State University Press, 2015), 23.

132. Flynn, "Call to Action," 1.

133. "Women Are Ready to Go to Jail," *Vinita Daily Chieftain*, November 16, 1909, 1; "Women Invite Imprisonment in Defense of Free Speech," *Santa Cruz News*, December 28, 1909, 1; "On the Road for Spokane," *Industrial Worker*, January 8, 1910, 2.

134. May, "Hobo Orator Union," 160.

135. "Synopsis Spokane Free Speech Fight," *Industrial Worker*, March 26, 1910, 3.

136. "Girl at IWW Helm," *Spokesman-Review*, November 12, 1909, 7; Fargo, *Spokane Story*, 220; Benjamin H. Kizer, "Elizabeth Gurley Flynn," *Pacific Northwest Quarterly* 57, no. 3 (July 1966): 110–112.

137. Ronald A. Myers, "Labor Pains," *Inlander*, September 9, 1998, 12; Mayer, *Beyond the Rebel Girl*, 33.

138. Joyce Kornbluh mentions the legendary incident in *Rebel Voices*, 95.

139. Flynn, *Rebel Girl*, 108.

140. Dubofsky offers an account of police brutality in Spokane. See Melvyn Dubofsky, *We Shall Be All: A History of the IWW* (New York: Quadrangle, 1969), 179.

141. "Driven Naked through the Streets by the Spokane Police," *Industrial Worker*, January 29, 2010, 2.

142. "IWW Fight Gets Tame," *Spokesman-Review*, November 16, 1909, 7.

143. "Eat, Mr. IWW, Spite Spokane," *Spokesman-Review*, November 22, 1909, 8; Elizabeth Gurley Flynn, "Do You See the Point?," *Industrial Worker*, November 24, 1909, 1; "Jury Hears Roast," *Spokane Chronicle*, February 11, 1910, 7.

144. "IWW Fight Gets Tame," 7.

145. See, for example, Nicole Hahn Rafter, *Partial Justice: Women, Prisons, and Social Control* (New Brunswick, N.J.: Transaction Publishers, 1995); and Clarice

Feinman, "An Historical Overview of the Treatment of Incarcerated Women: Myths and Realities of Rehabilitation," *Prison Journal* 63, no. 2 (1984): 12–26. For discussion of how prisons remain gendered organizations despite the implementation of seemingly gender-neutral practices and policies, see Jill A. McCorkel, "Embodied Surveillance and the Gendering of Punishment," *Journal of Contemporary Ethnography* 32, no. 1 (February 2003): 41–76.

146. Elizabeth Gurley Flynn, "The Shame of Spokane," *International Socialist Review* 10 (January 1910): 612.

147. Flynn, 615.

148. Flynn, 616.

149. Elizabeth Gurley Flynn, "I Have No Regrets," *Woman Today*, April 1937, 26.

150. Agnes Thecla Fair, "Miss Fair's Letter," *Workingman's Paper*, November 20, 1909, 1.

151. Fair, 1.

152. Fair, 1.

153. Mayer, *Beyond the Rebel Girl*, 36–38.

154. "Idlers Invade City to Assist IWW," *Spokesman-Review*, November 30, 1909, 7.

155. "E. Gurley Flynn and Others Pinched," *Industrial Worker*, December 1, 1909, 1.

156. Elizabeth Gurley Flynn, "Story of My Arrest and Imprisonment," *Industrial Worker*, December 15, 1909, 1.

157. Flynn, 1.

158. Elizabeth Gurley Flynn, "Mayor N.S. Pratt: Withdraw Your Statement or Sue Me for Criminal Libel," *Spokane Press*, January 8, 1910, 2; "News of Spokane Free Speech Fight," *Industrial Worker*, January 22, 1910, 1; Elizabeth Gurley Flynn, "Latest News from Spokane," *International Socialist Review* 10 (March 1910): 828–834.

159. "News of Spokane Free Speech Fight," *Industrial Worker*, December 25, 1909, 1; Engle, "Benefiting a City," 137.

160. "Struggle for Free Speech and Free Press," *Industrial Worker*, January 1, 1910, 3.

161. "Synopsis Spokane Free Speech Fight," *Industrial Worker*, March 19, 1910, 3.

162. "Thanksgiving Ceremonies in Fort Wright Bastille," *Industrial Worker*, December 25, 1909, 1; "Resolutions Adopted in Spokane Jail," *Industrial Worker*, January 8, 1910, 4.

163. "Juror Fights to Attend Court," *Spokesman-Review*, February 23, 1910, 9.

164. "News of Spokane Free Speech Fight," *Industrial Worker*, January 22, 1910, 1; "Plan to Intimidate Flynn Jurors Is Seen," *Spokesman-Review*, February 20, 1910, 1.

165. "Sorry She Was Freed," *Spokane Chronicle*, February 25, 1910, 1; "Filigno Is Found Guilty; Gurley Flynn Acquitted," *Spokesman-Review*, February 25, 1910, 1.

166. Flynn, *Rebel Girl*, 110.

167. Mari Boor Tonn, "Militant Motherhood: Labor's Mary Harris 'Mother' Jones," *Quarterly Journal of Speech* 82, no. 1 (February 1996): 1–21. This tactic is not limited to early twentieth-century American women. See, for example, Valeria Fabj, "Motherhood as Political Voice: The Rhetoric of the Mothers of Plaza De Mayo," *Communication Studies* 44, no. 1 (1993): 1–18.

168. Flynn, *Rebel Girl*, 109.

169. "Free Speech in Spokane," *Industrial Worker*, November 17, 1909, 2; "Free Speech," *Industrial Worker*, December 15, 1909, 1; E. D. Northrup, "To the Mayor of Spokane," *Industrial Worker*, January 22, 1910, 1.

170. Elizabeth Gurley Flynn, "News from the Front: Free Speech vs. Law," *Industrial Worker*, November 17, 1909, 1; Ben Reitman, "My Dear Brave Friends," *Industrial Worker*, November 24, 1909, 4; "Free Speech and Free Press," *Industrial Worker*, December 5, 1909, 2.

171. Katherine Flynn, "New York, November 12, 1909," *Industrial Worker*, November 24, 1909, 5; "Resolutions from Oakland, California," *Industrial Worker*, November 24, 1909, 5; "Minneapolis, November 21, 1909," *Industrial Worker*, November 24, 1909, 5; "Butte, Montana, November 19, 1909," *Industrial Worker*, November 24, 1909, 5; "The Scandinavians of Spokane," *Industrial Worker*, November 24, 1909, 5; "Mayor Presides at Rousing Protest Meeting," *Industrial Worker*, December 1, 1909, 4; "Resolutions from Portland," *Industrial Worker*, December 1, 1909, 4; "Resolutions Adopted at Arcade Hall, November 14, 1909," *Industrial Worker*, December 1, 1909, 4; "At a Mass Meeting of the Membership of Denver County Local S.P. of Colorado," *Industrial Worker*, January 1, 1910, 2; "Resolutions from Reading, PA," *Industrial Worker*, January 1, 1910, 2; "Scandinavian Socialist Local," *Industrial Worker*, January 22, 1910, 3; "Astoria, Oregon, January 13, 1910," *Industrial Worker*, January 22, 1910, 4; "Glass Workers Pass Resolutions Pledging Support to IWW Free Speech Fight," *Industrial Worker*, January 29, 1910, 3.

172. "Synopsis Spokane Free Speech Fight," 3.

173. "International Labor Notes," *Industrial Worker*, January 22, 1910, 2; "From over the Sea," *Industrial Worker*, April 2, 1910, 3.

174. "Unemployed Go to Spokane," *Ogden Standard*, November 18, 1909, 1.

175. "Making Anarchists," *Tacoma Times*, November 11, 1909, 4; "Freedom in Spokane," *Los Angeles Herald*, January 11, 1910, 4.

176. "Oh, It's Coming," *Scott County Kicker*, November 13, 1909, 1.

177. "John Mitchell and Freedom of Speech," *Intermountain Catholic*, December 11, 1909, 4.

178. "Spokane and Free Speech," *Wenatchee Daily World*, November 19, 1909, 4.

179. "Take IWW Chief; Calm Follows," *Spokesman-Review*, November 3, 1909, 9.

180. Flynn, *Rebel Girl*, 111.

181. "Spokane Sane Again," reprinted in *Industrial Worker*, April 10, 1910, 1.

182. Flynn, "I Have No Regrets," 26.

183. "Gurley Flynn Is Mother," *Spokesman-Review*, May 28, 1910, 9.

184. On the distinction between abstract rights and material goods necessary for organizing, see Duda, *Wanted!*, 3.

185. Barrett, "Bottom Up," 996–1020.

186. Flynn, "Do You See?," 1.

187. Duda, *Wanted!*, 3.

Chapter 2: The Fight for Free Speech in Paterson, New Jersey

1. Elizabeth Gurley Flynn, *The Rebel Girl: An Autobiography, My First Life (1906–1926)* (New York: International Publishers, 1955), 118.
2. Flynn, 123.
3. Flynn, 120–121.
4. Flynn, 118–119.
5. "Woman Socialist Freed," *Philadelphia Inquirer*, June 13, 1911, 9; Flynn, *Rebel Girl*, 122.
6. "'Joan of Arc' of Labor Movement Will Speak Here," *Bridgeport Times and Evening Farmer*, April 5, 1911, 8.
7. See, for example, "The New Unionism," *Chat*, April 1, 1911, 8.
8. "Says Some Union Leaders Work for Selves Only," *Newark Star-Eagle*, April 29, 1911, 6.
9. Charles Willis Thompson, "The New Socialism That Threatens the Social System," *New York Times*, March 17, 1912, SM1.
10. Peter Cole, David Struthers, and Kenyon Zimmer, introduction to *Wobblies of the World* (London: Pluto Press, 2017), 1.
11. Ahmed White notes the high likelihood of Wobblies being citizens in *Under the Iron Heel: The Wobblies and the Capitalist War against Workers* (Oakland: University of California Press, 2022), 139.
12. Quoted in Thompson, "New Socialism," SM1.
13. Helen C. Camp, *Iron in Her Soul: Elizabeth Gurley Flynn and the American Left* (Pullman: Washington State University Press, 1995), 29.
14. Michael Miller Topp, "The Lawrence Strike: The Possibilities and Limitations of Italian American Syndicalist Transnationalism," in *Italian Workers of the World: Labor Migration and the Formation of Multiethnic States*, ed. Donna R. Gabaccia and Fraser M. Ottanelli (Urbana: University of Illinois Press, 2001), 143.
15. "Unfit Food in 'Swell' Places," *Akron Beacon Journal*, January 14, 1913, 1; "Woman Leader of Striking Waiters in New York City," *Buffalo News*, January 15, 2013, 3.
16. See, for example, "Riot Reveals Romance," *Boston Globe*, January 25, 1913, 3; and Flynn, *Rebel Girl*, 153.
17. See, for example, "Gurley Flynn in New England," *Missoulian*, November 1, 1912, 9; "Leads Big Strike in New York City," *Pensacola Journal*, January 30, 1913, 3; and "Miss Flynn an Able Orator," *Washington Standard*, February 14, 1913, 7.
18. Flynn, *Rebel Girl*, 156.
19. Marcia Dente, *Paterson Great Falls: From Local Landmark to National Historical Park* (Charleston, S.C.: History Press, 2012), 94.
20. Kenyon Zimmer, "'A Cosmopolitan Crowd:' Transnational Anarchists, the I.W.W., and the American Radical Press," in *Wobblies of the World*, ed. Peter Cole, David Struthers, and Kenyon Zimmer (London: Pluto Press, 2017), 30.
21. Jennifer Guglielmo, *Living the Revolution: Italian Women's Resistance and Radicalism in New York City, 1880–1945* (Chapel Hill: University of North Carolina Press, 2010), 139.

22. Nunzio Pernicone and Fraser M. Ottanelli, *Assassins against the Old Order: Anarchist Violence in Fin de Siècle Europe* (Urbana: University of Illinois Press, 2018), 123–153. On the Fatti di Maggio, see also Louise A. Tilly, "I Fatti di Maggio: The Working Class of Milan and the Rebellion of 1898," in *Modern European Social History*, ed. Robert J. Bezucha (Lexington, Mass.: D. C. Heath, 1972), 1881–1911; and "Structure and Action in the Making of Milan's Working Class," *Social Science History* 19, no. 2 (Summer 1995): 243–259.

23. Nunzio Pernicone, *Carlo Tresca: Portrait of a Rebel* (New York: Palgrave, 2005), 64.

24. Pernicone, 64–65.

25. Kenyon Zimmer, *Immigrants against the State: Yiddish and Italian Anarchism in America* (Urbana: University of Illinois Press, 2015), 79.

26. Pernicone, *Carlo Tresca*, 66; Zimmer, *Immigrants against the State*, 84.

27. "A Situation of Vital Importance to Paterson," *Paterson Evening News*, February 21, 1913, 4.

28. Quoted in "Situation of Vital Importance," 4.

29. Mark Purcell, "Excavating Lefebvre: The Right to the City and Its Urban Politics of the Inhabitant," *GeoJournal* 58, no. 2 (2002): 102–103.

30. Flynn, *Rebel Girl*, 83.

31. Flynn, 155.

32. Flynn, 161.

33. *New York Call*, February 26, 1913, 1.

34. "Strike Leaders in Jail," *New York Tribune*, February 26, 1913, 16.

35. Steve Golin, "Bimson's Mistake: Or, How the Paterson Police Helped to Spread the 1913 Strike," *New Jersey History* 100, no. 3/4 (1982): 57–86.

36. Joyce Kornbluh, *Rebel Voices: An IWW Anthology* (Chicago: Charles H. Kerr, 1998), 198.

37. "Home Rule Halts Strike," *New York Tribune*, February 28, 1913, 16.

38. "Home Rule," 16.

39. "Strong Local Union May Grow out of Silk Strike," *Paterson Evening News*, March 13, 1913, 10.

40. "Strong Local Union," 10.

41. "Strong Local Union," 10.

42. Steve Golin, *The Fragile Bridge: Paterson Silk Strike, 1913* (Philadelphia: Temple University Press, 1992), 81.

43. Golin, 81–82; Anne Huber Tripp, *The I.W.W. and the Paterson Silk Strike of 1913* (Urbana: University of Illinois Press, 1987), 76.

44. "Lessig and Miss Flynn Out on Bail; Tresca and Quinlan Are in the County Jail," *Paterson Evening News*, April 26, 1913, 9.

45. "The Infamous Influence of the IWW in Paterson: Article No. 2," *Paterson Evening News*, March 12, 1913, 11.

46. John Fitch, "The I.W.W.: An Outlaw Organization," *Survey* 30 (June 7, 1913), 357.

47. Elizabeth Gurley Flynn, "Figures and Facts," *Solidarity*, April 19, 1913, 1; Flynn, *Rebel Girl*, 159.

48. "Police Prevent Meetings and Bar Agitators from Paterson, N.J.," *Solidarity*, September 11, 1915, 4.

49. New Jersey Bureau of Industrial Statistics, *Thirty-Sixth Annual Report of the Bureau of Statistics of Labor and Industries of New Jersey for the Year Ending October 31st, 1913* (Paterson, N.J.: News Printing Co., State Printers, 1914), 176.

50. Fitch, "I.W.W.," 355; see Charles Hill and Steven Cohen, "John A. Fitch and the Pittsburgh Survey," *Western Pennsylvania Historical Magazine* 67, no. 1 (January 1984): 17–32.

51. Fitch, "I.W.W.," 355.

52. Zimmer, *Immigrants against the State*, 84.

53. On the instrumental and expressive power of the mobile picket, see Mary Heaton Vorse, *A Footnote to Folly: Reminiscences of Mary Heaton Vorse* (New York: Farrar and Rinehart, 1935), 11–13.

54. On the significance of the strike as a method for halting production, see Joe Burns, *Reviving the Strike: How Working People Can Regain Power and Transform America* (New York: Ig Publishing, 2011), especially chapters 1 and 2.

55. Witnesses who testified at her trial recalled that Flynn gave them this advice. See "Flynn Defense on Today," *Paterson Evening News*, July 1, 1913, 1 and 9; and Thomas Flynn, "Trial of Gurley Flynn," *Solidarity*, December 11, 1915, 1.

56. Quoted in "Miss Flynn Urges Workers to Get on the Picket Line," *Paterson Evening News*, May 8, 1913, 10.

57. "Large Crowds at Open Air Session Last Night," *Paterson Evening News*, June 6, 1913, 9.

58. "Large Crowds," 9.

59. "Final Report and Testimony," 2631.

60. Melvyn Dubofsky, *We Shall Be All: A History of the IWW* (New York: Quadrangle, 1969), 278.

61. Pernicone, *Carlo Tresca*, 70–71.

62. "Bury Striker with Honors," *New York Times*, July 6, 1913, 2.

63. "Contract Slavery in Paterson Silk Mills," *Solidarity*, April 26, 1913, 4.

64. "Hannah Silverman Leads Strikers to Coney Island," *Paterson Evening News*, June 21, 1913, 7.

65. Quoted in *Paterson Evening News*, April 1, 1913, 1.

66. Pernicone, *Carlo Tresca*, 69.

67. Golin, *Fragile Bridge*, 62.

68. Golin, 58.

69. The attack on Baronio / Mrs. Gallo is recounted in Paul Avrich, *Anarchist Voices* (Princeton: Princeton University Press, 1995), 83.

70. Quoted in *Final Report and Testimony Submitted to Congress by the Commission on Industrial Relations Created by the Act of August 23, 1912*, vol. 3 (Washington, D.C.: U.S. Government Printing Office, 1916), 2525.

71. "Arrest Socialist Editor," *New York Times*, May 18, 1913, 2.

72. Golin, *Fragile Bridge*, 54.

73. "IWW Will Boycott Germania Assembly Rooms," *Paterson Evening News*, April 26, 1913, 9.

74. "General Strike Threatened," *Paterson Evening News*, March 3, 1913, 7.

75. Golin, *Fragile Bridge*, 151.

76. "Strikers Will Be Welcomed to Haledon by Mayor Brueckmann," *Paterson Evening News*, February 28, 1913, 2; "General Strike Threatens: 12,000 Workers Now Out," *Paterson Evening News*, March 3, 1913, 1, 7.

77. Elizabeth Gurley Flynn, "The Truth about the Paterson Strike," in *Words on Fire: The Life and Writing of Elizabeth Gurley Flynn*, ed. Rosalyn Fraad Baxandall (New Brunswick and London: Rutgers University Press, 1987), 117.

78. See, for example, "Greatest Meeting Yet at Haledon," *Solidarity*, May 31, 1913, 1.

79. Golin, *Fragile Bridge*, 153–154; Guglielmo, *Living the Revolution*, 195.

80. "None in Union Square," *New York Times*, June 8, 1913, 2; "The Social War in New Jersey," *Current Opinion* 55 (August 1913): 80–81; Mercer Green Johnson, *Patriotism and Radicalism: Addresses and Letters* (Boston: Sherman, French, 1917), 143–149.

81. Quoted in "Complain at Closing up of City Streets," *Paterson Evening News*, May 26, 1913, 7.

82. "Mayor Served with Papers in Hall Cases," *Paterson Evening News*, May 23, 1913, 14.

83. "Socialism and Strikes," *New York Times*, May 16, 1913, 10; "The I.W.W.," *New York Times*, May 20, 1913, 10; "Closing the Halls Will Not End the Strike," *Paterson Evening News*, May 20, 1913, 4.

84. "Miss Flynn Wants Churches for Women's Meeting," *Paterson Evening News*, May 23, 1913, 14.

85. "2,000 Met in Backyards of Ellison St," *Paterson Evening News*, May 26, 1913, 1.

86. "Historic Headquarters for IWW Strikers," *Solidarity*, June 14, 1913, 4.

87. "Historic Headquarters," 4.

88. "Historic Headquarters," 4.

89. "Historic Headquarters," 4.

90. "Strikers Meet in Pouring Rain on Their Own Property," *Paterson Evening News*, May 28, 1913, 1.

91. "Another Battle over Holding of Strike Meetings," *Paterson Evening News*, June 2, 1913, 1.

92. "Drum Corps at Practice and Auto with Bells Made Holding of Strike Meeting Difficult," *Paterson Evening News*, June 4, 1913, 1.

93. Flynn, *Rebel Girl*, 167.

94. "IWW Men Driven out of Bayonne," *New York Times*, May 28, 1913, 22.

95. "New Haven Refuses to Permit IWW to Hold Meeting," *Paterson Evening News*, June 21, 1913, 7.

96. "Labor Parades in Many Cities: Children of Paterson Strikers Principal Feature in New York," *San Francisco Call*, 2 May 1913, 11.

97. Golin, *Fragile Bridge*, 133–135; Tripp, *I.W.W.*, 117–119; Pernicone, *Carlo Tresca*, 67.

98. Flynn, "Truth about the Paterson Strike," 119.

99. "Committee on Industrial Relations," 2541; Golin, *Fragile Bridge*, 102.

100. "Elizabeth Gurley Flynn to the Bar," *Solidarity*, June 21, 1913, 2.

101. "Jury out in Flynn Case," *Paterson Evening News*, July 1, 1913, 1, 9; "Flynn Jury Deadlocked in Disagreement," *Paterson Evening News*, July 2, 1913, 1.

102. "Jury Disagrees," *Paterson Evening News*, July 3, 1913, 7.

103. Krishan Kumar and Ekaterina Makarova, "The Portable Home: The Domestication of Public Space," *Sociological Theory* 26, no. 4 (December 2008): 324; "Fear Jury Deadlock in Flynn Case: Locked up over Night and Woman Defendant Expects a Disagreement," *New York Times*, July 3, 1913, 18.

104. Golin, *Fragile Bridge*, 191–192.

105. Golin, 196.

106. Camp, *Iron in Her Soul*, 54.

107. Eugene M. Tobin, "Direct Action and Conscience: The 1913 Paterson Strike as Example of the Relationship between Labor Radicals and Liberals," *Labor History* 20, no. 1 (1979): 78.

108. Flynn, *Rebel Girl*, 171.

109. Flynn, 182.

110. Elizabeth Gurley Flynn to Mary Heaton Vorse, July 5, 1914, Mary Heaton Vorse Papers, box 54, Walter Reuther Library, Wayne State University (hereafter MHV Papers); Flynn to Vorse, July 19, 1914, MHV Papers, box 54.

111. Camp, *Iron in Her Soul*, 62.

112. "Police Prevent Meetings," 4.

113. "Police Take Drastic Stand in Keeping IWW Agitators from Speaking in Paterson," *Paterson Evening News*, September 4, 1915, 1.

114. Pernicone, *Carlo Tresca*, 69.

115. "Free Speech in Paterson," 692.

116. "Police Prevent Meetings," 1.

117. Quoted in "'Free Speech Is on Trial—Not I!' Says Elizabeth Gurley Flynn," *Day Book* 5, December 1, 1915, 13–14.

118. "Good for Paterson," *New York Times*, September 14, 1915, 10.

119. "Good for Paterson," 10.

120. Flynn, *Rebel Girl*, 172.

121. "IWW Appeals to President Wilson in Free Speech Battle," *Paterson Evening News*, September 17, 1915, 1.

122. "Paterson's Official Brutality and Stupidity," *Solidarity*, October 9, 1915, 3.

123. On the Free Speech League, see David M. Rabban, "The Free Speech League, the ACLU, and Changing Conceptions of Free Speech in American History," *Stanford Law Review* 45, no. 1 (November 1992): 47–114.

124. John Davenport, "Gagging Free Speech," *Mother Earth* 8 (January 1914): 331–332.

125. "Will Not Allow Miss Flynn to Speak Here," *Paterson Evening News*, September 30, 1915, 1; Leonard Abbott, "What Happened in Paterson," *Public*, October 15, 1915, 998.

126. Elizabeth Gurley Flynn to Rose Pastor Stokes, n.d., MS no. 573, Rose Pastor Stokes Papers, Yale University.

127. "Free Speech in Paterson," 692.

128. "Elizabeth Flynn's Contest with Paterson," *Survey* 35 (December 11, 1915): 283.

129. "Miss Flynn Is Organizer of Local I.W.W.," *Paterson Evening News*, November 13, 1915, 1.

130. "Miss Flynn, in Disguise, Invades Paterson in Vain," *New York Tribune*, November 12, 1915, 1; Elizabeth Gurley Flynn to Comrade, n.d., RPS Papers, reel 68, Tamiment Library, NYU.

131. Flynn, *Rebel Girl*, 172.

132. Judith Schwartz, *Radical Feminists of Heterodoxy: Greenwich Village 1912–1940* (Lebanon, N.H.: New Victoria Publishers, 1982), 1–3.

133. Camp, *Iron in Her Soul*, 64.

134. "Treasurer's Report of the Elizabeth Gurley Flynn Defense Fund," n.d., RPS Papers, reel 68, Tamiment Library, NYU.

135. See Franklin Rosemont, *Joe Hill: The IWW and the Making of a Revolutionary Workingclass Counterculture*, 2nd ed. (Oakland, Calif.: PM Press, 2015).

136. "Monster Joe Hill Protest Meeting in New York," *Solidarity*, November 20, 1915, 1; Flynn, *Rebel Girl*, 191–192.

137. "Gurley Flynn Free; to Keep on Talking," *New York Times*, December 1, 1915, 1.

138. Flynn, "Trial of Gurley Flynn," 1.

139. Quoted in "In the Field of Labor," *Independent*, December 13, 1915, 427.

140. Joseph Ettor, "Gurley Flynn Acquitted," *Solidarity*, December 4, 1915, 4.

141. See, for example, "Seek Release of 'Pat' Quinlan," *Paterson Evening News*, December 7, 1915, 11; and Elizabeth Gurley Flynn to Rose Pastor Stokes, December 22, 1915, RPS Papers, reel 68, Tamiment Library, NYU.

142. "IWW Leaders Plan Meetings in Paterson," *Paterson Evening News*, December 3, 1915, 11.

143. "Ban Still upon Miss Flynn: Paterson Police Chief Says She Shan't Speak Till Mayor Relents," *New York Times*, December 2, 1915, 22.

144. "Free Speech Followers to Call on Mayor," *Paterson Evening News*, January 5, 1916, 1–2; "Mayor Allows Miss Flynn to Speak Here," *Paterson Evening News*, January 20, 1916, 1.

145. "The Ladies Tilt Their Lances at Free Speech Dragon," *New York Tribune*, November 21, 1915, 3.

146. "Women Trying to Save Paterson Orator," *Fort Wayne Journal-Gazette*, December 4, 1915, 14.

147. "Elizabeth Gurley Flynn: Labor Leader," *The Outlook*, December 15, 1915, 905.

148. See, for example, "IWW on the Job in Paterson," *Solidarity*, October 23, 1915, 4; "Paterson's Official Brutality," 3; and Dubofsky, *We Shall Be All*, 196.

149. Flynn, *Rebel Girl*, 21.

Chapter 3: War and Civil Liberties

1. Stéphane Audoin-Rouzeau and Annette Becker, *Understanding the Great War: 14–18*, trans. Catherine Temerson (New York: Hill and Wang, 2001), 94–101.

2. R. Craig Nation, *War on War: Lenin, the Zimmerwald Left, and the Origins of Communist Internationalism* (Durham, N.C.: Duke University Press, 1989), 10–20.

3. See, for example, William Maehl, "The Triumph of Nationalism in the German Socialist Party on the Eve of the First World War," *Journal of Modern History* 24 (March 1952): 15–41. As Maehl explains, "The SPD was the keystone of the International, and, when that keystone was torn from its position by the force of nationalism, the proud arch of working-class unity crumbled in an instant," 15.

4. Francis L. Carsten, *War against War: British and German Radical Movements in the First World War* (Berkeley: University of California Press, 1982), 11–35.

5. Eric Thomas Chester, *The Wobblies in Their Heyday: The Rise and Destruction of the Industrial Workers of the World during the World War I Era* (Amherst, Mass.: Levellers Press, 2014), 117–120.

6. "Jeanne d'Arc of I.W.W. Denounces Defense Moves," *St. Louis Post-Dispatch*, May 24, 1916, 13.

7. Kenneth Warren, *Bethlehem Steel: Builder and Arsenal of America* (Pittsburgh: University of Pittsburgh Press, 2008); Hugh Rockoff, "Until It's over, over There: The U.S. Economy in World War I," in *The Economics of World War I*, ed. Stephen Broadberry and Mark Harrison (Cambridge: Cambridge University Press, 2005), 313.

8. David Montgomery, *Workers' Control in America: Studies in the History of Work, Technology, and Labor Struggles* (Cambridge: Cambridge University Press, 1979), 97.

9. Elizabeth Gurley Flynn, *The Rebel Girl: An Autobiography, My First Life (1906–1926)* (New York: International Publishers, 1955), 199.

10. On the ethnic composition of the Mesabi Range, see John Sirjamaki, "The People of the Mesabi Range," *Minnesota History* 27, no. 3 (September 1946): 203–215.

11. Robert D. Cuff and Melvin I. Urofsky, "The Steel Industry and Price Fixing during World War I," *Business History Review* 44, no. 3 (Autumn 1970): 294.

12. Thomas K. McCraw and Forest Reinhardt, "Losing to Win: U.S. Steel's Pricing, Investment Decisions, and Market Share, 1901–1938," *Journal of Economic History* 49, no. 3 (September 1989): 598.

13. Melvyn Dubofsky, *We Shall Be All: A History of the IWW* (New York: Quadrangle, 1969), 320; Robert M. Eleff, "The 1916 Minnesota Miners' Strike against U.S. Steel," *Minnesota History* 51, no. 2 (Summer 1988): 64.

14. Nunzio Pernicone, *Carlo Tresca: Portrait of a Rebel* (New York: Palgrave, 2005), 89.

15. Gary Kaunonen, *Flames of Discontent: The 1916 Minnesota Iron Ore Strike* (University of Minnesota Press, 2017), 138.

16. Pernicone, *Carlo Tresca*, 89.

17. Pernicone, 89.

18. Helen C. Camp, *Iron in Her Soul: Elizabeth Gurley Flynn and the American Left* (Pullman: Washington State University Press, 1995), 69–72. Flynn, Vorse, and Cothren were not the only women to play a part in the strike. See David LaVigne, "Rebel Girls: Women in the Mesabi Iron Range Strike of 1916," *Minnesota History* 65, no. 3 (Fall 2016): 90–100.

19. Michael G. Karni, "Elizabeth Gurley Flynn and the Mesabi Strike of 1916," *Range History* 5, no. 4 (1981): 2–4; *Duluth Herald*, July 12, 1916, 17; LaVigne, "Rebel Girls," 90.

20. Camp, *Iron in Her Soul*, 73; Pernicone, *Carlo Tresca*, 91–93.

21. Lara Vapnek, *Elizabeth Gurley Flynn: Modern American Revolutionary* (New York: Routledge, 2015), 63–66; Flynn, *Rebel Girl*, 207–216; Michael M. Topp, *Those without a Country: The Political Culture of Italian American Syndicalists* (Minneapolis: University of Minnesota Press, 2001), 186–192; Pernicone, *Carlo Tresca*, 92–93. On the conflict over centralization, see Michael Goldfield, *The Southern Key: Class, Race, & Radicalism in the 1930s & 1940s* (Oxford: Oxford University Press, 2020), 212–214.

22. "Elizabeth Gurley Flynn Will Speak Here for IWW," *Seattle Star*, January 12, 1917, 5; "Elizabeth Gurley Flynn," *Northwest Worker*, January 18, 1917, 2; "Miss Flynn Coming," *Tacoma Times*, January 29, 1917, 3; Flynn, *Rebel Girl*, 224.

23. "Elizabeth Gurley Flynn Appeals for Aid for Men Held for 'Constructive Murder,'" *Daily Missoulian*, February 11, 1917, 1.

24. Mabel Abbott, "Human Storm Signal! That's Gurley Flynn," *Tacoma Times*, March 7, 1917, 2.

25. As Dorothy Sue Cobble notes, there is no necessary connection between a union's structural form and its political orientation; see "Pure and Simple Radicalism: Putting the Progressive Era AFL in Its Time," *Labor: Studies in Working-Class History in the Americas* 10, no. 4 (Winter 2013): 73.

26. Ahmed White, *Under the Iron Heel: The Wobblies and the Capitalist War against Workers* (Oakland: University of California Press, 2022), 59–62; Chester, *Wobblies in Their Heyday*, 227–229; Dubofsky, *We Shall Be All*, 344–346.

27. See Julie Greene, *Pure and Simple Politics: The American Federation of Labor and Political Activism, 1881–1917* (New York: Cambridge University Press, 1999).

28. Jennifer Luff, *Commonsense Anticommunism: Labor and Civil Liberties between the World Wars* (Chapel Hill: University of North Carolina Press, 2012), 32–46; Alex Goodall, *Loyalty and Liberty: American Countersubversion from World War 1 to the McCarthy Era* (Urbana: University of Illinois Press, 2013), 104–105.

29. Joseph McCartin, *Labor's Great War: The Struggle for Industrial Democracy and the Origins of Modern Labor Relations, 1912–1921* (Chapel Hill: University of North Carolina Press, 1997), 56–57.

30. Montgomery, *Workers' Control in America*, 96.

31. David Montgomery, *The Fall of the House of Labor: The Workplace, the State, and American Labor Activism, 1865–1924* (Cambridge: Cambridge University Press, 1987), 332.

32. Robert Justin Goldstein, *Political Repression in Modern America from 1870 to the Present* (Boston: G. K. Hall, 1978), 100–101.

33. On the social, psychological, and political aspects of Italian anarchist violence at the end of the nineteenth century, see Nunzio Pernicone and Fraser M. Ottanelli, *Assassins against the Old Order: Anarchist Violence in Fin de Siècle Europe* (Urbana: University of Illinois Press, 2018).

34. Zechariah Chafee, *Freedom of Speech* (New York: Harcourt, Brace, 1920), 187–188.

35. William Preston observes that in passing the 1917 law "Congress abandoned the conviction that radicalism could be a home-grown phenomenon." See *Aliens and Dissenters: Federal Suppression of Radicals—1903–1933* (Cambridge, Mass.: Harvard University Press, 1963), 75.

36. Quoted in John Milton Cooper, *Woodrow Wilson: An Autobiography* (New York: Vintage, 2011), 377.

37. Dominique Pinsolle, "Sabotage, the IWW, and Repression: How the American Reinterpretation of a French Concept Gave Rise to a New International Conception of Sabotage," trans. Jesse Cohn, in *Wobblies of the World*, ed. Peter Cole, David Struthers, and Kenyon Zimmer (London: Pluto Press, 2017), 44–45.

38. See Walker Smith, *Jersey Justice at Work: First Decision on the Advocacy of Sabotage in the United States Courts* (New York: I.W.W. Publishing Bureau, 1913).

39. Elizabeth Gurley Flynn, *Sabotage: The Conscious Withdrawal of the Workers' Industrial Efficiency* (Chicago: IWW Publishing Bureau, 1916), 4.

40. Flynn, 5.

41. Flynn, 4, 12, 16, 20.

42. Rosemary Feurer, "Mary Harris 'Mother' Jones and Elizabeth Gurley Flynn: Radical Women of the Irish Diaspora," in *The Famine Diaspora and Irish American Women's Writing*, ed. Marguerite Corporaal, Jason King, and Peter D. O'Neil (London: Palgrave MacMillan, 2024), 163.

43. Philip S. Foner, *History of the Labor Movement in the United States, Vol. 4: The Industrial Workers of the World 1905–1917* (New York: International Publishers, 1965), 160–167.

44. Robert C. Sims, "Idaho's Criminal Syndicalism Act: One State's Response to Radical Labor," *Labor History* 15, no. 4 (September 1974): 512.

45. Ahmed A. White, "The Crime of Economic Radicalism: Criminal Syndicalism Laws and the Industrial Workers of the World, 1917–1927," *Oregon Law Review* 649, no. 3 (2006): 652, https://scholar.law.colorado.edu/faculty-articles/383.

46. Sims, "Idaho's Criminal Syndicalism Act," 514.

47. White, "Crime of Economic Radicalism," 652.

48. Woodrow Wilson, "Address at Independence Hall," July 4, 1914, http://www.gutenberg.org/files/17427/17427.txt.

49. Wilson.

50. Wilson.

51. Woodrow Wilson, "Third Annual Message to Congress," December 7, 1915, https://millercenter.org/the-presidency/presidential-speeches/december-7-1915-third-annual-message.

52. Wilson.

53. Woodrow Wilson, "Acceptance of Democratic Nomination," December 2, 1915, https://millercenter.org/the-presidency/presidential-speeches/september-2-1916-speech-acceptance.

54. Wilson.

55. Wilson.

56. "An Address in Washington to the League to Enforce Peace, 27 May 1916," *Papers of Woodrow Wilson: Vol 37, May 9–August 7, 1916*, ed. Arthur S. Link (Princeton: Princeton University Press, 1981), 113–117.

57. Woodrow Wilson, "22 January, 1917, 'Address of the President of the United States to the Senate,'" University of Michigan, Dearborn, accessed December 27, 2024, http://www-personal.umd.umich.edu/~ppennock/doc-Wilsonpeace.htm.

58. See Erez Manela, *The Wilsonian Moment: Self-Determination and the International Origins of Anticolonial Nationalism* (Oxford University Press, 2007); and Karen Stanbridge, "Nationalism, International Factors and the 'Irish question' in the Era of the First World War," *Nations and Nationalism* 11, no. 1 (2005): 32–33.

59. Hans Vought, "Division and Reunion: Woodrow Wilson, Immigration, and the Myth of American Unity," *Journal of American Ethnic History* 13, no. 3 (Spring 1994): 34; Thomas J. Noer, "The American Government and the Irish Question during World War I," *South Atlantic Quarterly* 72, no. 1 (1973): 95–99.

60. Woodrow Wilson, "Second Inaugural Address," March 4, 1917, http://www.gutenberg.org/files/17427/17427-h/17427-h.htm.

61. Manela, *Wilsonian Moment*, 37–38.

62. *United States Statutes at Large*, vol. 40, 65th Cong. (Washington, D.C.: U.S. Government Printing Office, 1918), 553.

63. Margaret A. Blanchard, *Revolutionary Sparks* (New York: Oxford University Press, 1992), 70.

64. Philip M. Glende, "Victor Berger's Dangerous Ideas: Censoring the Mail to Preserve National Security during World War I," *Essays in Economic and Business History* 26, no. 1 (2008): 8.

65. Donald Johnson, "Wilson, Burleson, and Censorship in the First World War," *Journal of Southern History* 28, no. 1 (February 1962): 53; Blanchard, *Revolutionary Sparks*, 77.

66. Blanchard, *Revolutionary Sparks*, 75.

67. Ira Kipnis, *The American Socialist Movement 1897–1912* (Chicago: Haymarket Books, 1952), 254–257.

68. Rachel Cutler Schwartz, "The Rand School of Social Science 1906–1924: A Study of Worker Education in the Socialist Era" (PhD diss., State University of New York–Buffalo, 1984).

69. Cornelius L. Bynum, "The New Negro and Social Democracy during the Harlem Renaissance, 1917–37," *Journal of the Gilded Age and Progressive Era* 10, no. 1 (January 2011): 95–96.

70. Mary Anne Trasciatti, "Athens or Anarchy? Soapbox Oratory and the Early Twentieth-Century American City," *Buildings & Landscapes* 20, no. 1 (Spring 2013): 43–68.

71. For the commission's report, see *Industrial Relations: Final Report and Testimony Submitted to Congress by the Commission on Industrial Relations Created by the Act of August 23, 1912* (Washington, D.C.: U.S. Government Printing Office, 1916).

72. McCartin, *Labor's Great War*, 105.

73. On labor's gains during the war, see McCartin, 94–175.

74. Goldstein, *Political Repression*, 119–121; David M. Kennedy, *Over Here: The First World War and American Society* (New York: Oxford University Press, 1980), 83.

75. David M. Rabban, *Free Speech in Its Forgotten Years, 1870–1920* (Cambridge: Cambridge University Press, 1997), 4–7. See also Christoper M. Finan, *From the Palmer Raids to the Patriot Act: A History of the Fight for Free Speech in America* (Beacon Press, 2008) and David M. Kennedy, *Over Here: The First World War and American Society* (Oxford University Press, 2004).

76. On the idea of "horizontal" processes for influencing public opinion about the war, see Audoin-Rouzeau and Becker, *Understanding the Great War*, 109–112.

77. Christopher Capozzola explores the distinction between vigilance and vigilantism, especially during the First World War, in *Uncle Sam Wants You: World War I and the Making of the Modern American Citizen* (New York: Oxford University Press, 2008), 117–143.

78. David A. Johnson, "Vigilance and the Law: The Moral Authority of Popular Justice in the Far West," *American Quarterly* 33, no. 5 (Winter 1981): 558–86; Richard Slotkin, *Gunfighter Nation: the Myth of the Frontier in Twentieth-Century America* (Norman: University of Oklahoma Press, 1998), 173–74.

79. Michael Cohen, "'The Ku Klux Government': Vigilantism, Lynching, and the Repression of the IWW," *Journal for the Study of Radicalism* 1, no. 1 (2006): 35.

80. Dubofsky, *We Shall Be All*, 391–393.

81. Norman Hapgood, *Professional Patriots* (New York: Albert and Charles Boni, 1927), 1–12; Robert D. Ward, "The Origin and Activities of the National Security League, 1914–1919," *Mississippi Valley Historical Review* 47, no. 1 (June 1960): 51–65.

82. Kennedy, *Over Here*, 165–166; Joan M. Jensen, *The Price of Vigilance* (Chicago: Rand McNally, 1968), 17–31.

83. Jensen, *Price of Vigilance*, 173.

84. Jensen, 74–76; Dubofsky, *We Shall Be All*, 406–408.

85. White, *Under the Iron Heel*, 119–25; Joseph R. Conlin, "William D. 'Big Bill' Haywood: The Westerner as Labor Radical," in *Labor Leaders in America*, ed. Melvyn Dubofsky and Warren Van Tine (Urbana: University of Illinois Press, 1987), 128.

86. Flynn, *Rebel Girl*, 236.

87. Robert C. Cottrell, *Roger Nash Baldwin and the American Civil Liberties Bureau* (New York: Columbia University Press, 2000), 73.

88. The tactic is not without its critics. Melvyn Dubofsky, who admits that logic favored her approach, asserts that "certain inescapable realities suggested a different course." These realities include the superior resources of the federal government to conduct a slew of legal cases, the anonymity of most of the defendants, and their commitment to stand together in defense of principles rather than subject themselves to false allegations of criminal conduct. See Dubofsky, *We Shall Be All*, 425–428.

89. Philip S. Foner, *The Case of Joe Hill* (New York: International Publishers, 1965), 77.

90. For a discussion of how ideas about gender-appropriate behavior figured in the cases of women radicals during the First World War, see Kathleen Kennedy, *Disloyal Mothers and Scurrilous Citizens: Women and Subversion during World War I* (Bloomington: Indiana University Press, 1999).

91. Elizabeth Gurley Flynn to Woodrow Wilson, January 10, 1918, File 188032-146, Record Group 60, Department of Justice, National Archives.

92. Flynn to Wilson.

93. Frances H. Early identifies the beginnings of a peace culture in New York City within the context of civil liberties and prodemocracy movements during the war years in *A World without War: How U.S. Feminists and Pacifists Resisted World War I* (Syracuse: Syracuse University Press, 1997), 27–28. On early feminist antiwar protests, see Kennedy, *Over Here*, 30.

94. Rabban, *Free Speech*, 300–303.

95. Early, *World without War*, 21–26.

96. On the involvement of feminists in World War I era civil liberties organizations, see Frances H. Early, "Feminism, Peace, and Civil Liberties: Women's Role in the Origins of the World War I Civil Liberties Movement," *Women's Studies* 18, nos. 2–3 (1990): 95–115.

97. Flynn, *Rebel Girl*, 172; E. G. Flynn Defense Committee to "My Dear . . . ," November 8, 1917, RPS Papers, reel 68, Tamiment Library, NYU; "The Arrest of Elizabeth Gurley Flynn," n.d., RPS Papers, reel 68, Tamiment Library, NYU; Fannie May Witherspoon to Elizabeth Gurley Flynn, December 20, 1918; Flynn to Witherspoon, December 29, 1918, New York Bureau of Legal Advice (NYBLA) Records, reel 2, Tamiment Library, NYU; Fannie May Witherspoon to Arthur S. Leeds, February 28, 1919, NYBLA Records, reel 1, Tamiment Library, NYU.

98. Cottrell, *Roger Nash Baldwin*, 61–79.

99. See, for example, "The Congressional Election of 1918," *Messenger* 2 (January 1918): 6; "Free Speech," *Messenger* 2 (January 1918): 9–10; and Chandler Owen, "Psychology Will Win this War," *Messenger* 2 (July 1918): 19–21.

100. "League Formed for Defense of IWW," *New York Evening Call*, March 5, 1918, 6; "League Formed to Defend IWW and Socialists," *New York Evening Call*, March 13, 1918, 3.

101. "Liberty-Defense League Organization Complete," *New York Evening Call*, March 8, 1918, 7.

102. "Defense Union to Assist Free Speech Victims," *New York Evening Call*, April 1, 1918, 3; "Defense Union Work Grows, Cash Is Needed," *New York Evening Call*, April 5, 1918, 1, 3; "National Aid for Liberty Defense Union," *New York Evening Call*, April 13, 1918, 3; "Radical Press Backs Liberty Defense Union," *New York Evening Call*, April 24, 1918, 1, 3.

103. "City Labor to Form Liberty Defense Body," *New York Evening Call*, July 26, 1918, 1; "U.H.T. for Labor Defense Body," *New York Evening Call*, July 27, 1918, 2; "Many Bodies Join Defense Conference," *New York Evening Call*, July 30, 1918, 1–2; "Liberty Defense Union Conference Tonight," *New York Evening Call*, July 31, 1918, 1; "Rose Pastor Stokes Denounces Enemies of Freedom," *New York Evening Call*, August 1, 1918, 1–2; "Liberty Union to Get Fund by Defense Stamps," *New York Evening Call*, August 2, 1918, 1–2; "Defense Union Holds Vital Meeting Tonight," *New York Evening Call*, August 22, 1918, 1.

104. Flynn, *Rebel Girl*, 244–245.

105. Flynn, 246.

106. "Workers' Defense Union," New York: Workers' Defense Union, 1919, 4–5, Workers' Defense Union Collection, EGF Papers, State Historical Society of Wisconsin (hereafter WDUC EGF Papers).

107. Flynn, *Rebel Girl*, 245.

108. Flynn, 247.

109. Flynn, 247.

110. Theodore Draper, *The Roots of American Communism* (New York: Viking Press, 1957), 97–130.

111. Luff, *Commonsense Anticommunism*, 57–59.

112. McCartin, *Labor's Great War*, 184–185.

113. Interchurch World Movement, *Public Opinion and the Steel Strike: Supplementary Reports of the Investigators to the Commission of Inquiry, The Interchurch World Movement*, reprint ed. (New York: Da Capo Press, 1970), 101.

114. Commission of Inquiry of the Interchurch World Movement, *Report on the Steel Strike of 1919* (New York: Harcourt, Brace and How, 1920), 235–238.

115. Jeremy Brecher, *Strike!* (Oakland, Calif.: PM Press, 2014), 122–123.

116. Brecher, 123.

117. Theodore Kornweibel Jr., *"Investigate Everything": Federal Efforts to Control Black Loyalty during World War I* (Bloomington: Indiana University Press, 2002), 80.

118. John Keegan, *The First World War* (New York: Vintage Books, 1998), 374.

119. Kornweibel, *"Investigate Everything,"* 77.

120. Kornweibel, 76–117.

121. Kornweibel, 276.

122. Glenda Elizabeth Gilmore, *Defying Dixie: The Radical Roots of Civil Rights, 1919–1950* (New York: W. W. Norton, 2008), 36–38.

123. Don Hutchison, *The Great Pulp Heroes* (New York: Mosaic Press, 1995), 202.

124. Arthur Guy Empey, "Treat 'Em Rough on Bolshevism," *Treat 'Em Rough* 2, no. 3 (March 1919): 10, New York Historical Society.

125. Empey, 10.

126. Emphasis in original. Arthur Guy Empey, "The Soviet Government of America," *Treat 'Em Rough* 2, no. 4 (April 1919): 9–10, New York Historical Society.

127. Empey, 10.

128. "Empey Suggests Axe and Education as Alternate Remedies," *New York Call*, April 3, 1919, 1. After Empey served briefly (six days) as a captain in the U.S. Army's Adjutant General Department, his commission was rescinded, allegedly because he made disparaging comments about American soldiers who had had to be coerced into the army through conscription. He reenlisted in the army as a private but was discharged five months later. See "Truth about Empey Damages Him $100,000, Sues the Call for It," *New York Evening Call*, April 2, 1919, 1–2.

129. "Soldiers and Sailors Break up Meetings," *New York Times*, May 2, 1919, 3; "Sh! Treating Reds Rough Is Anarchism!," *Chicago Daily Tribune*, September 9, 1919, 1 and 5; "School Song Angers Reds," *New York Times*, January 30, 1920, 4.

130. "State Laws against Free Speech: The Facts about the Criminal Syndicalist and Sedition Laws, with Court Decisions," New York: American Civil Liberties Union, 1925, 1–2, Frank P. Walsh Papers, box 108, New York Public Library.

131. "State Laws against Free Speech," 1–2.

132. "State Laws against Free Speech," 1–2.

133. "State Laws against Free Speech," 3.

134. Todd J. Pfannestiel, *Rethinking the Red Scare: The Lusk Committee and New York's Crusade against Radicalism, 1919–1923* (New York and London: Routledge, 2003), 19–36.

135. On the Soviet Bureau, see Todd Pfannestiel, "The Soviet Bureau: A Bolshevik Strategy to Secure U.S. Diplomatic Recognition through Economic Trade," *Diplomatic History* 27, no. 2 (April 2003): 171–193.

136. M. J. Driscoll to R. W. Finch, October 30, 1919, Records of the Joint Legislative Committee to Investigate Seditious Activities, N.Y., L0029, New York State Archives, Albany, N.Y. (hereafter NYS Archives).

137. Camp, *Iron in Her Soul*, 88.

138. Untitled Press Release, Workers' Defense Union, November 24, 1919, ACLU of Maryland Records, University of Baltimore.

139. Workers' Defense Union, "2nd Financial Statement of the Workers Defense Union of New York," December 1919, 3, ACLU of Maryland Records, University of Baltimore.

140. Flynn, *Rebel Girl*, 247.

141. "Brothers and Comrades!," 1.

142. Eugene Lyons, "The Epidemic of Reactionary Laws," *Workers' Defense Bulletin*, September 8, 1919, 2, ACLU of Maryland Records, University of Baltimore.

143. Lyons, 3.

144. Eugene Lyons, "The Menace of Deportation," *Workers' Defense Bulletin*, September 8, 1919, 4, ACLU of Maryland Records, University of Baltimore.

145. Flynn, *Rebel Girl*, 255.

146. Flynn, 255.

147. Flynn, 255.

148. Flynn, 257.

149. Workers' Defense Union, "2nd Financial Statement," 8.

150. "The Regular Delegates Meeting of the Workers' Defense Union," February 11, 1920, 1–2, ACLU of Maryland Records, University of Baltimore; "Minutes of the Meeting of the Workers Defense Union," New York, March 10, 1920, ACLU of Maryland Records, University of Baltimore.

151. Deportees Defense and Relief Committee, "Help the Deportees!," *Liberator* 3 (February 1920): 58.

152. "Financial Statement Deportees Defense and Relief Fund," n.d., ACLU of Maryland Records, University of Baltimore.

153. Fred Biedenkapp to Comrades and Fellow Workers, January 24, 1920, ACLU of Maryland Records, University of Baltimore.

154. Alexander Trachtenberg and Benjamin Glassberg, eds., *The American Labor Year Book 1921–1922* (New York: Rand School of Social Science, 1922), 42, Rand School Collection, Tamiment Library, NYU.

155. "Minutes of the Meeting of the Delegates of the Workers Defense Union," New York, June 1919, 2, ACLU of Maryland Records, University of Baltimore.

156. "Radicals Open Parley to Bring about Return of Liberties," *New York Call*, February 23, 1919, 1–2.

157. Elizabeth Gurley Flynn to "Dear Comrades," March 25, 1919, Workers' Defense Union Collection, EGF Papers, State Historical Society of Wisconsin.

158. Workers' Defense Union, *Using the Espionage Act to Terrorize Labor: Some Judicial Atrocities*, n.d., Records of the Joint Legislative Committee to Investigate Seditious Activities, N.Y., L0029, NYS Archives.

159. Gilmore, *Defying Dixie*, 36; Workers' Defense Union, "2nd Financial Statement," 7.

160. "Workers' Defense Union Minutes of Delegates Meeting," October 24, 1919, 1, Records of the Joint Legislative Committee to Investigate Seditious Activities, N.Y., L0029, NYS Archives.

161. "Red-Hot Mass Meeting," flyer, n.d., Records of the Joint Legislative Committee to Investigate Seditious Activities, N.Y., L0038, NYS Archives; Mark Ellis, *Race, War, and Surveillance: African Americans and the United States Government during World War I* (Bloomington: Indiana University Press, 2001), 112.

162. "The Hun in America," *Messenger* 2 (July 1919): 5.

163. "Red-Hot Mass Meeting."

164. "M.J. Driscoll, Special Agent, to Chief Clerk, C.L. Converse, New York, July 13, 1919," Records of the Joint Legislative Committee to Investigate Seditious Activities, N.Y., L0029, NYS Archives.

165. "Verbatim Report of Mass Meeting Called by The Committee of Justice to the Negro at the Harlem Casino, November 30, 1919," Records of the Joint Legislative Committee to Investigate Seditious Activities, N.Y., L0029, NYS Archives.

166. "Verbatim Report," 45–46.

167. "Verbatim Report," 47.

168. "Verbatim Report," 47–48.

169. "Verbatim Report," 49.

170. "Verbatim Report," 51.

171. "For Immediate Release," Workers' Defense Union, New York, July 2, 1919, NYBLA Records, reel 4, Tamiment Library, NYU.

172. "Justice Later," n.d., Workers' Defense Union, New York, 2, Records of the Joint Legislative Committee to Investigate Seditious Activities, N.Y., L0029, NYS Archives.

173. "Justice Later," 2–3. See also "Is Opinion a Crime?," n.d., League for Amnesty of Political Prisoners, New York, 3, ACLU of Maryland Records, University of Baltimore; and "Workers' Defense Union of Baltimore, Maryland, Auditing Committee Report," 1920, Workers' Defense Union of Baltimore, 2, ACLU of Maryland Records, University of Baltimore.

174. "Workers' Defense Union," 1919, Workers' Defense Union, New York, 1, ACLU of Maryland Records, University of Baltimore.

175. "Workers' Defense Union," 16.

176. "Workers' Defense Union," 16; "Defense Union Delegates to Meet Sunday," *New York Call*, January 18, 1919, 6.

177. "Will You Make a Liberty Loan?," Workers' Defense Union, New York, September 5, 1919, ACLU of Maryland Records, University of Baltimore.

178. Workers' Defense Union, *Using the Espionage Act*, 1.

179. Vapnek, *Elizabeth Gurley Flynn*, 76; "Trials of Christ and Debs Unfair, Says Miss Flynn," *Brooklyn Daily Eagle*, March 31, 1919, 8.

180. "Defense Union Delegates," 6.

181. Ernest Freeberg, *Democracy's Prisoner: Eugene V. Debs, the Great War, and the Right to Dissent* (Cambridge, Mass.: Harvard University Press, 2010), 190–201.

182. On the general amnesty campaign as a counter-reactionary force, see Freeberg, *Democracy's Prisoner*, 194–195.

183. See, for example, "Why?," *New York Times*, February 28, 1920, 10; "Palmer Won't Free Political Prisoners," *New York Times*, September 15, 1920, 11; Robert Ferrari, "The Trial of Political Criminals Here and Abroad," *Dial*, June 28, 1919, 647; Robert Ferrari, "Political Crime," *Columbia Law Review* 20, no. 3 (March 1920): 308–316; Robert Ferrari, "Political Crime in Europe," *World Tomorrow* 3, no. 12 (December 1920): 375–378; and M. Greenwood, "'Political Prisoners.' Debs Not in Jail for His Opinions but for Obstructing Recruiting," *New York Times*, April 7, 1921, 14.

184. Padraic Kenney, *Dance in Chains: Political Imprisonment in the Modern World* (Oxford University Press, 2017).

185. Christina Heatherton, "University of Radicalism: Ricardo Flores Magón and Leavenworth Penitentiary," *American Quarterly* 66, no. 3 (September 2014): 557–581.

186. David M. Struthers, "IWW Internationalism and Interracial Organizing in the Southwestern United States," in *Wobblies of the World*, ed. Peter Cole, David Struthers, and Kenyon Zimmer (London: Pluto Press, 2017), 74–88.

187. Kelly Lytle Hernández, *City of Inmates: Conquest, Rebellion, and the Rise of Human Caging in Los Angeles 1771–1965* (Chapel Hill: University of North Carolina Press, 2017), 92–130.

188. Flynn, *Rebel Girl*, 181.

189. Robert G. Lee, "The Hidden World of Asian Immigrant Radicalism," in *The Immigrant Left in the United States*, ed. Paul Buhle and Dan Georgakas (Albany: SUNY Press, 1996), 273.

190. Friends of Freedom for India, *Back to the Hangman* (New York: Friends of Freedom for India, 1919); "India News Service of the Friends of Freedom for India," Friends of Freedom for India, February 14, 1920; Basanta Koomar Roy, *The Labor Revolt in India* (New York: Friends of Freedom for India, 1920); Surendra Karr, "British Inquisition in India," Friends of Freedom for India, 1920.

191. News that *The Labor Revolt in India* had been banned in India was published in the *News Letter of the Friends of Irish Freedom* (Washington, D.C.: Friends of Irish Freedom, 1920), 7.

192. "National Convention of the Friends of Freedom for India," *Independent Hindustan* 1 (January 1921): 113.

193. "National Convention," 114.

194. Flynn, *Rebel Girl*, 269.

195. Harald Fischer-Tiné, "Indian Nationalism and the World Forces: Transnational and Diasporic Dimensions of the Indian Freedom Movement on the Eve of the First World War," *Journal of Global History* 2, no. 3 (November 2007): 333–335.

196. On the ties between Irish and Indian anti-imperialists, see, for example, Maia Ramnath, *Haj to Utopia: How the Ghadar Movement Charted Global Radicalism and Attempted to Overthrow the British Empire* (Berkeley: University of California Press, 2011); and Manela, *Wilsonian Moment*, 172.

197. Flynn, *Rebel Girl*, 186.

198. Ellen McKibben, "Divided Loyalties: Irish American Women Labor Leaders and the Irish Revolution, 1916–1923," *Éire-Ireland* 51, nos. 3–4 (Fall/Winter 2016): 178.

199. McKibben, 179.

200. Flynn, *Rebel Girl*, 269.

201. "Calls Working Classes to Oppose Ku Klux Klan," *Winston-Salem Journal*, February 10, 1921, 2.

202. "National Convention," 114.

Chapter 4: From Civil Liberties Icon to Communist Menace

1. "Minutes of the Conference to Reorganize the National Civil Liberties Bureau," January 12, 1920, 7, ACLU Papers, vol. 20.

2. "Minutes of the Conference," 7.

3. "Gossip of Gotham Town," *Rising Son*, October 25, 1906, 3; "Montana Socialists Storm County Jail," *Riverside Daily Press*, October 6, 1909, 1.

4. "All around Appreciative," *Daily People*, February 17, 1908, n.p.

5. "All around Appreciative," n.p.

6. "Only 19, She Braved Motherhood in Cell to Struggle for Free Speech," *Tacoma Times*, December 29, 1909, 7.

7. "Husband of Radical Seeks a Separation," *Bay City Tribune*, July 31, 1921, 5.

8. See, for example, "Death Puts End to Honeymoon," *Duluth News Tribune*, September 13, 1920, 2; "Waves Rob Him of Bride," *Kansas City Star*, September 13, 1920, 1; "Chicago Man Lost Wife on Honeymoon," *Riverside Daily Press*, September 13, 1920, 2; and "Death Ends Honeymoon," *Idaho Statesman*, September 14, 1920, 2.

9. *Industrial Worker*, January 20, 1917, NYU EGF Papers, box 1.

10. "Who's Who in Leadership of Organized Bolshevist Movement in the U.S.," *St. Louis Post-Dispatch*, January 5, 1919, 26.

11. "Police Raiders Arrive Just as Radicals Get Started," *Public Ledger* (Philadelphia), March 7, 1921, 1.

12. "Philadelphia to Clean-Up Reds," *Wilmington Evening Journal*, July 22, 1922, 1.

13. "Ford Hall Forum Complete Program 1922–1923 Season," 1922, NYU EGF Papers, box 1.

14. On the radical vision of the early ACLU, see Laura Weinrib, *The Taming of Free Speech: America's Civil Liberties Compromise* (Cambridge, Mass.: Harvard University Press, 2016).

15. "Suggestions for Reorganization of the National Civil Liberties Bureau," n.d., ACLU Papers, vol. 120.

16. "A New Civil Liberties Union," *Survey* 43 (January 31, 1920): 480.

17. "Socialist Speaker Fined," *New York Times*, October 14, 1920, 2; "Say Orators Will Sue," *New York Times*, October 14, 1920, 32; "Anti-Socialist Law Turned down by Justice Keogh," *Evening World*, October 14, 1920, 3; "Socialists Win," *Springfield Daily Republican*, October 19, 1920, 14; "Three Street Talkers Held," *Brooklyn Daily Eagle*, October 21, 1920, 4.

18. "Labor to Test Right to Speak in Union Square," *New York Call*, August 20, 1920, 1.

19. "Labor Day to Mark the Marne Victory," *New York Times*, September 6, 1920, 2.

20. "Labor Day to Mark," 2.

21. "Do Not Forget! Political Prisoners Are Still Rotting in the Bastilles of American Capitalism," *Liberator* 5 (May 1922), 35. "Labor Men and Women! Political Prisoners Are Still in Jail in America," *Labor Age* 11 (May 1922): 29.

22. Labor Defense Council, *Help Repel This Attack upon Labor!* (Chicago: Labor Defense Council, November 1922); James R. Barrett, "Boring from Within and Without: William Z. Foster, the Trade Union Educational League, and American Communism in the 1920s," in *Labor Histories: Class, Politics, and the Working-Class Experience*, ed. E. Arnesen, J. Greene, and B. Laurie (Urbana: University of Illinois Press), 319.

23. Elizabeth Gurley Flynn, *The Rebel Girl: An Autobiography, My First Life (1906–1926)* (New York: International Publishers, 1955), 299.

24. "Sacco and Vanzetti Are Found Guilty of First Degree Murder," *Boston Herald*, July 15, 1921, 1; "Find Italians Guilty in Paymaster Murder," *New York Times*, July 15, 1921, 5; "Sacco e Vanzetti Ritenuti Colpevoli di Duplice Assassinio," *Il Progresso Italo-Americano*, July 16, 1921, 1. On press coverage of the executions, see Mary Anne Trasciatti, "Framing the Sacco-Vanzetti Executions in the Italian American Press," *Critical Studies in Media Communication* 20, no. 4 (December 2003): 407–430.

25. Lisa McGirr, "The Passion of Sacco and Vanzetti: A Global History," *Journal of American History* 93, no. 4 (March 2007): 1085–1115.

26. Flynn, *Rebel Girl*, 299–300.

27. Flynn, 300.

28. The original Sacco-Vanzetti Defense Committee included a Spanish anarchist, Frank Lopez.

29. Flynn, *Rebel Girl*, 302.

30. John Nicholas Beffel, "Workers' Defense Union," press release, n.d., John Nicholas Beffel Papers, box 12, Tamiment Library, NYU.

31. Flynn, *Rebel Girl*, 302.

32. For a full account of Flynn's work for Sacco and Vanzetti, see Mary Anne Trasciatti, "Elizabeth Gurley Flynn, the Sacco-Vanzetti Case, and the Rise and Fall of the Liberal-Radical Alliance," *American Communist History* 15, no. 2 (2016): 191–216.

33. Sacco-Vanzetti Defense Committee News Service, December 14, 1924, Aldino Felicani Collection, Boston Public Library.

34. Gloria Garrett Sampson, *The American Fund for Public Service: Charles Garland and Radical Philanthropy* (Westport, Conn.: Greenwood, 1996), 112–115.

35. Philip V. Cannistraro, "Mussolini, Sacco-Vanzetti, and the Anarchists: The Transatlantic Context," *Journal of Modern History* 68, no. 1 (March 1996): 31–62.

36. Michael Jay Tucker, *And Then They Loved Him: Seward Collins and the Chimera of an American Fascism* (New York: Peter Lang, 2006), 141–142; John P. Diggins, *Mussolini and Fascism: The View from America* (Princeton: Princeton University Press, 1972), 20–31; Nunzio Pernicone, *Carlo Tresca: Portrait of a Rebel* (New York: Palgrave, 2005), 145; Gaetano Salvemini, *Italian Fascist Activities in the United States*, ed. Philip Cannistraro (New York: Center for Migration Studies, 1977), xxix.

37. Diggins, *Mussolini and Fascism*, 80; Philip V. Cannistraro, *Blackshirts in Little Italy, Italian Americans and Fascism, 1921–1929* (West Lafayette, Ind.: Bordighera Press, 1999), 1–7.

38. Salvemini, *Italian Fascist Activities*, 39–42.

39. Rudolph J. Vecoli, "The Making and Un-making of the Italian American Working Class," in *The Lost World of Italian American Radicalism*, ed. Philip Cannistraro and Gerard Meyer (New York: Praeger, 2003), 54–55.

40. Flynn, *Rebel Girl*, 334.

41. Pernicone, *Carlo Tresca*, 300.

42. Diggins, *Mussolini and Fascism*, 91.

43. Elizabeth Gurley Flynn to Fred H. Moore, February 3, 1923, Aldino Felicani Collection, Boston Public Library.

44. Fraser M. Ottanelli, "'If Fascism Comes to America We Will Push It Back into the Ocean': Italian American Antifascism in the 1920s and 1930s," in *Italian Workers of the World: Labor Migration and the Formation of Multiethnic States*, ed. Donna R. Gabaccia and Fraser M. Ottanelli (Urbana: University of Illinois Press, 2001), 190.

45. Bureau of Investigation, "Anti-Fascisti: Italian Anarchist Activities, Providence, RI," File no. 61-1335-152, October 29, 1923.

46. "Hillman, Sigman to Lend Aid in War on Fascisti," *New York Call*, June 18, 1923, 1.

47. Untitled, *Il Voglio*, Wilkes-Barre, Pa., 1922, n.p., NYU EGF Papers, box 1; "Labor, the 'Klan' Spirit and One Hundred Percent Americanism," flyer, Community Church of New York, 1923, NYU EGF Papers, box 1; "Fascist Activities in America," *Evening Star*, February 17, 1924, 25, NYU EGF Papers, box 1; "Fascisti Compared to Ku Klux Klan in Hot Attack by Woman Speaker," *Washington (D.C.) Herald*, February 19, 1924, n.p., NYU EGF Papers, box 1; "Says Fascisti at Work in America," *Buffalo Courier*, February 25, 1924, 10, NYU EGF Papers, box 1; "Elizabeth Gurley Flynn Warns of Fascist Menace," *Daily Worker*, April 14, 1924, 2, NYU EGF Papers, box 1; "Woman Radical Calls Fascisti and Klan Alike," *Ithaca Journal*, April 26, 1924, 7, NYU EGF Papers, box 1; "Conferenza," advertisement, Ant-Fascisti Alliance of North America Local Buffalo, May 4, 1924, NYU EGF Papers, box 1.

48. Ottanelli, "'If Fascism Comes,'" 182.

49. "Baltimore Open Forum," *Baltimore Evening Sun*, February 14, 1925, 9.

50. Flynn, *Rebel Girl*, 334.

51. Diggins, *Mussolini and Fascism*, 121; Pernicone, *Carlo Tresca*, 163–164.

52. Flynn, *Rebel Girl*, 334.

53. "Italians Here Riot: Denounce Fascisti," *New York Times*, June 27, 1924, 21.

54. Diggins, *Mussolini and Fascism*, 121–134; "They Mustn't Import Their Quarrels," *New York Times*, August 18, 1925, 18; "They Should Go Home for Fighting," *New York Times*, October 30, 1925, 20.

55. Flynn, *Rebel Girl*, 335.

56. Pernicone, *Carlo Tresca*, 152–156.

57. Pernicone, 244.

58. Rosalyn Fraad Baxandall, *Words on Fire: The Life and Writing of Elizabeth Gurley Flynn* (New Brunswick, N.J.: Rutgers University Press, 1987), 20–23; Helen C.

Camp, *Iron in Her Soul: Elizabeth Gurley Flynn and the American Left* (Pullman: Washington State University Press, 1995), 112–114.

59. Mary Heaton Vorse, "Elizabeth Gurley Flynn," *Nation*, February 17, 1926, 175–176.

60. "Extremists Join to Fete Labor Queen," *New York American*, February 1926, NYU EGF Papers, box 1.

61. Esther Lowell, "Elizabeth Flynn's 20 Years for Labor Honored," Federated Press Eastern Bureau, sheet 2, no. 1781, February 15, 1926, 1, NYU EGF Papers, box 1.

62. Lowell, 1; Bartolomeo Vanzetti to Elizabeth Gurley Flynn, February 11, 1926, NYU EGF Papers, box 1; "Joan of Arc of America Sees Labor Improvement," *New York Telegram*, February 5, 1926, NYU EGF Papers, box 1; "Workers to Fete Women Leader," *New York City Graphic*, February 13, 1926, NYU EGF Papers, box 1; "Radicals Hold Dinner," *New York Times*, February 15, 1926, 21; "La Festeggiata," *Il Nuovo Mondo*, February 17, 1926, NYU EGF Papers, box 1.

63. Lowell, "Elizabeth Flynn's 20 Years," 1.

64. See, for example, "The Passaic Textile Strike Encounters the Courts," *Labor Defender*, April 1926, 57–58; "Framing Up in Passaic," *Labor Defender*, September 1926, 151–152; and Hollace Ransdell, "Greasing the Wheels for Passaic Strikers," *Labor Defender*, January 1927, 4 and 15.

65. Elizabeth Gurley Flynn to Mary Heaton Vorse, September 11, 1926, NYU EGF Papers, box 14.

66. Flynn to Vorse, September 11, 1926.

67. "Bomb Square Quiets Uproar in Meeting," *New York Times*, May 3, 1926, 7; "All Hands to the Dykes," flyer, September 26, 1926, ACLU Papers; Irma Watkins-Owens, "Stepladder to Community," in *Mighty Change, Tall Within: Black Identity in the Hudson Valley*, ed. Myra B. Young Armstead (Albany: State University of New York Press, 2003), 153–154; "To Oppose Greeting Queen," *New York Times*, October 18, 1926, 2; "Labor Leader Addresses Porters," *New York Amsterdam News*, November 10, 1936, 2.

68. On Cannon and the formation of the ILD, see Bryan D. Palmer, *James P. Cannon and the Origins of the American Revolutionary Left, 1890–1928* (Urbana: University of Illinois Press, 2017), 261–268.

69. Palmer, 274–279; Rebecca Hill, *Men, Mobs, and Law: Anti-lynching and Labor Defense in U.S. Radical History* (Durham, N.C.: Duke University Press, 2009), 196–208, 231–235.

70. Jennifer Ruthanne Uhlmann, "The Communist Civil Rights Movement: Legal Activism in the United States, 1919–1946" (PhD diss., University of California–Los Angeles, 2007), 95–176; "International Labor Defense Membership Drive," reprinted in *Hearings before a Special Committee to Investigate Communist Activities in the United States of the House of Representatives* (Washington, D.C.: U.S. Government Printing Office, 1930), 1511.

71. Quoted in Fred Mann, "The Spirit of the I.L.D. in Conference," *Labor Defender*, October 1926, 171.

72. "Flynn on Tour," *Labor Defender*, December 1926, 214; "The Flynn Tour for I.L.D.," *Labor Defender*, January 1927, 7.

73. "Labor Defense in Pictures," *Labor Defender*, February 1927, 18; Camp, *Iron in Her Soul*, 125.

74. Elizabeth Gurley Flynn to Mary Heaton Vorse, December 23, 1926, NYU EGF Papers, box 14.

75. Carlo Tresca to Marie Equi, January 11, 1927, NYU EGF Papers, box 14.

76. The first and only full-length work on Marie Equi is Michael Helquist, *Marie Equi: Radical Politics and Outlaw Passions* (Corvallis: Oregon State University Press, 2015).

77. "Elizabeth Gurley Flynn," *Labor Defender*, January 1928, 19.

78. Elizabeth Gurley Flynn to Mary Heaton Vorse, March 22, 1929, NYU EGF Papers, box 14.

79. Flynn to Vorse, March 22, 1929.

80. Elizabeth Gurley Flynn to Comrades, July 29, 1929, NYU EGF Papers, box 19.

81. Helquist, *Marie Equi*, 219–232.

82. Elizabeth Gurley Flynn to Mary Heaton Vorse, January 25, 1930; February 5, 1930; and May 16, 1930, NYU EGF Papers, box 14.

83. Elizabeth Gurley Flynn to Mrs. Roosevelt, July 18, 1934, and July 31, 1934, NYU EGF Papers, box 18.

84. Elizabeth Gurley Flynn to Kathie Flynn, August 6, 1955, quoted in Baxandall, *Words on Fire*, 32.

85. See, for example, Camp, *Iron in Her Soul*, 130–131.

86. Helquist, *Marie Equi*, 222.

87. Baxandall, *Words on Fire*, 33.

88. *Elizabeth Gurley Flynn Speaks to the Court* (New York: New Century Publishers, 1952), 11.

89. Camp, *Iron in Her Soul*, 142–143; Lara Vapnek, *Elizabeth Gurley Flynn: Modern American Revolutionary* (New York: Routledge, 2015), 104–105.

90. "A Duty to Those behind Prison Bars," *Daily Worker*, December 24, 1936, 2.

91. "Italians Here to Protest Intervention," *Daily Worker*, March 3, 1937, 2; "Famous Woman Leader Fights against Fascism," *Daily Worker*, March 19, 1937, 7.

92. Camp, *Iron in Her Soul*, 142; Elizabeth Gurley Flynn, "It Didn't Take the First Time," draft manuscript, quoted in Baxandall, *Words on Fire*, 36.

93. Fraser M. Ottanelli, *The Communist Party of the United States: From the Depression to World War II* (New Brunswick, N.J.: Rutgers University Press, 1991), 17–48.

94. Ottanelli, 84–87.

95. *Elizabeth Gurley Flynn Speaks*, 11–12.

96. Mark Naison, "Remaking America: Communists and Liberals in the Popular Front," in *New Studies in the Politics and Culture of U.S. Communism*, ed. Michael E. Brown, Randy Martin, Frank Rosengarten, and George Snedeker (New York: Monthly Review Press, 1993), 43.

97. Ottanelli, *Communist Party*, 137–157.

98. "Lincoln Brigade Rally April 24 in Mecca Temple," *Daily Worker*, April 14, 1937, 2; "Bard to Speak on Spain: Lincoln Battalion Meeting to Hear Talk on Fighting," *Daily Worker*, April 22, 1937, 1 and 5.

99. "Marcantonio Talks July 4 in Wash. Sq.," *Daily Worker*, June 30, 1937, 2.

100. "A Century's Setback," *Daily Worker*, April 3, 1938, 10.

101. Maurice Isserman, *Which Side Were You On? The American Communist Party during the Second World War* (Middletown, Conn.: Wesleyan University Press, 1982), 9–14; Ottanelli, *Communist Party*, 122–125.

102. Ottanelli, *Communist Party*, 151.

103. Judy Kutulas, *The Long War: The Intellectual People's Front and Anti-Stalinism, 1930–1940* (Durham, N.C.: Duke University Press, 1995), 106–114; Ottanelli, *Communist Party*, 166–167.

104. Baxandall, *Words on Fire*, 39.

105. Camp, *Iron in Her Soul*, 147–150.

106. See, for example, "The Communist Party Has the Ear of the People," *Daily Worker*, September 26, 1939, 5.

107. Elizabeth Gurley Flynn to Mary Heaton Vorse, September 28, 1939, NYU EGF Papers, box 14.

108. "Words Are Weapons for Good or Evil," *Daily Worker*, December 3, 1939, 6.

109. Peggy Lamson, *Roger Baldwin: Founder of the American Civil Liberties Union* (Boston: Houghton Mifflin, 1976), 201.

110. Samuel Walker, *In Defense of American Liberties: A History of the ACLU* (New York: Oxford University Press, 1990), 96–97.

111. Walker, 118–119.

112. "Statement on the Attitude of the American Civil Liberties Union to Current Issues of Civil Rights by the Board of Directors," March 1937, 1, ACLU Papers, vol. 970.

113. "Statement on the Attitude of the American Civil Liberties Union," 3.

114. For a detailed overview of sit-down strikes, see Jim Pope, "Worker Lawmaking, Sit-Down Strikes, and the Shaping of American Industrial Relations, 1935–1938," *Law and History Review* 24, no. 1 (Spring 2006): 45–113.

115. Sidney Fine, *Sit-Down: The General Motors Strike of 1936–1937* (Ann Arbor: University of Michigan Press, 1969); Joshua Murray and Michael Schwartz, "Moral Economy, Structural Leverage, and Organizational Efficacy: Class Formation and the Great Flint Sit-Down Strike, 1936–1937," *Critical Historical Studies* 2, no. 2 (Fall 2015): 219–259.

116. Roger Baldwin to Walter Frank, March 11, 1937, ACLU Papers, vol. 970; Roger Baldwin to the Board of Directors, March 12, 1937, ACLU Papers, vol. 970.

117. Weinrib, *Taming of Free Speech*, 274; "Statement on So-Called Sit-Down and Stay-In Strikes Adopted by the National Committee of the American Civil Liberties Union," April 1937, ACLU Papers, vol. 970; "Stand on Sit-Down Defined by Union," *Civil Liberties Quarterly* (June 1937), 3; Arthur Garfield Hays to Gentlemen, March 19, 1937, ACLU Papers, vol. 970.

118. Edward Parsons to Roger Baldwin, March 31, 1937, ACLU Papers, vol. 970; Harry Elmer Barnes to Roger Baldwin, April 12, 1937, ACLU Papers, vol. 970.

119. A. J. Muste to Roger Baldwin, April 2, 1937, ACLU Papers, vol. 970; Frederick Howe to Roger Baldwin, April 21, 1937, ACLU Papers, vol. 970.

120. Edward Tittmann to Board of Directors, April 3, 1937, ACLU Papers, vol. 970; Clough Turrill Burnett to Roger Baldwin, April 7, 1937, ACLU Papers, vol. 970; William Pickens to Roger Baldwin, April 22, 1937, ACLU Papers, vol. 970.

121. Baruch Charney Vladeck to Roger Baldwin, April 12, 1937, ACLU Papers, vol. 970; Margaret DeSilver to Roger Baldwin, April 22, 1937, ACLU Papers, vol. 970.

122. Vote on ACLU Statement on Sit-Down Strike, April 12, 1937, ACLU Papers, vol. 970.

123. Elizabeth Gurley Flynn to American Civil Liberties Union, April 11, 1937, ACLU Papers, vol. 970.

124. "U.S. Reports: Labor Board v. Fansteel Corp.," 306 U.S. 240 (1939), https://tile.loc.gov/storage-services/service/ll/usrep/usrep306/usrep306240/usrep306240.pdf.

125. Irving Bernstein, *The Turbulent Years: A History of the American Worker, 1933–1941* (Chicago: Haymarket Books, 2010), 738–741.

126. Walker, *Defense of American Liberties*, 102; Myron Gollub, "The First Amendment and the N.L.R.A.," *Washington University Law Review* 27, no. 2 (January 1942): 242–263.

127. John Haynes Holmes to Harry Ward, February 8, 1938, ACLU Papers, vol. 1080.
128. Harry Ward to John Haynes Holmes, February 10, 1938, ACLU Papers, vol. 1080.
129. John Haynes Holmes to Harry Ward, February 11, 1938, ACLU Papers, vol. 1080.
130. Roger Riis to Roger Baldwin, May 12, 1938, ACLU Papers, vol. 2037.

131. Roger William Riis, "Watch-Dog of Liberty," *Reader's Digest* 33, no. 199 (December 1938): 32–37.

132. Walker, *Defense of American Liberties*, 103.

133. Walter Goodman, *The Committee: The Extraordinary Career of the House Committee on Un-American Activities* (New York: Farrar, Straus and Giroux, 1964), 13–23.

134. "House Inquiry Hunts Officials' Link Bridges," *New York Herald Tribune*, August 17, 1938, 58, ACLU Papers, vol. 1090; Evidence compiled by HUAC, 218, ACLU Papers, vol. 2181; United States Congress Special Committee to Investigate Un-American Activities, *Investigation of Un-American Propaganda Activities in the United States, Hearings before a Special Committee on Un-American Activities, House of Representatives, Seventy-Fifth Congress, Third Session* (Washington, D.C.: U.S. Government Printing Office, 1938), 277–518.

135. "Dies Takes Rap at Probe Critics," *Washington (D.C.) Star*, August 30, 1938, 106, ACLU Papers, vol. 1090.

136. "Should the Dies Committee Die?," January 24, 1939, 21–22, ACLU Papers, vol. 2079; "Dies Inquiry Wins Year's Extension in House, 344–35," *New York Times*, February 4, 1939, 1.

137. "Transcript of Testimony before the Special Committee to Investigate Un-American Activities-October 23, 1939," October 31, 1939, 231–34, ACLU Papers, vol. 2076.

138. Adam Lapin, "Alliance between Dies and Jittery Liberals Grows at Cocktail Party," *Daily Worker*, November 24, 1939, 4; Judy Kutulas, *The American Civil Liberties Union and the Making of Modern Liberalism, 1930–1960*, new ed. (Chapel Hill: University of North Carolina Press, 2006), 68–70.

139. Cletus Daniels, *The ACLU and the Wagner Act: An Inquiry into the Depression-Era Crisis of American Liberalism* (Ithaca: New York State School of Industrial and Labor Relations, Cornell University, 1980), 133.

140. "A.C.L.U. Resolution of February 5, 1940," reprinted in Corliss Lamont, *The Trial of Elizabeth Gurley Flynn by the American Civil Liberties Union* (New York: Modern Reader, 1968), 44–45.

141. "Gurley Flynn Spikes Press Slanders on Her ACLU Status," *Daily Worker*, February 21, 1940, 4; "Proposed Statement by the Board of Directors," n.d., ACLU Papers, vol. 2162.

142. For a summary of the criticism, see Walker, "American Liberties," 130–131.

143. "Letter of Resignation, March 2, 1940, from Dr. Harry F. Ward, Chairman of the ACLU Board of Directors, 1920–1940," reprinted in Lamont, *Trial of Elizabeth Gurley Flynn*, 212.

144. "Reply of Elizabeth Gurley Flynn to Charges Filed by Dorothy Dunbar Bromley on March 4, at the Board of Directors Meeting of the American Civil Liberties Union," ACLU Papers, vol. 2162.

145. "Reply of Elizabeth Gurley Flynn."

146. "Reply of Elizabeth Gurley Flynn."

147. See Elizabeth Gurley Flynn, "Why I Won't Resign from the ACLU," *New Masses* 34, no. 13 (March 19, 1940): 11–12.

148. Elizabeth Gurley Flynn, "I Am Expelled from Civil Liberties!," *Daily Worker*, March 17, 1940, reprinted in Lamont, *Trial of Elizabeth Gurley Flynn*, 154.

149. Roger Riis to John Haynes Holmes, March 17, 1940, ACLU Papers, vol. 2162.

150. John Haynes Holmes to Roger Baldwin, March 19, 1940, ACLU Papers, vol. 2162.

151. "Elizabeth Gurley Flynn's Defense," reprinted in Lamont, *Trial of Elizabeth Gurley Flynn*, 101.

152. In a letter to Osmond K. Fraenkel, Thomas opined, "I do not think it necessary to ask Communists of fellow travelers, now on our board, to resign. I think it is necessary to see that they are not put in a position of responsibility as the chairmanship and I also think it inadvisable in the future to elect Communists or fellow travelers to the board." Norman Thomas to Osmond K. Fraenkel, December 21, 1939, ACLU Papers, vol. 2064. On the dispute between Socialists and Communists, see Ottanelli, *Communist Party*, 56–57; Fraenkel warned Thomas not to let the dispute influence ACLU board politics. Fraenkel to Thomas, December 15, 1939, ACLU Papers, vol. 2064.

153. Weinrib, *Taming of Free Speech*, 302.

154. Beverly Gage, *G-Man: J. Edgar Hoover and the Making of the American Century* (New York: Viking, 2022), 283–285.

155. Jerold Auerbach shares my interpretation, observing that "in a tragic twist or irony, an organization whose raison d'être was the defense of civil liberties imposed a political test that curtailed freedom of expression and made guilt by association the inevitable consequence." See Jerold Auerbach, "The Depression Decade," in *The Pulse of Freedom: American Liberties 1920–1970s*, ed. Alan Reitman (New York: W. W. Norton, 1975), 91–102. The quote is from page 102. See also Ellen Schrecker, *Many Are the Crimes: McCarthyism in America* (Boston: Little, Brown and Company, 1998), 84–85.

Chapter 5: From the Little Red Scare to the Big Red Scare

1. Elizabeth Gurley Flynn, "Mine Eyes Have Seen the Glory," *New Masses* 31, no. 6 (May 2, 1939): 4.

2. M. J. Heale, "Citizens versus Outsiders: Anti-Communism at State and Local Levels, 1921–1946," in *Little "Red Scares": Anti-Communism and Political Repression in the United States, 1921–1946*, ed. Robert Justin Goldstein (New York: Routledge, 2016), 45.

3. "Gurley Flynn Speaks of Fascism; Tear Gas Raid Makes It Real," *Daily Worker*, October 25, 1938, 3; "Tear Gas for Children," *Sunday Worker*, November 6, 1938, 9; "Probe Sought in Break-Up of Communist Meeting in Ohio," *American Civil Liberties Union Bulletin*, no. 841, November 5, 1938, 2, Mudd Manuscript Library, Princeton University.

4. See Kenneth O'Reilly, "The Dies Committee v. the New Deal: Real Americans and the Unending Search for Un-Americans," in Goldstein, *Little "Red Scares,"* 237–260.

5. Rebecca Hill, "The History of the Smith Act and the Hatch Act: Anti-Communism and the Rise of the Conservative Coalition in Congress," in Goldstein, *Little "Red Scares,"* 320.

6. Michal R. Belknap, *Cold War Political Justice: The Smith Act, the Communist Party, and American Civil Liberties* (Westport, Conn.: Greenwood, 1977), 36; Robert Justin Goldstein, *Political Repression in Modern America from 1870 to the Present* (Boston: G. K. Hall, 1978), 215–216, 247–248.

7. Hill, "History of the Smith Act," 317.

8. Ellen Schrecker, *Many Are the Crimes: McCarthyism in America* (Boston: Little, Brown and Company, 1998), 106.

9. *United States of America Congressional Record, Proceedings and Debates of the 76th Congress*, vol. 86, part 8, June 13–July 8, 1940 (Washington, D.C.: U.S. Government Printing Office, 1940), 9034.

10. *United States Statutes at Large*, vol. 54, 76th Cong., 2nd and 3rd Sess. (Washington, D.C.: U.S. Government Printing Office, 1941), 670–671.

11. Hill, "History of the Smith Act," 321.

12. See, for example, *I Vote My Conscience: Debates, Speeches, and Writings of Vito Marcantonio*, reprint edition, ed. Annette T. Rubinstein and Associates (New York: John D. Calandra Italian American Institute, 2002), 129–130.

13. "Civil Liberties Union Hits Smith 'Alien' Bill," *Daily Worker*, July 17, 1939, 3; "ILD Warns of Rule by Political Force," *Daily Worker*, June 3, 1940, 5; "Emergency Rally to Fight Alien Drive," *Daily Worker*, June 4, 1940, 5; "Mass Rally Tonight against Anti Alien Bills," *Daily Worker*, June 7, 1940, 5; "Foreign Born Group Asks Smith Bill Veto," *Daily Worker*, June 26, 1940, 3; "Aid in Thwarting This 'Detestable Thing,'" *Daily Worker*, June 26, 1940, 6; "Marcantonio Broadcasts Tomorrow on Alien Bills," *Daily Worker*, July 27, 1940, 5; "Marcantonio Announces Nationwide Drive to Repeal Alien Registration Act," *Daily Worker*, August 26, 1940, 1; "Marcantonio Sponsors Bill for Repeal of Alien Registration Law," *Daily Worker*, August 30, 1940, 1; "Call Conference to Defeat Drive on Foreign Born," *Daily Worker*, September 11, 1940, 3; "Welfare Workers Denounce Anti-Alien Campaign," *Daily Worker*, June 28, 1940, 3; Carey McWilliams, "Stand by Civil Liberties," *New Masses* 35, no. 11 (June 4, 1940): 9.

14. "An Un-American Bill," *Daily Worker*, June 29, 1939, 6; "Sen. Reynolds' Crocodile Tears," *Daily Worker*, June 20, 1939, 6.

15. "Civil Liberties Union Hits," 3.

16. "Congress in Wild Attack on Labor, Non-Citizens," *Daily Worker*, May 28, 1940, 4.

17. "American Citizenship on 'New Citizens Day,'" *Daily Worker*, June 2, 1939, 6; "Strike a Blow for Liberty," *Sunday Worker*, July 2, 1939, 6; "Full Senate Committee to Get Anti-Alien Bill," *Daily Worker*, May 27, 1940, 2; "'Anti-Alien' Bills a Menace to All," *Sunday Worker*, June 2, 1940, 4; "Swift Action Needed to Kill Repressive Bills," *Daily Worker*, June 13, 1940, 4; "Smith Anti-Alien Bill Can Still Be Stopped," *Daily Worker*, June 21, 1940, 1; "Warn of Menace of Smith Bill," *Daily Worker*, June 21, 1940, 5; "Kill the Smith Anti-Alien Bill," *Daily Worker*, June 22, 1940, 6; "Aid in Thwarting This," 6; "Tell the White House to Veto this Shameful Measure," *Daily Worker*, June 27, 1940, 1; "Tell Him to Veto It," *Daily Worker*, June 28, 1940, 6; "A Dragnet Laid for the Whole People," *Daily Worker*, July 2, 1940, 6; "Real Fifth Column against Declaration of Independence," *Daily Worker*, July 4, 1940, 6; "The Registration Director Tips His Hand," *Daily Worker*, August 13, 1940, 6; "What Organizations-? A Menace to the Nation," *Daily Worker*, August 14, 1940, 6.

18. "Sen. Reynolds' Crocodile Tears," 6.

19. "Tories Get Right of Way for Anti-Alien Bills," *Daily Worker*, July 1, 1939, 5.

20. Gale Thorne, "Those Alien and Sedition Acts Return," *New Masses* 34, no. 4 (January 16, 1940): 11.

21. "Congress in Wild Attack," 1.

22. Greg Robinson, *By Order of the President: FDR and the Internment of Japanese Americans* (Cambridge, Mass.: Harvard University Press, 2001), 49–50.

23. Elizabeth Gurley Flynn, "Tom Paine Was an Alien Too," *New Masses* 38, no. 9 (February 18, 1941): 41.

24. Flynn, 41.

25. Donna Haverty-Stack, *Trotskyists on Trial: Free Speech and Political Persecution Since the Age of FDR* (New York: NYU Press, 2016), 1–5.

26. Haverty-Stack, 5.

27. Haverty-Stack, 6–7.

28. Milton Howard, "The Prosecution of the Minneapolis Trotzkyites," *Daily Worker*, August 16, 1941, 5; Carl Winter, "Minneapolis Trial Shows Labor Wary of Trotzkyites," *Daily Worker*, December 19, 1941, 5.

29. Dorothy Ray Healy and Maurice Isserman, *California Red: A Life in the American Communist Party* (Urbana: University of Illinois Press, 1990), 174.

30. Fraser M. Ottanelli, *The Communist Party of the United States: From the Depression to World War II* (New Brunswick, N.J.: Rutgers University Press, 1991), 191–194, 203.

31. "Browder Appeals for Loans for Defense Fund," *Daily Worker*, October 26, 1939, 1.

32. "William Weiner," in *Biographical Dictionary of the American Left*, ed. Bernard K. Johnpoll and Harvey Klehr (New York: Greenwood, 1986), 409.

33. Schrecker, *Many Are the Crimes*, 96.

34. Robin D. G. Kelley, *Hammer and Hoe: Alabama Communists during the Great Depression* (Chapel Hill: University of North Carolina Press, 1990), 214–215.

35. Ottanelli, *Communist Party*, 204–205; James Douglas Rose, *Duquesne and the Rise of Steel Unionism* (Urbana: University of Illinois Press, 2001) 204; "1,000 Waiting to Testify in Petition Trial," *Pittsburgh Post-Gazette*, October 7, 1940, 22.

36. Maurice Isserman, *Which Side Were You On? The American Communist Party during the Second World War* (Middletown, Conn.: Wesleyan University Press, 1982), 51–53; for a firsthand account of what it was like to go underground at this time, see Steve Nelson, James R. Barrett, and Rob Ruck, *Steve Nelson, American Radical* (Pittsburgh: University of Pittsburgh Press, 1981), 50–52.

37. Schrecker, *Many Are the Crimes*, 119–121.

38. Helen C. Camp, *Iron in Her Soul: Elizabeth Gurley Flynn and the American Left* (Pullman: Washington State University Press, 1995), 151; "Sick Veteran Sends $250 to Bail Fund," *Daily Worker*, October 31, 1939, 1; "Answer Dies and War-Mongers with Aid for Bail Fund, Foster Urges," *Daily Worker*, November 1, 1939, 1, 4.

39. "Browder's Appeal for C.P. Defense Fund Gets Swift Response," *Daily Worker*, October 27, 1939, 4.

40. "U.S. War Vet Offers Savings to C.P. Fund," *Daily Worker*, October 28, 1939, 4.

41. "Gurley Flynn Honors Son with Defense Fund Gifts," *Daily Worker*, May 18, 1940, 5.

42. Jodi Dean, *Comrade: An Essay on Political Belonging* (London, Verso: 2019), 9–10.

43. *Daily Worker*, March 29, 1941, 3.

44. Elizabeth Gurley Flynn to Mary Heaton Vorse, January 7, 1940, MHV Papers, box 66.

45. *They Shall Not Die! Stop the Legal Lynching! The Story of Scottsboro in Pictures* (New York: League of Struggle for Negro Rights, 1932), 3.

46. Kelley, *Hammer and Hoe*, 76.

47. *Equality, Land, and Freedom: A Program for Negro Liberation* (New York: League of Struggle for Negro Rights, 1933), 27–31.

48. *The South Comes North in Detroit's Own Scottsboro Case* (New York: League of Struggle for Negro Rights, 1934), 2.

49. Kelley, *Hammer and Hoe*, 122, 176.

50. On the emergence of civil rights law, see Risa Goluboff, *The Lost Promise of Civil Rights* (Cambridge, Mass.: Harvard University Press, 2007), 16–50; on the lingering implications of the civil rights–civil liberties split, see Christopher W. Schmidt, "The Civil Rights–Civil Liberties Divide," April 2014, http://scholarship.kentlaw.iit.edu/fac_schol/807.

51. Elizabeth Gurley Flynn, "Defend the Civil Rights of Communists!," *Communist* 18, no. 12 (December 1939), 1115.

52. Flynn, 1115.

53. "Bail Fund $30,000; 'Hurry the Rest,' Gurley Flynn Asks," *Sunday Worker*, December 3, 1939, 5.

54. "Recovering from Grippe at Home, Gurley Flynn Talks about Bail Fund," *Daily Worker*, December 29, 1939, 5.

55. "Recovering from Grippe," 5.

56. "Flynn to Lead Discussion on Civil Liberties and War," *Swarthmore Phoenix*, December 5, 1939, 2; "Gurley Flynn Hits Persecution of Browder at City College Meeting," *Daily Worker*, December 8, 1939, 4; "Students Eager to Hear Browder, E.G. Flynn Says," *Daily Worker*, December 12, 1939, 4.

57. Author interview with Bob Lewis, June 25, 2010.

58. "Notebook of Autobiographical Events," 1937–1948, 26, NYU EGF Papers, box 3.

59. Citizens' Committee to Free Earl Browder, "The Browder Case," September 1941, 6–11.

60. Camp, *Iron in Her Soul*, 151.

61. "Washington Civil Rights Parley Ends Sessions," *Daily Worker*, April 23, 1940, 1.

62. "Washington Civil Rights Parley," 4.

63. "Washington Civil Rights Parley," 4.

64. House Special Committee on Un-American Activities, "Investigation of Un-American Propaganda Activities in the United States," 1944, 652.

65. See, for example, National Federation for Constitutional Liberties, "Committee on Election Rights—1940," October 1, 1940, Correspondence-Labor and Liberal Organizations, vol. 2205, ACLU Papers; and "2,000 at Rally Demand Defense of Minority Ballot Rights," *Daily Worker*, October 10, 1940, 4.

66. Roger Baldwin to "Our Local Committees," November 26, 1940, Correspondence-Labor and Liberal Organizations, vol. 2205, ACLU Papers.

67. House Committee on Un-American Activities, "Guide to Subversive Organizations," March 3, 1951, 40.

68. Elizabeth Gurley Flynn, "How to Free Earl Browder," *Communist* 20 (June 1941): 508–512; "Forward in the Browder Recruiting Drive," *Daily Worker*, May 20, 1941, 5.

69. Flynn, "Free Earl Browder," 509.

70. Flynn, 511.

71. Flynn, 312.

72. "Mooney from Sick Bed Appeals for Browder," *Daily Worker*, September 26, 1941, 5.

73. Elizabeth Gurley Flynn, "Carry on for Tom Mooney," *Daily Worker*, March 11, 1942, 5.

74. "Prominent Citizens Form Committee for Nationwide Campaign," *Daily Worker*, August 18, 1941, 1.

75. Elizabeth Gurley Flynn, *Earl Browder: The Man from Kansas* (New York: Workers Library Publishers, November 1941), 3.

76. "Notebook of Autobiographical Events," 29, 35; Sadie Van Veen, "Elizabeth Gurley Flynn, Mother, Poet, Leader," *Sunday Worker*, February 1, 1942, 6.

77. "Keep 'Em Sailing Is Union Seamen's Motto," *Sunday Worker*, February 8, 1942, 6.

78. "Gurley Flynn Broadcast for Browder Thursday," *Daily Worker*, February 10, 1942, 1; "Browder Broadcast Features Gurley Flynn and Freedom Songs," *Sunday Worker*, February 22, 1942, 7; "Gurley Flynn on Browder Congress, WHOM," *Daily Worker*, March 31, 1942, 7.

79. Camp, *Iron in Her Soul*, 170; James G. Ryan, *Earl Browder: The Failure of American Communism* (Tuscaloosa: University of Alabama Press, 1997), 212–213.

80. "Rallies for Earl Browder," *Daily Worker*, March 11, 1942, 5; "Flynn, Billings to Address Boston Rally," *Daily Worker*, March 22, 1942, 4.

81. John Haynes Holmes to Citizens Committee to Free Earl Browder, March 24, 1942, vol. 2364, ACLU Papers.

82. Roger Baldwin to O. John Rogge, October 8, 1941, vol. 2277, ACLU Papers; Arthur Garfield Hays, "Memorandum on the Browder Case," December 3, 1941, 4, vol. 2363, ACLU Papers.

83. Roger Baldwin to Morris Ernst, September 30, 1941, vol. 2277, ACLU Papers.

84. Roger Baldwin to Dear Friends, November 28, 1941, vol. 2364, ACLU Papers.

85. Roger Baldwin to Arthur Garfield Hays, October 22, 1941, vol. 2277, ACLU Papers.

86. Roger Baldwin, John Haynes Holmes, and Arthur Garfield Hays to Franklin Roosevelt, November 27, 1941, vol. 2364, ACLU Papers.

87. Roger Baldwin to Francis Biddle, January 9, 1942, vol. 2364, ACLU Papers.

88. "Browder Returns; FDR Act Praised," *Daily Worker*, May 18, 1942, 1.

89. Schrecker, *Many Are the Crimes*, 105.

90. Nat Low, "Great Fighting Champion Comes back to the Garden," *Daily Worker*, July 4, 1942, 8.

91. "Lewis Shadow Hangs over Anthracite," *Daily Worker*, March 23, 1945, 3; "Coal Miners Hour of Trial," *Daily Worker*, March 28, 1945, 2; "Gurley Flynn Shows up Lewis' Stooge," *Daily Worker*, April 2, 1945, 7; "Did Miners Vote Overwhelmingly for Strike?," *Daily Worker*, April 4, 1945, 7.

92. "Anti-Semitism Poisons Our United War Effort," *Sunday Worker*, January 31, 1943, 14; "We Can Elect TWO Communists to Council," *Sunday Worker*, October 31, 1943, 11; "Connolly's Hopes of Eire's Role," *Daily Worker*, March 17, 1945, 6.

93. Elizabeth Gurley Flynn, "Notes on People," 1944, 3–5, NYU EGF Papers, box 3.

94. "In Sorrowful Memory of My Dearly Beloved Only Son Fred Flynn," *Sunday Worker*, March 29, 1942, 2.

95. Camp, *Iron in Her Soul*, 185–194.

96. Flynn, "Notes on People," 9.

97. *Daily Worker*, March 30, 1945, 10.

98. These columns are great. See, for example, "Sister Kathie Says: Elizabeth, You're a Sinatra Fan!," *Sunday Worker*, December 10, 1944, 11; "Elizabeth Asks: Kathie, Is You Is or Is You Ain't?," *Sunday Worker*, January 7, 1945, 11; "Sister Kathie Says: Obey the 11th Commandment," *Sunday Worker*, January 28, 1945, 11; "Sister Kathie Says: Speaking? There's Nothing to It!," *Sunday Worker*, February 11, 1945, 11; and "Sister Kathie Says: Now There Was an Irishman!," *Sunday Worker*, April 1, 1945, 11.

99. Kate Weigand, *Red Feminism: American Communism and the Making of Women's Liberation* (Baltimore: Johns Hopkins University Press, 2001), 164n33.

100. See, for example, "America Is Learning That It's a War," *Daily Worker*, May 23, 1943, 14; "Let's Heave Jim Crow over Right Now," *Sunday Worker*, November 14, 1943, 11; and "Negro Women Who Made History," *Daily Worker*, February 19, 1945, 7.

101. Elizabeth Gurley Flynn, *Women in the War* (New York: Workers Library Publishers, 1942), 17.

102. Flynn, 19.

103. Flynn, 23.

104. Weigand, *Red Feminism*, 46–50.

105. Elisabeth Armstrong, "Before Bandung: The Anti-Imperialist Women's Movement in Asia and the Women's International Democratic Federation," *Signs: Journal of Women in Culture and Society* 41, no. 2 (Winter 2016): 305–331.

106. "Notebook of Autobiographical Events," 54.

107. Autobiographical Notes on Trips, n.d., NYU EGF Papers, box 3.

108. Flynn even published an eyewitness account of the French Communist Party. See "First Party of France," *Sunday Worker Magazine*, February 24, 1946, 1, 8.

109. Joseph Starobin, *American Communism in Crisis, 1943–1957* (Berkeley: University of California Press, 1972), 119–120.

110. Despite their resistance to the feminist label, Kate Weigand argues that Communist women helped build the ideological and organizational foundations for second wave feminism. See Weigand, *Red Feminism*, 1–11.

111. Clare Coss, "Veteran Activist Leads Long Courageous Life," *New Directions for Women* 16, no. 2 (March/April 1987): 4.

112. Maurice Isserman, *Reds: The Tragedy of American Communism* (New York: Basic Books, 2024), 209–216.

113. Ottanelli, *Communist Party*, 208–212.

114. "Notice of Dissolution," *Daily Worker*, January 11, 1944, 2.

115. Elizabeth Gurley Flynn to Earl Browder, February 26, 1944, Earl R. Browder Papers, box 19, Special Collections Research Center, Syracuse University.

116. Isserman, *Reds*, 218.

117. "Notebook of Autobiographical Events," 49.

118. "Speech by Elizabeth Gurley Flynn," *Political Affairs* 24, no. 7 (July 1945): 613.

119. "Notebook of Autobiographical Events," 7.

120. Starobin, *American Communism in Crisis*, 119; Rosalyn Fraad Baxandall, *Words on Fire: The Life and Writing of Elizabeth Gurley Flynn* (New Brunswick, N.J.: Rutgers University Press, 1987), 51; see also Baxandall, 280n102.

121. "Speech by Elizabeth Gurley Flynn," 617.

122. Nelson, Barrett, and Ruck, *Steve Nelson, American Radical*, 397.

123. Camp, *Iron in Her Soul*, 203.

124. For a detailed exploration of these events, see Starobin, *American Communism in Crisis*, 51–120; Isserman, *Which Side Were You On?*, 187–243; and Ottanelli, *Communist Party*, 207–212.

125. "Red Organizer Claims Midwest Only Pacifist," *Scottsbluff Daily Star-Herald*, May 22, 1946, 5.

126. "Communist Rally Tonight," *Nashua Telegraph*, October 11, 1946, 7.

127. Elizabeth Gurley Flynn, *Meet the Communists* (New York: CPUSA, 1946), 13.

128. See, for example, "Communist Leaders," *Sunday Worker Magazine*, August 11, 1946, 1–2; and "What Is a Plenum?," *Daily Worker*, January 9, 1947, 7.

129. "Gurley Flynn to Spur City Communist Recruiting Drive," *Daily Worker*, June 24, 1946, 5.

130. "Notebook of Autobiographical Events," 55–62.

131. On the party's rededication to the "Negro question," see Starobin, *American Communism in Crisis*, 134–135.

132. Mammoth Rally in Union Square, *People's Voice*, March 9, 1946, 4; "Thousands Storm Union Square Freeport Protest Meeting," *People's Voice*, March 16, 1946, 4; "Canada Lee Slated for Longshore Dance," *People's Voice*, July 20, 1946, 9; "1,000 Visit Clark on Lynchings," *Daily Worker*, July 30, 1946, 12; "Harlem Rally on Housing Tomorrow," *Daily Worker*, April 19, 1947, 4; "All Out May 14 to Protest," *People's Voice*, May 10, 1947, 6.

133. "The Civil Rights Congress," *Daily Worker*, April 24, 1946, 9.

134. "Communist Tells Trials of Early IWW Days," *Salt Lake Telegram*, May 17, 1946, 17.

135. William C. Kelly, "High Time to Revive the Art of the Streetcorner Speaker," *Daily Worker*, July 20, 1946, 11.

136. "Why Am I a Communist?," *Sunday Worker Magazine*, September 15, 1946, 1.

137. "Why Am I a Communist?," 1.

138. Camp, *Iron in Her Soul*, 204–205.

139. "What Is Democracy Worth to You?," *Daily Worker*, March 14, 3.

140. "What Is Democracy Worth to You?," 3.

141. "Proud to Be Treasurer," 12.

142. "The People Tell with $$ What Liberty's Worth," *Daily Worker*, March 23, 1947, 3.

143. "Fighting Fund Tops $124,000 in One Week," *Daily Worker*, March 24, 1947, 5; Elizabeth Gurley Flynn, "Over the Top and Not Stopping," *Sunday Worker*, April 6, 1947, 9.

144. Robert Justin Goldstein, *American Blacklist: The Attorney General's List of Subversive* Organizations (Lawrence: University Press of Kansas, 2008), 51.

145. Harry S. Truman, "On the Veto of the Taft-Hartley Bill," March 12, 1947, UVA Miller Center, https://millercenter.org/the-presidency/presidential-speeches/june-20-1947-veto-taft-hartley-bill.

146. Schrecker, *Many Are the Crimes*, 317–333.

147. "CRC to Seek End of 'Un-American' Body," *Daily Worker*, November 24, 1937, 3.

148. "Life of the Party," *Daily Worker*, November 28, 1947, 11.

149. "The American People Are Eager for Third Party," *Daily Worker*, January 2, 1948, 11.

150. See Starobin, *American Communism in Crisis*, 155–194.

151. "Notebook of Autobiographical Events," 64.

152. "And the Communist Party's Name Led All the Rest," *Daily Worker*, December 8, 1947, 11.

153. "Yellow Press Screams Red Raids—History Repeats Itself," *Daily Worker*, November 17, 1947, 11.

154. "What We're Fighting For," *Daily Worker*, September 17, 1947, 7.

155. "Battle of Loudspeakers," *Daily Worker*, August 23, 1947, 7.

156. See, for example, "Crown Heights Wins a Free Speech Fight," *Daily Worker*, January 19, 1948, 11.

157. "Justice Department Hits All-Time Low—The Attack on Claudia Jones," *Daily Worker*, January 23, 1948, 11.

158. "Harlem Acts to Help Free Claudia Jones," *Daily Worker*, January 26, 1948, 3, 10.

159. "Notebook of Autobiographical Events," 67–68, 72; Elizabeth Gurley Flynn, "A Woman's Meeting of Vital Importance," *Daily Worker*, February 9, 1948,

11; "Cleveland Negro Women Respond to Defense Appeal," *Daily Worker*, March 8, 1948, 11.

160. "American Jewish League against Communism Charges Reds with Fomenting Racial Strife," *New York Age*, July 31, 1948, 1.

Chapter 6: The Smith Act Trials of Communists in New York

1. Harry Raymond, "Brand Bid to Bar School to CP Denial of Rights," *Daily Worker*, January 13, 1948, 3.

2. Helen C. Camp, *Iron in Her Soul: Elizabeth Gurley Flynn and the American Left* (Pullman: Washington State University Press, 1995), 205.

3. Harry Raymond, "Hail Court Victory on Crown Heights Meeting," *Daily Worker*, January 15, 1948, 16.

4. Elizabeth Gurley Flynn, "Crown Heights Wins a Free Speech Fight," *Daily Worker*, January 19, 1948, 11.

5. "The Miami Gutter Press Launches a Lynch Campaign," *Daily Worker*, March 3, 1948, 11.

6. "What You Can Do to Save Mrs. Ingram and Her Two Sons," *Daily Worker*, March 1, 1948, 11; "Cleveland Negro Women Respond to Defense Appeal," *Daily Worker*, March 8, 1948, 11; "The Women of Canton, O; Akron Rallies for Deportees," *Daily Worker*, March 12, 1948, 11.

7. "Force and Violence against the Negro People," *Daily Worker*, March 19, 1948, 11.

8. "Top o' the Morning to the Irish," *Daily Worker*, March 17, 1948, 11.

9. "Top o' the Morning," 11.

10. "Force and Violence against the Negro People," 11.

11. Elizabeth Gurley Flynn, "Life of the Party," *Daily Worker*, June 11, 1948, 10.

12. Flynn, 10.

13. Rob F. Hall, "7,500 Lobby in Capital, Protest Mundt Bill, Picket White House on Negro Rights," *Daily Worker*, June 3, 1948, 1; "Art against War," *Daily Worker*, June 3, 1948, 9.

14. "Last Long Step—into Fascism," *Daily Worker*, May 3, 1948, 10.

15. "Last Long Step," 10.

16. Elizabeth Gurley Flynn, *My Life as a Political Prisoner: The Rebel Girl Becomes "No. 11710,"* revised edition of *The Alderson Story* (New York: International Publishers, 2019), 12.

17. *Daily Worker*, July 23, 1948, 10.

18. *Daily Worker*, July 28, 1948, 10.

19. Michal R. Belknap, *Cold War Political Justice: The Smith Act, the Communist Party, and American Civil Liberties* (Westport, Conn.: Greenwood, 1977), 52.

20. Elizabeth Gurley Flynn, "They Must Go Free!," *Political Affairs* 27, no. 12 (December 1948): 1076.

21. Ellen Schrecker, *Many Are the Crimes: McCarthyism in America* (Boston: Little, Brown and Company, 1998), 191.

22. Schrecker, 190–203.

23. Belknap, *Cold War Political Justice*, 52, 58–59.

24. "On Arrests and Indictments," August 6, 1948, 1–2, NYU EGF Papers, box 4.

25. "On Arrests and Indictments," 2–3.

26. "On Arrests and Indictments," 3.

27. Elizabeth Gurley Flynn, *The Twelve and You: What Happens to Democracy Is Your Business, Too!* (New York: New Century Publishers, 1948), 5.

28. Flynn, 9.

29. Flynn, 11.

30. Flynn, 21.

31. Flynn, 6–14.

32. She also urged that women demand the abolition of the HUAC and an end to politically motivated deportations. See Elizabeth Gurley Flynn, *An Appeal to Women* (New York: CPUSA, 1949), 4.

33. Flynn, 2–3.

34. Rosalyn Fraad Baxandall, *Words on Fire: The Life and Writing of Elizabeth Gurley Flynn* (New Brunswick, N.J.: Rutgers University Press, 1987), 60.

35. Elizabeth Gurley Flynn, "Life of the Party," *Daily Worker*, January 3, 1949, 10.

36. My account of the trial relies primarily on Michael Belknap's comprehensive treatment, *Cold War Political Justice*.

37. "Trial of '12' Costs $10,000 a Week," *Daily Worker*, February 1, 1949, 4.

38. "The '12', the '6' and Many More," *Daily Worker*, February 2, 1949, 5.

39. *Daily Worker*, February 11, 1949, 10.

40. "To Spark Defense of '12,'" *Daily Worker*, February 22, 1949, 2.

41. "Call Madison Square Rally on Jury-Rigging," *Daily Worker*, February 27, 1949, 10.

42. "Trial of Commie Leaders Has Deep Significance for Nation," *Brooklyn Daily Eagle*, January 23, 1949, 18; "Eleven vs. the U.S.A.," *New York Age*, February 5, 1949, 4.

43. "U.S. Communists Will Oppose Wall St. War, Say Foster, Dennis," *Daily Worker*, March 3, 1949, 3.

44. "Kremlin Shift," *New York Times*, March 6, 1949, E1.

45. Flynn insisted these moves were not delaying tactics. See, for example, "Help Tell Story of Trial of '12,'" *Daily Worker*, February 8, 1949, 7.

46. Schrecker, *Many Are the Crimes*, 194.

47. Belknap, *Cold War Political Justice*, 79.

48. Belknap, 82.

49. Schrecker, *Many Are the Crimes*, 196–197.

50. Elizabeth Gurley Flynn, "Stool Pigeon" (New York: New Century Publishers, 1949), 17.

51. *Daily Worker*, August 23, 1949, 8.

52. "30th Anniversary of the Communist Party," *Daily Worker*, September 1, 1949, 5.

53. *Daily Worker*, September 9, 1949, 8; *Daily Worker*, September 20, 1949, 10.

54. Ronald K. L. Collins and Sam Chaltain, *We Must Not Be Afraid to Be Free: Stories of Free Expression in America* (New York: Oxford University Press, 2011), 96.

55. "100 Come from Illinois to Watch Frame-Up Trial in Foley Square," *Daily Worker*, September 13, 1949, 3; "From Chicago to Foley Square," *Daily Worker*, September 19, 1949, 5.

56. Herbert Aptheker, "Paul Robeson and the Negro People's Historic Fight against Imperialist Wars," *Daily Worker*, May 11, 1949, 12.

57. Martin Duberman, *Paul Robeson* (New York: Alfred A. Knopf, 1988), 364–377; Roger M. Williams, "A Rough Sunday at Peekskill," *American Heritage* 27, no. 3 (April 1976), https://www.americanheritage.com/rough-sunday-peekskill.

58. Elizabeth Gurley Flynn, "Life of the Party," *Daily Worker*, September 29, 1949, 10; and Elizabeth Gurley Flynn, "Life of the Party," *Daily Worker*, October 5, 1949, 10.

59. "Statement by President Truman in Response to First Soviet Nuclear Test," September 23, 1949, History and Public Policy Program Digital Archive, Department of State Bulletin, vol. 21, no. 533, October 3, 1949, http://digitalarchive.wilsoncenter.org/document/134436.

60. "We All Have a Date with Ben," *Daily Worker*, October 12, 1949, 7.

61. "Communist Trial Ends with 11 Guilty," *Life* 27 (October 24, 1949): 34.

62. Elizabeth Gurley Flynn, "On Behalf of the 12 Sons of the American Working Class, I Thank You," *Daily Worker*, October 25, 1949, 5.

63. See, for example, "Millions Will Rally," *Cairo Record*, November 11, 1949, 6.

64. Elizabeth Gurley Flynn, "Life of the Party," *Daily Worker*, November 15, 1949, 10.

65. *Daily Worker*, January 20, 1950, 9.

66. Elizabeth Gurley Flynn, "Mass Action Can Free the Eleven," *Political Affairs* 4, no. 5 (May 1950): 153.

67. Elizabeth Gurley Flynn, "Life of the Party," 10.

68. Flynn, "Mass Action," 152.

69. Flynn, 154.

70. Schrecker, *Many Are the Crimes*, 197.

71. Samuel Frody, Letter to the Editor, *Daily Worker*, April 28, 1950, 6.

72. Elizabeth Gurley Flynn, "Life of the Party," *Daily Worker*, January 10, 1950, 8.

73. Belknap, *Cold War Political Justice*, 124.

74. Belknap, 125–131.

75. *United States Statutes at Large*, vol. 64, 81st Cong., 2nd Sess. (Washington D.C.: U.S. Government Printing Office, 1950), ch. 1024, pp. 987–1031.

76. "It's Your Choice, The Bill of Rights or the McCarran Act," n.d., NYU EGF Papers, box 6.

77. Kevin M. Baron, *Presidential Privilege and the Freedom of Information Act* (Edinburgh: Edinburgh University Press, 2019), 34–35.

78. "Dennis v. United States" 34 U.S. 494, 1951, https://tile.loc.gov/storage-services/service/ll/usrep/usrep341/usrep341494/usrep341494.pdf.

79. Elizabeth Gurley Flynn, "What Is to Be Done: A Plan of Action to Get Rehearing for Communist '11,'" *Daily Worker*, June 11, 1951, 1, 9.

80. Flynn, *My Life*, 9.

81. Flynn, 12.

82. Belknap, *Cold War Political Justice*, 160–162.

83. *Daily Worker*, June 21, 1951, 3, 9; *Daily Worker*, July 5, 1951, 5.

84. Flynn, *My Life*, 15.

85. Elizabeth Gurley Flynn, *Daily Worker*, July 5, 1951, 5; "News on the Bail Struggle," *Daily Worker*, July 24, 1951, 5.

86. Roger Baldwin to Elizabeth Gurley Flynn, July 15, 1951, and July 15, 1951, NYU EGF Papers, box 6; Patrick Murphy Malin to Elizabeth Gurley Flynn, September 5, 1951, NYU EGF Papers, box 6.

87. Flynn, *My Life*, 11.

88. *Stack v. Boyle*, 342 U.S. 1, 72 S. Ct. 1, 96 L. Ed. 3, 1951.

89. Baxandall, *Words on Fire*, 56; James R. Barrett, *William Z. Foster and the Tragedy of American Radicalism* (Urbana: University of Illinois Press, 1999), 238–239; Joseph Starobin, *American Communism in Crisis, 1943–1957* (Berkeley: University of California Press, 1972), 219–220, 306–307; Frederick V. Field to Elizabeth Gurley Flynn, July 2, 1951, NYU EGF Papers, box 6.

90. Elizabeth Gurley Flynn, "Right of Political Asylum," *Daily Worker*, October 19, 1951, 5.

91. See, for example, Elizabeth Gurley Flynn, "Further Hostages and Reprisals," *Daily Worker*, July 17, 1951, 5; "The Five Lawyer Victims of the Fascist Smith Act," *Daily Worker*, September 6, 1951, 5; "Brief of Negro Attorney on Smith Act Ruling," *Daily Worker*, October 4, 1951, 5; "Civil Rights Highlights," *Daily Worker*, October 23, 1951, 5; "Salute to the Imprisoned Communist Leaders," *Daily Worker*, December 6, 1951, 5; and "The Smog Screen of 1952, Fear Grips Our Ancestors," *Daily Worker*, February 19, 1952, 5.

92. "U.S. Communists Ask to Meet Acheson on North Korea Cease Fire," *Daily Worker*, August 27, 1951, 8; "Judge Forbids Communists to Take Plan for Korea Peace to Acheson," *Daily Worker*, October 1, 1951, 2.

93. Marion Bachrach and Elizabeth Gurley Flynn to Dear Friend, August 26, 1951, NYU EGF Papers, box 6.

94. Flynn, *My Life*, 10–12.

95. "Smith Act Victims Seek $250,000 Defense Fund," *Daily Worker*, December 2, 1951, 4; Frederick Woltman, "Buy Seals? Yule Help the Reds," *Pittsburgh Press*, December 27, 1951, 24.

96. Katherine Flynn, "My Sister Elizabeth," reprinted in *Daily Worker*, January 27, 1952, 3–4.

97. Belknap, *Cold War Political Justice*, 222.

98. Flynn, *My Life*, 13.

99. Harold Ickes to Elizabeth Gurley Flynn, July 29, 1951, NYU EGF Papers, box 6; Arthur Garfield Hays to Elizabeth Gurley Flynn, October 9, 1951, Mary Kaufman Papers, Sophia Smith Collection, Smith College.

100. Elizabeth Gurley Flynn to Sylvester Ryan, August 13, 1951, NYU EGF Papers, box 6; Flynn, *My Life*, 13.

101. Baxandall, *Words on Fire*, 60; Flynn, *My Life*, 15.

102. Flynn, *My Life*, 22.

103. Belknap, *Cold War Political Justice*, 170.

104. Richard O. Boyer, "Smith Act Trial Begins, Books, Ideas at Stake," *Daily Worker*, April 20, 1952, 4.

105. *Elizabeth Gurley Flynn Speaks to the Court* (New York: New Century Publishers, 1952), 3.

106. *Elizabeth Gurley Flynn Speaks*, 4–11.

107. *Elizabeth Gurley Flynn Speaks*, 9.

108. *Elizabeth Gurley Flynn Speaks*, 21.

109. *Elizabeth Gurley Flynn Speaks*, 17.

110. *Elizabeth Gurley Flynn Speaks*, 13.

111. Elizabeth Gurley Flynn, "1948—A Year of Inspiring Anniversaries for Women," *Political Affairs* 27, no. 3 (March 1948), 259–265; Angela Y. Davis, *Women, Race & Class*, New York: Random House, 1981, 96.

112. See, for example, Elizabeth Gurley Flynn, "Thought Control in Prison," *Daily Worker*, May 8, 1952, 5; and "America's Political Prisoners," *Daily Worker*, May 22, 1952, 4.

113. Jacques Duclos to Elizabeth Gurley Flynn, February 26, 1952, and March 12, 1952, NYU EGF Papers, box 4.

114. Jacques Duclos Sworn Statement (in French), April 1, 1952, NYU EGF Papers, box 4.

115. "Soviet Aid to Reds in U.S. Denied Here," *New York Times*, June 26, 1952, 4; "Miss Flynn Denies Anti-U.S. Attitude," *New York Times*, June 27, 1952, 8.

116. Harry Raymond, "Flynn Tells McCarran Board Her Life of Labor Struggles," *Daily Worker*, June 29, 1952, 4, 6.

117. "Release Miss Flynn Says Pat Devine," *Irish Democrat* 93 (September 1952), 3.

118. "Faster Pace Is Urged for Fund to Defend '16,'" *Daily Worker*, February 7, 1952, 1; Elizabeth Gurley Flynn, "We Need Help Pronto," *Daily Worker*, February 7, 1952, 5.

119. Elizabeth Gurley Flynn, *Daily Worker*, August 1952, 5.

120. Belknap, *Cold War Political Justice*, 152–157.

121. Elizabeth Gurley Flynn, "A Liberal's Education," *Political Affairs* 33, no. 8 (August 1954): 81.

122. Joseph North, "She Tells the Truth about Communism, but the Papers Hide It," *Daily Worker*, October 26, 1952, 4.

123. *Daily News*, July 18, 1951, 9; *Daily News*, November 8, 1952, 71; *Democrat and Chronicle*, January 23, 1953, 18; *Pittsburgh Press*, February 2, 1953, 1; *Daily News*, February 4, 1953, 13.

124. Author interview with Bob Lewis, June 25, 2010; Mary E. Dreier to Kathie Flynn, February 28, 1953, and John S. Codman to Elizabeth Gurley Flynn, November 14, 1954, NYU EGF Papers, box 5.

125. See, for example, "Hit Jailing of Women under Smith Act Hysteria," *Daily Worker*, August 5, 1951, 8; Sean Nolan to Elizabeth Gurley Flynn, August 16, 1952, NYU EGF Papers, box 5; "Irish Workers Hail Elizabeth Gurley Flynn's Birthday," *Daily Worker*, September 3, 1952, 2; and George Hardy to Elizabeth Gurley Flynn, July 29, 1954, and Hardy to Flynn, August 9, 1954, MSS 0099, F0922, George Hardy letters to Elizabeth Gurley Flynn, Special Collections, University of Delaware Library.

126. Albert Vetere Lannon, *Second String Red: The Life of Al Lannon, American Communist* (Washington, D.C.: Lexington Books, 1999), 130.

127. "Elizabeth Flynn's Stand Hailed by Defendants," *Daily Worker*, November 21, 1952, 8; Claudia Jones, "Her Words Rang Out Beyond the Walls of the Courthouse," *Daily Worker*, November 21, 1952, 3.

128. James Reston, "Would Open Talks: Soviet Premier Willing to Start Negotiations to Ease Tension," *New York Times*, December 25, 1952, 1.

129. Belknap, *Cold War Political Justice*, 170; Mark Rohr, "Communists and the First Amendment: The Shaping of Freedom of Advocacy in the Cold War Era," *San Diego Law Review* 28, no. 1 (1991): 61; Harry Raymond, "Free Us and Save American Honor," *Daily Worker*, January 11, 1953, 4; "What Gurley Flynn Told the Court about 'Present Danger,'" *Daily Worker*, January 12, 1953, 5.

130. Elizabeth Gurley Flynn, "Summation Speech," January 6, 1953, NYU EGF Papers, box 5.

131. *Daily News*, February 3, 1953, 4.

132. Elizabeth Gurley Flynn, "The Right to Travel," *Daily Worker*, March 19, 1953, 5; "McCarran Act-Blueprint for Fascism," *Daily Worker*, April 23, 1953, 5; "Political Discrimination in Prison," *Daily Worker*, May 28, 1953, 4; "Into the Fight to Save the Rosenbergs, Communist Party Statement Declares," *Daily Worker*, June 12, 1953, 1; Harry Raymond, "Will Appeal 'Foreign Agent' Slander of SACB, Says Communist Party," *Daily Worker*, April 26, 1953, 8.

133. Elizabeth Gurley Flynn, "Let's Talk about Socialism," *Daily Worker*, October 6, 1953, 5; "A Report from Your Columnist," *Daily Worker*, December 8, 1953, 4.

134. Barrett, *William Z. Foster*, 240–446; Starobin, *American Communism in Crisis*, 195–213.

135. "Life of the Party," *Daily Worker*, February 28, 1950, 8.

136. Terry Pettus to Elizabeth Gurley Flynn, February 25, 1954, NYU EGF Papers, box 7.

137. Elizabeth Gurley Flynn to Steve Nelson, October 14, 1953, Abraham Lincoln Brigade Archives (ALBA) Records, box 1, Tamiment Library, NYU.

138. Elizabeth Gurley Flynn to Mary Kaufman, October 1, 1953, Mary Kaufman Papers, Sophia Smith Collection, Smith College; Elizabeth Gurley Flynn to Steve Nelson, December 8, 1953, ALBA Records, box 1, Tamiment Library, NYU.

139. Sidney Schechter, MD, Certification of Treatment of EGF in August 1953, January 22, 1955, Mary Kaufman Papers, Sophia Smith Collection, Smith College.

140. Dwight D. Eisenhower, "Annual Message to the Congress on the State of the Union," January 7, 1954, https://www.presidency.ucsb.edu/documents/annual-message-the-congress-the-state-the-union-13.

141. *Expatriation Act of 1954*, 68 Stat, 1146, Pub. L. no. 772, 83rd Cong., 2nd Sess. (Washington, D.C.: U.S. Government Printing Office, 1954).

142. "CP Submits Brief Extolling Stoolies," *Daily Worker*, August 12, 1954, 2; Elizabeth Gurley Flynn, "Canvassing in the Bronx," *Daily Worker*, August 26, 1954, 5; Milton Howard, "Gurley Flynn's 'Got a Right,' Bronxites Tell Canvassers," *Daily Worker*, September 5, 1954, 11; "Communists Asked to Give Priority to Flynn Drive," *Daily Worker*, September 13, 1954, 1; Elizabeth Gurley Flynn, "Congratulations," *Daily Worker*, September 28, 1954, 5; "CP Will Sue Today to End Tax Harassment," *Daily Worker*, October 11, 1954, 2.

143. Virginia Gardner, "They Can't Jail You for That, the Cab Driver Told Kathie," *Daily Worker*, January 30, 1955, 6, 11.

144. Harry Raymond, "Hearing Today on Matusow Subpoena," *Daily Worker*, February 8, 1955, 1; Belknap, *Cold War Political Justice*, 215–219.

Chapter 7: The Struggle Continues

1. Alexandra Marks, "The Prison That Martha Stewart Will Call Home," *Christian Science Monitor*, October 8, 2004, https://www.csmonitor.com/2004/1008/p01s01-usju.html.

2. Elizabeth Gurley Flynn to Anna K. Flynn, January 25, 1955, NYU EGF Papers, box 7.

3. Elizabeth Gurley Flynn, *My Life as a Political Prisoner: The Rebel Girl Becomes "No. 11710,"* revised edition of *The Alderson Story* (New York: International Publishers, 2019), 27.

4. Al Richmond, *A Long View from the Left: Memoirs of an American Revolutionary* (New York: Delta, 1972), 370. Starobin notes that "virtually everyone who had anything to do with the underground" left the party between mid-1956 and mid-1957; see Joseph Starobin, *American Communism in Crisis, 1943–1957* (Berkeley: University of California Press, 1972), 223.

5. Emphasis in original. Flynn, *My Life*, 29.

6. Flynn, 37.

7. Flynn, 32.

8. Elizabeth Gurley Flynn, "An Irish-American Childhood," *Masses & Mainstream*, August 8, 1956, 8–25; *I Speak My Own Piece: Autobiography of "The Rebel Girl"* (New York: Masses & Mainstream, 1955).

9. Elizabeth Gurley Flynn to Al Richmond, March 16, 1964, NYU EGF Papers, box 14.

10. Dorothy Rose Blumberg to Scott Nearing, April 19, 1956, NYU EGF Papers, box 5; Kathie Flynn, "Speech on Mother's Day," May 4, 1956, NYU EGF Papers, box 5; William Patterson, "Greetings to Elizabeth Gurley Flynn," n.d. [Spring 1956], NYU EGF Papers, box 5; Gina and Ben Davis to Families of the Smith Act Victims, May 4, 1956, NYU EGF Papers, box 5; Scott Nearing to Dorothy Rose Blumberg, April 24, 1956, NYU EGF Papers, box 5; Roger Baldwin to Dorothy Rose Blumberg, April 23, 1956, NYU EGF Papers, box 5.

11. Elizabeth Gurley Flynn, "On the Declaration of Independence," *Alderson Eagle*, July 4, 1956, reprinted in *My Life*, 217–221.

12. Elizabeth Gurley Flynn to Kathie Flynn, January 25, 1955, NYU EGF Papers, box 7.

13. John Gates, *The Story of an American Communist* (New York: Thomas Nelson, 1958), 166–168.

14. Joseph Clark, "Joseph Stalin: Three Years Later," *Daily Worker*, March 12, 1956, 5; Alan Max, "U.S. Marxists and Soviet Self Criticism," *Daily Worker*, March 13, 1956, 4.

15. William Z. Foster, "The Reevaluation of Stalin's Work," *Daily Worker*, March 16, 1956, 2.

16. Elizabeth Gurley Flynn to Muriel Symington, March 24, 1956, NYU EGF Papers, box 7.

17. Eugene Dennis, *The Communists Take a New Look* (New York: New Century Publishers, 1956), 21, 24, 41–42.

18. Steve Nelson, James R. Barrett, and Rob Ruck, *Steve Nelson, American Radical* (Pittsburgh: University of Pittsburgh Press, 1987), 387. Richmond also discusses the emotional reaction to Khrushchev's speech in *Long View*, 367–368.

19. Elizabeth Gurley Flynn to Kathie Flynn, June 8, 1956, NYU EGF Papers, box 7.

20. Harrison E. Salisbury, "Khrushchev Talk on Stalin Bares Details of Rule Based on Terror; Charges Plot for Kremlin Purges," *New York Times*, June 5, 1956, 1; "Stalin's Repressions Spelled Out in Khrushchev Speech Made Public Here," *Daily Worker*, June 5, 1956, 2, 5; Elizabeth Gurley Flynn to Kathie Flynn, June 16, 1956, NYU EGF Papers, box 7.

21. Elizabeth Gurley Flynn to Clemens France, June 16, 1956, NYU EGF Papers, box 7.

22. Maurice Isserman, *Reds: The Tragedy of American Communism* (New York: Basic Books, 2024), 258–270.

23. "COMMUNISTS: Never Again?," *Time*, June 25, 1956, https://content.time.com/time/subscriber/article/0,33009,824248-1,00.html.

24. Elizabeth Gurley Flynn to Muriel Symington, June 23, 1956, NYU EGF Papers, box 7.

25. Joseph R. Starobin, "A Communication," *Nation*, August 25, 1956, 158, 168.

26. Elizabeth Gurley Flynn to Muriel Symington, September 1, 1956, NYU EGF Papers, box 7.

27. Elizabeth Gurley Flynn to Kathie Flynn, June 29, 1956, NYU EGF Papers, box 7.

28. Elizabeth Gurley Flynn to Muriel Symington, June 30, 1956, NYU EGF Papers, box 7.

29. Elizabeth Gurley Flynn to Kathie Flynn, July 14, 1956, NYU EGF Papers, box 7; Elizabeth Gurley Flynn to Clemens France, August 8, 1956, NYU EGF Papers, box 7.

30. "Draft Resolution for the 16th National Convention of the Communist Party of the U.S.A. Adopted September 13, 1956," New York: New Century Publishers, 1956, 59.

31. "Draft Resolution," 55, 61, 62.

32. William Z. Foster, "On the Party Situation," *Political Affairs* 35, no. 10 (October 1956): 15–45.

33. On the diversity among reformers, see Richmond, *Long View*, 379–380. On Foster's response to the Draft Resolution and to the struggle within the party generally, see James R. Barrett, *William Z. Foster and the Tragedy of American Radicalism* (Urbana: University of Illinois Press, 1999), 252–272.

34. Elizabeth Gurley Flynn to Muriel Symington, October 13, 1956, NYU EGF Papers, box 7. In a letter to Clemens France, Flynn referred to Stone's comments as "carping criticisms." Elizabeth Gurley Flynn to Clemens France, October 13, 1956, NYU EGF Papers, box 7.

35. Elizabeth Gurley Flynn to Kathie Flynn, October 27, 1956, NYU EGF Papers, box 7.

36. Gates, *Story of an American Communist*, 178–181.

37. Peter Khiss, "Soviet Attack Hit by Daily Worker," *New York Times*, November 6, 1956, 23; Elizabeth Gurley Flynn to Clemens France, November 22, 1956, NYU EGF Papers, box 7.

38. Elizabeth Gurley Flynn to Kathie Flynn, January 19, 1957, NYU EGF Papers, box 7.

39. Gates, *Story of an American Communist*, 182–183.

40. Richmond, *Long View*, 381–382.

41. Steve Nelson, James R. Barrett, and Rob Ruck, *Steve Nelson, American Radical* (Pittsburgh: University of Pittsburgh Press, 1981), 397.

42. Elizabeth Gurley Flynn to Muriel Symington, February 22, 1957, NYU EGF Papers, box 7; Elizabeth Gurley Flynn to Clemens France, February 25, 1957, NYU EGF Papers, box 7.

43. Flynn to France, February 25, 1957.

44. Elizabeth Gurley Flynn to Muriel Symington, January 26, 1957, NYU EGF Papers, box 7; Elizabeth Gurley Flynn to Clemens France, March 3, 1957, NYU EGF Papers, box 7; Flynn to Symington, March 16, 1957, NYU EGF Papers, box 7; Flynn to France, March 23, 1957, NYU EGF Papers, box 7.

45. Flynn to France, May 4, 1957, NYU EGF Papers, box 7.

46. Flynn to France, May 10, 1957, NYU EGF Papers, box 7.

47. Elizabeth Gurley Flynn to Muriel Symington, May 17, 1957, NYU EGF Papers, box 7.

48. Marion Bachrach, "Elizabeth Gurley Flynn Looks Quite Different, But Is Still the Same," *Daily Worker*, June 2, 1957, 4–5.

49. Elizabeth Gurley Flynn to Kathie Flynn, September 15, 1956, NYU EGF Papers, box 7; Helen C. Camp, *Iron in Her Soul: Elizabeth Gurley Flynn and the American Left* (Pullman: Washington State University Press, 1995), 289.

50. "U.S. Reports: Watkins v. United States," 354 U.S. 178 (1957), https://tile.loc.gov/storage-services/service/ll/usrep/usrep354/usrep354178/usrep354178.pdf; "U.S. Reports: Yates v. United States," 354 U.S. 298 (1957), https://tile.loc.gov/storage-services/service/ll/usrep/usrep354/usrep354298/usrep354298.pdf.

51. Virginia Gardner, "1,600 Honor Freed Communist Leaders," *Daily Worker*, July 26, 1957, 1.

52. Gardner, 7.

53. Dorothy Ray Healy and Maurice Isserman, *California Red: A Life in the American Communist Party* (Urbana: University of Illinois Press, 1990), 174.

54. "Gurley Flynn Will Run for City Council," *Daily Worker*, August 23, 1957, 1, 5.

55. See George Morris, "The Challenge of the Flynn Campaign," *Daily Worker*, September 6, 1957, 5.

56. See "Hail East Side Response to Gurley Flynn," *Daily Worker*, September 13, 1957, 2; and William Z. Foster, "The Flynn Signature Campaign," *Daily Worker*, September 17, 1957, 4.

57. "Fall Elections Offer Preview for Ballot in '58 and '60," *National Guardian* 9, no. 49, September 23, 1957, 5.

58. "For Gurley Flynn Canvassing," *Daily Worker*, August 27, 1957, 4.

59. "Elizabeth Gurley Flynn Campaign Schedule," 1957, NYU EGF Papers, box 8.

60. "Proposed Program of Elizabeth Gurley Flynn, Candidate for City Council, 24th District," 1957, NYU EGF Papers, box 8.

61. "A Day with Elizabeth Gurley Flynn," *Worker*, November 3, 1957, 5.

62. "Gurley Flynn's Name to Appear on Row H," *Daily Worker*, October 16, 1957, 2; "Women Voters to Hear Flynn," *Daily Worker*, October 21, 1957, 1; "Practice What You Teach," *Daily Worker*, October 30, 1957, 2; "Total Red Vote Is Only 710 Here," *New York Times*, November 7, 1957, 38.

63. "Total Red Vote," 38; Evelyn Wiener, "The Elizabeth Gurley Flynn Campaign," *Political Affairs* 37, no. 1 (January 1958): 14–15.

64. Elizabeth Gurley Flynn, "Celebrating Gil Green's Birthday," *Daily Worker*, September 17, 1957, 3; "Let These Men Go Free," *Daily Worker*, December 8, 1957, 7; "On Your Guard," *Daily Reporter*, February 22, 1958, 2.

65. Elizabeth Gurley Flynn, "From My Post-Prison Diary," *Daily Worker*, December 15, 1957, 6–7.

66. "Dear Teenager," n.d. [December 1957], NYU EGF Papers, box 8.

67. "School Cancels Red's Speech," *Eau Claire Reader*, December 18, 1957, 24; "Wisconsin Speech Ban on Communist Speaker Hit by ACLU," ACLU Papers, box 704, Mudd Manuscript Library, Princeton University.

68. "No Hall for Free Press?," *Daily Worker*, November 21, 1957, 1.

69. National Executive Committee, CPUSA, "Statement on the Declaration of 12 Parties," *Political Affairs* 37, no. 1 (January 1958), 1–4.

70. William Z. Foster, "The Party Crisis and the Way Out, Part II," *Political Affairs* 37, no. 1 (January 1958), 49–65.

71. Elizabeth Gurley Flynn, "Johnny, I Hardly Knew Ye," *Daily Worker*, January 26, 1958, 16.

72. Elizabeth G. Flynn, "Gurley Flynn Says: Build Worker," *Daily Worker*, January 13, 1958, 2.

73. "From Our Letter Bag," *Worker*, March 2, 1958, 1; Elizabeth Gurley Flynn, "Where Have You Been?," *Worker*, March 23, 1958, 6.

74. "May Day Rallies Reflect Resurging Enthusiasm," *Worker*, May 11, 1958, 3; "Elizabeth Gurley Flynn Travel Notes," *Worker*, May 25, 1958, 9; "Elizabeth Gurley Flynn Travel Notes," *Worker*, June 29, 1958, 9.

75. "Elizabeth Gurley Flynn: Defend Negro Women of South Africa," *Worker*, August 2, 1959, 9; "Elizabeth Gurley Flynn: Votes for All Negro Women," *Worker*, October 25, 1959, 9; "Elizabeth Gurley Flynn: Amnestia ... for 6,000," *Worker*, February 28, 1960, 9.

76. Elizabeth Gurley Flynn to Friend Unknown, April 5, 1959, Freedom of Information Act (FOIA) File 100-1287, NYU EGF Papers, box 9.

77. "Elizabeth Gurley Flynn: Holidays in Prison," *Worker*, November 30, 1958, 9.

78. "Elizabeth Gurley Flynn: Attention Congressman Celler," *Worker*, March 22, 1959, 9.

79. See, for example, "Elizabeth Gurley Flynn: The Easiest Way," *Worker*, July 26, 1959, 9.

80. "U.S. Reports: Uphaus v. Wyman," 355 U.S. 16 (1957), https://tile.loc.gov/storage-services/service/ll/usrep/usrep355/usrep355016/usrep355016.pdf.

81. "U.S. Reports: Barenblatt v. United States," 360 U.S. 109 (1959), https://tile.loc.gov/storage-services/service/ll/usrep/usrep360/usrep360109/usrep360109.pdf.

82. "Elizabeth Gurley Flynn: Supreme Court Retreats," *Worker*, July 5, 1959, 9.

83. "CP Charts Course for Peaceful Coexistence, Peace Economy," *Worker*, December 20, 1959, 1.

84. Camp, *Iron in Her Soul*, 293.

85. "Elizabeth Gurley Flynn Writes from Copenhagen," *Worker*, May 1, 1960, 10.

86. Camp, *Iron in Her Soul*, 307.

87. Elizabeth Gurley Flynn to Unknown, November 21, 1960, FOIA File 100-1287, NYU EGF Papers, box 9.

88. Camp, *Iron in Her Soul*, 310–313.

89. Elizabeth Gurley Flynn to Steve Nelson, August 9, 1960, ALBA Records, box 1, Tamiment Library, NYU; Edward J. Hickey to J. Edgar Hoover, January 14, 1960, NYU EGF Papers, box 9.

90. "Elizabeth Gurley Flynn: Flying into Socialism," *Worker*, May 22, 1960, 7.

91. "Elizabeth Gurley Flynn: A Soviet Rest Home," *Worker*, August 21, 1960, 7.

92. Elizabeth Gurley Flynn to Unknown, January 3, 1961, FOIA File 100-1287, NYU EGF Papers, box 9.

93. Flynn to Nelson, August 9, 1960.

94. "Elizabeth Gurley Flynn: Impressions on Return," *Worker*, January 29, 1961, 7.

95. Elizabeth Gurley Flynn, "Gene Dennis—Comrade and Valiant Leader," *Worker*, February 12, 1961, 4.

96. "Elizabeth Gurley Flynn Named Chairman of CP," *Worker*, March 19, 1961, 1.

97. "Elizabeth Gurley Flynn: Out by the Golden Gate," *Worker*, April 31, 1961, 7.

98. Marion Bachrach to Elizabeth Gurley Flynn, July 1957, NYU EGF Papers, box 8.

99. David A. Shannon, *Decline of American Communism: A History of the Communist Party of the United States Since 1945* (New York: Harcourt, Brace and Company, 1959), 360; Isserman, *Reds*, 268.

100. "Elizabeth Gurley Flynn: Revisiting Portland, Ore.," *Worker*, April 23, 1961, 7.

101. "Elizabeth Gurley Flynn Pierces Press Curtain," *Worker*, May 28, 1961, 7.

102. Art Shields, "Will Fight for Bill of Rights, CP Leaders Tell Newsmen," *Worker*, June 18, 1961, 1, 10.

103. "U.S. Communists Assail Ruling; Party to Fight for Legal Rights," *New York Times*, June 6, 1961, 16; Anthony Lewis, "Law Tightens on U.S. Communists: Party's Existence Threatened by Demand for Full Self-Exposure," *New York Times*, June 11, 1961, E8; National Committee, Communist Party USA, "An Open Letter to the American People," *New York Times*, June 22, 1961, 20.

104. Elizabeth Gurley Flynn to Unknown, June 28, 1961, FOIA File 100-1287, NYU EGF Papers, box 9.

105. Elizabeth Gurley Flynn, *Freedom Begins at Home* (New York: New Century Publishers, 1961), 7.

106. John Pittman, "Moscow Says Farewell," *Worker*, September 10, 1961, 3.

107. Elizabeth Gurley Flynn to Unknown, October 13, 1961, FOIA File 100-1287, NYU EGF Papers, box 9.

108. Flynn to Unknown, October 13, 1961.

109. "Elizabeth Gurley Flynn: Three Days in Stalingrad," *Worker*, November 5, 1961, 7.

110. Camp, *Iron in Her Soul*, 296.

111. "Penalizing Communists: Party Official Asks for Support for Her Defiance of the McCarran Act," *New York Times*, November 22, 1961, 32.

112. On the Chelsea Hotel, see Sherill Tippins, *Inside the Dream Palace: The Life and Times of New York's Legendary Chelsea Hotel* (New York: Mariner Books, 2013). The Behan anecdote is on page 55.

113. Fred Gillman, "Phony Tax Suit Vs. CP Follows McCarran Arrests," *Worker*, March 25, 1962, 1.

114. "Memo to Director, FBI, 100-1287, Re: Elizabeth Gurley Flynn," March 18, 1960, NYU EGF Papers, box 9; "Memo to Director, FBI, 100-1287, Re: Elizabeth

Gurley Flynn," March 23, 1960, NYU EGF Papers, box 9; "Vindictive and Nasty," *Worker*, February 13, 1962, 2.

115. Robert Justin Goldstein, *Political Repression in Modern America from 1870 to the Present* (Boston: G. K. Hall, 1978), 425; Michael Heale, *American Communism: Combating the Enemy Within, 1830–1970* (Baltimore: Johns Hopkins University Press, 1990), 197–199.

116. "Defense Committee Organized," *Worker*, April 3, 1962, 7.

117. "Defense Committee Organized," 7; "Gurley Flynn Tells of Plans in Hall-Davis Defense Drive," *Worker*, April 10, 1962, 3.

118. "Gurley Flynn Tells," 3; "Elizabeth Gurley Flynn: I'm Back," *Worker*, April 22, 1962, 7.

119. Elizabeth Gurley Flynn to "Folks," February 19, 1962, NYU EGF Papers, box 9.

120. Goldstein, *Political Repression*, 415; Mike Davidow, "Gus Hall's Coast Visit Helps Deliver Blow to Ultra Right," *Worker*, February 11, 1962, 3; "Benjamin Davis Free Speech Issue Comes to Campus at Wilmington," *Worker*, February 11, 1962, 3.

121. Martin J. Broekhuysen and Ronald J. Greene, "Davis Calls McCarran, Smith Acts American 'Blueprints for Fascism,'" *Harvard Crimson*, April 19, 1962, https://www.thecrimson.com/article/1962/4/19/davis-calls-mccarran-smith-acts-american/; "Students Assail Curb on Reds," *New York Times*, May 20, 1962, 49.

122. *Ben Davis on the McCarran Act at the Harvard Law Forum* (New York: Gus Hall–Benjamin J. Davis Defense Committee, 1962). See, for example, Daniel J. Chasan, "Editor, Youth Leader Attack McCarran Act for 'Stifling Debate,'" *Harvard Crimson*, December 13, 1963, https://www.thecrimson.com/article/1963/12/13/editor-youth-leader-attack-mccarran-act/; and George Morris, "Clothing Union to President: End McCarranism!," *Worker*, July 1, 1962, 1.

123. A succinct and informative history of the Passport Division and national security concerns is Sam Lebovic, "No Right to Leave the Nation: The Politics of Passport Denial and the Rise of the Security State," *Studies in American Political Development* 34, no. 1 (April 2020): 170–193.

124. See, for example, Charles M. Whelan, "Passports and Freedom of Travel: The Conflict of a Right and a Privilege," *Georgetown Law Review* 41, no. 1 (1952): 63–90; and Leonard B. Boudin, "The Constitutional Right to Travel," *Columbia Law Review* 56, no. 1 (1956): 47–75. Flynn argued for a domestic as well as international right to travel. See, for example, "Court Curbs N.Y. Travel Rights of '13,'" *Daily Worker*, March 3, 1953, 6.

125. "Memorandum to Mr. W.C. Sullivan, Re: Elizabeth Gurley Flynn," April 20, 1962, NYU EGF Papers, box 8.

126. Frances G. Knight to Elizabeth Gurley Flynn, July 17, 1962, NYU EGF Papers, box 7.

127. "Flynn, Aptheker Passport Suit Procedure Set," *Worker*, May 7, 1963, 7; "Affidavit in Support of Plaintiff's Motion for Summary Judgement," n.d., NYU EGF Papers, box 8.

128. "Elizabeth Gurley Flynn: Along the Overland Trail," *Sunday Worker*, May 13, 1962, 9.

129. "Elizabeth Gurley Flynn: Farewell to San Francisco," *Worker*, June 24, 1962, 9.

130. "Hundreds Hear Elizabeth Flynn at Detroit Anti-McCarran Picnic," *Worker*, July 15, 1962, 4.

131. "Albertson Is First of 10 Targets in New McCarran Persecutions," *Worker*, September 2, 1962, 3, 14.

132. "Elizabeth Gurley Flynn: Coast SACB Hearings," *Worker*, December 2, 1962, 8.

133. "Elizabeth Gurley Flynn: Negro Leaders Are Included," *Worker*, December 16, 1962, 7.

134. "Assail McCarran Act Hounding of More," *Worker*, April 16, 1963, 1.

135. Elizabeth Gurley Flynn, "The McCarran Act Today," *Political Affairs* 41, no. 10 (October 1962): 13–17; Elizabeth Gurley Flynn, "The Borders Are My Prison," *Political Affairs* 41, no. 11 (November 1962): 26–30; *The McCarran Act: Fact and Fancy* (New York: Gus Hall–Benjamin J. Davis Defense Committee, 1963).

136. Flynn, "Borders Are My Prison," 27.

137. Ronald J. Krotoszynski Jr., "Transborder Speech," *Notre Dame Law Review* 94, no. 2 (2019): 474; Flynn, "Borders Are My Prison," 29.

138. Flynn, "Borders Are My Prison," 29.

139. "The McCarran Act: The Right to Travel," n.d., NYU EGF Papers, box 8.

140. See Elizabeth Gurley Flynn, "The Communist Party in the Dock," *Political Affairs* 41, no. 12 (December 1962): 25–32.

141. "CP Faces Witch-Hunt Trial," *Workers World*, December 7, 1962, 2.

142. "Elizabeth Gurley Flynn: Awaiting a Date," *Worker*, January 13, 1963, 7; see also "Call That a Trial?," *Political Affairs* 42, no. 2 (February 1963): 7–13.

143. "Elizabeth Gurley Flynn: McCarran Act Trial Challenges," *Worker*, March 31, 1963, 7; "Ruling on Communists: Fifth Amendment," *New York Times*, December 22, 1963, E2.

144. Mary Anne Trasciatti, foreword to Flynn, *My Life*, ix–xi.

145. Osmond K. Fraenkel, "Brief for American Civil Liberties Union for Amicus Curiae," n.d., NYU EGF Papers, box 8.

146. Elizabeth Gurley Flynn, "Why Can't I Go to Ireland?," *Worker*, August 11, 1963, 7.

147. Flynn acknowledged her reputation in "Elizabeth Gurley Flynn: McCarran Act Trial Challenges," *Worker*, March 31, 1963, 7.

148. "Elizabeth Gurley Flynn: Boston Revisited," *Worker*, May 12, 1963, 7.

149. Elizabeth Gurley Flynn to Al Richmond, June 3, 1963, NYU EGF Papers, box 8.

150. Flynn to Richmond, June 14, 1963, NYU EGF Papers, box 8.

151. Flynn to Richmond, July 8, 1963, NYU EGF Papers, box 8.

152. Anders Stephanson, "Interview with Gil Green," in *New Studies in the Politics and Culture of U.S. Communism*, ed. Michael E. Brown, Randy Martin, Frank Rosengarten, and George Snedeker (New York: Monthly Review Press, 1993), 316–326; Isserman, *Reds*, 271–285.

153. John Abt to Elizabeth Gurley Flynn and Herbert Aptheker, October 9, 1963, NYU EGF Papers, box 7.

154. Elizabeth Gurley Flynn to Al Richmond, July 18, 1963, NYU EGF Papers, box 14; "A Message from Elizabeth Gurley Flynn," *Worker*, October 20, 1963, 8. Just prior to the letter from Abt, Flynn had published a *Political Affairs* article on the CPUSA's long history of fighting for its rights in the face of relentless political persecution, "The Communist Party Fights for Its Rights, 1919–1963," *Political Affairs* 42, no. 9 (September 1963): 33–39.

155. Elizabeth Gurley Flynn to Al Richmond, September 14, 1963, NYU EGF Papers, box 14.

156. "Argue McCarran Appeal, See Long, Costly Struggle," *Worker*, November 6, 1963, 3; *McCarran Act: Fact and Fancy*; "Supreme Court to Hear McCarran Act Passport Cases," *Worker*, December 8, 1963, 2.

157. Anthony Lewis, "High Court Hears Passport Appeal," *New York Times*, April 22, 1964, 28.

158. Elizabeth Gurley Flynn, "I Visit Lowell House," *Worker*, April 26, 1964, 7.

159. "Memorandum to Mr. W.C. Sullivan, Re: Passport Violation of Elizabeth Gurley Flynn," March 13, 1962, NYU EGF Papers, box 9.

160. "Memo to Director of FBI (100-1287), Re: Elizabeth Gurley Flynn," July 16, 1964, NYU EGF Papers, box 9.

161. "Memo from Department of State Re: Citizenship and Passports: Elizabeth Gurley Flynn," August 14, 1964, NYU EGF Papers, box 9.

162. Elizabeth Gurley Flynn to Unknown, August 12, 1964, NYU EGF Papers, box 9.

Epilogue

1. Grace Hutchins to Anne Burlak Timpson, September 16, 1964, Anne Burlak Timpson Papers, Sophia Smith Collection, Smith College.

2. Dorothy Day, "Red Roses for Her," *Catholic Worker*, November 1964, 4.

3. As reported in Edith Evans Asbury, "ACLU Reverses Ouster of Elizabeth Gurley Flynn," *New York Times*, June 22, 1976, 38.

4. Henry Schwarzschild to Paul R. Meyer, April 6, 1976, ACLU Records, box 624, Mudd Manuscript Library, Princeton University.

5. Burt Neuborne, "Of Pragmatism and Principle: A Second Look at the Expulsion of Elizabeth Gurley Flynn from the ACLU's Board of Directors," *Tulsa Law Review* 41, no. 4 (Summer 2006): 799–815.

6. Andrew Jeong, "New Hampshire Removes Historical Marker for Feminist with Communist Past," *Washington Post*, May 17, 2023, https://www.washingtonpost.com/history/2023/05/17/new-hampshire-elizabeth-gurley-flynn-communist/; Mary Anne Trasciatti, "Cancelling Elizabeth Gurley Flynn," *LaborOnline*, May 24, 2023, https://www.lawcha.org/2023/05/24/cancelling-elizabeth-gurley-flynn/.

INDEX

Abbott, Leonard, 35, 68
Abraham Lincoln Brigade, 145, 171. *See also* Spanish Civil War
Abrams v. the United States, 233
Abt, John, 249, 261, 282, 285, 289
Act to Prevent Pernicious Political Activities (Hatch Act), 164
Albertson, William, 181, 283, 289
Alderson Federal Industrial Institute for Women, 169, 243, 245, 247, 248, 261–262
Alderson Story, The, 285–286
Alien and Sedition Acts (1798), 166, 167, 223
Alien Registration Act (Smith Act): conspiracy provision of, 205, 214; criticism of, 167–168, 239–240; efforts to repeal, 167, 221, 228–229, 241; hearings on, 165–166; implication of *Yates v. United States* decision for, 263; membership clause of, 275; passage and terms of, 166; trial of Socialist Workers Party members for violating, 169–140; as violation of First Amendment, 212, 222, 224, 237. *See also United States of America v. Elizabeth Gurley Flynn, et al.*; *United States of America v. Eugene Dennis, et al.*

American Civil Liberties Union (ACLU): advocates for release of Browder, 182; advocates for Sacco and Vanzetti, 124, 128; anti-Communism of, 154–162; California branch of, 283; cooperates with Popular Front organizations, 149; early years of, 122–124; expels Flynn, 159–161; Flynn criticizes, 178, 237, 246; founding of, 119–120; opposes Smith Act, 165, 167; political standing after Flynn expulsion, 161–162; political tensions among leadership, 149–154; reinstates Flynn, 291–292; responds to Smith Act indictments of Communists, 206, 222, 226, 229; supports Flynn's passport case, 286–287; Wisconsin branch of, 267
American Committee for the Protection of the Foreign Born, 149, 165, 167
American Federation of Labor (AFL): anti-Communism of, 144; and Passaic strike, 136–137; and Paterson strike, 46; position on IWW free speech fights, 26, 32; response to wage labor system, 15; rivalry with IWW, 9, 46, 78–79; and WWI, 74, 78–79, 87, 124

American Fund for Public Service (Garland Fund), 129, 136, 142
Americanism: as political identity, 89, 98, 186, 192; as political language, 5, 18, 40, 43, 49, 61, 146, 207, 293
American Labor Party, 166, 206, 217
American Legion, 132, 217
American Protective League (APL), 89–90
American Veterans Committee, 206
Amnesty Alliance for New York State Political Prisoners, 124
Amter, Israel, 147, 225, 228
anti-Communism: in ACLU, 154–162; effect of international events on, 156, 164–165, 171, 174–176, 196, 202, 219, 222–224, 239; at federal level, 164–167, 170–171, 174–175, 194–210, 214, 221–242, 270–271, 275–283, 286; fueled by U.S. press, 223; at state and local levels, 164, 171, 217
antifascism: Anti-Fascist Alliance of North America, 131; Antifascist Committee of Soviet Women, 187; and collapse of Nazi-Soviet Pact, 180; compromised by Nazi-Soviet Pact, 147–149, 167–168; effect of Matteotti murder upon, 133–134; and Flynn, 131–133, 143, 145–146; and opposition to repressive legislation, 168–169, 203, 209; origins among Italian radicals, 13; and Popular Front, 144–147; and postwar CPUSA, 191; and Tresca, 133–134
Anti-Fascist Alliance of North America (AFANA), 131
Aptheker, Herbert, 278–279, 282, 286–287, 288
Aptheker v. Secretary of State, 289–290
Ashley, Jessie, 69, 93

Bachrach, Marion, 225–228, 261–262, 274
bad tendency test, 88
Baldwin, Roger: advocates against deportation, 105; advocates for conscientious objectors, 94; advocates for release of Browder, 182; allies with anti-Communists, 156; defends Sacco and Vanzetti, 129; and Flynn's Smith Act trial, 227; founds ACLU, 119–120, 123–124; founds League for Mutual Aid, 135; founds Liberty Defense Union, 95; opposes Smith Act, 165; on publication of Flynn's autobiography, 248; reacts to Nazi-Soviet Pact, 149; role in expulsion of Flynn from ACLU, 157–160; supports Indian independence, 114–115; supports Popular Front, 150; and tensions among ACLU leaders, 150–151; view of National Federation for Constitutional Liberties, 178
Barenblatt v. United States, 271
Baron, Kevin, 223
Barrett, James, 18, 39
Baxandall, Rosalyn Fraad, 190, 210, 299n4
Begun, Isidore, 225, 230
Belknap, Michael, 214
Berger, Victor, 106, 135, 205
Berkman, Alexander, 67, 88, 104, 106
Billings, Warren, 139, 182, 285
Bimson, John, 41, 47, 50, 55, 59, 66, 70
Bittelman, Alexander, 198, 201, 225, 262
blacklisting, 48, 65, 67, 177, 195, 201, 208
Blackshirts, 129–131
Bloor, Ella Reeve "Mother," 95, 136
Blumberg, Albert, 264
Blumberg, Dorothy Rose, 247
Boas, Franz, 114, 178
Botto, Eva, 54
Botto, Maria and Pietro, 57, 65
Botto House, 57–60, 65, 296
Boyd, Frederic Sumner, 56, 65, 80–81
Boyer, Richard O., 231
Brazier, Richard, 29–30
Bromley, Dorothy Dunbar, 159

Browder, Earl: arrest, trial, and imprisonment, 170–172, 177–178; arrest under Michigan criminal syndicalism law, 124; ascends to leadership of CPUSA, 144; on Communism and Americanism, 146; criticism from Moscow and expulsion from CPUSA, 188–192; defense campaign for, 172–173, 174, 179–182; denied readmission to CPUSA, 216; dissolves CPUSA and forms Communist Political Association, 188–189; during Popular Front period, 147; release from prison, 182–183; vilified by party leadership, 250
Browder v. United States, 178
Budenz, Louis, 215, 230, 231
Burleson, Albert, 85–86

Cannon, James P., 135, 139, 144, 169
Cannon, Joseph, 117
Carlson, Grace, 169
Chafee, Zechariah, Jr., 284
Charney, George, 225, 243
Citizens' Committee to Free Earl Browder, 179, 181
Citizens Emergency Defense Conference, 230–231
City Beautiful Movement, 12–13, 23, 24, 28
Civil Rights Congress, 178, 192, 195–196, 206, 211, 217, 226–227
Clark, Joseph, 250, 265
Clark, Tom C., 216, 271
clear and present danger standard, 107, 169, 223–224, 239, 241, 263
Cohen, Michael, 88–89
Cold War: Communists' perception of, 263; as historical paradigm, 2; impact on domestic politics, 202, 212–214, 224; implications for civil liberties, 221, 231; as rationale for passport denials, 281; Stalin's comments on, 239

Colson, William N., 108
Comitato Generale di Difesa Contro Il Fascismo, 131
Commission on Industrial Relations, 87
Communist Control Act, 242
Communist front organizations, 155–156, 171, 178, 235, 240
Communist Information Bureau (Cominform), 199, 202
Communist International (Comintern), 144, 188, 236
Communist Party of the Soviet Union (CPSU), 144, 199, 250, 276
Communist Party of the United States (CPUSA): advocates for civil rights for members, 173–179; in Alabama, 171, 174; in California, 193, 227, 229, 259, 263, 269, 283; campaign against homosexuality, 240; contest over direction of the party, 251–252, 263–269, 271; disbands the *Daily Worker*, 267–269; and Draft Resolution, 255–256, 259; elects Flynn as first female chair, 273–274; and expulsion of unions from the CIO, 196; factionalism in the 1920s, 144; Flynn joins, 144; forms International Labor Defense, 139; impact of tensions between China and the Soviet Union on membership, 288; "imperialist war" phase of, 169, 171, 175, 177; and Moscow Trials, 147; and Nazi-Soviet Pact, 148; in New York, 145–146, 269, 287–288; opposes McCarran Act, 275–276, 278–285, 288–289; organizing prowess, 145; orientation toward Franklin Roosevelt, 144–145, 168, 171, 179, 183; and Passaic strike, 136–138; during Popular Front era, 145–149, 163; and postwar reorganization as Communist Political Association, 188–191;

Communist Party of the United States (*continued*): reacts to Khrushchev's revelations about Stalin, 250–255; reacts to Soviet invasion of Hungary, 257–259; reconstituted as CPUSA, 191–192; relationship with ACLU, 161–162; response to arrest of Browder, 170–172, 177–183; supports Wallace presidential campaign, 196; and "third-period" analysis, 144; and women's issues, 185–188; works for Black liberation, 139, 149, 173, 185–186, 201–202, 208–209, 234, 283, 288

Communist Party of the United States v. Subversive Activities Control Board, 275, 285

Communist Political Association (CPA), 188–191, 235

comradeship, 172–173

Conference on Constitutional Liberties, 178

Congress of American Women (CAW), 187, 192

Congress of Industrial Organizations (CIO): contributions of Communists to, 145, 146, 257; expels Communist-led unions from, 196; supports Smith Act defendants, 206, 217

Connolly, James, 9, 10, 116, 126, 287

Connolly, Nora, 116

Connolly Association, 236

conscientious objectors, 93–95

conspiracy charge: and Espionage Act indictments, 90, 106; and Expatriation Act, 242; and Paterson strike, 47, 64, 70; and Smith Act trial of first-string Communists, 205, 214–215, 223–224; and Smith Act trial of second-string Communists, 225–226, 231, 239; and Smith Act trial of Trotskyists, 169; and Spokane free speech fight, 29, 34–35, 36, 39

constructive legal offenses, 77, 111

Coolidge, Calvin, 117, 134

Cothren, Marion, 70, 76, 93–94

Council for National Defense (CND), 78, 87

Cram, Edith, 65, 70

criminal anarchy, 79–80, 101, 103, 107, 116, 124

criminal syndicalism, 81–82, 101, 103, 149, 165, 175, 255

Crocket, George, 211, 217

Daily Worker. See Communist Party of the United States

Daniels, Cletus, 156

Davis, Angela, 234

Davis, Benjamin: and controversy over reforming CPUSA, 268; defends civil rights for Communists, 195; and Flynn's autobiography, 248; and Flynn's run for New York City Council, 264; McCarran Act case and defense campaign for, 278–280, 282–283, 285; as party leader, 269, 275, 277; position on Soviet invasion of Hungary, 257; and Smith Act case, 204, 216; supports Browder during CPA controversy, 189

Day, Dorothy, 238, 286, 291

Dean, Jodi, 172

Debs, Eugene, 41, 88–89, 106, 113, 149, 179

Declaration of Independence, 30, 40, 111, 126, 248

Declaration of Twelve Communist and Workers Parties, 267

Defense Committee for Civil Rights for Communists (DCCRC), 172–176

Dennis, Eugene: comments on Smith Act indictments, 209; confers with Flynn on Budenz testimony, 230; and controversy over reforming CPUSA, 251–252, 254, 256, 259, 264, 268; dies, 273; elected to party

leadership, 269, 271; and Flynn, 254, 255, 273; as own counsel during Smith Act trial, 216; responds to formation of NATO, 213; responds to Soviet invasion of Hungary, 257; sojourns in the Soviet Union, 255
Dennis, Peggy, 247
Dennis v. the United States, 224
Department of Justice (DOJ), 89
deportation: of Berkman and Goldman, 88; CPUSA opposition to, 167; Flynn's opposition to, 96, 103–105, 112, 113, 115, 126, 138, 168, 198; of Claudia Jones, 197–198, 201, 287; of Larkin, 116, 128; as penalty under the Espionage Act, 91, 96, 104, 114; of Potash, 262; provision under Anarchist Exclusion Act, 80
Deportation Act, 104
Deportees Defense and Relief Committee, 105
DeSilver, Albert, 101
DeSilver, Margaret, 155
Dies, Martin, 155–156
Dies Committee, 155–156, 158, 164, 170–171, 177–178. *See also* House Un-American Activities Committee
Dimitrov, Georgi, 144–145, 209, 232
Dimock, Edward S., 230–231, 234–235, 238–239, 243, 254
Division of Passport Control, 278, 280–282
Domingo, W. A., 108
Dublin Lockout, 68, 116
Du Bois, W. E. B., 98, 114, 115, 182, 281
Duclos, Jacques, 188, 235, 259
Duclos article, 188–189
Dunn, Robert, 150

Easter Rising, 115–116
Eastman, Crystal, 94
Eisenhower, Dwight D., 239, 241–242, 263, 271, 274

Eisler, Gerhardt, 197
Elaine Massacre, 100, 110
Emergency Civil Liberties Committee, 275
Emerson, Marion, 126
Emerson, Ralph, 165
Emerson, Thomas, 230
Empey, Arthur Guy, 100–101
Equi, Marie, 70, 77, 107, 140–143
Ernst, Morris, 149, 155–156, 158, 161, 182
Espionage Act: criticism of, 111–112; Debs indictment under, 89; enforcement of, 88; impact on civil liberties movement, 92–95; IWW indictments, 89–92; other indictments, 106–107, 113–115; passage and terms of, 84–86
Ettor, Joseph: advocates for Paterson silk workers, 62; Espionage Act indictment of, 90–92; and Flynn, 140, 144; and Lawrence strike, 42, 43, 64; and Mesabi Range strike, 76; reports on Flynn's Paterson trial, 70
Everett Massacre, 77–78
Executive Order 9383, 195
Expatriation Act, 242

Fair, Agnes Thecla, 33–34, 36
Families Committee of Smith Act Victims, 247, 248
Fargo, Lucile F., 25
fascism: Americans react to, 130, 134; causes conflict among Italian Americans, 131, 133–134; criticized as antidemocratic, 131, 183; equated with communism, 150, 154, 156, 166, 210; and "fascism is coming" mentality of Communists, 203, 204–205, 209, 219–221, 225, 226, 239; in Italy, 129; Ku Klux Klan as American version of, 132, 185; as reason for Europeans fleeing to the United States, 168; and relationship to capitalism, 179; and violence in Europe, 133

Fascist League of North America (FLNA), 130, 133
Fast, Howard, 253–254
Federal Bureau of Information (FBI): colludes with Passport Office, 278; informants for, 215, 243, 272, 282; investigates Socialist Workers Party, 169–170; origin of, 78; raids CPUSA offices, 171; reports on German spy ring, 166; sends agents to Smith Act trials, 231; and Smith Act arrests of CPUSA leaders, 204, 206, 225; and surveillance, 165, 246
Federici, Silvia, 15
Feurer, Rosemary, 81
fifth column, 166
Filigno, C. L., 19–20, 36, 39
Fitch, John, 51
Flynn, Elizabeth Gurley: acquires national reputation, 41–42, 120–122; advocates for Black workers, 108–111, 138–139; advocates for civil rights for Communists and Black Americans, 173–179, 195–196, 201–202; advocates for Indian independence, 115–116; advocates for Joe Hill, 69–70; advocates for recognition of political prisoners in the United States, 112–113; advocates for right to travel, 283–285; advocates for women's issues, 185–188; appeals to Wilson for clemency, 91–92; assumes provisional leadership role in party, 211–212; betrayal by Tresca and sister Sabina Flynn, 134–135; and brother Tom Flynn, 143; builds diverse labor defense constituency, 102, 105–106; chairs own Smith Act defense campaign, 228–230; charged with contempt, 238; and James Connolly, 9; and Nora Connolly, 116; criticizes Black women's oppression, 185–186; criticizes civil liberties implications of Smith Act, 228; criticizes Frankfurter, 271; criticizes Hobbs "Concentration Camp" Bill, 168–169; criticizes informants, 215; criticizes Mundt-Nixon Bill, 203; criticizes Paterson Pageant, 63; defends Browder, 170, 172, 178–182; defends CPUSA against anti-Communism, 194–197; defends Everett IWWs, 77; defends "first-string" Smith Act defendants, 206–207, 216, 219–221, 224–225; defends Claudia Jones, 197–198, 200; defends Mesabi Range strikers, 76; defends Sacco and Vanzetti, 124–129; dies in Soviet Union, 290; divorces husband, 39; and early ACLU, 123–124; early life, 7; elected first female chair of CPUSA, 274–275; election to National Executive Committee, 269; embraces internationalism, 113–115; embraces syndicalism, 10; encourages women strikers, 54–55; endorses party line on Moscow Trials, 148–149; ends formal relationship with IWW, 76; and Equi, 140–142; Espionage Act indictment of, 91; expelled from ACLU executive board, 159–161; exposes a prison prostitution ring, 34–36; and father Thomas Flynn, 7, 70, 121, 135; first labor defense campaign, 9; and founding of ACLU, 119; and founding of Irish Socialist Federation, 10; founds Workers' Defense Union, 95–96; gives birth to son, 39; and Hall-Davis Defense Committee, 278–279; health issues, 240, 241; and husband Jack Jones, 11; imprisoned at Alderson, 243; and International Labor Defense, 139–140, 142; and Irish American identity, 9–10, 74, 110–111, 115–116, 136, 175, 177, 183, 201–202, 215, 222,

232, 236, 238, 247, 278, 287; isolated from American political mainstream, 207–208, 209, 212, 267; joins CPUSA, 143–146; joins IWW, 8–9; justifies Nazi-Soviet Pact, 148–149; and Larkin, 68, 116, 128; launches activist career, 7–8; leads hotel workers strike, 44; leads Lawrence strike, 42–43; leads Missoula free speech fight, 14, 16–18, 20–22; leads Paterson free speech fight, 66–70; leads Paterson strike, 47–49, 50, 52–53; leads Spokane free speech fight, 29, 31–32; meets Tresca, 43–44; and mother Annie Gurley, 7, 135, 142, 143, 160; and Nelson, 240–241; and nephew Peter Martin, 249; opposes deportations, 103–105; opposes McCarran Act, 224, 275–277, 282–283; opposes Mussolini and fascism, 131–134, 142; opposes World War I, 74; and Passaic Strike, 136–138; passport canceled, 280–282; passport reinstated, 288–289; as political prisoner, 246–247; position on future of CPUSA, 259–260, 262–264; position on NLRB Ford decision, 153–155; position on reorganization of CPUSA into CPA, 188–191; position on sit-down strike, 150–153; and pregnancy, 36–37; and publication of autobiography, 247–248; publishes prison memoir, 285–286; raises money for strikers and IWW defendants, 62, 65; rallies support for war, 183–184; reacts to criticism of Communists, 253–254; reacts to Dennis's report, 254–255; reacts to Draft Resolution, 256–257; reacts to Khrushchev's speech, 250–253; reacts to prison, 245–246; reacts to Soviet invasion of Hungary, 257–258; recruits for reconstituted CPUSA, 191, 193–194; released from prison, 260–262; as remembered by Healy, 170, 264; as remembered by Nelson, 190, 259; responds to ACLU's Communazi resolution, 157–159; runs for Congress in New York, 242; runs for New York City Council, 264–266; and *Sabotage* pamphlet, 80–81; and sister Kathie Flynn, 185, 225, 229, 243, 249, 259, 270, 277; and sister Sabina Flynn, 143, 184; and Skeffington, 116; Smith Act arrest and indictment of, 225–227; and Smith Act trial, 230–239; and son Fred Flynn, 142, 160, 172–173, 184; testifies at Smith Act trial, 237–238; testifies before Subversive Activities Control Board, 235–236; travels to Soviet Union, 272–273; travels west with IWW, 13–14; tried for conspiracy, 36–37, 64, 70; and "triple jeopardy" thesis, 234; and Wallace presidential campaign, 196; writes article on Declaration of Independence, 248–249

Flynn, Fred "Buster," 38–39, 41, 64, 135, 141–143, 159–160, 172–173, 184–185

Flynn, Kathie: comments on Flynn's incarceration, 259; corresponds with Flynn at Alderson, 245, 249, 252, 254, 257–258; dies, 277; edits Flynn's autobiography, 247; and Flynn's release from Alderson, 261; fundraises for Flynn's Smith Act defense, 229; illness and convalescence, 270, 277; interviewed for *Daily Worker* profile of Flynn, 243; shares apartment with Flynn, 185, 225; speaks at celebration of Flynn's autobiography, 245; travels to Nigeria, 262

Flynn, Sabina (Bina), 134–135, 138, 143, 184

Flynn, Thomas, 7, 70, 121, 135, 184, 236

Flynn v. Rusk, 286–287
Foley Square, 211, 214, 225, 229, 238
Fordyce, Robert, 66–67, 70
Foreign Agents Registration Act, 164
Forer, Joseph, 280, 281–282, 285, 289
Fort-Whiteman, Lovett, 107, 108
Foster, William Z.: ascends to CPUSA leadership, 191; as co-leader of CPUSA, 144; dies in Soviet Union, 276; directs party members to go underground, 227; opposes NATO, 213–214; opposes Subversive Activities Control Act, 203; public persona and reputation, 207–208; reacts to Khrushchev's speech, 250; reacts to proposals for reform of the Party, 252, 256–259, 265, 268, 271; reacts to Soviet invasion of Hungary, 257; relationship with Flynn, 189, 264; rivalry and conflict with Browder, 188–189; and Smith Act arrest, 198, 204; and Smith Act trial, 214, 216, 219; warns against dangers of defense work, 206, 240–241
four-loom system, 45, 46, 65
Fraenkel, Osmond, 165, 333n152
France, Clemens, 249, 253, 258, 259, 260, 261–262
Frankfurter, Felix, 135, 271, 275
free speech fights: as catalyst for debate about the First Amendment and free speech, 37–38; controversy among Wobblies about, 39, 72; definition of, 11; Flynn's position on, 39–40, 72; significance to civil liberties history, 12, 39–40
Free Speech League, 29, 67
Frenette, Edith, 21–22, 30, 32–34, 70
Friends of Freedom for India (FFI), 114–115
Friends of Irish Freedom, 115
Furriers Union, 95, 172, 217

Gannes, Harry, 171
Gannett, Betty, 226–227, 243, 246–247, 285
Gardner, Virginia, 243
Garland Fund, 129, 136, 142
Gates, John, 204, 216, 220, 256–259, 264–265, 267–268
Gerson, Simon, 211, 225, 230
Gerstle, Gary, 18
Giovannitti, Arturo, 42, 43, 56, 64, 90–92, 135, 144
Goldman, Emma, 67, 88, 104, 106, 135, 290
Goldwater-Rhodes Bill, 240
Gompers, Samuel, 15, 74, 78–79, 87, 97
Great Depression, 144, 152
Green, Gil, 204, 216, 220, 227, 262, 266, 269
Greene, Julie, 78
Greene, Nathan, 150
Greeni, Joe, 75
Greenwich Village, 63, 69, 135
guilt by association doctrine, 162, 334n155
Gurley, Annie, 7, 43, 64, 116, 135, 160

Hall, Gus, 204, 216, 220, 227–228, 271, 275, 277–283, 285
Hall-Davis Defense Committee, 278, 280–281, 283, 285
Hand, Learned, 222, 224
Harlan, John Marshall, 263
Harmon, Constance, 201
Harrison, Hubert, 56–57
Haverty-Stack, Donna, 169
Hays, Arthur Garfield, 151, 154, 156, 182, 206, 229
Haywood, William D. "Big Bill": and Espionage Act indictment, 91–92; founds International Labor Defense, 139; and Haywood, Moyer, and Pettibone defense, 9–10; and Lawrence strike, 42; and Paterson free speech fight, 67; and Paterson strike, 47, 53, 56–57, 63; plans for

reorganization of IWW, 77; splits with Flynn, 76
Heale, M. J., 164
Healy, Dorothy, 170, 264, 267–268, 283
Heatherton, Christina, 113–114
Herndon, Angelo, 149
Heslewood, Fred, 38
Hill, Joe, 69–70, 120
Hill, L. Barron, 200
Hill, Rebecca, 166
Hobbs "Concentration Camp" Bill, 168–169
hoboes, 20, 25, 31, 33. *See also* migratory workers
Hollywood Ten, 195
Holmes, Oliver Wendell, 107, 194, 233
Holmes, Reverend John Haynes: and anti-Communism, 119, 149, 154–155; on "Battle of the Overpass," 153–154; and Elizabeth Gurley Flynn Defense Committee, 70; and Flynn's expulsion from ACLU, 157–161; free speech activism of, 123; and Liberty Defense Union, 95; and National Civil Liberties Bureau, 94; negotiates for release of Browder, 182; reacts to Flynn's prison memoir, 286
Hoover, J. Edgar, 104, 116, 161, 164, 206, 263, 279
hotel and restaurant workers strike (1913), 43–44
House Un-American Activities Committee (HUAC), 155, 211, 263, 270–271, 276–277, 279. *See also* Dies Committee
Hudson, Roy, 189, 191
Hutchins, Grace, 226

Ibarruri, Dolores, 187, 286
Ickes, Harold, 229
Indian independence movement, 114–115, 116

Industrial Workers of the World (IWW): 1908 convention, 10–11; advocates sabotage, 80–81; campaigns for Espionage Act defendants, 91, 94; and controversy over centralization, 90–92; embraces syndicalism, 10; Espionage Act indictments, 89–90, 106; as example of dangers of defense campaign, 207; Flynn joins, 8; and Flynn's conspiracy trial during Paterson strike, 64–65, 70–72; founding, philosophy, and mission of, 9; Haywood's plan for reorganizing, 78–79; and hotel and restaurant workers strike, 43–44; influences early ACLU, 123; and Lawrence strike, 42–44, 51–52, 62; and Mesabi Range strike, 75–78; and Missoula free speech fight, 12–23; organizing strategy of, 11, 299n4; orientation toward wage labor, 15–16; and Paterson free speech fight, 66–72; and Paterson strike, 44–63; position on World War I, 74–75; rivalry with AFL, 9, 46, 78–79; rivalry with Salvation Army, 16–17, 23, 25, 28; sentences of Espionage Act defendants, 117; and Spokane free speech fight, 24–40; and Workers' Defense Union, 106–108, 124
Ingram, Rosa Lee, 201
Internal Securities Act (McCarran Act): as amended by Communist Control Act, 242; Communist opposition to, 275–278, 282–283; conspiracy provision of, 226; Flynn opposition to, 278–279, 283, 289; Section 6 and passport denials, 280–282, 286–287, 289; student protests against, 280; and Subversive Activities Control Board, 235, 240, 278; terms of, 225; and trial of CPUSA, 284–285

International Labor Defense (ILD), 137, 138, 139–143, 167
International Women's Assembly, 272
International Workers Order (IWO), 172
Irish independence movement, 9, 84, 115–117, 201, 215
Irish Socialist Federation, 9, 10, 37, 116
I Speak My Own Piece, 247–248
Isserman, Abraham, 150, 211, 229

Jackson, James, 272
Janney, Russell, 217
Jerome, V. J., 225
John Birch Society, 274, 275, 278
Johnson, Arnold, 225, 266
Johnson, James Weldon, 99, 110, 119, 136
Joint Legislative Committee to Investigate Radical Activities in New York State (Lusk Committee), 102, 110, 124
Jones, Claudia: advocates for civil rights, 269; arrest of (1948), 197–198, 200–201; deportation of, 252, 285; and Flynn, 185, 234; imprisonment at Alderson, 246–247; Smith Act case, 225, 226, 228, 238, 243
Jones, John Archibald "Jack," 11, 14, 20, 31, 39, 121–122
Jones, Joseph J., 107, 108
Jones, Mary Harris "Mother," 36, 121

Kaufman, Mary, 230, 237, 241, 249, 262
Kelley, Robin D. G., 174
Kennedy, John F., 278, 287
Kennedy, Robert, 282–283
Kenney, Padraic, 113
Kent, Rockwell, 281, 286
Kent v. Dulles, 281
Khrushchev, Nikita, 250–253, 255, 257, 271, 272
Knight, Frances G., 282
Koettgen, Ewald, 60

Korea, 84, 222–224, 228, 239
Krotoszynski, Ronald J., 284
Ku Klux Klan, 116, 117, 132, 208, 285

Labor Defender. *See* International Labor Defense
Labor Defense Council, 124
LaGuardia, Fiorello, 3, 134
Lannon, Albert, 225
Larkin, James (Jim), 68, 116, 124, 128
Lawrence strike, 42–44, 51–52, 62
League for Amnesty of Political Prisoners, 113
League for Mutual Aid, 135
League of Struggle for Negro Rights (LSNR), 173–174
League of Women Voters, 177, 266
Leavenworth Prison, 106, 113–114, 117
LeFebvre, Henri, 22. *See also* right to the city
Lenin, Vladimir, 162, 256
Lessig, Adolph, 57, 60–61, 68
Lewis, Bob, 177
Lewis, John L., 183
Liberty Defense Union (LDU), 95
Lightfoot, Claude, 271
Little, Frank, 14, 75, 89, 90
Lovestone, Jay, 144
Lowe, Caroline, 77
Lowell, Esther, 135, 136
Loyalty Review Board (LRB). *See* Executive Order 9383
Lusk Committee, 102, 110, 124
Lyons, Eugene, 128

MacMahon, Thomas, 136, 137, 138
Magón, Ricardo Flores, 113–114
Maloney, James B., 199–200
Marcantonio, Vito, 166–167, 181, 182, 203, 236
marketplace of ideas metaphor, 161, 231
Marshall Plan, 199, 209, 213
Martin, Peter, 134–135, 249

Marxism-Leninism, 214–215, 223, 232–233, 252
Masses & Mainstream. See Communist Party of the United States
Matteotti, Giacomo, 133
Max, Alan, 250
May, Matthew, 20
McBride, Andrew, 48, 59–60, 66
McCarran Act. *See* Internal Securities Act
McCarthyism, 161–162
McGohey, John, 211
McTernan, John, 230
Medina, Harold, 211, 214, 216–217, 219, 221, 222, 230
Mesabi Iron Range strike, 75–76, 291
Messenger, The, 94, 99, 108
Meyer, Paul R., 292
migratory workers, 12–14, 19–20, 24, 26–27, 30
Mindel, Jacob, 225
Minor, Robert, 128, 137–138, 172, 182, 189, 191
Missoula free speech fight: background and causes of, 12–16; Flynn's arrest, 21–22; Flynn's leadership of, 14–18, 20–21; and Frenette, 21–22; outcome of, 23; police retaliation against, 20–21; recruitment of free speech fighters for, 17–20. *See also* free speech fights; Industrial Workers of the World
Montgomery, David, 79
Moon, Henry Lee, 212
Moore, Fred H., 27, 125, 127, 129, 131, 189
Moore, Richard B., 138
Mortimer, Wyndham, 151
Moscow Trials, 147, 150
Mosk, Stanley, 280
Mundt-Nixon Bill, 202–203, 221
Mussolini, Benito, 129–135, 143, 146

Naison, Mark, 145
Nathenson, Carol, 217
National Association for the Promotion of Labor Unionism among Negroes, 117
National Civil Liberties Bureau, 94, 95, 106, 112, 119, 123, 173
National Federation for Constitutional Liberties, 178
National Free Browder Congress, 182
National Labor Relations Act (NLRA), 152, 193, 195. *See also* Wagner Act
National Labor Relations Board (NLRB), 153–155, 158, 178
National Lawyers Guild, 206, 230
National Negro Congress, 178
National War Labor Board (NWLB), 87, 97
Nazism, 134, 146, 253
Nazi-Soviet Pact: announcement of, 147–149; collapse of, 179, 183; implications for Browder defense campaign, 176; influences Communists' orientation to World War II, 167–168; as validation of anti-Communism, 156, 164–165, 171, 174, 175–176, 196
Nearing, Scott, 88, 248
Nelson, Steve, 190, 227, 240–241, 251–252, 259, 272, 273
Neuborne, Burt, 292
New Deal: challenges to, 164, 191; Communists' views of, 143, 144, 145, 149, 164, 188, 192, 249
New Deal liberalism, 149–150, 164, 166
New Jersey Bureau of Industrial Statistics, 50–51
New York Bureau of Legal Advice (NYBLA), 93–94
NLRB Ford decision, 153–155, 158, 160
NLRB v. Fansteel, 152
Norman, William, 211
North, Joseph, 237
North American Committee to Aid Spanish Democracy, 149

North Atlantic Treaty Organization (NATO), 213

O'Casey, Sean, 286
O'Connor, Harvey, 275
O'Hare, Kate Richards, 88, 106
Onipede, Frances, 185
Ottanelli, Fraser, 147, 188
Ovington, Mary White, 115
Owen, Chandler, 86, 94, 99, 108

Palmer Raids, 104–105, 112, 125, 126
Parker, Roscoe, 283
Passaic textile strike, 136–138, 140
Paterson free speech fight: background and causes of, 66–67; conflict between Flynn and law enforcement during, 68–69; differences from other IWW free speech fights, 67; Free Speech League support for, 67–68; outcome of, 70; support from suffragists for, 69, 71–72. *See also* free speech fights; Industrial Workers of the World
Paterson Pageant, 63, 69
Paterson strike: anarchist influence on, 45–46; arrival and arrest of Flynn, Tresca, and Haywood, 47–48; background and causes of, 44–45; blacklisting of strikers, 48; as catalyst for debate about free speech, 59–60; and conspiracy trial of Flynn, 64–65, 70; meeting halls and other spaces, 55–56, 59–62; outcome, 65; participation of women in, 53–55; and Paterson Pageant, 63; picketing and other tactics, 51–53; police brutality, 53; relationship between Flynn and strikers, 48–49, 55; use of Botto House for meetings, 57–58. *See also* Paterson free speech fight
Pauker, Ana, 187
peace movement (World War I), 92–94

Peekskill riot, 217. *See also* Robeson, Paul
People's Republic of China, 219, 221
People's Rights Party, 242, 264
Perry, Pettis, 225, 228, 231, 235, 264
pickets: as contested form of political speech, 3, 52–53, 72, 98, 209; as site of violence, 53, 208–209; as strike tactic, 51, 61, 63, 136–137; women's involvement in, 53, 55, 69
Political Prisoner Defense and Relief Committee, 112–113
political prisoner status, 96, 112–113, 143, 174, 235, 240, 246, 269–270
Popova, Nina, 187
popular constitutionalism, 1
Popular Front, 145–146, 149–150, 163, 174, 188
Potash, Irving, 204, 262, 266
prison: conditions for early twentieth-century female prisoners, 21, 32–36; Flynn's ideas for reform of, 245–246, 270; as site of politics, 20, 113–114
Progressive Party, 196, 204, 206

Quill, Mike, 201
Quinlan, Patrick, 10, 47, 56, 57, 59, 65, 70

Rabban, David M., 12
Randolph, A. Philip, 86, 94, 99, 108, 116–117, 138
Rand School of Social Science, 86, 96, 102
red flag laws, 101–102
Red Summer (1919), 99
Regeneración, 114
Reichstag fire, 209
Reston, James, 238–239
Reuther, Walter, 153
Richmond, Al, 248, 259, 287
right to the city, 22, 46. *See also* LeFebvre, Henri